Bringing Literacy Home

KaiLonnie Dunsmore
and Douglas Fisher, Editors

INTERNATIONAL
Reading Association
800 BARKSDALE ROAD, PO BOX 8139
NEWARK, DE 19714-8139, USA
www.reading.org

D1221899

The International Reading Association attempts, through its publications, to provide a forum for a wide spectrum of opinions on reading. This policy permits divergent viewpoints without implying the endorsement of the Association.

Executive Editor, Books   Corinne M. Mooney
Developmental Editor   Charlene M. Nichols
Developmental Editor   Tori Mello Bachman
Developmental Editor   Stacey L. Reid
Editorial Production Manager   Shannon T. Fortner
Design and Composition Manager   Anette Schuetz

Project Editors   Tori M. Bachman and Rebecca A. Stewart

Cover   Design, Lise Holliker Dykes; Photography (background image) © iStockphoto.com/
Kertlis, (images in house) © Shutterstock

The publisher would appreciate notification where errors occur so that they may be corrected in subsequent printings and/or editions.

Library of Congress Cataloging-in-Publication Data
Bringing literacy home / KaiLonnie Dunsmore and Douglas Fisher, editors.
　　p. cm.
　Includes bibliographical references and index.
　ISBN 978-0-87207-711-9
　1. Family literacy programs--United States. 2. Home and school--United States. 3. Education--
Parent participation--United States. I. Dunsmore, KaiLonnie, 1970- II. Fisher, Douglas, 1965-
　LC151.B74 2010
　302.2'244--dc22

　　　　　　　　　　　　　　　　　　　　　　　　　　　　　　　　　　　　2009045460

CONTENTS

SECTION 1
Supporting Families in School-Based Literacy Practices

SECTION 2
Connecting School With Home Culture

SECTION 3
Implications for Family Literacy Research and Scholarship

KaiLonnie Dunsmore is the Director of Literacy Initiatives at The Ball Foundation, Glen Ellyn, Illinois, USA. She is a former elementary and middle school teacher who developed inclusion practices designed to support students who struggle with school-based literacy. Subsequently, she spent nearly a decade working as a college/university professor where she engaged in federal and state funded intervention research that involved collaboration with classroom teachers to develop literacy programs for special education and at-risk student populations. She has taught numerous courses and workshops that help teachers develop instructional and assessment practices to support the literacy development of all students, particularly in those populations that tend to be socially and educationally marginalized. Her published articles, book chapters, and local and national presentations have focused on differentiated instruction, writing, content area literacy, literacy coaching, and family literacy.

KaiLonnie is committed to hands-on work with teachers, school administrators, and regional educational agencies that transforms instructional and organizational practices in order to support high levels of student achievement, especially for those on the margins of classrooms and society. As the mother of a toddler, her interest in family literacy has become deeply personal. KaiLonnie can be reached at kdunsmore@ballfoundation.org.

Douglas Fisher is a professor of language and literacy education in the Department of Teacher Education at San Diego State University (SDSU), California, USA, and a classroom teacher at Health Sciences High and Middle College (HSHMC) in San Diego. He is the recipient of an International Reading Association (IRA) Celebrate Literacy Award, the Farmer Award for excellence in writing from the National Council of Teachers of English, and a Christa McAuliffe Award for excellence in teacher education from the American Association of State Colleges and Universities. He is a past chair of IRA's Adolescent Literacy Committee.

Doug has published numerous articles on reading and literacy, differentiated instruction, and curriculum design as well as books such as *In a Reading State of Mind: Brain Research, Teacher Modeling, and Comprehension Instruction* (with Nancy Frey and Diane Lapp), *Creating Literacy-Rich Schools for Adolescents* (with Gay Ivey), *Better Learning Through Structured Teaching: A Framework for the Gradual Release of Responsibility* (with Nancy Frey), and *Teaching English Language Learners: A Differentiated Approach* (with Carol Rothenberg). He has taught a variety of courses in SDSU's teacher-credentialing program as well as graduate-level courses on English-language development and literacy. An early intervention specialist and language development specialist, he has taught high school English, writing, and literacy development to public school students. Doug can be reached at dfisher@mail.sdsu.edu.

CONTRIBUTORS

Julio Cammarota
University of Arizona
Tucson, Arizona, USA

Catherine Compton-Lilly
University of Wisconsin—Madison
Madison, Wisconsin, USA

Brooke David
Boston University
Boston, Massachusetts, USA

Patricia A. Edwards
Michigan State University
Lansing, Michigan, USA

Nancy Frey
San Diego State University
San Diego, California, USA

Geneva Gay
University of Washington, Seattle
Seattle, Washington, USA

Shirley Brice Heath
Brown University
Providence, Rhode Island, USA

Kathleen V. Hoover-Dempsey
Vanderbilt University
Nashville, Tennessee, USA

Gay Ivey
James Madison University
Harrisonburg, Virginia, USA

Barbara Krol-Sinclair
Boston University
Boston, Massachusetts, USA
Chelsea Public Schools
Chelsea, Massachusetts, USA

Melanie R. Kuhn
Boston University
http://www.jiunlimited.com/en/index
Boston, Massachusetts, USA

Gloria Ladson-Billings
University of Wisconsin—Madison
Madison, Wisconsin, USA

Diane Lapp
San Diego State University
San Diego, California, USA

Alan L. Mendelsohn
New York University School of
   Medicine and Bellevue Hospital
   Center, Department of Pediatrics
New York, New York, USA

Luis C. Moll
University of Arizona
Tucson, Arizona, USA

Lesley Mandel Morrow
Rutgers University
New Brunswick, New Jersey, USA

Rosario Ordoñez-Jasis
California State University, Fullerton
Fullerton, California, USA

Jeanne R. Paratore
Boston University
Boston, Massachusetts, USA

Flora V. Rodríguez-Brown
University of Illinois at Chicago
Chicago, Illinois, USA

Nancy Roser
University of Texas at Austin
Austin, Texas, USA

Adina Schick
New York University
New York, New York, USA

Denny Taylor
Hofstra University
Hempstead, New York, USA

Manya C. Whitaker
Vanderbilt University
Nashville, Tennessee, USA

INTRODUCTION

The chapters in this book originated from a conversation, funded by The Ball Foundation, in which each contributing author was invited to come together in Chicago, share their work, and help create consensus about the kind of family literacy practices and research we as a field need to create true home–school–community partnerships. Some of those present viewed themselves as knowledgeable about literacy but less so about the family and community contexts that supported it; others had significant experience in creating interventions for and studying *early* literacy in the family; still other scholars had significant expertise in involvement in schooling more generally. What was created, then, was a meeting place where our diverse experiences and expertise created a broader conversation about the nature and function of literacy in the juxtaposition of family, community, and school. As one participant noted, "the past 30 years of research have contributed to an unfortunate bifurcation between home and school"; she then wondered aloud about the role her own research and writing had played in that process. Another commented that it was the most "intellectually rigorous" conversation she had been part of for quite some time. The diverse scholarly traditions and experiences present allowed us to examine and reconstruct potentials for family literacy as a field of inquiry that would truly transform the academic outcomes as well as relational practices for students, especially those most on the margins of our society.

While there are a plethora of sessions at educational conferences on family literacy, there is often little sustained effort to seriously interrogate our own field and the foundational concepts, dominant methods and theories, and organizing purposes that guide work in the domain of family literacy. This collective work, begun as a face-to-face dialogue and then represented in this book, is an effort to develop a conversation about school-based literacy routines in which understanding the patterns and practices of home life is central to all planning for and teaching of students.

Family literacy is often construed with parent–child book reading routines. Yet, literacy in the 21st century involves new, complex, and multimodal forms of interaction with symbols and text in which home–school–community connections are myriad and changing. The conversation started in this book endeavors

From *Bringing Literacy Home* edited by KaiLonnie Dunsmore and Douglas Fisher.
© 2010 by the International Reading Association.

to connect analysis of the multiple literacies present in students' lives with the patterns and practices of home, school, and community life. That is, we want to bring to the home the same sophisticated sets of tools and understandings that we apply to the development of new literacy standards.

Bringing Literacy Home also recognizes the reflexivity of professional and personal life. The scholars whose work is found in this volume reflect to a great degree the demographic diversity in our schools. This means that research on family literacy and teaching now posits teachers' own identities as well as the content of their discipline as directly situated in particular sociocultural contexts. It is important that practitioners understand that school-based literacy practices are cultural homes to some individuals and often not to others. We must develop strategies that help students see the goals and tasks of school literacy as a lens into understanding the meanings and values of the home. In addition, we must begin to explore the deeply personal and culturally situated nature of our own literacy research and practice.

This often happens in the moments that we tend to view as peripheral to our "real" work. In the symposium in which these chapters were first presented, talk about work during the formal presentations as well as during meal times and breaks was liberally peppered with stories about the children important in our lives and our struggles to juxtapose our work as professionals with our love, commitment, and passion for these children. Collectively we are literacy/learning professionals; that is, we make our living from teaching teachers about effective practices, writing articles and books, giving presentations, doing research, and leading workshops related to educational design. We're also parents, aunts or uncles, grandparents, and cousins. We are deeply invested in the educational success of the children so close to our hearts as well as very knowledgeable about current research on effective literacy strategies, instructional routines, and pedagogical practices. We lead busy lives in which we must work very intentionally to integrate our understanding of the academic literacies of school with the culture, values, and practices that are meaningful within our own homes. Our awareness of the social capital teachers bestow on children for their parents' involvement in school activities—that may have nominal impact on children's cognitive development—provides extra impetus for engagement in practices that at times seem less central to our family and professional goals. We too struggle with the imperatives about what parents should be doing at home and what families ought to look like. Very practically, the conversation surrounding the discussion of the chapters and the interactions around the authors themselves served to make very public the ways that literacy as a professional field of inquiry is also uniquely situated in the interactions and practices in our own homes. Our talk continued to bring the literacy of our work home in our own images, stories, and experiences with our children.

Because we all serve also in various ways as teacher educators, we were tasked with constructing chapters that would contribute to a change in the conversation that teachers have with one another about what it means to construct school practices that support family literacy. *Bringing Literacy Home* intentionally addresses the field of family literacy, of which the history is well documented in a number of chapters in this volume, particularly in the opening chapter. Foundations, professional organizations, corporations, legislators, school administrators, and community activities are often at the forefront of creating materials and publicizing expectations for how family routines and practices support the literacy development of children. Partnering with parents has become an axiom of successful school programs along with defined expectations for particular forms of literate routines in the home for school readiness markers. The opening chapter traces, through an unparalleled examination of three generations of family life, the ways in which the literate routines of the home are nested in broader economic, political, social, and geographical forces.

The first section of this book, "Supporting Families in School-Based Literacy Practices," examines some of the research on programs designed to assist parents in accessing the knowledge about how schools work, understanding the home practices that model and support school-based literacy routines, developing confidence and skill in using home routines to develop literacy practices, and creating relationships between families and teachers that allow parents to reflect on and at times interrogate the literacy routines of the school with respect to home. We know that rarely do parents intentionally take actions intended to deprive their children of important learning objectives; research repeatedly confirms that parents want better opportunities for their children, greater choice, and more certain school success.

In Chapter 1 of this volume, Shirley Brice Heath—who is one of the earliest scholars working in and defining this field—traces the economic, cultural, and educational research that has informed the development of family literacy as a field of study. Heath is best known for providing the rich linguistic and ethnographic portraits of families that repositioned the study of literacy in families of poverty and cultural diversity from a deficit perspective to one which acknowledged and explored the complex and multifaceted ways in which all families differentially use language. Particularly compelling in this chapter is that in tracing the evolution of families and communities over the past 40 years and the research that has surrounded them, Heath now raises questions about how decreased intergenerational activities and conversations have led to a loss of linguistic patterns important in supporting particular cognitive functions. Because she highlights this work by describing the community, family, and school contexts of several generations of children, she provides a uniquely personal perspective on family literacy as a professional field of inquiry.

In Chapter 2, Nancy Frey suggests that if we aim for true reciprocity and partnership with parents, we need to examine how to make schools more home-like rather than making homes more school-like. She invites us to ask ourselves hard questions about what we mean by dialogue, partnership, and reciprocity, in order to create organizational structures that can become a cultural and intellectual home to the diverse stakeholders represented in our classrooms. Family literacy that truly transforms students' opportunities might do better, Frey suggests, if they assist families—especially those who are most disenfranchised from the educational system—in developing tools that allow them to interrogate, challenge, teach, and question school practices and content. Frey argues that we need to work to create schools in which parents and students find in their classroom learning extensions of the values, goals, and activities of the home as opposed to passively accepting increased demands on the home. Frey's chapter serves not merely as prescience to subsequent chapters but rather as a conceptual frame for defining the transactional relationships between home and school that the authors in this book advocate.

In Chapter 3, Kathleen V. Hoover-Dempsey and Manya C. Whitaker examine dimensions of "relationship" between families and schools that are bidirectional. That is, concerns of the family and not just of the school inform the nature and character of the partnership. Their chapter provides an extensive survey of the research on parent engagement as a lens for examining literacy development and instruction. Scholarship in this field indicates the multiple and varied ways that home activities and parent interactions support, extend, and create new forms of cognitive engagement in children. This strongly suggests that in developing a model for parent involvement, a teacher or school needs to both recognize the multiple trajectories family engagement might take and work to create learning conditions that use these to form a true partnership, informed by the needs and values identified by the families, not only those identified by school staff.

In Chapter 4, Lesley Mandel Morrow, Alan L. Mendelsohn, and Melanie R. Kuhn begin with the reminder that family members are "children's first teachers" and children's teachers for "the longest time." They describe and then identify the common characteristics of three family literacy programs Morrow and her colleagues developed that were successful (based upon standardized measures of student achievement) in helping parents of young children engage in home literacy routines or activities with their children that supported or built school-based literacy practices (e.g., through at-home conversations, play, activities, speech acts). These programs were effective, the authors note, in part because of their attention to the adult learning conditions and infrastructure needed to support the participation of families, especially those of poverty. This raises important questions about the availability of funding to support models found to be effective, when such programs are often viewed as peripheral to the work of teachers and classroom learning.

In Chapter 5, Nancy Roser notes that children talk about books in the ways that the adults in their lives do. Children's interactions with texts are, thus, in her words *nestled* in relationships with families and the community and linked to goals that have situated meanings, functions, and definitions. Roser reviews a number of studies that examine the beliefs and practices of families of poverty and how community resources (or their lack) contribute to the literacies present in the home. This creates a more nuanced understanding of the role that socioeconomic status has on the availability and use of texts in daily life. In addition, Roser raises important questions about how texts privilege and objectify certain forms of experiences and examines ways in which teachers can create in classrooms the "intimate" conversations that help children gain skills at making meaning from representational forms.

In Chapter 6, Diane Lapp presents the case of an African American student and his family with whom she developed a long-term and multifaceted relationship in which she served as a teacher, mentor, advocate, friend, and learner. Lapp shares how she took what she learned from this relationship to construct new kinds of experiences for students in her teacher education classes and created curriculum and programs for public school students that intentionally connected to interests and practices of the home. The power in this chapter lies in how researchers can create relationships of reciprocity where learning about the lives and experiences of families provides meaningful change in the structures of the programs and practices in which researchers themselves are engaged.

The authors in Section 2, "Connecting School With Home Culture," argue that teachers need to develop new understandings both of the cultural resources and practices of students from nonmainstream backgrounds as well as to develop a broader understanding of the relationship between the interests, practices, and values students carry between multiple contexts, especially those of home and school. Although some of the authors start with the needs of nonmainstream populations (e.g., ethnic or linguistic minorities, recent immigrants, children of poverty), others start with the instructional routines of the classroom and examine the degree to which students' identities are represented, supported, and become resources to support engagement in the literacy practices of the classroom or provide motivation and contexts for ongoing skill development. In this section, student engagement in learning is clearly situated in the transactions between life in and out of school, and family literacy is addressed not merely through the interaction that children have with their parents but also through the degree to which "the familiar" is represented in the texts, goals, interaction patterns, and norms of the classroom. The chapters in this section raise questions about the classroom pedagogies and teacher expertise needed to effectively use the knowledge and interests that students bring into the classroom as resources for the academic literacies of school.

Geneva Gay, in Chapter 7, draws from her own research and that of others to illustrate the powerful motivational and cognitive support provided to conventional literacy instruction when teachers intentionally recognize, use, and celebrate the cultural literacies students bring with them. She suggests that instructional practices that enable students to learn with the tools gained from their family interactions, communities, and cultural traditions provide important aids to the development of academic literacy. Gay examines teachers as learners themselves, suggesting that recognition of one's own self as a cultural being creates a reflexive space for understanding how culturally situated norms, expectations, and routines inform pedagogical decision making and differentially support student success.

In Chapter 8, Patricia A. Edwards speaks intentionally as an African American family literacy scholar to provide a context for understanding the convictions about power and access that guide her work on the literacy development of students from marginalized communities. She notes that criticism of intervention programs that help parents acquire the literate routines privileged in schools often suggest that they minimize the rich, varied, and complex literacies present in the life of African American families. She argues, however, that her own lived reality demonstrates the need for parents and students to both understand and have access to the literacies that allow them in to the codes, institutions, and knowledge of the cultural mainstream. Teachers' recognition of multiple literacies must not mask the cultural hegemony of American institutions in which particular ways of knowing are privileged, rendering certain forms of literacy as barriers to participation and others as bridges.

In Chapter 9, Flora V. Rodriguez-Brown provides a detailed examination of a program she and her colleagues developed to support new immigrant Latino families in becoming active participants in their children's school experiences and literacy learning. She explores as well the theoretical relationship between learning and culture and the means by which university research programs serve an important resource to community organization. The description of Project FLAME (Family Literacy: Aprendiendo, Mejorando, Educando [Leading, Improving, Educating]) illustrates how a program can simultaneously provide functional and critical literacy skills and use a curriculum in which the participants' ownership allows for evolution and transformation. Rodriguez-Brown argues that effective family literacy programs are characterized by a philosophical orientation and practice in which respect for and acceptance of the contributions families themselves bring is central.

Chapter 10, by Gloria Ladson-Billings, provides data snapshots from three projects in which teachers in various contexts are struggling to find ways to successfully teach African American students. As she notes, her stories are less of "triumph" than of an ongoing commitment by teachers to learn from their students and examine their own teaching strategies. Another characteristic of successful instruction for marginalized students was these teachers' abilities to help students learn how to access the knowledge and skills they already possessed to use as tools in new and unfamiliar contexts. Ladson-Billings suggests that pedagogical ideologies and deficit views of students and their families can hinder teachers from placing student learning at the heart of instructional decision making, creating a culture in which students from particular families had permission to fail. She argues that if teachers make an unequivocal commitment to student learning and place student literacy achievement as the focus, teachers are then positioned to learn how the culture, practices, and skills that students bring to the classroom provide ready fodder for instructional strategies. What are evaluated and seen as wanting in such classrooms are strategies and pedagogies, not students.

In Chapter 11, Gay Ivey provides insight into the curricular and pedagogical contexts that support adolescent literacy development. She acknowledges that family literacy has never been a label applied to her work. This chapter, however, serves significantly to recast family literacy from an intervention for the teachers or parents of young children to a framework in which all teacher curricular decision making places culturally situated identity at its heart. "Family" and "family literacy" in this context represent the broader pattern of students' lives and experiences, which must inform the way we define and teach our school disciplines. The terms *home*, *school*, and *community* are arbitrary ways of dividing up the identities that students carry whole across geographical spaces and that affect their perception of the meaningfulness or utility of classroom tasks. Effective adolescent literacy pedagogies, Ivey notes, are those which engage individual (cultural) beings in reading, writing, or speaking activities that matter to them and draw from the repertoire of resources and interests with which they enter the classroom.

In Section 3, implications for family literacy research and scholarship are explored. Because most of the literature on family research has targeted young children and policies and funding for such work tends to be oriented around text-based interventions in the home rather than the challenging and changing of instruction in the school, we must begin to examine the characteristics needed in our own work as scholars to challenge rather than to contribute to relationships that lack the reflexivity needed for true transformation to occur. We need sophisticated analytic frameworks for understanding the role that culturally patterned norms around social interaction play in examining minute-by-minute encounters with reading, or how values and identities shape what and how students interact with texts in school. Questions are raised about the kinds of knowledge about students' lives that are essential in developing effective instructional routines in the classroom, as well as about the methodological tools and lenses needed for creating knowledge that changes how we understand students and schools. Educational scholars commonly cite the increasing linguistic and ethnic diversity of the student population engaging with a relatively homogeneous teaching population as problematic, but scholars do not clearly delineate the ways that literacy instruction in schools can and should change to create new opportunities and new forms of knowledge for students and their families. The issues raised in this section caution us as a field about how the research we do (and do not do) mediates the expectations teachers and schools hold for what family support of literacy entails. If we wish to caution teachers about identifying narrowly defined (and culturally situated) tasks as the only (essential) precursors to school-based literacy and about assuming that it must be parents alone who will reorganize the patterns of their daily life, then we must produce research that teaches, reveals, and informs.

In Chapter 12, Jeanne R. Paratore, Barbara Krol-Sinclair, Brooke David, and Adina Schick examine the long-term effects on student success and educational trajectory gained when family members participate in a program designed to build on participants' own knowledge to learn the codes of school-based literacy routines. Through gathering interviews and personal stories as well as more formal standardized achievement evidence, they demonstrate that the Intergenerational Literacy Program (ILP) provides significant gains for students on a range of dimensions long after program participation ends. Students whose families have participated show increased graduation rates, higher GPAs, more pursuit of postsecondary educational opportunities, and better school attendance among other factors. Furthermore, longer participation is correlated with increased outcomes both for these students and for siblings born subsequently. The ILP provides insights into possibilities for an educational system in which family (children, parents, grandparents, siblings, aunts or uncles, and cousins) are all invited into conversations and activities designed to reveal the norms and routines of school, develop facility in English-language literacy, and call on the cultural norms and traditions of the home to support school-based literacy routines.

In Chapter 13, Luis C. Moll and Julio Cammarota cite earlier work, for which they are well known, that examines the funds of knowledge of students from cultural and linguistic communities that are not mainstream in the U.S. schooling context and how these can serve as resources to support learning in school disciplines. The focus in this chapter is on a particular school program that assists students in cultivating new funds of knowledge that serve as resources for individual students as well as for their families and communities. The importance of biliteracy and selective acculturation of new forms of knowledge is discussed within the context of preserving family and community identity as well as more pragmatically supporting student achievement. Moll and Cammarota demonstrate how academic success in school need not be at the expense of cultural identity for nonmainstream students but is, in fact, inextricably linked to the preservation and privileging of family and community relationships. They suggest that the "participation of families becomes both process and outcome" of school-based learning (p. 303).

Chapter 14, by Catherine Compton-Lilly, is an invited reaction to themes arising in the conversation and writing of the previous chapters and their authors. Compton-Lilly responds through attending to how family literacy researchers approach the issue of time in delineating appropriate units of analysis for studying families, intervention programs, and literacy actions. She presents a selection from a broader critical literature review of family literacy research (under preparation at the time of this publication) that examines citation patterns, methodology, and theoretical lenses. She notes that how we invoke and delineate time indicates how we make sense of experience and identify those relationships that are of central importance. She suggests family literacy research needs to include a broader and more longitudinal portrait of literacy practices so that actions in the moment are understood as nested in larger social histories. The literature review reveals citation patterns that inform us about how educational scholars have constructed the field. She suggests that attending to timescales and in particular increasing the breadth of our lens may allow us to recast families as agents of their own transformations.

Chapter 15 presents an invited reaction by Rosario Ordoñez-Jasis, who examines the goals and practices that undergird literacy programs designed for families, especially those from oppressed populations. She calls attention to the ways in which ideologies reflected in programs for nondominant families reveal assumptions about the skills and tools families possess, the value of these practices, and the essential goals of literacy. Drawing on the theoretical and methodological tools of critical literacy, Ordoñez-Jasis suggests that our programs and curricular practices should invite social critique and social change, because to do otherwise masks and reifies existing inequalities of economic, political, and cultural power and privilege. She argues that family literacy programs must intentionally become places where families from subordinate cultures are allowed to develop voice, re-examine personal and institutional relationships, and own the direction of their own change. To do otherwise, she suggests, is both to render such programs ineffective for educational transformation and success as well as to continue the subordination and oppression of parts of U.S. society.

The concluding chapter in this volume, by Denny Taylor, provides an emotionally evocative portrait of the material context of words. Taylor uses the stylistic convention of "Everybody's Child" to present vignettes taken from her work with children affected by humanitarian and natural disasters, as well as trauma in her own and her friends' lives to explore the juxtaposition of material, emotional, and physical experiences that color our relationships with words and text. She provides a window into the psychological dimension of literacy development, as words studied formally as vocabulary and identified in the narrative and expository content materials of the classroom become detached from the embodiment of meaning in personal experience. Taylor points out that rarely is there a place in school for the kind of cognitive sense-making necessary to develop complex understandings of word meanings needed for a literacy that can support personal and collective transformation. If our scholarship contributes to stripping language and literacy of its connection to sensorial experience, it becomes truly academic in the pejorative—incapable of giving life, meaning, purpose, and tools to carry children into new and imagined futures.

Bringing Literacy Home is only in part about ensuring that family practices intentionally support school-based literacy routines. It is even more deeply about ensuring that the definitions of literacy we hold and pedagogies we employ at school are first and foremost deeply rooted in the meanings and identities children construct at home. We must bring our scholarship, educational practices, and academic strategies into radical juxtaposition so that home and community goals and values are viewed as key reformers of how we construct and make sense of school learning. Thus, while the research highlighted in this book examines the knowledge and practices we know are effective in helping parents engage in tasks at home that lead to statistically significant improvement in school learning outcomes, the authors also raise questions about power, access, and the forms of knowledge that are privileged. We raise questions about the institutional, political, and philosophical demands of "true" partnerships in which each party has the right to interrogate the other and each claims the responsibility of learning from and with the other as we collectively work to form a community that is home to all voices.

A portion of the proceeds from the sales of this book will benefit the International Reading Association's Teacher as Researcher Grant and Ronald W. Mitchell Convention Travel Grant.

—KaiLonnie Dunsmore and Douglas Fisher

Supporting Families in School-Based Literacy Practices

CHAPTER 1

Family Literacy or Community Learning? Some Critical Questions on Perspective

Shirley Brice Heath

For more than 30 years, I have followed the 300 families of Roadville, a working-class white community, and Trackton, a working-class black community, both in the southeastern United States. As a linguistic anthropologist, I began studying these families in 1969. I reported in *Ways With Words: Language, Life, and Work in Communities and Classrooms* and subsequent follow-up publications (Heath, 1983, 1990) the changing nature of language socialization in the lives of the original families I studied and their children and grandchildren. Through their economic setbacks and breaks of good luck, geographic relocations across the country, and numerous crises of health and natural disasters, I have followed these families and their descendants in the course of their changing patterns of socializing the young through and into oral and written language uses.

What follows in this chapter is a brief general overview of what I learned about the realities of changing family life across more than three decades. Some families have lived just on the cusp of disaster and economic wipe-out, while others have flourished. Others have little left in their lives that might be called "family." The patterns of oral and written language uses that emerge from their lives tell us much about changes in the values surrounding family literacy—reading and writing carried out jointly between adults and children in the home (Heath, in press).

From *Bringing Literacy Home* edited by KaiLonnie Dunsmore and Douglas Fisher.

Family Literacy—A Look Back

In the late 1970s, historian Christopher Lasch (1977) opened his controversial volume on "the family besieged" by stating an idea with which few public figures then or now would disagree:

> As the chief agency of socialization, the family reproduces cultural patterns in the individual. It not only imparts ethical norms, providing the child with his [sic] first instruction in the prevailing social rules, it profoundly shapes his character, in ways of which he is not even aware. The family instills modes of thought and action that become habitual. (p. 3)

Lasch (1977) goes on to say, "Because of its enormous emotional influence, it [the family] colors all of a child's subsequent experience" (p. 3). His volume traces the "invasion" of the family by social, medical, and educational services. His book is an extended warning of the consequences that will follow as families lose their traditional forms and purposes. He believes modern families have little resistance and, moreover, few resources with which to sustain the home as the haven it needs to be for children growing up in an increasingly cruel outside world.

Just about the time Lasch's (1977) widely publicized volume appeared, the concept and practice of "family literacy" came into the public realm of American education. Governmental and educational institutions wanted to turn around the negative effects they feared poverty and cultural "deprivation" brought to the academic success of America's children. During the 1970s, the United Nations renewed efforts worldwide to educate mothers, in the belief that they in turn could bring literacy goals and skills to their own children. In the United States, individuals still fired with the drive for civil rights and greater equity pushed for early childhood programs, some starting at birth. These programs were to supplement whatever parents living in poverty could provide and also to engage parents as partners to promote home reading, language development, and awareness of numeracy. Implicit in promotions of literacy in the home was the idea that reading together should be a core family activity, because books instilled values. Books and reading brought the literate ways of thinking that were highly prized in school into habitual practice and gave family members common ground for talking, joking, and cross-referencing observations of everyday life.

Following the Civil Rights era, policymakers in the United States promoted the power of equal educational opportunities to elevate rates of secondary-school graduation and college entry. Gradually, education, publicly defined as legitimization by the formal institution of schooling, became primary to goals and dreams parents held for their children as a preface to college entry and "success" in a future career. Many parents in the 1970s saw their own education as deficient and believed strongly that success in school could open opportunities to their children they themselves had been denied.

However, belief and action often do not match.

In the 1970s, anthropologists and linguists began to study families in the United States as closely as they had, in prior decades, examined households in regions scattered around the world. In communities within the United States, social scientists spent extended periods of time living closely with families of different social classes and cultural memberships. They documented paths of immigration for settlers in different regions of the country. They examined economic opportunities, patterns of religious beliefs, work in factories, and self-started small businesses. Their longitudinal studies of schools described ways that family norms of immigrants from all parts of the world both differed from and coordinated with the norms of formal schooling in the United States.

In some of their studies, these social scientists also detailed vast differences in language socialization contexts shaped not only by ideologies of family, home, religion, and respect, but also by the limited financial, time, and material resources that families had for matching school norms (Young, 1970). Social scientists, particularly anthropologists such as George and Louise Spindler and their many graduate students, documented home and school contexts of learning for multiple communities—Native American, African American, immigrant, and regional—in the extensive publications of the series Anthropology and Education. The Spindlers also collected several volumes of reports of studies that were later published as books (e.g., Spindler 1982). This work strongly influenced the studies of many students of education in graduate schools across the United States into the early 1990s. These social scientists did not find the "invasion" of social, medical, and educational services in impoverished and working-poor families that Lasch (1977) had foretold. Instead they found families struggling very much alone in communities—under-resourced and ill-prepared for the shifting demands of both school and work. Growing economic and educational aspirations of families were no match for the realities of their limited discretionary time and money. Families who previously lived by the rhythms of agricultural life, which offered some downtime and seasonal shifts, were now migrating steadily to manufacturing jobs that kept parents working day and night in unfamiliar rhythms that disrupted family life. Farming families had been accustomed to working with their children in gardens, on hunting expeditions, and in projects of home repair and maintenance. Now as millworkers, they saw their hours spent in joint adult–child activities severely curtailed. Social scientists cautioned that less time for talk and joint planning, telling of stories, working, and playing together would have repercussions for the "paths to success" so many families now dared to dream of for their children (Harrington & Boardman, 1997).

During the 1980s, economic recession and an increase in migration to urban centers brought rapid changes to almost every detail of family life that had been valued and practiced as recently as the past two decades. Families no longer knew their neighbors. Extended families were broken up by public housing rules that restricted the number of family members living in apartments. Outdoor spaces for gardening, safe play, spontaneous ballgames, and family cookouts were fast-fading memories for many families. Leaving behind wage-based employment and familiar religious and small-town or rural neighborhood social networks, families who migrated to mid-size cities and urban areas entered low-salary jobs or set up small businesses. They struggled with previously unknown forces—inner-city crime, the vagaries and costs of public transport, crowded living conditions, the appeal of the crack-cocaine trade for the young, and the dangers to children of play in open spaces away from the direct surveillance of family members.

These same issues met families who entered the country through economic migration or refugee status following the Vietnam War and upheavals and loss of human rights in their home countries. These families had to struggle not only to survive financially but also to learn a new language and to understand American schooling. They had little time for understanding the necessity of adopting literacy habits and family interactional patterns essential to success in that schooling. In many cases, their countries and cultures told stories orally and did not rely on written literature dedicated to children. Their patterns of respect for the authority of elders often had little tolerance for talking with their children over books and allowing children conversational time in the presence of adults.

Teachers often interpreted silence from immigrant children as ignorance or resistance. Homework, especially assignments involving extended multimodal projects, embarrassed immigrant parents whose inability to help their children meant that they lost respect in their children's eyes. These parents saw their dreams for what American education could provide their children begin to slip away as they stood by, watching helplessly as their children gravitated more and more to peer interactions away from home.

Believing in Equality

Numerous volumes in the 1970s and 1980s written by teachers who entered urban classrooms generally unprepared for immigrant children and children bused to new schools by desegregation rulings told stories of idealistic teachers and resistant students as well as stubborn teachers and creative young learners. Textbooks and teachers reflected little knowledge or understanding of the realities in the lives of students' families. White teachers, many of them male, often entered urban classrooms fresh from their participation in Civil Rights protests of the 1960s. Some of these teachers documented the painful and tedious lessons from their students who wanted to show their teachers that believing in equality did not make it so. Protests and legislation could not cure the social inequities that meant poor children in the United States lived in families whose time, space, aspirations, and inspirations could not move them toward equality.

Teachers who initially documented their learning experiences in urban classrooms moved beyond schools to look to social infrastructural supports for the academic success held out as the epitome of the American way. Herb Kohl and Jonathan Kozol led the way in these examinations (Kohl, 1967, 2009; Kozol, 1991). Entire communities got behind "block schools," claiming the right to have "a school of our own" (Roderick, 2001). Unique storefront schools, set up literally in storefronts of Harlem and inner-city Chicago and Detroit, offered alternatives to customary curricula and expectations of schooling (Rist, 1972).

Key individuals started family literacy programs (see the chapters by Gay, Edwards, and Rodríguez-Brown in this book). The National Family Literacy Center, funded by the Toyota Foundation, and numerous bilingual/bilerate programs for parents and children funded by the Ford Foundation, spread across the country. Social scientists paired up with state school officers and heads of state departments of education to prepare materials and workshops to help teachers learn more about the language and home backgrounds of the children they taught (Heath, 1972). Philosophers and social scientists despaired over the lack of preparation young teachers from white, middle-class backgrounds would have for life in urban classrooms or with immigrant students (Greene, 1973). They urged these teachers to try to see anew and to think through their own cultural backgrounds and to learn openly from those with different social class, immigration, and racial histories. John Dewey's ideas were renewed in experiential learning programs and grassroots, community-based organizations and documented in engaging and widely popular published accounts.

As the experiential and project-based bandwagon rolled forward, however, some few cautioned that much about experiential and creative learning that gave children opportunities for discovery in learning had little to do with the values many families held. For example, African Americans who had migrated from southern states often embraced expectations grounded in religious and social norms that accepted authority, hard work, and discipline (Delpit, 1996). These families expected teachers to hold high expectations, demand much of their children, and to be in authoritative control. The same was true of many immigrant families who had in their home countries grown accustomed to the norm that the teacher is the disciplinarian, the ultimate authority.

Though born of good intentions and a desperate sense of need, most of the progressive initiatives of the 1980s lasted only a few years. Infrastructural means were lacking to continue the institutional learning needed to integrate principles (and not just practices) into preservice and inservice teacher education and school schedules and norms. Students needed instruction in basics: phonics, multiplication tables, and problem sets in mathematics and science. Yet to feel, see, and deeply learn how to build from the basics for creative and critical thinking, they also needed immersion in experiential learning. Some students, especially those working in their second, third, or fourth language, also needed additional instructional time outside of school. They needed extensive practice with the basics to benefit from the joys of applying what they had learned to experiential projects, free reading, and library visits. Yet the combination of basics, sufficient practice in language, and motivation to imagine beyond the immediate could not be provided by urban schools or districts in rural areas of dwindling populations and resources.

State-based and federally supported initiatives became battlegrounds for competition among different school-reform ideas. Entrepreneurial individual educators and start-up for-profit companies offered wide-ranging solutions; most had little or no long-term research to back their claims of effectiveness. School-reform ideas competed fiercely with one another for adoption by those school districts whose public financing could support the spread of specific ideas for reform as well as new roles in education administration and practice. Some districts added literacy coaches, along with highly innovative programs of reading and writing instruction, and fostered family literacy opportunities. In some districts, however, governmental and public enthusiasm for comparative assessment of academic achievement led to decisions that narrowed or eliminated exploratory opportunities for learning in schools and defined *literacy* narrowly as comprehension of printed textual material.

Throughout the 1980s and well into the 1990s, strong leadership by notable educators pointed to the persistent and increasing diversity of students in classrooms across the United States and the importance of multicultural education (see the chapters by Hoover-Dempsey and Whitaker and by Ladson-Billings, in this book). Yet the majority of state-adopted materials for reading instruction stuck to neutral topics, ascribed grade-level vocabulary usage, and heightened emphasis on phonics-based instruction. Foundations pulled back their support for family literacy programs and community efforts in bilingual or biliterate education, choosing instead to support school reforms.

Some museums and grassroots community organizations persisted in their efforts to draw in families from different cultural and linguistic backgrounds. But cultural expectations of after-school activities, along with lack of access to transport, meant that only a small portion of students could spend sufficient time in guided learning in informal settings to move their skills into intermediate and advanced learning.

Meanwhile, the push continued, largely instigated by schools, for parents to take more responsibility for their children's school behavior, preparation for literacy, and response to homework assignments. When student failures became part of schools' public identities, the schools often shifted blame to the shortcomings and failures of parents. Negative views of teenagers and the dangers they presented to society accelerated. Sweeping state-level changes in judicial policies regarding juvenile offenders resulted in longer prison terms that in turn led to higher recidivism rates for young males, particularly those of color (Males, 1996). Not only gang membership but also numbers and types of gangs increased, as young men (and women) turned to these hood-families for security, a sense of identity, and often protection. Schools became encircled by high fences and other security measures. Regulations regarding clothing and accessories attempted to neutralize evidence of youth memberships beyond school doors. Assistant principals, long the pals of adolescents who needed an adult friend, were forced to shift in responsibility from friendship and casual conversations to discipline and control. Equality could not hold up in the face of middle America's increasing calls for security and accountability.

Community in Action

Some observers during these decades perceived within communities the same kinds of loss of spirit and engagement that Lasch (1977) had noted in the 1970s for families. Social scientists and public commentators on education responded to the invasion of institutions such as schools on home values and community norms by pointing out the vital need for organizations, entities that, unlike institutions, resulted from people acting through consent with flexible structures and recognition of fallibility and the need for ongoing learning. Many national spokespersons rebelled against an increasingly "care-less society" (McKnight, 1995). Organizations could and must accommodate diversity, stimulate creativity, respond quickly, and build leadership across multiple roles. They could prepare individuals, especially the young, for real work roles in adulthood. Unlike institutions, organizations could, for example, operate through principles that insisted all staff members view young people as civic resources and advocates for the arts, environmental change, and community improvement. Within this framework of responsibility, young people would see literacy as essential for not only career development but also for full participation in the civic sector.

As schools focused more on preventing and controlling trouble and promoting assessment in schools, some (albeit too few) community organizations and spokespersons took note of the critical need for individuals to come together into forums for citizenship (Putnam, 2000; Putnam & Feldstein, 2003). Libraries, YMCAs, Boys and Girls Clubs, and soccer leagues, for example, found ways to accelerate and expand their activities during out-of-school hours in order to help two-working-parent families and single-parent families. Literacy, numeracy, decision making, critical thinking, and argumentation figured as central to daily life in many youth activities in these organizations.

A survey of 120 youth organizations across the United States in the mid-1990s indicated expanded hours and opportunities, increased use of volunteers, and growth in innovative partnerships bringing several types of organizations together (Heath & Smyth, 1999; McLaughlin, Irby, & Langman, 1994). Libraries and other centers available to children during their nonschool hours increased electronic resources for children and young people and widened programming to involve Readers Theatre, puppetry, and environmental programs. Inner-city and rural youth who had access to community libraries found them the safest and most accessible no-cost places to be during nonschool hours. Religious organizations, in an effort to recruit and hold onto a young membership, expanded means of worship and participation, adding opportunities in music, youth-led services, films and books, and dramatic performances. Grassroots community organizations, as well as nationally based groups such as the Scouts, Boys and Girls Clubs, 4-H, and Future Farmers of America, expanded locations of their activities, moving into housing development recreation centers and sponsoring diverse types of summer camps. By the opening of the 21st century, students in some communities and neighborhoods had already experienced strong differences between school instructional hours and their after-school opportunities for exploration, creativity, team-based competition, and development of community service through the arts (Halpern, 2003).

Through the 1990s, many of these community organizations took as part of their mission helping to save young people from destructive forces in society. These organizations were zones of safety, offering both refuge from tension-filled homes and streets and the chance for the young to do something meaningful. Moreover, some youth organizations provided job training and experience in small-business development through social enterprise. In committing to the "business of place," small business developments promoted crafts, arts, innovation, and community building as well as consensual decision making (cf. Abrams, 2005). Federal programs, such as Job Corps, and union-sponsored training programs linked with community organizations gained attention through their message of complementing school learning and preparing workers for the 21st century. Behind all these efforts lay a paradox: youth can be a danger and a drag for society, yet young people represent the society's promise and possibility. The message of "let's save them" saw the young as potential employees, community leaders, heads of families, and leaders in small businesses for their neighborhoods.

Television channels such as Bravo, along with evening news programs, youth newspapers, and feature stories in local and national newspapers, celebrated the achievements of programs that rescued young people who otherwise might not have made it. In many cases, the immediate forces from which the youth needed respite and even removal came from their own families, where control by physical and mental abuse had become destructive to their most vulnerable members. The premises of community organizations that put young people into meaningful real roles built high-risk opportunities for work and play and surrounded them with tough love—the idea that adults are there for you and with you, never against you. Running social enterprises, pitching accounts to civic and business leaders, rallying for altered zoning rules, and many such activities carried high risks, for success or failure would have lasting effects (Heath & McLaughlin, 1993; Heath & Smyth, 1999).

These organizations carried additional features. Young people from newcomer families, second-generation immigrant families, African American families, and European American families came to take part. Languages, oral and written, flowed through everyday events: theater productions in Spanish, bilingual poetry volumes and song lyrics, and graffiti arts production projects all meant meaningful practice and authentic authorship. Parents in immigrant families had too often judged English as essential for their children and thus diminished verbal contact in their mother tongue with their children. As children grew older, they felt less able and willing to talk with their parents, and opportunities for reading, talking, and thinking together around books, ideas, and projects seemed strange and impossible. Instead, peers became the draw for young people who wanted to be where the action is and who could not imagine anything really happening in sustained interaction with extended written texts. Community organizations proved otherwise while also giving immigrant students ample opportunity to hear English used in business-oriented and project-driven contexts.

The most fortunate among first- and second-generation youth in immigrant families lived in households where the mother tongue was kept alive through wide-ranging functions. In these famlies, young people talked with parents and other family members in the mother tongue and saw them read mail and newspapers from the homeland and listen to television programs and read books— some or all in a language other than English. The children of these families acquired not only the habits and values of literacy but also learned early in their lives to articulate explanations, narrate directions, and ask questions. Once their English reached even a modicum of fluency, these children could manage most academic requirements, such as homework and assigned projects, discussion in class, and questions about the content and the process of assignments. In their mother tongue, they had already acquired ways of talking that met discourse demands of academic literacy. Learning to perform these ways in English came far more easily to them than to children from families who had not socialized their children in their mother tongue to the genres, styles, and functions that characterized not only school life but public institutional life in general. Community organizations that put adolescents at the center reinforced and added valuable meaningful practice in a wide range of genres and for audiences of many different types and interests.

Following the recession of the early 1980s and the loss of low-skilled jobs in the 1990s, more and more students lived in poverty and in families of the working poor (Hart & Risley, 1995, 1999; Lareau, 2003). Many not only entered school but also went through their full 12 years of public school without having daily extended conversations with adults—their parents or teachers—about abstract ideas, reading materials, or future projects and plans. Sustaining a conversation on a single topic for 10 minutes seemed out of reach for children from an increasing portion of families of the working poor, single-parent households, and two-working-parent families (Heath, in press; Miller, 2006). Formulating a plan for something so seemingly simple to teachers as a project or a laboratory experiment often required language skills unfamiliar in most children's linguistic repertoire. Throughout this decade, juvenile justice officials increasingly reported misdemeanors and crimes that resulted from young people not thinking about the consequences of their actions (Venkatesh, 2006). Extensive practice in talking about actions into the future and developing plans that involved complexities of intentional and unintentional consequences often was not available to allow young people to internalize thinking about cause and effect.

Many grassroots organizations recognized this important need among their young members and provided roles that put them into positions where they had agency. These roles asked youth to think ahead, anticipate what others might do, and consider how their actions would affect the operations of the unit as a whole. As scholars reported long-term positive effects of community organizations, federal and state policymakers took note. However, as policymakers created legislation for after-school learning opportunities, they failed to consider the critical features of learning environments that gave young people responsibilities and roles as well as guidance and tough love. The strong desire for a quick fix or magic bullet to improve young people's chances in schools led politicians to take scholars' reports of community organizations' successes and make them into turn-around stories. They failed to heed the recommendations of what was needed from the American Youth Policy Forum and numerous philanthropic foundations who urged more systematic attention to the needs of American youth and young families (e.g., Larner, Zipporoli, & Behrman, 1999; Halperin, 1998).

Instead, quick-fix stories were simplified and twisted into rationales for federal and state policies and programs. The 21st Century Community Learning Centers had been initially formulated around the findings of reports from research scholars and foundations (e.g., Heath & McLaughlin, 1993; for a brief history, see McCallion, 2003). The original idea had been to provide expanded nonschool learning opportunities to help prepare young people for the challenges of production, creativity, and civic responsibility. In many centers developed in the first five years (1995–2000), grandparents and nonworking family members became intensely involved, sharing with youth organizations their hobbies, narratives, and special talents in cooking, gardening, mixing paints, and crafting woodwork. Most of the initial Centers partnered schools and community resources by bringing artists, museum curators, parks and recreation groundskeepers, and community garden developers together with teachers interested in art, science, and civic engagement for students. Acknowledged in the initial years of the 21st Century Learning Centers was the fact that schools and community organizations worked to give children the best of both worlds (Heath & McLaughlin, 1994).

In the second round (2000–2005) of 21st Century Community Learning Centers, pressure was on for these centers to be located within schools and to work as extensions of the school day. The focus shifted from skills projected for future workers to skills needed to do homework and prepare for standardized tests. Teachers—not artists, health professionals, or park rangers—became central actors within these Centers. This arrangement gave teachers opportunities to supplement their salaries and to reinforce basic skills for academically weak students—thereby improving chances for schools to raise test scores. Community partners became only occasional participants offering one-off performances, visits, and presentations and only occasionally being able to work on long-term projects with children and youth. The Centers evolved quickly into being less about partnering—an initial premise behind establishment of the Centers—and more about school personnel and priorities. After-school and before-school opportunities had become by the middle of the first decade of the 21st century extended times for tutoring, homework catch-up, and child care for mothers who did not get off work until several hours after the end of the normal school day. Key premises of the experiential learning opportunities and grassroots community organizations that had inspired the after-school movement could not find their way into school-based, extended-day sessions that featured teachers charged with improving student performance.

Exceptions came in community schools that, though few in number, stepped forward to incorporate the best possible practices of academic and civic work in communities while also offering medical, social, and neighborhood resources to needy children (Dryfoos, Quinn, & Barkin, 2005). Community schools, along with neighborhood community organizations for youth, recognized that expectations the schools could make of families of the working poor had to match realities. Neither discretionary time nor money was available in a majority of these families. Out of reach were activities, such as reading, playing adult-child games, planning joint projects or family vacations, and visiting parks and other informal learning environments, that were designed for families with the time and finances to think about leisure.

In the 1990s, young people fortunate enough to find their way to grassroots community organizations or affiliates of national organizations (such as 4-H, Boys and Girls Clubs, Scouts, and Girls, Inc.), had the chance to develop identities as artists, environmental stewards collecting trash and urging recycling, and civic agents, as well as team members playing soccer or swimming. Many of these organizations included literacy and numeracy as a matter of course in routine activities and built into their system opportunities for young people to advance in status (e.g., from Cub Scout to Eagle Scout) through successful achievement of project development.

However, by the end of the 1990s, the public climate—driven by ideas put forward in the No Child Left Behind Act—pressured anyone involved with children and youth—especially those without the resources of middle- and upper-income families—to view the young primarily as students whose academic standing had to be improved. Gone for the most part were opportunities during the nonschool hours for these youth to take on roles that advanced their sense of agency, initiative, and interdisciplinary learning demonstrated through performance. Now they had to learn to play well the primary role of student. Doing so meant being passive learners who focused on earning good scores on tests that relied exclusively on reading skills and, to a lesser extent, on writing skills.

Through the first decade of the 21st century, notions of equity narrowed to mean everyone reaching certain levels on standardized test measures of achievement. Popular media, educators, and political and legal spokespersons for underrepresented groups raised to national awareness the idea of the "achievement gap," or the disparity of scores among racial groups. Descriptors such as *minorities* or *inner-city* stuck to young people confined in their local schools. Busing mandates and equal-opportunity ideals fell away from policymakers and judicial systems; the equity these had strived for fell back onto the shoulders of individual teachers and occasionally their principals (Baldacci, 2004; Fisher, 2007; Thomas-El, 2003). They were left to take on both blame for the achievement gap and responsibility for closing it. Urban and rural schools alike in poor districts faced the realities of too few quality trained teachers (especially in mathematics and the sciences), safe school spaces, textbooks and laboratory equipment, and opportunities for extracurricular activities and field trips. The arts, science clubs, special-interest projects, and enrichment trips disappeared in many school districts. The comparative status of American public education to achievements in other economically advanced nations became a matter of national shame and a strong reminder that earlier rhetoric about equal opportunity for all had no match in current political and educational realities.

Families in the 21st-Century Economy

From the opening of the first decade of the 21st century, perhaps no topics entered public debate as frequently as those surrounding family. What makes the *family*? What about *working class* as a designation? Had this class of families simply become the *working poor*? (Ehrenreich, 2001; Hicks, 2002). Such questions surrounded controversial issues that ranged from adoption and abortion to real estate and retirement. Adopted children sought and gained access to information about the identity of their birth mothers. Long-term, live-together agreements meant that *legal parents* had to be rethought in pragmatic terms. Dual-mother lesbian couples or dual-father gay couples offered challenges not only to norms and expectations of gendered roles but also to what had long been school-based celebrations of Valentine's Day, Mother's Day, and Father's Day. Single-parent families, multiple-family households, and separate parenting obligations under custodial arrangements offered a host of challenges to those seeking signatures on parental permission forms.

Meanwhile, in many communities—rural and urban—children and youth working as entrepreneurs in the underground economy of trafficking drugs, guns, and sex supported their families. Yet when they entered classrooms, they were seen only as students, asked to take their seats, forego their agency and independence, and become passive learners (Venkatesh, 2006). The number of foster children and children living with grandparents skyrocketed. Identification of children with special needs (especially autism) was no longer a private matter for individual families but a national crisis for the United States and a challenge to the medical establishment (Grinker, 2007). Spousal and child abuse increased. Inevitably, teachers, counselors, community-organization leaders, and librarians witnessed the effects of children's firsthand and secondhand exposure to violence in their homes and communities. An entire genre of young adult literature recounted the ingenuity, resilience, and creativity of children whose families had turned violent and abusive. More and more children were abandoned, left largely on their own by parents who disappeared or were imprisoned for crimes against society.

Long-standing expectations of home and family have centered on a single space as *the* home of a student and on biological heterosexual parents as *the* responsible caregivers. However, by the opening of the 21st century, more and more public observers and scholars pointed out the discrepancy between expectation and fact. Homelessness, parents with addiction or mental health problems, and growth in the prison population left more and more children on their own. Multiplying patterns of living arrangements meant more and more children *stayed* more than they *lived* at certain addresses. Back-migrations to home countries, as well as the realities of a precarious existence for undocumented or illegal immigrants, challenged norms of permanency and the clear identification of parents. Adult family members tutored young children on how to give only just enough information to satisfy authorities and when to claim fictional family membership and addresses.

Religious and political organizations, social science reports, and individual spokespersons for nonprofit groups argued that "families still matter" (Bengtson, Biblarz, & Roberts, 2002). Yet more and more libraries and community organizations had to find ways around bureaucratic demands for a single address or head-of-family designation in requisite paperwork related to grant support, liability reporting, and so on. In urban centers and small towns across the United States, many homeless families consisted of a single parent and child on their way to somewhere else and in search of only temporary housing. Natural disasters, such as Hurricane Katrina, separated and scattered families not only from prior physical locations but also from school and medical records. The worst outcomes that might have been imagined from Lasch's (1977) predictions about intrusions into family life and the wiping away of traditions rolled in with the flood waters of Katrina and the extended aftermath of consequences—medical, social, and economic.

The economic recession at the end of the first decade of the 21st century brought to a rapid end the American dream for families that had undertaken mortgages far beyond the realities of their wages or salaries. Public media surrounding the recession, which many felt to be a depression, brought into the open the extraordinary variations in families created by class, regional, sexual orientation, and immigration differences. The development of niche marketing for products related to home design and decoration, vacation planning, parenting, and dieting laid open only some of the many types of families living in the United States. Special interests, choices of vacation spots and recreational activities, along with demographic data such as combinations of languages in homes and numbers of households owned by individuals, could be picked up from Internet research. Americans, with little regard for real income, became consumed with acquiring and purchasing. One author described this consumption as resulting from markets corrupting children, infantilizing adults, and swallowing citizens whole (Barber, 2007).

Behind the commercial facade, however, were the realities of immigration status, poverty, number and types of jobs held by family members, and access to health care and mental health stability. Today it is irresponsible, perhaps unethical, for educators and policymakers to tout the family, as though the ideal family whose description opens Lasch's (1977) book exists as the norm or even as representative for the making of policies for the opening of the 21st century.

Accounts of Hurricane Katrina pointed to the inadequate, inept, and often unjust governmental response to this crisis as the cause for the broad scattering of families in the United States. What fell under the flood waters and in subsequent revelations was a general public faith that individuals could expect to bring together physical home, personal possessions, and healthy family members into a vibrant safe community of friends, churches, and schools. The tear in the American social fabric rendered by Katrina reached much further than Louisiana, Mississippi, and Texas (cf. Eggers, 2009).

Citizens across the country identified with relentless portraits of families' dispersal and despair, as many other families felt their own internal storms and floods, whether in the spread of new forms of drugs, such as methamphetamine, or by unemployment and eviction (Reding, 2009). Estimates in several regions of the country claimed that the majority of foreclosed homes had been purchased by grandparents raising their grandchildren, single parents trying to start anew with their children, and dual-families created by second marriages of parents with children from previous marriages. All these arrangements of family gave would-be homeowners rationales for taking advantage of sub-prime loans, delayed payment of interest, and heavy consumption through purchases made with credit cards. The need for more and more space became the mantra of advertising that hawked everything from real estate developments to home renovations, gazebo construction, and second homes in remote locations. Multiple computers and televisions, as well as entertainment centers, sent children of middle- and upper-class families scattering into their own rooms. Meanwhile, parents in two-working-parent households and single-parent households scurried off to work or play on their own computers. Social networking through Twitter and other brief means of connecting electronically kept family members in touch with distant others more often than with those living in the same household. Carbon footprints multiplied from flying to vacation homes that increasingly needed to replicate the communication hook-ups, entertainment centers, and easy access to customary foods that primary homes offered. If books went along on these travels at all, they increasingly did so through technological means made possible by digital reading devices.

Where, Then, Is Family Literacy in the Future?

Since the 1970s, most social scientists have worked with keen awareness of designations of deficit that prevailed before the Civil Rights era for families, children, and youth of backgrounds diverse in immigration experiences, language backgrounds, and cultural heritage. Study after study has laid bare strengths and resources of multicultural identities, bilingualism, and diverse routes of growing up (Zentella, 1997, 2005). Social justice has been a primary goal of social science research. This work has increasingly exposed the expanding gap between democratic goals of schooling and exclusionary effects of policies and practices that prevail in formal education. Statisticians and demographers point out that the achievement gap so widely discussed at the end of the first decade of the 21st century does not reflect the underachievement of young learners so much as it reveals continuing inequities of economic and educational possibilities and misunderstanding by parents of what must be done to protect their children from electronic media (O'Connor, Tilly, & Bobo, 2001).

The achievement of equity in schooling, family time, and community organizational life—all of which stimulate and reward literacy—has proved elusive even as more members of ethnic and racial groups formerly held down by unjust laws and discriminatory practices enter the upper classes. Scholars reveal that consumer habits and lifestyle choices of middle- and upper-class minority families now contribute to differential school performance (Yeakey & Henderson, 2009). Philosophers, empiricists, and theoreticians urge academics and policymakers to take care in generalizing about the sources of the self, or roots of self-definition (Taylor, 1989). They caution that rapidly increasing global moves—of people, resources, labor, and conflicting values—bring instrumental and atomistic outlooks sure to devalue the traditional and the civic. This devaluation feeds a growing inability to take the long view and to project unintended consequences.

This inability results from the nation's loss of processes and incentives for deliberative discourse around matters of severe consequence for all citizens. Health care, environmental change, educational innovation, and public works respect no particular persons or groups; these issues apply to everyone. Yet greed and refusal to think beyond individual goals shut off civic reasoning. There can be no better illustration of these points than the worldwide economic recession at the end of the first decade of the 21st century. The course of this event resulted from consistent denial of the relationship between act and consequence in an unregulated system of artifice and greed encouraged and rewarded through public forces that appear to families to obligate acts of consumption and norms of separation. This sense of obligation centers on an ideology found among parents of all classes, regardless of immigration status, geographic location, or specific familial needs and demands (such as inclusion of a special-needs child).

These obligations reach into families on welfare, the working poor, and the middle class, as well as the wealthy. The pressure is on for parents to *give*—things, opportunities, and immediate gratification. Parents in families across all types of situations today speak of their struggle to make sure their children get ahead. From every angle, parents are encouraged to believe they must give their children every possible opportunity; accountings that parents ask for from children focus on how children are using these opportunities (cf. Ochs & Taylor, 1995). Unquestioned is the obligation of parents to give their children opportunities for high school completion and movement into higher education.

Higher education, with its demands for academic achievement, pursuit of extracurricular service and engagements, and development of special talents in art, science, and civic commitment, stands as the general measure of parents having met their obligation. Family ideology thrusts parents into the position of involving their children in both the institutional life of school (and its requisite homework) and organizational opportunities of child care, recreation, and entertainment. This ideology projects the child into a future in which benefits accrue from successful achievement in current engagements. Many of these engagements require special uniforms and equipment, transport to places of practice, extra lessons, spectator opportunities, and other investments of time and money by parents. Along with these engagements comes socialization into competition, rank ordering by power and achievement, and expectations of praise for trying even with relatively mediocre success.

Missing from messages of obligation, however, are two critical factors that have long been central to concepts of family literacy: sustained language interactions with children and real pleasure in doing and being *with* children in all stages of development from infancy into young adulthood. From its beginning years, family literacy programs have been based on an underlying principle that promotes enjoyment and delight, wonder and curiosity, playful thinking and leisurely work of children and parents doing something together. Across classes, these norms find little credence or promotion among those who push the idea that parents must give opportunities to the children. The preposition *to* seems all wrong; instead, the preposition *with* would wipe out any notion of one-way giving. Mutual benefit and exchange of talents, skills, insight, and humor come into projects undertaken by adults with children. Such projects, whether reading or acting out a book, writing or drawing one's own book, or building a robot under guidance of an illustrated text, bring two individuals together in unique experiences that become indelible in memory.

The preposition *with,* central to family literacy, has been wiped out for parents across classes through the dominance of equipment for children at every stage. Designed for the child's solo exploration, much of this equipment (often labeled as *educational toys* or *edutainment*) centers on spectatorship, repetitive hand-eye coordination, and mimicry of adult toys. Miniature mobile telephones, computers, DVD players, drive-and-ride automobiles, kitchen and workbench tool sets, and even recreational vehicles put children into actions that mirror those of adults in their work. In families with more discretionary income, children wear miniature versions of the same clothing their parents wear during their recreational pursuits: baseball caps, sweatshirts, activity vests, backpacks, helmets, and sports shoes. Similarly, bed linens, lunchboxes, purses, sports bags, and sweatshirts carry images of figures known to children only through electronic media.

As many child-development specialists and public intellectuals began to note early in the 21st century, peer play, as known for centuries, significantly decreased in most parts of the United States (Sutton-Smith, 1997). Exploration in nearby forests and parks, neighborhood bike rides, and peer-planned projects of building or creating backyard forts, all but vanished (Louv, 2005). Even walking to school became a thing of the past (Hoffman, 2009). With the loss of free play, the ability to roam the neighborhood, or to explore the "wilderness," children have lost many of the personal connections to reading childhood classics with parents that have been treasured in past generations (Chabon, 2009). Classics of children's literature set children loose to find crawl spaces through holes in fences, step through the backs of cupboards, and explore deep dark forests (e.g., *The Secret Garden*, The Chronicles of Narnia, *Alice in Wonderland*). Parents today live in fear of unknown strangers and potential harm to their children. Thus they hire intimate strangers (e.g., coaches and other organizational providers of services to children) to watch over and guide their children.

Often these strangers have control over the young between the hours of 3:00 and 7:00 p.m., guiding lessons, clubs, and teams. When dinner comes, food, not a meal, is consumed. Most of this food is outsourced—characterized by fat, salt, and sugar content and brought in from take-out or fast-food restaurants— or bought as frozen dinners, pizzas, or fries in bulk packages at wholesale clubs and stuck in the microwave (Kessler, 2009; Pollan, 2006). Regular times for talk, planning joint play and projects, and exploring parks and beaches has fallen almost out of the realm of possibility of parents and children.

Shopping for food, clothes, or sports equipment could be a time for such talk. Instead, it often becomes routinized, as either a quick order on the Internet or a run to the mall by a parent and one or more children. Significant in such occasions is the resulting freedom for one parent to do something else while the child is occupied by the other parent on the outing. Talk on such outings tends to center on what *is*; the objects currently present in the environment of the wholesale club, grocery, or deli and not on what *is to be* or *to come*. Conversations such as these (as well as those that surround doing homework) are action-scripted, both drawing from artifacts in the immediate environment and centering on the pacing of the current activity. Explanatory talk (Blum-Kulka & Snow, 2002) primarily includes spurts of short utterances centered again on the immediate (Goodwin, 2006) or in argument that lacks one or more of the usual triangle of components of *because, then,* and *since* (Andrews, 2005; Tannen, 1998). Similarly, such explanatory talk lacks conditionals that set up future plans, assess past events in terms of consequences, or offer extended accounts of past events.

Every generalization about family life, whether with regard to family literacy, child language and art, or informal learning of science, has to be seen as only one arena in the vast array of potential combinations of behavior and ideology of young people and the adults with whom they interact. Yet largely anachronistic ideologies of family and literacy persist so fiercely that little is likely to jar these long-standing ways of thinking significantly in the near future. Most people still use the term *family* as noun and descriptor (as in *family dinner*) with more than a hint of romanticism. Numerous ideas linked with literacy and family time around and with books appear not only in curricular materials but also in announcements that go home from school, public celebrations, and numerous advertisements.

For those who remain concerned with family literacy, it is worthwhile to take stock on a regular basis of at least some of the realities of both *literacy* and *family* in rapidly shifting economic conditions.

Looking at the Future Through the Keyhole of Language

I close this chapter and open this volume with a keyhole through which to look—that of language. To look through a keyhole means that though we look through a tiny aperture, we see a larger vista beyond.

No keyhole is more pertinent to family literacy than that of language. Between 2000 and 2009, my study of language use between adults and children and among peers between the ages of 12 and 18 has shown changes in syntax that relate to shifting patterns of peer play, transport, solitary time with technology, and structured time with intimate strangers.

In contrast to the corpora of language collected in the 1970s and 1980s, talk during the 1990s began to reflect simplified syntax, a shrunken genre range, and reduction in the range of verifiable sources of conversational content. In short, the young in the first decade of the 21st century talk less about more and with less use of the creative potential of language than did their counterparts in the two preceding decades. Though it is true that many children and adolescents talk unceasingly with peers about contemporary media artists and forms as well as about technologies, software programs, electronic games, and Internet sources, their knowledge of what lies behind and within the majority of these sources is relatively shallow. On the other hand, for areas of genuine interest to them as individuals or in peer groups, they can rattle off the equivalent of pages and pages of an encyclopedia. Pushed, however, to compare origins, styles, content, and genres within these interests, young experts often wind down quickly. Asked to think of historical counterparts or counterpoints, their silence persists. Verifiable sources and influences on even their major interest areas cluster in recency, with little use of historical references.

In short, both between adults and children and among peers, the locus of attention centers primarily on the here and now and the management of current interests. It follows that particular grammatical structures indicating past and future time and variable conditions for consequences, and extended narrative forms, appear more and more infrequently. In public interactions, service personnel within institutions and organizations manage their daily interactions on the back of certain language forms: direct answers to frequently asked questions and referrals to managers or supervisors for matters that go beyond written and rehearsed instructions and procedures. The phenomenon of the "tipping point" may be relevant here (Gladwell, 2002). In the near future, we may reach a tipping point at which certain syntactic forms and vocabulary domains all but disappear from daily interactional use. Examples of language change abound in social history in relation to cultural and economic shifts. Cognition is intimately related to culture (Tomasello, 1999). The use of subjunctive forms that posit hypothetical or might-be worlds offers one such example in English and other Romance languages. Though frozen forms remain (such as "If I were you,..."), today's corpora of conversations across a range of circumstances have fewer and fewer creative forms of the subjunctive. The same is true for vocabulary items that have come into English from Greek, Latin, French, and Italian, the most common foreign sources of lexical items in English. Words such as *penumbra*, *hermetic, bon appétit*, or *decimated* rarely enter conversations the young take part in or hear.

Changes in the economy have brought new patterns of work and play. With these have come radical alterations in time, the uses of space, and views of what is important for and to parents and children. With all these changes have come reductions in sustained interactions between young and old around books and the kind of talk that books generate and provide. While sales of picture books and specialty and series books for children and young adult readers stay steady and have even accelerated on occasion since the opening of the 21st century, the sharing of books between adults and children has dropped off sharply according to numerous reports from the American Library Association, National Endowment for the Humanities, and local library and school surveys. When children reach the age of 4 or 5—even in families with discretionary income and literate-oriented ideology—reading together all but disappears. Thus this valuable time for the meaningful practice of the kinds of language needed to reason out, explore, and argue with a dilemma, problem, or imagined scenario is not taking place in conversations around books between adults and the young.

Other types of opportunities may, however, be on the rise among families and within communities who have chosen to reject the fast life of consumption, over scheduling, and electronic communication take-overs. Some few community groups are now considering slow cooking, community gardening, community arts, and the green movement (Elizabeth & Young, 2006; Kingsolver, 2007). All these collaborative work projects resemble those practiced in the home countries of many immigrants and in rural life in the United States in earlier centuries (Klindienst, 2006). These engagements call for joint planning, actions counter to the mainstream, thoughtful justifications, civic deliberation, and family literacy. Deliberative discourse works in connection with reading sources of information and creating diaries, recipes, and records of garden life, as well as accounts of community arts and science projects. Grassroots opportunities for citizen participation in deliberative democracy may be on the rise in U.S. communities (Gutmann & Thompson, 2004; Mutz, 2006). The notion and practice of community literacy resurfaced at the end of the 20th century, often through the arts and led in a majority of instances across the nation by communities of immigrant origin and often by young people (Goldbard, 2006). Within a decade, journals and books, as well as several documentary films, were absorbed by citizen science and the green movement (for example, *Community Literacy Journal*). Barack Obama's successful campaign for the presidency of the United States in 2008 modeled the mingling of family and community talk with electronic media and the importance of keeping abreast of new forms of communication such as twittering. Such literacies mean reading the media for instrumental, project-based means, but also comparing one's thoughts, activities, processes, and products with those of others. Doing so builds reading comprehension and critical reading and writing skills (Hobbs, 2007).

Activities and incentives for joint work and play that generate deliberative talk rely primarily on a mix of novice and expert, young and old. Times together abound with stories, explanations, questions, counterexamples, and bits and pieces of information from written texts and other verifiable retrievable sources, such as the Internet, films, and television programs. But there are already some hints that commercialization will transform even these efforts by private citizen groups and individuals into demands for special products and equipment. For example, in 2009 the phenomenon of slow cooking, a "new" old idea taken up in the popular press, was treated in only a handful of books and then primarily in relation to a product or piece of equipment. Dozens of books newly celebrated the slow cooker (first introduced under the trade name Crock-Pot in the 1980s for women who needed to leave dinner to cook in the pot all day while they worked at jobs outside the home). The slow cooker was the focus of cookbooks setting out recipes and explaining ways to use the cooker. Other project-based think-and-do-together activities, such as garden composting, quickly found their way into the world of niche marketing and the hawking of "essential" products and pieces of equipment meant to make these projects faster, easier, and more efficient.

Family literacy, however, like all forms of reading, will never lend itself to being fast, easy, or efficient. Reading together calls for real time committed and unattached to a specific goal or tangible reward. Intangible are the rewards that reading together gives: social intimacy, laughter, fulfillment of curiosity, and contemplation of the wonders of real and imagined worlds. These values and pleasures cannot be co-opted by consumerism; as a consequence, they do not lend themselves to widespread adoption or promotion. Thus family literacy proponents and educators who depend on reading, writing, and talking within families to support the work of schools may be faced with a constantly receding horizon of what can be expected of family interaction and discourse. The accumulation of material goods, mediation through technologies, and limits on time and space for comaintenance and generation of projects by family members are sure to continue to influence changes in language structures and uses. Fluency or practiced competence with certain linguistic forms (such as those related to self-monitoring and self-regulation) may well continue to decline in usage among the young. As this fluency recedes, so may children's abilities to self-monitor their sense of order, predictability, and control.

Perhaps, however, we may take some solace in reminders such as that of writer George Eliot in *Middlemarch*: "But let the wise be warned against too great readiness at explanation: it multiplies the sources of mistake, lengthening the sum for reckoners sure to go wrong" (2003, p. 422). The pace of change in the current era adds intensity to Eliot's warning. Change in matters of intellect today come rapidly, particularly through the dizzying pace of research in the neurosciences and robotics. Before the end of the first decade of the 21st century, scientists predict that robots may go in thought and action further than their human creators intended. Moreover, neuroscientific breakthroughs promise to make possible devices to be implanted in the brain to control impulsive behavior and misfiring neurons.

As intelligent creativity flourishes, it is sure to bring not only entirely new and previously unimagined changes to older technologies and bodies of knowledge but also innovations not yet dreamed of. Changing forms of family and literacy will hold some role. But we also must expect more community literacies, ranging from targeted advertising and marketing based on patterns of Web surfing to communal responses to dwindling supplies of clean air, water, and safe food. In all these will be texts, oral and written, visual and verbal, inherent to projects of joint work and play upon which the futures of human life and the planet depend.

REFERENCES

Abrams, J. (2005). *The company we keep: Reinventing small business for people, community, and place.* White River Junction, VT: Chelsea Green.

Andrews, R. (2005). Models of argumentation in educational discourse. *Text, 25*(1), 107–127. doi:10.1515/text.2005.25.1.107

Baldacci, L. (2004). *Inside Mrs. B's classroom: Courage, hope, and learning on Chicago's South Side.* New York: McGraw-Hill.

Barber, B. (2007). *Consumed: How markets corrupt children, infantilize adults, and swallow citizens whole.* New York: W.W. Norton.

Bengtson, V.L., Biblarz, T.J., & Roberts, R.E. (2002). *How families still matter: A longitudinal study of youth in two generations.* New York: Cambridge University Press.

Blum-Kulka, S., & Snow, C.E. (2002). *Talking to adults: The contribution of multiparty discourse to language acquisition.* Mahwah, NJ: Erlbaum.

Chabon, M. (2009). Manhood for amateurs: The wilderness of childhood. *The New York Review of Books, 56*(12), 17–18.

Delpit, L. (1996). *Other people's children: Cultural conflict in the classroom.* New York: New Press.

Dryfoos, J., Quinn, J., & Barkin, C. (Eds.). (2005). *Community schools in action: Lessons from a decade of practice.* New York: Oxford University Press.

Eggers, D. (2009). *Zeitoun.* New York: McSweeney's.

Ehrenreich, B. (2001). *Nickel and dimed: On (not) getting by in America.* New York: Metropolitan.

Eliot, G. (2003). *Middlemarch.* New York: Fine Creative Media.

Elizabeth, L., & Young, S. (Eds.). (2006). *Works of heart: Building village through the arts.* Oakland, CA: New Works.

Fisher, M.T. (2007). *Writing in rhythm: Spoken word poetry in urban classrooms.* New York: Teachers College Press.

Gladwell, M. (2002). *The tipping point: How little things can make a big difference.* Boston: Little, Brown.

Goldbard, A. (2006). *New creative community: The art of cultural development.* Oakland, CA: New Village.

Goodwin, M. (2006). Participation, affect and trajectory in family directives/response sequences. *Text and Talk, 26*(4–5), 515–543.

Greene, M. (1973). *Teacher as stranger: Educational philosophy for the modern age.* Belmont, CA: Wadsworth.

Grinker, R.R. (2007). *Unstrange minds: Remapping the world of autism.* New York: Basic.

Gutmann, A., & Thompson, D.F. (2004). *Why deliberative democracy?* Princeton, NJ: Princeton University Press.

Halperin, S. (Ed.). (1998). *The forgotten half revisited: American youth and young families,*

1988–1998. Washington, DC: American Youth Policy Forum.

Halpern, R. (2003). *Making play work: The promise of after-school programs for low-income children*. New York: Teachers College Press.

Harrington, C.C., & Boardman, S.K. (1997). *Paths to success: Beating the odds in American society*. Cambridge, MA: Harvard University Press.

Hart, B., & Risley, T.R. (1995). *Meaningful differences in the everyday experience of young American children*. Baltimore: Paul H. Brookes.

Hart, B., & Risley, T.R. (1999). *The social world of children learning to talk*. Baltimore: Paul H. Brookes.

Heath, S.B. (1972). *Children's language*. Columbia, SC: State Department of Education.

Heath, S.B. (1983). *Ways with words: Language, life, and work in communities and classrooms*. Cambridge, England: Cambridge University Press.

Heath, S.B. (1990). The children of Trackton's children: Spoken and written language in social change. In J.W. Stigler, R.A. Shweder, & G.S. Herdt (Eds.), *Cultural psychology: Essays on comparative human development* (pp. 496–519). New York: Cambridge University Press.

Heath, S.B. (in press). *Intergenerational ways with words: Language, life, and work in families and communities*. Cambridge, England: Cambridge University Press.

Heath, S.B., & McLaughlin, M.W. (Eds.). (1993). *Identity and inner-city youth: Beyond ethnicity and gender*. New York: Teachers College Press.

Heath, S.B., & McLaughlin, M.W. (1994). The best of both worlds: Connecting schools and community youth organizations for all-day, all-year learning. *Educational Administration Quarterly, 30*(3), 278–300. doi:10.1177/0013161X94030003004

Heath, S.B., & Smyth, L. (1999). *Artshow: Youth and community development*. Washington, DC: Partners for Livable Communities.

Hicks, D. (2002). *Reading lives: Working-class children and literacy learning*. New York: Teachers College Press.

Hobbs, R. (2007). *Reading the media: Media literacy in high school English*. New York: Teachers College Press.

Hoffman, J. (2009, September 13). Why can't she walk to school? *The New York Times* [Styles], pp. 1, 14.

Kessler, D. (2009). *The end of overeating: Taking control of the insatiable American appetite*. New York: Rodale.

Kingsolver, B. (2007). *Animal, vegetable, miracle: A year of food life*. New York: HarperCollins.

Klindienst, P. (2006). *The earth knows my name: Food, culture, and sustainability in the gardens of ethnic Americans*. Boston: Beacon.

Kohl, H.R. (1967). *36 children*. New York: New American Library.

Kohl, H.R. (2009). *The Herb Kohl reader: Awakening the heart of teaching*. New York: New Press.

Kozol, J. (1991). *Savage inequalities: Children in America's schools*. New York: Harper.

Lareau, A. (2003). *Unequal childhoods: Class, race, and family life*. Berkeley: University of California Press.

Larner, M.B., Zipporoli, L., & Behrman, R.E. (1999). When school is out: Analysis and recommendations. *The Future of Children, 9*(2), 4–20.

Lasch, C. (1977). *Haven in a heartless world: The family besieged*. New York: Basic.

Louv, R. (2005). *Last child in the woods: Saving our children from nature-deficit disorder*. Chapel Hill, NC: Algonquin.

Males, M. (1996). *The scapegoat generation: America's war on adolescents*. Monroe, ME: Common Courage Press.

McCallion, G. (2003). *21st century community learning centers in P.L. 107-110: Background and funding*. Washington, DC: Congressional Research Service, Library of Congress.

McKnight, J. (1995). *The careless society: Community and its counterfeits*. New York: Basic.

McLaughlin, M.W., Irby, M.A., & Langman, J. (1994). *Urban sanctuaries: Neighborhood organizations in the lives and futures of inner-city youth*. San Francisco: Jossey-Bass.

Miller, S. (2006). *Conversation: A history of a declining art*. New Haven, CT: Yale University Press.

Mutz, D.C. (2006). *Hearing the other side: Deliberative versus participatory democracy.* New York: Cambridge University Press.

O'Connor, A., Tilly, C., & Bobo, L.D. (Eds.). (2001). *Urban inequality: Evidence from four cities.* New York: Russell Sage.

Ochs, E., & Taylor, C. (1995). The "father knows best" dynamic in dinnertime narratives. In K. Hall & M. Bucholtz (Eds.), *Gender articulated: Language and the socially constructed self* (pp. 97–120). New York: Routledge.

Pollan, M. (2006). *Omnivore's dilemma: A natural history of four meals.* New York: Penguin.

Putnam, R.D. (2000). *Bowling alone: The collapse and revival of American community.* New York: Simon & Schuster.

Putnam, R.D., & Feldstein, L.M. (2003). *Better together: Restoring the American community.* New York: Simon & Schuster.

Reding, N. (2009). *Methland: The death and life of an American small town.* New York: Bloomsbury.

Rist, R.C. (1972). *Restructuring American education: Innovations and alternatives.* New Brunswick, NJ: Transaction.

Roderick, T. (2001). *A school of our own: Parents, power, and community at the East Harlem Block schools.* New York: Teachers College Press.

Spindler, G.D. (1982). *Doing the ethnography of schooling: Educational anthropology in action.* New York: Holt, Rinehart and Winston.

Sutton-Smith, B. (1997). *The ambiguity of play.* Cambridge, MA: Harvard University Press.

Tannen, D. (1998). *The argument culture: Stopping America's war of words.* New York: Ballantine.

Taylor, C. (1989). *Sources of the self: The making of modern identity.* Cambridge, MA: Harvard University Press.

Thomas-El, S. (2003). *I choose to stay: A black teacher refuses to desert the inner city.* New York: Kensington.

Tomasello, M. (1999). *The cultural origins of human cognition.* Cambridge, MA: Harvard University Press.

Venkatesh, S.A. (2006). *Off the books: The underground economy of the urban poor.* Cambridge, MA: Harvard University Press.

Yeakey, C., & Henderson, R. (2009). *Surmounting all odds: Education, opportunity, and society in the new millennium.* New York: New Information Age.

Young, V.H. (1970). Family and childhood in a Southern Negro community. *American Anthropologist, 72*(2), 269–288. doi:10.1525/aa.1970.72.2.02a00030

Zentella, A.C. (1997). *Growing up bilingual.* Oxford, England: Blackwell.

Zentella, A.C. (2005). *Building on strengths: Language and literacy in Latino families and communities.* New York: Teachers College Press.

CHAPTER 2

Home Is Not Where You Live, But Where They Understand You

Nancy Frey

Educators agree that family literacy programs are at their best when they create a caring community of language and literacy that envelops everyone involved (e.g., Bryk & Schneider, 2002; Comer, 1995). And yet in too many cases, the school stands curiously distanced from the process. On the one hand, literacy educators devote great time and thought to crafting programs that are effective (as measured by achievement scores and contact hours), and sustainable (through outside funds, grant monies, and existing resources). The efforts of these teachers and parent educators are focused on research-based practices that foster phonological and comprehension skills that will serve children well in their school-based literacy lives. In addition, many family literacy programs also seek to positively influence the literacy levels of the adults who bring their children to school each day, especially through English-language classes. On the other hand, it is the school that is the arbiter of literacy services, while families are traditionally the consumers. The school itself remains unchanged, and the family literacy program is viewed as a means for perpetuating school-based practices.

To borrow a reading comprehension concept, there is a difference between a transmission model, where knowledge emanates from an authority (the author), and a transactional model, where meaning is a co-construction between the reader and the text (Rosenblatt, 1995). Reading educators understand that what the reader brings to the text enriches and extends it beyond the author's words. It is this fundamental quality that fosters discussion among readers. Likewise, a family literacy program that situates itself as the authority limits the discussion—it becomes a one-sided lecture with none of the exchange of ideas that leads to new understandings. Yet when the school itself remains open to the possibility of being changed through an interface with families, innovation can blossom.

German poet Christian Morgenstern is credited with writing almost a century ago, "Home is not where you live, but where you are understood" (1918, n.p.). In a place like school, where symbols of preferred knowledge such as academic reading and writing abound (see Chapter 7 in this volume), some families may be unintentionally alienated because they do not see a clear link to home life. School then remains misunderstood because these families avoid entering it, sometimes feeling as though they are intruding into a space where they have nothing to offer (Lapp, Fisher, Flood, & Moore, 2002). This is the transmission model come to fearful life—another generation learns that school is a place to be avoided as an adult, and another generation of students pass through classrooms as learners who are detached from their families, and who are therefore not fully understood by their teachers. The family assumes the role of a rare creature, spoken of by the child but only glimpsed briefly by the teacher. As educators, we are left to peer through the doorway and wonder what we might do differently to involve families in the literacy lives of their children. We return to the drawing board, tweak the activities, offer a new incentive, and hope that attendance will increase.

A transactional approach to family literacy programming could help these efforts more fully realize their promise. By examining the characteristics of strong families, schools could foster those same elements in their organizational structure. In other words, redefining school as a place where families are understood can correct a fundamental flaw in traditional family literacy programs: Our job is not to make homes more school-like, but to make school more home-like.

Making School More Like Home

What might be the effects on a school that became more home-like? Researchers in this book discuss the merits of a home-like school, albeit indirectly. When Paratore, Krol-Sinclair, David, and Schick (Chapter 12 in this volume) investigated the trajectory of the lives of participants in a family literacy program called the Intergenerational Literacy Program (ILP), they discovered that shared time with other family members was an important element; "the ILP is my other home," said one participant (p. 284). As well, in their review of the literature on family literacy, Hoover-Dempsey and Whitaker (Chapter 3 in this volume) describe how a sense of efficacy is vital in order for a parent to help a child learn. They caution that this is not cultivated through a prescribed list of activities but rather "is shaped by personal experiences of involvement success, observation of similar others', verbal persuasion by trusted others, and personal emotional and cognitive investment in their children's school success" (pp. 56–57). The BELLE Project (described in Chapter 4 in this volume) seeks to tap into this social network by positioning itself within well-child visits at the pediatrician's office. Each of these researchers indirectly highlights a factor that, collectively, could represent a next step in improving schools for families.

However, if school is to become more home-like, then we as educators must understand what home means. Too often we superimpose our own family experiences onto the members of a community and use those experiences as a yardstick for determining whether they measure up. The problem is that an examination of one's own personal history is inexorably bound in the context of the time and the culture of the community in which we lived. These differences are further compounded when the family histories of teachers and their students are widely disparate. Consider the national demographic statistics for school-aged children in the United States (Annie E. Casey Foundation, 2008):

- 32% are members of a single-parent household
- 18% live below the federal poverty level
- 22% are members of an immigrant family (at least one parent is foreign-born)
- 6% do not live with either parent
- 41% do not have Internet access at home
- 31% do not have a computer at home

Compare these to the national demographic portrait of teachers, collected during the 2000–2001 census ("Teacher Demographics," 2004):

- 90% are white
- 79% are female
- Median age is 46
- 56% have a master's degree

In addition, society itself has changed in many ways from the family structures of the 1960s, when many of those teachers were children themselves. Mobility rates have increased, leaving more people living at great distances from their extended families. More women have entered the workplace, resulting in a higher need for after-school care and supervision. One national survey reported that up to 60% of families with children in the home reported feeling stressed by the tension between work lives and time spent with family (Jacobs & Gerson, 2005).

It comes as little surprise that those who design family literacy programs are likely to begin with assumptions about what constitutes a family. Even those who are knowledgeable about the needs of the community are still vulnerable to assumptions about what constitutes a "good" and "supportive" parent. These measures typically include attendance at parent–teacher conferences, school performances, open houses, and PTA/PTO meetings. The common thread here is that first and foremost what is valued is family attendance at school functions. In fact, throughout this book, family attendance is reported as a chief measure of success. However, the ability to attend school functions is mitigated by practical considerations like the ability to take time away from work and to obtain transportation. If parents do not attend, they are viewed as being unsupportive and uninvolved. In their study of teacher perceptions of new immigrants, Suárez-Orozco, Suárez-Orozco, and Todorova (2008) put it succinctly: "Coming to school [is] a critical symbol of parent involvement" (p. 76). This attitude comes at a high cost. Weiss, Kreider, Lopez, and Chatman (2005) caution, "All too often, school personnel treat poor parents from a deficit perspective, which becomes a barrier to family involvement" (p. xvii).

On the other hand, a strengths-based approach can reveal new insights into the ways in which a school–home connection can be fostered. It is the family structure itself that should inform this direction.

Understanding the Characteristics of Family

To borrow a phrase, seek first to understand before being understood (Covey, 2004). The literature on family dynamics is vast but relatively unknown to educators. This is ironic, given that schools represent the second organizational structure a child will know. Family systems theory applies a biological model to understand symbiotic and supportive relationships that occur within a family structure. Importantly, it also recognizes that there are subsystems within the overall structure, such as the relationship between parents and relationships among siblings (for a thorough review, see Beels, 2002). Application of family systems theory is perhaps best seen in the health-care field, where treatment protocols invariably include plans for addressing the needs of the family. Both the American Psychiatric Association and the American Medical Association require that the family of the patient is considered in the treatment plan and recognize that the family may benefit from specialized care themselves. Although it may seem obvious, it is important that schools recognize these subsystems and acknowledge that the school's relationships with various members of a family will differ and will require specialized supports that work best given the person's position within the family.

Family systems researchers have sought to define the qualities that mark resilient families whose members are capable of supporting one another. Note that these qualities are not bound by defined roles because a family unit has less to do with blood relationships and more to do with affinity. These qualities include the following (Stinnett & DeFrain, 1985):

- Affection and appreciation
- Commitment
- Positive communication
- Ability to cope with a crisis
- Time together

These qualities could describe a home-like school setting as well. In what follows, I will explore each of these qualities through the lens of family literacy and make recommendations for further expansion of quality family literacy programs to build home-like qualities.

Affection and Appreciation

The direction of a journey is often determined with the first step. Similarly, the adoption of a belief system influences every subsequent aspect of a program's implementation. A strong family literacy program that is designed to augment resilient family structures is oriented toward an overall sense of affection and appreciation for what the community can offer. Moll and Cammarota's discussion of funds of knowledge (see Chapter 13, this volume) describes "methods to help define working-class families as possessing valuable cultural resources for instruction [and] challenging any perception that they would be lacking in such assets" (p. 289). In particular, the discussion of selective acculturation, which balances the school-based culture with home culture, provides a bridge to the concept of mutual appreciation. Using the lens of selective acculturation, the school is cognizant of the potential rifts that can be created within a family when children grow distant from a home culture that relies on certain language and communication styles. Moll and Cammarota note that parents' ability to provide guidance and discipline for their children is a linchpin to school-based success. A design approach that assesses a community's funds of knowledge can represent an important first step in creating a home-like school.

Commitment

A second quality of resilient families is their commitment to one another over a lifetime. In a similar fashion, a home-like school follows students not only across the grade span of the school but also beyond as students enter feeder schools. The role of a parent liaison can be critical for accomplishing this element. Parent liaisons are employed by a school to foster family involvement and a sense of self-efficacy within families (Sanders, 2008). Hoover-Dempsey and Whitaker (Chapter 3 in this volume) emphasize the importance of parents' self-efficacy in making schooling decisions and assuming an active role in their children's learning. They note that self-efficacy is built through both direct and vicarious mastery experiences. We often conceive of mastery as being experienced by an individual, but the authors note that the observation of other parents being successfully involved in the school serves as an important motivator for families who are not yet ready to become active members of the school community. The parent liaison can provide insights into the ways in which families can witness such events from a safe distance. For example, Sanders (2008) describes a reading event that shifted location from the school to a large apartment building where many of the school's students and former students lived. Families could participate or observe the event in a more comfortable and less intimidating setting. Partnership teams across schools can also coordinate events so that older and younger siblings can participate, which is vital for families with children attending more than one school, who must otherwise make choices to miss one event in order to attend another.

Positive Communication

For many families, the only opportunities they have to communicate with the school come in the form of parent–teacher conferences. These meetings are fraught with anxiety as parents brace themselves for negative feedback about their child. Some parents feel that they lack the language to fully participate or view the formal social and hierarchical structures of school as off-putting.

Lee (2005) interviewed first generation Korean parents whose children attended U.S. schools and who were labeled as "uncooperative" by the school because they did not participate in school functions and rarely responded to communications. She discovered that a number of barriers existed that made communication and participation unlikely. In particular, she discovered that scheduled events often conflicted with work responsibilities and unintentionally preferred families who had a stay-at-home parent or who worked in a 9 to 5 job. Families that worked more than one job, had complicated child-care schedules, or worked in the late afternoon and early evening could not attend (Lee, 2005). She also found that oral communication left many families feeling uncomfortable as they were likely to misunderstand the American social norms of interruption, turn taking, and disagreement. Indeed, the expectation by school personnel that parents are expected to ask questions and challenge ideas often differs from societal expectations in other countries (Suárez-Orozco, Suárez-Orozco, & Todorova, 2008). One Korean parent reported that it was "barbarian" to disagree with the teacher (Lee, 2005, p. 305). The same study also reported that the brief and decontextualized nature of written school communications (e.g., field trip notices, bus schedule changes, and school event announcements) made it difficult for families to determine what was important, especially when only some items were translated. One parent told the researcher that "she only read what was translated into Korean, leaving out information relevant to the whole school. She assumed that information directly affecting her children would be translated into Korean, when this was not the case" (Lee, 2005, p. 305).

Sociologist Annette Lareau (2003) conducted an ethnographic study of poor, working-class, and middle-class parents across several racial and ethnic groups. Her findings are a caution to educators to remember that differences in culturally bound communication styles should not be confused with personality traits:

> The same parents we observed silently accepting different teachers' (sometimes contradictory) assessments of their children were firmly vocal with their cable companies,

landlords, and local merchants. Working-class and poor parents are capable of being demanding with other adults. Rather, they do not define this approach as appropriate when dealing with school or medical professionals, perhaps in part because they lack the requisite vocabulary to effectively challenge such individuals. (p. 199)

Schools can develop a culturally responsive approach to communication (Gay, Chapter 7 in this volume) by using tools as a form of differentiation. Within a given class, some parents may prefer to receive communication logs—an ongoing journal of written notes that travels in the child's backpack. Others may wish to receive information in the form of a phone call. Still others want to communicate directly in informal arrangements, such as during a conversation that takes place at the classroom door after school. Just as it is unlikely that every child in the class will learn in exactly the same way, it is also true that families will have preferred communication modes. As families become more comfortable with relaxed communication styles, they will become more at ease with asking questions, making requests, and offering new ideas.

Ability to Cope With a Crisis

When faced with a problem, some families will draw together to pool resources and support one another, growing stronger in the process. Others fracture because the crisis overwhelms the family system. The ability to weather problems is referred to as resilience, and it has many parallels to the home-like school. While the term *crisis* connotes a large scale problem, in fact we can reinterpret its meaning as a challenge in the context of a school. Students in our schools face crossroads related to their academic and personal lives, and a home-like school sees itself as part of the extended family system. This may require that the school look for imaginative locations for delivering supports and services outside of the school walls, such as within the doctor's office in the Reach Out and Read program (Morrow, Mendelsohn, & Kuhn, Chapter 4 in this volume).

One of the most innovative programs in the United States today is the Harlem Children's Zone (HCZ), the brainchild of Geoffrey Canada. The HCZ is really a network of school and family supports and includes Foster Care Prevention Services that seek to strengthen families who are in crisis. One location is the Midtown Family Place, which combines a literacy program with a food pantry and after-school care (Tough, 2008). Several essential assumptions underlie this approach. First is the assumption that educational systems should play an important role in meeting the emotional, psychological, and learning needs of families. Second, HCZ acknowledges that it is difficult for families in crisis to be fully involved in their children's school lives, and therefore it is important to meet with parents where they are, both literally and figuratively. Importantly, the Midtown Family Place and the Beacon Centers (located in school buildings) are open until 9:00 p.m., six days a week.

Time Together

Time together is arguably the most valued element of all for resilient families. As noted earlier in this chapter, a majority of families feel that they do not have enough time to spend together as a family (Jacobs & Gerson, 2005). It is understandable that busy families who already feel that they are not together enough are going to be unwilling to sacrifice more time for school-related activities. However, if events are structured so that families see these events as time to spend together, they might be more likely to attend. Family literacy programs that are designed to maximize quality time spent together can provide families with valued services. Paratore, Krol-Sinclair, David, and Schick (see Chapter 12, this volume) report that intergenerational literacy programs like the one implemented in Boston play an important role in the lives of the families involved. When a participant reports that the family literacy program is "my other home," it indicates that the physical and psychological spaces created by the program have achieved an important goal.

But Are We Asking the Right Questions?

I have discussed the hallmarks of a strong and resilient family system and likened them to elements of effective family literacy programs. But I am left with a gnawing feeling that our efforts to justify the continuation of these elements are causing us to ask the wrong questions, or at least to overlook questions we should be asking. In nearly every chapter of this book, the studies cited report on the academic achievement results of family literacy programs, especially as measured by standardized test scores, attendance rates, and continued schooling experiences. More rarely, studies in the literacy field have looked at family results as they relate to educational attainment and career advancement. These measures are important, of course, and serve as indicators of change. But if Lareau (2003) is correct, then a major barrier to parent involvement in the school lives of their children has to do with understanding the vocabulary of education. This vocabulary extends beyond the technical use of language to the communication tools used to make oneself understood. The vocabulary of parent involvement and family literacy includes the ability to question, to disagree, to ask for help, to request clarification, and to make suggestions. Is it possible that this is the true literacy of families that we should be aiming for?

Future research in the field of family literacy could extend the ideas of authors in this book by using qualitative and quantitative methodologies to answer the following questions:

- What are the characteristics of family literacy programs that result in increased discourse between parents and school personnel?
- In what ways can schools create pathways for parents to assume leadership positions?
- How are schools changed due to parent empowerment?

I began this chapter with the quote, "Home is not where you live, but where you are understood" (Morganstern, 1918, n.p.). Family literacy projects have resulted in important changes in the lives of students and families, but schools remain relatively untouched by the process. In order for a program to be truly transactional, all stakeholders must be willing to risk change. Maintaining the status quo is inadequate; we have too many failing students to continue as before. In addition, we are serving communities that are enriched because of their diversity of language and culture. To reach real understanding, we must be willing to teach families the language of resistance and action along with the grammar and syntax of literacy.

REFERENCES

Annie E. Casey Foundation. (2008). *Kids count data center.* Retrieved December 13, 2008, from www.kidscount.org/datacenter

Beels, C. (2002). Notes for a cultural history of family therapy. *Family Process, 41*(1), 67–82. doi:10.1111/j.1545-5300.2002.401020000 67.x

Bryk, A.S., & Schneider, B. (2002). *Trust in schools: A core resource for improvement.* New York: Russell Sage Foundation.

Comer, J.P. (1995). *School power: Implications of an intervention project.* New York: Simon & Schuster.

Covey, S. (2004). *The 7 habits of highly effective people: Powerful lessons in personal change.* New York: Free Press.

Jacobs, J.A., & Gerson, K. (2005). *The time divide: Work, family, and gender inequality.* Cambridge, MA: Harvard University Press.

Lapp, D., Fisher, D., Flood, J., & Moore, K. (2002). "I don't want to teach it wrong": An investigation of the role families believe they should play in the early literacy development of their children. In D. Schallert, C. Fairbanks, J. Worthy, B. Maloch, & J. Hoffman (Eds.), *51st yearbook of the National Reading Conference,* (pp. 275–287). Oak Creek, WI: National Reading Conference.

Lareau, A. (2003). *Unequal childhoods: Class, race, and family life.* Berkeley: University of California Press.

Lee, S. (2005). Selective parent participation: Structural and cultural factors that influence school participation among Korean parents. *Equity & Excellence in Education, 38*(4), 299–308. doi:10.1080/10665680500299734

Morgenstern, C. (1918). *Stufen eine entwickelung in aphorismen und tagebuch-notizen.* Project Gutenberg e-book retrieved from www.gutenberg.org/etext/15898

Rosenblatt, L. (1995). *Literature as exploration.* New York: Modern Language Association.

Sanders, M.G. (2008). How parent liaisons can bridge the home-school gap. *The Journal of Educational Research, 101*(5), 287–296. doi:10.3200/JOER.101.5.287-298

Stinnett, N., & DeFrain, J. (1985). *Secrets of strong families.* Boston: Little, Brown.

Suárez-Orozco, C., Suárez-Orozco, M.M., & Todorova, I. (2008). *Learning a new land: Immigrant students in American society.* Cambridge, MA: Harvard University Press.

Teacher demographics. (2004, April/May). *Reading Today, 21*(5), p. 36.

Tough, P. (2008). *Whatever it takes: Geoffrey Canada's quest to change Harlem and America.* Boston: Houghton Mifflin.

Weiss, H.B., Kreider, H., Lopez, M.E., & Chatman, C.M. (Eds.). (2005). *Preparing educators to involve families: From theory to practice.* Thousand Oaks, CA: Sage.

CHAPTER 3

The Parental Involvement Process: Implications for Literacy Development

Kathleen V. Hoover-Dempsey and Manya C. Whitaker

Across recent decades, an increasingly informative body of research has suggested strongly that students learn most successfully when their families are actively engaged in supporting their learning. These findings have underscored parental involvement's strong links to several important student learning outcomes, including the development of skills, beliefs, and behaviors essential to effective learning across subjects and performance on summary measures of learning as well as achievement across the school years (e.g., Fan & Chen, 2001; Jeynes, 2003). Research on literacy learning too has suggested strongly that family involvement offers critical support for the development of skills and motivations central to literacy development (see Heath, Chapter 1; Morrow, Mendelsohn, & Kuhn, Chapter 4; Roser, Chapter 5; or Edwards, Chapter 8, this volume, for reviews of this literature).

In this chapter, we describe a model of the parental involvement *process* as a framework for understanding specific steps that literacy development programs might take to further enhance the incidence and effectiveness of family support for students' literacy learning. We begin with description and discussion of the model, move to brief consideration of principles undergirding effective applications of the model, and conclude with a sample of applications for using the model to enhance program support for effective family engagement in students' literacy development.

From *Bringing Literacy Home* edited by KaiLonnie Dunsmore and Douglas Fisher.
© 2010 by the International Reading Association.

The Parental Involvement Process

Grounded in prior work on parental involvement, Hoover-Dempsey and Sandler (1995) offer a model of the parental involvement process focused on understanding *why* parents become involved in their children's education and *how* their involvement, once engaged, influences student learning. As further developed in subsequent work (Green, Walker, Hoover-Dempsey and Sandler, 2007; Hoover-Dempsey & Sandler, 1997; Hoover-Dempsey et al., 2005; Walker, Wilkins, Dallaire, Sandler, & Hoover-Dempsey, 2005), the model suggests that the parental involvement process moves through several different levels (see Figure 3.1).

The process begins in parents' *motivations* for becoming involved (Level 1), continues in their selection of varied involvement *forms* (Level 1.5), and focuses then on parents' selection and use of varied *learning mechanisms* in the course of involvement activities (Level 2). The model suggests next that parental involvement's influence on student learning depends in part on *students' perceptions* of involvement (Level 3). At Level 4, the model suggests that parental involvement has its strongest and most direct influence on student learning through its support for students' development of varied *skills and attributes* that are often essential to effective learning across the course of schooling, including literacy learning. The model concludes in Level 5, which suggests that the learning skills and attributes students develop in the context of family involvement—when *engaged* by students across learning settings and tasks—offer critical support for their learning accomplishments throughout the course of schooling.

The model thus highlights the multiple and complex ways through which parental involvement influences students' school learning. It provides insights into why and how parents become involved, and it suggests that understanding of the process must include attending to the learning mechanisms parents engage during involvement and attending to students' perceptions of that involvement. In focusing on the outcomes of parental involvement, the model suggests that its primary outcomes are to be found in students' development of attributes and skills that, when used by students in the course of learning, support achievement across domains of schooling. The model thus offers schools, programs, teachers, and families information that may be essential to expanding the depth and effectiveness of school support for family involvement as well as the effectiveness of the involvement process itself.

The model's focus on involvement as a process may challenge assumptions about why parents are—or are not—involved; it may challenge easy

Figure 3.1. Model of the Parental Involvement Process

Level 5

Student Achievement (Varied Summary Measures)

↑

Level 4

Student Proximal Learning Attributes Conducive to Achievement, e.g.:			
Academic Self-Efficacy	Intrinsic Motivation to Learn	Self-Regulatory Strategy Knowledge & Use	Social Self-Efficacy for Relating to Teachers

↑

Level 3

(Mediated by) Student Perceptions of Learning Mechanisms Engaged by Parents			
Encouragement	Modeling	Reinforcement	Instruction

↑

Level 2

Learning Mechanisms Engaged by Parents during Involvement Activities, e.g.:			
Encouragement	Modeling	Reinforcement	Instruction

↑

Level 1.5

Parent Involvement Forms. e.g.,:			
Values, Goals, Expectations, Aspirations.	Involvement Activities at Home	Parent/ Teacher/School Communications	Involvement Activities at School

↑

Level 1

Personal Motivators		Parent's Perceptions of Contextual Invitations to Involvement			Life Context Variables		
Parental Role Construction for Involvement	Parental Efficacy for Helping the Student Succeed in School	General School Invitations	Specific Teacher Invitations	Specific Student Invitations	Parental Knowledge & Skills	Parental Time & Energy	Family Culture

Note. Adapted from Hoover-Dempsey & Sandler, 1995, 1997, 2005.

assumptions that involvement is basically a set of activities that thoughtful parents "do" with their children to help them learn. This focus offers often expanded perspectives on the multiple ways in which families may model, support, and encourage their children's learning, as well as expanded perspectives on parents' contributions to students' learning in literacy and across domains of early childhood, elementary, and secondary schooling. The model also essentially suggests that the most important contributions of effective family involvement are found in families' support for students' beliefs about themselves as learners, students' motivations for learning, and students' development of effective learning strategies. Applied to literacy development in childhood and adolescence, the model suggests fundamentally that when the involvement process is supported by schools, programs, teachers, and communities and is construed as a productive *relationship* between program and family, it offers resources essential for effective student learning. Please note that while the model and related literature in parental involvement are broadly pertinent to literacy learning across the early childhood through adolescent years, applications in this chapter—following the preponderance of work in both parental involvement and literacy development—are focused primarily on the early childhood and elementary years. For background and suggestions regarding parental involvement in adolescence, see Hoover-Dempsey, Ice, and Whitaker (2009) and Ivey, Chapter 11 in this volume.

We turn now to describing each level of the model in somewhat more detail. Consistent with the major purposes of this book, references are kept to a minimum; readers may consult works cited in the first paragraph of this section for additional information.

What Motivates Parents to Become Involved? (Level 1)

The model suggests first that parents' decisions about actively supporting their children's learning in literacy and across domains of school learning are grounded in three major sources of motivation: personal psychological motivators, contextual motivators, and school or program responsiveness to important elements of family life contexts (Level 1, Figure 3.1).

Personal Psychological Motivators of Involvement. Personal psychological motivators of involvement include parents' role construction for involvement (what parents believe they are supposed to do in supporting their children's school learning) and parents' self-efficacy beliefs for helping their children succeed in school (what parents believe about the likelihood that their involvement activities will make a difference in their children's learning). *Role construction* for involvement is shaped by parents' understanding of important others' expectations for their involvement in their children's education. These "important others" generally include family, members of parents' social support systems, and others (e.g., children's teachers) who may offer important contributions to parents' decisions about involvement. Parents' *sense of efficacy* for helping their children learn is shaped by personal experiences of involvement success, observation of similar others' (e.g., parents "like me") successful involvement, verbal persuasion by trusted others (e.g., family members, friends, teachers), and personal emotional and cognitive investment in their children's school success. A sense of efficacy for helping the child learn influences not only parents' decisions about involvement but also their persistence in supporting their children's learning in the face of challenges.

Very important from the perspective of all current and potential participants (families, schools, communities), role construction and efficacy are both subject to notable influence by teachers and school or program staff, especially when these school or program staff members are perceived by parents to be trustworthy, knowledgeable, and helpful.

Research on parents' role construction for involvement and sense of efficacy for helping their children learn has suggested that both factors exert important influence on parents' decisions about active engagement in their children's learning. Thus, the more active parental role construction is and the more positive parents' sense of efficacy is, the more likely parents are to be actively and productively engaged (with teachers and school personnel, if a positive and trusting relationship is in place) in supporting their children's learning.

The importance of role construction and sense of efficacy to parents' decisions about becoming actively involved in supporting their children's learning has been noted often in work on literacy development. For example, Lapp, Fisher, Flood, and Moore (2002) and Edwards (1995) note the very negative effects of weak or passive parental role construction on parents' decisions about involvement. Morrow and Young's (1997) quotation from an interview with parents who participated in a family literacy program offers a strong endorsement of self-efficacy's importance to decisions about involvement: "I learned how to help my child *and that I could*" (p. 740, emphasis added).

Overall, the evidence suggests that when parents believe they should be involved, believe that they know what to do when they're involved, *and* experience their involvement as making a positive difference in their children's learning, they are most likely to be actively and consistently involved in supporting their children's literacy development.

Contextual Motivators of Involvement. The next contributor to parents' decisions about involvement (Level 1, Figure 3.1) suggests that parents' motivations are strongly influenced by their perceptions of invitations to involvement from others directly engaged in the child's education. The others who are notably important in offering those invitations include school or program staff, teachers, and the student.

General invitations from the school or program are generally reflected in program-wide practices emphasizing that the school values and *wants* parents' active engagement in student learning. These invitations are often most effective when teachers and other program staff offer interesting and manageable opportunities for family engagement in student learning. They are also effectively developed when schools convey clearly that they are committed to building *relationships* with families characterized by trust, meaningful roles for family members, and consistently respectful communications and interactions.

Specific invitations from teachers, too, play a critical role in parents' decisions about involvement. Teachers' invitations appear particularly powerful when they include manageable suggestions for *specific* and manageable steps that families can take to support student learning. Parents spoke frequently of such invitations during one study (Hoover-Dempsey, Bassler, & Burow, 1995); they identified teachers' suggestions that were focused, specific, and manageable within the contexts of their own lives—as well as those offering specific information in response to parents' questions. For example, one parent asked his child's teacher about how he should think about and support his son's reading. According to this father, the teacher's response was,

> Let him read for 15 minutes, and have him read out loud so you can hear him. And when he makes mistakes, don't say, "No, you know better than that...." Go in there and say, "I think you've misread this" and "Let's go over this together." The parent added, "It really helps.... She's fantastic [and] we need more like her." (p. 443)

Very importantly, teachers' direct and responsive suggestions (offered without direct request or in response to parents' questions) also actively affirm the value of parents' engagement in supporting their children's learning. Their suggestions also often encourage parents' sense of partnership *with* teachers and the school in supporting students' learning success.

Specific invitations from the student are often notably powerful in motivating involvement, in part because parents generally want their children to succeed and want to support their development and respond effectively to their needs. Student invitations may come in direct requests (e.g., "I don't get this; can you help me?") and in more implicit forms, as parents observe children's learning processes, successes, frustrations, and difficulties. The power of students' requests has been noted in several studies. For example, there were numerous occasions on which parents spontaneously described requests from a child and their own responses (e.g., "*If she has a question about something she is doing,* we will sit down and read the instructions together and talk about it, or maybe have to look in her books and see the explanations or something"; Hoover-Dempsey et al., 1995, p. 441, emphasis added). Within the context of their own study, Morrow and Young (1997) emphasize that the parent–child *interactions* growing out of joint engagement in learning activities in response to children's questions and interests are a critical element of family support for students' literacy learning.

Teachers may also play an important role in supporting student invitations to involvement. Most often, they do so by designing homework tasks that require interactions with family members (e.g., Epstein & Van Voorhis, 2001) or by structuring assignments in ways that require students to seek information from parents related to parents' experiences or expertise (e.g., González, Andrade, Civil, & Moll, 2001).

Research on the effects of contextual invitations to involvement thus has underscored the power of school, program, teacher, and child invitations to involvement. We suggest that school or program invitations are more powerful when they are grounded in assumptions of partnership and when the invitations convey that the school or teacher values family involvement. The power of specific teacher invitations is likely linked to many parents' expressed desire to know what they can do that will be helpful in supporting their children's learning, and the power of children's invitations to involvement quite likely emerges from parents' wishes to respond well to their children's needs.

Overall, the findings suggest that literacy programs whose qualities invite, support, and inform parents' engagement in their children's learning—and whose teachers and staff members offer respectful, responsive, specific, and manageable suggestions for involvement—are likely to experience notable family support for students' literacy development.

Responsiveness to Important Elements of Family Life Context. The model's first level suggests that a third major motivator of parental involvement is found in school, program, and teacher responsiveness to elements of family life context relevant to parents' thinking about involvement. These elements include parents' perceptions of the skills and knowledge they bring to involvement, the time and energy they can give to involvement, and their past experience of school, program, and teacher responsiveness to important elements of family culture. Consistent with these factors, work on parental involvement has suggested that if parents believe that their *skills and knowledge*, as well as *time and energy*, are sufficient for the demands of a particular learning task or activity, they will generally engage in that task and will be pleased to help.

We've found (as have several literacy investigators) many examples of parents working to integrate active support for their children's learning into the routine demands of everyday family life. One parent in our study, for example, told us that she cooks while her child reads (Hoover-Dempsey et al., 1995). In that process, she continued,

> If [a word] didn't sound right, [then] I make him go back and read it over again. And if he skips over it again, or it sounded the same way, I go back and I read it. [Then I will] tell him, "C., this is not right, that word is something else.... Don't skip over the words; you've got to break it down and read what it is." (p. 443)

As is true of others, we have also found that if parents believe their skills or knowledge are *not* adequate to a learning task—or that their time and energy are stretched too thin—they may seek alternative sources of help, try to do what they can, or simply avoid involvement.

Family culture clearly plays a significant role in many parents' thinking about involvement in children's learning. Of particular concern to many families and professionals are school or program practices that (a) reflect, implicitly or explicitly, a belief that parents who "don't show up at school" are uninterested in or don't care about their children's learning; (b) encourage and support—or ignore and negate—the richness of families' contributions to their children's learning; and (c) attend well to—or ignore and fail to address—barriers to effective parental involvement. Such concerns underscore the importance of school and program efforts to develop effective and mutually supportive relationships with students' families. These relationships are often critically important, simply because it is often only in the context of such relationships that families' hopes and aspirations for their children's education may be made known, their funds of knowledge engaged to support student learning, and their insights into their children's learning interests, needs, and strengths recognized by those working with the child at school.

Considerable work in literacy development, emerging from a range of perspectives, has underscored the particular importance of school responsiveness to family culture and circumstances to many parents' thinking about the options available for supporting their children's literacy learning. The results of research in these areas point to the often critical importance of school and program efforts explicitly focused on valuing the strengths that families may bring to supporting their children's literacy learning (for examples see Morrow et al., Chapter 4; Lapp, Chapter 6; Gay, Chapter 7; Edwards, Chapter 8; Rodriguez-Brown, Chapter 9; Ladson-Billings, Chapter 10; and Moll & Cammarota, Chapter 13).

What Is Parental Involvement? (Level 1.5)

Assuming that families are motivated to be actively involved in supporting their children's learning across the school years and across specific domains of learning, they generally have several forms of involvement from which they may choose. Contrary to an assumption about students' families that is sometimes heard in schools (e.g., "They're never at school; they just don't care"), parents may be quite actively involved in supporting their children's learning in several different ways. Four are included in the model (Level 1.5, Figure 3.1).

One incorporates parents' clear communication with their children about their *personal and family values, goals, expectations,* and *aspirations* for children's learning. This communication generally offers important support for the development of student beliefs and behaviors conducive to learning, such as paying attention, working hard on learning tasks, and persisting in the face of challenge (e.g., Clark, 1983; Trevino, 2004).

Families also offer considerable support for student learning through *involvement activities at home.* These often include such activities as talking about school, expressing interest in the student's learning, monitoring and reviewing student work, encouraging student effort, offering help with assignments, and responding to teachers' suggestions for specific learning support activities (e.g., Hoover-Dempsey et al., 2001).

Effective *family–school communications* are also often very important to students' progress across domains of learning. The value of these communications is generally strongest when the communications are consistently characterized by mutual respect, careful listening, and school responsiveness to parents' questions, ideas, suggestions, and concerns.

Finally, parents' *involvement at school* may be focused on multiple goals. Comer's (1995) work, for example, has suggested strongly that when programs focus on encouraging (or requiring) parents' involvement at school, parents' knowledge of school expectations and procedures is enhanced, as are opportunities for involving families in school events, volunteer work, governance, or school-related events in the community. Parents' presence in the school or program may also increase parents' access to teachers, staff members, and other parents as sources of information and support for student learning; such benefits may be most likely when parents have relatively low levels of education themselves (Dearing, Kreider, Simpkins, & Weiss, 2006) and when schools support parent or family resource rooms and programs (e.g., Mapp, Johnson, Strickland, & Meza, 2008).

Parents may thus be productively and actively involved in supporting student learning in many different ways, activities, and locations. This observation strongly suggests that involvement's importance and influence are not derived from the specific activities in which parents engage (or from the location of those activities), but rather from the extent to which their involvement activities fit students' learning needs as well as the mix of skills, time, and values that individual families bring to involvement.

Across the many specific involvement activities that parents may enact, student learning is generally best served when involvement occurs in the context of a home–school relationship that supports the complementary roles of family and school in that process. This suggests in turn that program and school approaches to family involvement are likely to be most successful when they are grounded in recognition that multiple forms of involvement offer valid and important support for student learning. The success of involvement programs is also likely to be served best when schools attend not only to school-generated ideas about parents' involvement, but also to the needs, values, and preferences of families and communities served by the schools' programs.

How Does Parental Involvement Influence Student Learning? (Level 2)

Once engaged, how does family involvement work (i.e., *how* does it support student learning)? The broad answer is that family involvement in student learning generally works because parents, in the course of specific activities, engage a number of the learning mechanisms that support much of children's learning—across cognitive, social, and emotional domains, and across home, school, and community settings. The model suggests that the mechanisms of encouragement, modeling, reinforcement, and instruction are among those most often and most effectively engaged (Level 2, Figure 3.1). It is important to note that just as several different forms of involvement may offer valuable support for student learning, so too may parents' use of varied learning mechanisms.

Encouragement—parents' explicit affective support for students' learning activities, efforts, and accomplishments—may emerge in many different parental behaviors (e.g., explicitly appreciating and valuing students' learning efforts, engaging students' interests, encouraging students to seek help and persist when confronted with difficulties, affirming students' accomplishments). Parental encouragement may be particularly helpful when students are developing new knowledge or learning strategies, when their interest is flagging, when they are working to overcome negative perceptions of their own competence, or when parents wish simply to affirm the value of the child's efforts and reaffirm recent learning successes. Work on parental involvement in general and in literacy in particular has underscored the value of parental encouragement in supporting important learning progress (e.g., Clingenpeel & Pianta, 2007; Taylor, Anthony, Aghara, Smith, & Landry, 2008).

Parents' *modeling* of learning-related values and behaviors also generally offers a powerful stimulus for student learning. Modeling theory (e.g., Bandura, 1997) suggests this is so because children generally have ample opportunity to observe parents' behaviors, and—because children generally perceive their parents as competent, responsive, and powerful—parents' behaviors are often particularly important to students' development of attitudes and strategies central to successful learning. Positive parental modeling of learning-related beliefs and behaviors has been linked to students' development of attributes (e.g., personal motivation, goal-setting, self-monitoring, and problem solving; Pomerantz, Grolnick, & Price, 2005). In literacy in particular, parents' modeling behaviors—for example, demonstrating personal interest in books, reading, and writing; expressing (verbally and behaviorally) personal enjoyment of reading and related literacy activities; modeling overt valuing of storytelling, reading, writing, and other literacy-related activities—have all been linked to children's development of the skills, values, and motivations central to successful literacy learning (e.g., Dearing et al., 2006).

Parents' *reinforcement* of student behaviors central to learning success across domains of learning also offers important contributions to students' school-related accomplishments. Reinforcement theory and research (e.g., Bandura, 1997) suggests that children learn and repeat behaviors when they associate those behaviors and outcomes with positive consequences. Parents are often quite effective in offering reinforcement because they generally know what reinforcements are effective for shaping and maintaining desired learning behaviors in their children. The importance of positive reinforcement by family members has been affirmed often and in studies of children's literacy development in particular. Morrow and Young (1997), for example, noted that parents who participated in a successful family literacy support program were "encouraged to answer children's questions about reading and writing and to reward literacy activities by saying, 'I'm happy to see you are reading and writing,' and 'Can I help you?'" (p. 737).

Parents' *instruction* also often contributes in very important ways to students' learning and school success. Instruction that is indirect may include participation in activities during which parents express interest and questions, help the student plan and organize longer-term tasks, and use scaffolding strategies to support development of increasingly complex skills and understandings. More direct forms of instruction often focus on actively teaching new factual, procedural, or conceptual material; engaging the student in reviewing and strengthening responses to varied learning tasks; and preparing for exams and assessments of learning. When used effectively (especially when it offers affective support for literacy activities and is informed by parents' knowledge, teachers' suggestions, and parent–teacher interactions), parents' use of instruction in the course of involvement has been related to students' development of skills and motivations essential to effective literacy learning (e.g., Sénéchal & LeFevre, 2002; Sonnenschein & Munsterman, 2002).

These findings suggest fundamentally that parents support their children's learning in many different ways. Schools' most important contributions to the effectiveness of parents' involvement, in literacy as in other domains of learning, may be found in schools' active encouragement (in conversations, discussions, and sharing of specific information) of parents' use of varied learning mechanisms (including but not limited to the examples above) that support the active development of motivations and skills essential to successful learning.

What Student Learning Outcomes Does Parental Involvement Support? (Levels 3–5)

The model suggests that parental involvement—influenced in part by student perceptions of family involvement activities (Level 3)—supports students' development of specific "proximal" learning attributes and skills. These proximal outcomes (so labeled because they are the learning outcomes most directly influenced by parents' involvement) include such student attributes and skills as academic self-efficacy, intrinsic motivation, self-regulatory knowledge and skills, and social self-efficacy for relating to teachers (see Level 4). These proximal learning outcomes in turn are used by students in classroom, home, group, and individual learning situations, thus offering often critical support for students' longer term—or "distal"—learning outcomes (learning accomplishments generally assessed through summary measures such as achievement test results) across domains of school learning, including literacy.

The Role of Student Perceptions (Level 3). Consistent with social-cognitive learning theory (e.g., Bandura, 1997), the model suggests (Level 3, Figure 3.1) that what students perceive and how they process information that is shared and observed in the course of parents' engagement in their learning influences what they actually learn from involvement. Thus, parents' ability to perceive and respond to their children's interests and understandings during involvement influences students' attentiveness to the tasks at hand, their personal engagement in those tasks, and what they learn from involvement.

Consistent with this observation, children's learning in literacy has been closely tied to the quality of parent–child interactions during involvement. For example, the quality of parent–child attachment has been positively linked to young children's literacy development (Bus & van IJzendoorn, 1995), the affective qualities of parent–child interactions during reading have been found to influence children's interest in reading (Sonnenschein & Munsterman, 2002), and mothers' responsiveness during involvement (including affective warmth and sensitivity to the child's needs, interests, and current understandings) has been positively related to students' reading comprehension (Taylor et al., 2008). Consistent with these findings, literacy programs may benefit from offering considerable support for parents' experience and expression of affective warmth during literacy-related interactions and from focusing clearly on supporting parents' engagement of children's interest and understanding during involvement activities.

The Proximal Outcomes of Parental Involvement (Level 4). The model next suggests that parental involvement—mediated by students' perceptions of their involvement as we've described—contributes to the development of student beliefs, behaviors, and skills that are often critically important for effective learning. These beliefs, behaviors, and skills, or proximal learning outcomes (Level 4, Figure 3.1), are generally developed over time and are subject to direct parental influence from early childhood through adolescence. These outcomes are arguably the most important consequences of parental involvement because as these student beliefs, behaviors, and skills develop, they come to serve as valuable resources students may use in supporting their own learning efforts across multiple domains, tasks, and contexts. The model includes a sample of four proximal learning outcomes that are frequently and directly related to students' learning success: *academic self-efficacy*, *intrinsic motivation*, *self-regulation*, and *social self-efficacy* for relating to teachers.

Academic self-efficacy, student beliefs about personal ability to succeed in school work and learning, is supported by parental involvement, as are student gains in several related areas, including perceptions of personal competence, achievement motivation, mastery orientation toward learning, and personal academic aspirations. Consistent with theory and research regarding the sources of self-efficacy development (Bandura, 1997), parents' influence on students' sense of efficacy for learning is well supported by parents' positive responses to students' learning successes and consistent verbal encouragement for students' learning efforts. Work in literacy has affirmed the importance of this set of learning outcomes. Baker and Wigfield (1999), for example, reported positive relationships between children's sense of self-efficacy for learning and their motivation for reading.

Students' *intrinsic motivation for learning*, most often defined as an interest in learning for its own sake rather than for the external rewards it may offer, has also been related to effective parental involvement in general and in children's literacy learning in particular. While extrinsic motivation is also a normal part of much learning across the life span, children's intrinsic motivations for learning—and adults' support of their interests—are often critical to successful engagement in learning over time (e.g., Baker & Wigfield, 1999). Because parents are likely to be aware of their children's interests and because students' interests are often directly linked to their motivations for learning, parents' active support of motivation and interest may be particularly important to students' learning success in general and in literacy in particular (e.g., Pintrich, 2003). Deckner, Adamson, and Bakeman (2006), for example, report that students' interests influenced parent–child interactions during literacy activities and were positively linked to children's letter knowledge and expressive language.

Self-regulatory strategies and skills focus on enabling learners to activate, adapt, and maintain learning processes even in the absence of external structuring. They encompass a wide set of cognitions, metacognitions, and behaviors, including goal setting, planning, self-monitoring, evaluating one's learning strategies, and adjusting strategies as needed across learning tasks and circumstances. Stronger knowledge and skills in these areas have been associated with higher levels of learning success (e.g., Xu, 2005; Zimmerman & Martinez-Pons, 1990). Parents' engagement with students in developing such strategies may be particularly helpful, as parents are often aware of their students' interests and learning preferences (e.g., Hoover-Dempsey et al., 1995). As students' literacy learning occurs in adolescence, a focus on self-regulation may be particularly helpful in supporting links among students' personal interests, developmentally grounded increases in personal autonomy seeking, and ability to access specific help as needed in the course of literacy learning (see Chapter 11 for related ideas).

Social self-efficacy for relating to teachers may also be quite important across the school years and domains of learning, including literacy development. Grounded in self-efficacy theory, the construct suggests that students' beliefs about the usefulness and appropriateness of seeking help from knowledgeable others influences the likelihood that they will seek help when needed. The construct also includes student beliefs that engaging with teachers and knowledgeable others will in fact in fact yield useful help (e.g., Patrick, Hicks, & Ryan, 1997). Parents' focused involvement in helping students develop self-questioning skills and strategies for effective help seeking (perhaps especially through parental modeling and direct suggestion) is quite likely to offer important support for student learning.

The proximal learning outcomes included in the model are generally developed across a wide range of tasks and activities undertaken by students across time and across a range of contexts, including home, school, and community. Schools and literacy development programs are likely to benefit from explicitly recognizing that families contribute to these student outcomes in varied ways, across varied contexts. Such recognition, and a commitment to working with families in developing these attributes, promises notable benefits for students' learning in literacy as well as in other domains.

Distal Outcomes of Parental Involvement (Level 5). The model's Level 4 thus suggests that family involvement in student learning is important because it supports the development of beliefs, behaviors, and skills (proximal learning outcomes) that—when actively used by students during school learning tasks—support their achievement of *distal learning outcomes* (Level 5, Figure 3.1). These distal learning outcomes generally include achievement in several domains of knowledge (e.g., verbal skills, math, science), including literacy.

Several investigators have offered evidence supporting the proposition that parental involvement in student learning supports students' school achievement. Fan and Chen (2001) and Jeynes (2003, 2007), for example, report on meta-analyses that identified important positive links between parental involvement and various summary measures of achievement. Other investigators have focused on longitudinal evaluations of early intervention programs that include parental involvement. Comparison of program participants with control group members has offered notable evidence of positive links between parental involvement in early interventions for at-risk students and various developmental outcomes in adolescence and adulthood. Schweinhart and colleagues (2005), for example, report that students participating in the HighScope/Perry Preschool program, when compared with control group members, recorded lower drop-out rates, lower rates of pregnancy, and lower rates of criminal behavior during adolescence; in adulthood, they achieved higher rates of full-time employment, higher paying jobs, and higher rates of home ownership. Investigators attributed the findings in part to parents' learning and engagement during the program itself and to their continued capacities for effective involvement in their students' development and schooling as students matured.

Across a variety of inquiries, therefore, evidence suggests that the parental involvement process plays an important role in supporting student learning, and that schools and programs often play critically important roles in encouraging, enabling, focusing, and supporting families' considerable influence on their children's learning.

Grounded in this evidence, we next identify four principles supported by past and ongoing work in parental involvement and related fields. With several investigators who have also focused on parental involvement in students' literacy development, we suggest that programs' active use of these principles is likely to offer substantial support for effective family engagement in students' effective literacy learning.

Following the introduction of the principles, we offer specific suggestions for applying the model to encourage and support parents' contributions to their children's literacy development. We suggest that the active use of the principles through these applications will lend further strength to families' and schools' success in developing students' literacy.

The Parental Involvement Process and Literacy Development

Many literacy support efforts have experienced notable success, grounded in expert knowledge of the experiences, skills, and motivations often essential to effective literacy development (see, for example, National Council on Family Literacy, 2008; Wasik, Dobbins, & Hermann, 2002), and various other chapters in this book). This work, in combination with work on parental involvement in education from early childhood through adolescence, suggests four broad principles that appear central to successful family engagement in supporting children's literacy learning.

Respecting and Working With Family Perspectives and Contributions

The first principle suggests that the effectiveness of parental involvement in students' literacy learning is often directly linked to program success in attending well to the skills, resources, needs, values, and perspectives that families bring to the literacy development process. The principle suggests strongly that the goals of literacy development programs are often most effectively realized if program staff and teachers seek information about participating families' hopes, goals, and aspirations for their children's literacy development and work to discern, understand, and use those resources in the course of literacy education. Families' cultural contexts as well as their ideas about what they should, could, or might bring to support their children's literacy learning should be understood by school and program staff and respectfully accessed in support of students' literacy development (see Chapters 6, 7, and 9 for illustrations and greater discussion of this point).

Creating a Collaborative Relationship

The second principle suggests that school and family contributions to student literacy learning are enhanced when members of both systems (school and family) create interactive and mutually respectful communications focused on developing a collaborative and trusting relationship. Often, it is only in the context of such collaboration and trust that families may hear, accept, and work with program suggestions for supporting children's learning. Of equal importance, it is also often only in the context of such relationships that families are consistently likely to offer information, questions, and suggestions that may enhance school and family support for literacy learning. Particularly if parents believe that their own education and skills may offer little of value to their children's literacy development, teachers and program staff are often well advised to take the first steps (and many subsequent steps, as needed) and invite parents into effective and collaborative relationships that support student learning.

Morrow and Young (1997), for example, offer several observations about the value of strong teacher and program support for parents' active engagement in their children's literacy development. Near the conclusion of the program, participating parents noted that program staff really helped them feel comfortable about being in school and participating; they also noted their emerging willingness to share their ideas and concerns with program staff and ask for help as needed. Teachers, who affirmed their support (before the program started) for the idea that families and schools should function as partners in children's literacy development, observed later that they hadn't realized how important the program (i.e., a specific and well-supported effort to involve families) would be in "bringing parents, students, and teachers *together* in working toward the literacy development of children" (p. 741, emphasis added). Also important and not to be missed as preface to the next principle was parents' affirmation of their own enjoyment of helping their children learn.

Focusing on the Parent–Child Relationship and Its Influence on Learning

The third principle suggests that family involvement in students' literacy learning is most likely to be successful if grounded in understanding that qualities of the parent–child relationship influence parents' effectiveness in supporting student learning. Thus, program efforts to support effective family engagement in students' literacy development are best served when they focus not only on essential skills and motivations but also on the importance of parents' positive affective engagement with their children in the course of their involvement efforts and related learning activities.

Considerable evidence in developmental psychology suggests that responsive, positive and caring parent–child relationships undergird the effectiveness of parents' involvement in multiple domains of children's learning across childhood and adolescence. Maccoby's (1992) insightful review notes, for example, that parents' positive mood during interactions with their children influences children's responses to their parents; for example, children are more likely to pay attention and to be willing to do what parents ask them to do in the context of generally positive—rather than affectively flat or negative—interactions. Maccoby also notes considerable support for the observation that parents' long-term influence on their children's learning is often dependent on the development over time of a generally positive and responsive relationship between parent and child.

Bus and van IJzendoorn (1995) underscore the importance of a positive, secure attachment between parent and child for children's literacy learning during parent–child interactions. More recently, Taylor and colleagues (2008) highlight the importance of parenting behaviors that are accepting and responsive (e.g., generally relaxed, positive interactions with the child; sensitivity to children's cues, needs, and interests) to children's literacy development, particularly reading comprehension. Added to the observations of others (e.g., Morrow & Young, 1997; Maccoby, 1992), studies of parents' roles in literacy development thus also suggest the importance of program attention to supporting parents' positive engagement (e.g., interactions that are often positive and enjoyable for both parties) in their children's literacy learning.

Focusing on the Motivations and Skills Essential to Literacy Development

The fourth principle suggests that parents' involvement in supporting children's literacy development is likely to be most effective when the efforts and tasks involved focus on supporting the motivations *and* skills essential to full literacy learning. Considerable work in literacy has examined skills that are generally critical to successful literacy development (e.g., phonological awareness, letter/word recognition and identification, expressive and receptive language, vocabulary, spelling and reading skills, and fluency and comprehension; see Chapters 4, 5, and 8 for thoughtful attention to supporting parents' contributions in these areas). Work has also focused, although somewhat less often, on the issues of motivation that are also essential to literacy development. These include, for example, developing a personal interest in literacy learning, gaining a sense of personal competence and self-efficacy for literacy learning and activities, and coming to experience personal enjoyment of reading and other literacy activities (e.g., Baker & Wigfield, 1999; Ivey & Broaddus, 2007).

Efforts to engage parents in support of literacy learning are likely to be most effective when they address parents' contributions to students' emergent literacy skills *and* their emergent motivations for literacy activities and learning. In offering support for both critical contributors to literacy, programs may benefit also from discerning and attending to parents' own areas of "comfortable" and preferred involvement tasks (i.e., the areas and tasks where parents are also most likely to experience and convey positive attitudes about the tasks and related learning as they work with their children). Because parents influence their children's learning in many arenas, programs' support for effective parental involvement are also likely to benefit from attending not only to school-identified or school-like tasks but also—through interactive engagement with families—to multiple arenas of family life and parent–child interaction where motivations and skills important to literacy also receive support.

Model-Based Suggestions for Enhancing Students' Literacy Learning: Building Family Capacities for Effective Parental Involvement

We turn now to a sample of model-based suggestions for supporting families' active and productive engagement in children's literacy development. These suggestions are offered with the understanding that the strongest and most useful applications for any program will emerge from program efforts to identify and build on current program strengths, address concerns of particular importance to the program and its families, and support family involvement in ways consistent with knowledge and needs of program members, participating families, and the communities they serve. We focus most heavily on suggestions related to supporting parents' motivations for involvement (Level 1) because parents' motivations are the first and most essential step in the full involvement process.

As an introduction to the importance of parents' motivations, we first focus briefly on the role and value of family–school relationships to any program's success in encouraging, supporting, nurturing, and reaping the benefits of effective family engagement in student learning.

Developing the Foundation

As suggested above, many families' success in supporting their children's literacy development is best accomplished when literacy programs focus clearly on creating and sustaining effective, interactive relationships with participating families. This is important because it is often primarily in the context of relationship that family and school may identify and use information about what families are already doing that supports their children's literacy learning. Particularly for families who may feel uncertain about the value of their potential contributions to children's literacy, the school and program can most effectively demonstrate their support for family contributions by initiating and developing consistent two-way communications with families in which (a) both parties offer ideas, concerns, and suggestions and (b) program staff explicitly appreciate family contributions and use parents' suggestions and ideas.

Supporting Parents' Motivations for Involvement (Level 1): Personal Motivations, Contextual Motivations, and Responsiveness to Life Context

Personal Motivations: Role Construction and Efficacy. Teachers and other program staff may offer significant support for the development or affirmation of parents' personal motivations for involvement when they explicitly acknowledge or help parents believe that they indeed have a significant and important role to play in their children's literacy development and they are indeed able to offer important support for their children's literacy learning (i.e., what they can do *and* what they can learn to do really does make a difference in the child's learning success). Examples of specific steps that program staff may take to support parents' active role construction and positive sense of efficacy include the following:

- Working with parents to identify current family practices that support student literacy learning, emphasizing the importance of these family practices to children's understanding of literacy and its importance in family life (e.g., reading to and with children, writing letters to grandparents, making shopping lists)

- Offering parents specific points of information about how these family practices and activities support children's development of the motivations and skills essential to effective literacy learning
- Suggesting other specific literacy support activities that family members might reasonably add to their repertoire and maintaining regular contact to check on and encourage progress in family use of those activities
- Arranging, as possible within the program, school, or neighborhood, opportunities for parents to observe other (similarly situated) parents' successful engagement in literacy activities with children, as well as opportunities to share their own experiences with supporting their children's literacy, and—as parents become comfortable with their own roles in the program—offer suggestions that other parents might find helpful

Contextual Motivators: School Invitations, Teacher Invitations, Child Invitations. Programs, teachers, and program staff may play important roles in actively inviting parents to participate in supporting children's literacy learning at school and home.

- School invitations may include involving administrative, teaching, and support staff in creating welcoming and visually appealing entryways; developing simple hospitality practices (i.e., noting, caring, and appreciating that families are present) that ensure all parents are greeted on entry and have access to supportive conversation (perhaps including an offer of coffee or refreshments); and creating a parent/family room (or rooms) where parents may talk with each other, interact informally with program staff and teachers, and find resources that may be helpful in their literacy activities with their children.
- Specific teacher invitations to involvement may be offered by requesting that parents use specific, manageable, and time-limited activities with the child at home; developing an interactive "report book" where teacher and parent offer comments about the child's responses to learning tasks or ask questions daily or weekly; inviting the parent to observe the child's learning; and maintaining regular contact and invitations in whatever ways are feasible for teacher and family.
- Child invitations to involvement may be well supported by teachers in asking that children engage parents in specific, short, and manageable literacy activities at home (with advance word and materials given to parents

as helpful); encouraging parents to attend closely to the child's apparent understandings in the course of literacy support activities at home; or emphasizing the importance of responding supportively to the student's questions and interests.

Responsiveness to Family Life Context. Often of concern here—for families and for teachers—are questions about the skills and knowledge needed for supporting children's literacy, the time and energy that parents may have for involvement, and the extent to which school expectations and family culture fit together so that at least some expectations held by each are shared or amenable to discussion for the development of common understanding and action. Some of the contributions that schools, teachers, and support staff may make in working to create a fit between family and school needs and expectations include the following:

- Addressing parents' skills and knowledge concerns directly; keying specific requests to activities that program staff (based on conversations with parents) know are manageable for the family and targeted to parents' skills, interests, and family routines; working to develop skills and knowledge that parents want to develop as part of their engagement in supporting student learning

- Discerning and understanding various families' experiences of other demands on their time and energy (e.g., holding a job that doesn't offer flextime for parent visits to school; having only intermittent or no access to transportation); offering program sessions in community sites that are accessible; developing support for program activities and home visits at times convenient for the family

- Demonstrating responsiveness to family culture through respect for families and adaptation of program or home activities to fit participating families' skills, schedules, and needs; developing program support for translators who are available as needed; tailoring student work to family "funds of knowledge" (González et al., 2001), including literacy-relevant resources, interests, and skills; making strong efforts to ensure that the invitations offered to families fit their life circumstances and contexts; offering regular and positive feedback to parents on specific ways in which their various involvement activities support the motivations and skills essential to successful literacy development

Supporting Parents' Choice of Involvement Forms (Level 1.5)

Perhaps most important in the area of family choice of involvement forms is active understanding (and active program support for *families'* understanding) that many forms of involvement may be used to enhance children's literacy development. This means in part that families should be encouraged to use the forms they believe are most feasible given family circumstances and with which they feel most comfortable and productive. At the same time, programs are often well advised to act from an awareness that families may *become* comfortable with involvement options that may have initially been less preferred. Parents' addition of varied literacy support strategies to the family repertoire seems most likely when program staff members are active in offering parents specific information about how families might use specific involvement strategies well and why the suggested activities are likely to support students' literacy learning. There are several understandings that are notably important to many program efforts in this domain, including the following:

- Most families may offer effective support for the values and goals of literacy learning; similarly, most families may develop and consistently express positive family expectations, hopes, and aspirations for children's successful learning. (It is important to note that these family activities are not dependent on parents' own literacy skills or knowledge but rather on their willingness to express their hopes and aspirations for their children's learning and engage in activities that support those hopes and aspirations.)

- Families may engage many literacy-supportive activities at home. While these are often not seen by program personnel (and thus, unfortunately, sometimes discounted or ignored by schools), home-based activities may benefit from program knowledge of steps parents are already taking in support of literacy development; parents and children may also benefit from specific suggestions for family support activities appropriate to individual family needs and goals for student learning.

- Family–program communications are an often critical component of successful parental involvement in literacy development by creating specific support for regular home–school communications in ways that offer useful answers to questions families may have about involvement in their children's literacy development.

- Involvement activities at school may be particularly important for the opportunities they afford parents to observe children's learning activities, talk with teachers and support staff, and talk with other parents about involvement successes and questions. Programs may also work to create school-based involvement opportunities that are schedule- and location-friendly for participating families. One caution, however, is that simultaneous and strong support for parents' personal motivations for involvement—Do parents believe they should play an active role in their children's literacy development? Do they believe that their activities will make a positive difference in their children's learning?—is often essential to the success of efforts to offer family-friendly involvement opportunities. Such simultaneous efforts to enhance parents' active role construction and positive sense of efficacy may address periodic staff laments that "We did *everything*—child care, bus transportation, pizzas—and *still* just a few people came!"

Supporting Parents' Use of Learning Mechanisms During Involvement (Level 2)

Perhaps most important at Level 2 of the involvement process are program, teacher, staff, and family understandings that parents may engage in effective involvement through the use of many different learning mechanisms: the four identified in the model as well as others used in various literacy development programs. Programs may offer important encouragement for families' involvement and effectiveness in supporting their children's literacy learning by doing the following:

- Helping parents understand that they may effectively support their children's learning by encouraging their children's literacy learning interests, motivations, activities, efforts, and successes; modeling the value and uses of varied literacy-related activities; reinforcing their children's literacy learning interests, motivations, efforts, and successes; and instructing their children in varied literacy-supportive skills and tasks
- Offering specific information about and examples of each learning mechanism and its uses
- Encouraging and supporting conversations with staff members (and other parents, when parent resource programs have been developed) about perceived challenges, problems, and successes in using each mechanism;

these efforts may contribute substantially to parents' sense of efficacy and their experience of success in using varied learning mechanisms in the course of involvement

Across the varied learning mechanisms that different programs may support, families also often benefit from active encouragement for using learning mechanisms—known to be effective and relatively familiar (or comfortable)—for family members' use. Such active encouragement may be supported through family-friendly meetings with staff and other parents to answer questions about learning mechanisms, offer demonstrations of what they are and how they may be used, discuss the benefits that may accrue by using each one, and give examples of each mechanism that parents may bring to the group.

Supporting Parents' Understanding of Students' Perceptions of Involvement (Level 3)

Literacy development programs may have an especially critical role to play in supporting families' understanding that students' perceptions of their involvement activities (i.e., how their children attend to those activities, how they feel about the activities, and how they understand the activities) play a significant role in shaping what students learn from involvement. For example, focusing with parents on the importance of encouraging and offering positive reinforcement for student effort, interest, and accomplishment may be particularly important to the development and maintenance of a positive, warm, and responsive relationship, which, in turn, offers support for student attention to and processing of information offered by parents. Similarly, parents' efforts to model the importance of literacy activities and events in their own family activities and work may engage student attention and interest in ways that support their active processing of parents' information regarding specific literacy activities and the value of those activities to daily life.

Supporting Parents' Understanding of Student Proximal Learning Outcomes (Level 4)

When parents understand the ways their involvement supports student's learning success, their commitment to and motivation for active engagement in supporting students' literacy development may benefit substantially. Parents and their children may benefit from parents' understanding that (a) involvement's major contributions to student learning are often found in consistent support for beliefs, attitudes, behaviors, and skills that enhance students' literacy development and (b) those same beliefs, attitudes, behaviors, and skills are also often essential to effective learning across the school years in other subjects as well.

Specific approaches to supporting parents' focus on proximal learning outcomes may center on the proximal outcomes identified in the model, as well as on others important to program-specific goals. Academic self-efficacy, for example, may be well supported by parental emphases on the child's learning successes, efforts, and interests; similarly, children's intrinsic motivation for literacy learning may receive substantial support from parents' explicit linking of specific student interests with information available through several different kinds of literacy activities. Students' self-regulatory knowledge and skills—focused, for example, on the student's development of personal abilities to plan work in various areas, set immediate and longer term learning goals, and monitor personal need for help—may be very well supported by teachers' and parents' articulated modeling of such steps in varied literacy-related learning events and many daily routines of school and family life. Students' self-efficacy for relating to teachers and other helpers may be similarly supported by parents' and teachers' focus on helping children identify when and for what purposes seeking help from knowledgeable others may be particularly useful. Across important proximal outcomes, program staff may provide the most significant help by offering explicit support for parents' understanding of (a) what each outcome is, (b) how each may best be supported, and (c) why and how these outcomes make a positive difference in students' learning in literacy and in many other domains of schooling and life.

Supporting Parents' Understanding of Links Between Proximal Learning Outcomes and Students' Literacy Development (Levels 4 and 5)

Finally, the model suggests that children's literacy learning may be supported by parents', teachers', and students' understanding that the development of beliefs, skills, and behaviors related to successful learning (proximal learning outcomes), in turn, support students' learning success in the classroom and on summary measures of achievement. Although this final stage of the involvement process as articulated in the model is likely less salient to or important for younger children's explicit understanding, adolescents—with their increasingly well-developed cognitive capacities—may benefit substantially from understanding how and why the proximal or intermediate goals of parents' active involvement in student learning offer critically important support for students' longer term learning goals and aspirations.

NOTES

We gratefully acknowledge support for portions of this work from the Institute for Education Sciences (formerly Office for Educational Research and Improvement), U.S. Department of Education (see Hoover-Dempsey & Sandler, 2005, for further details). Many thanks to other members of our research lab who have contributed much to our understanding of the parental involvement process over the years, especially Joan M.T. Walker and Christa L. Ice. We also offer hearty thanks to KaiLonnie Dunsmore of the Ball Foundation for insightful and most helpful suggestions.

REFERENCES

Baker, L., & Wigfield, A. (1999). Dimensions of children's motivation for reading and their relations to reading activity and reading achievement. *Reading Research Quarterly, 34*(4), 452–477. doi:10.1598/RRQ.34.4.4

Bandura, A. (1997). *Self-efficacy: The exercise of control.* New York: W.H. Freeman.

Bus, A.G., & van IJzendoorn, M.H. (1995). Mothers reading to their 3-year-olds: The role of mother-child attachment security in becoming literate. *Reading Research Quarterly, 30*(4), 998–1015. doi:10.2307/748207

Clark, R.M. (1983). *Family life and school achievement: Why poor black children succeed or fail.* Chicago: University of Chicago Press.

Clingenpeel, B.T., & Pianta, R.C. (2007). Mothers' sensitivity and book-reading interactions with first-graders. *Early Education and Development, 18*(1), 1–22.

Comer, J.P. (1995). *School power: Implications of an intervention project.* New York: Simon & Schuster.

Dearing, E., Kreider, H., Simpkins, S., & Weiss, H.B. (2006). Family involvement in school and low-income children's literacy: Longitudinal associations between and within families. *Journal of Educational Psychology, 98*(4), 653–664. doi:10.1037/0022-0663.98.4.653

Deckner, D.F., Adamson, L.B., & Bakeman, R. (2006). Child and maternal contributions to shared reading: Effects on language and literacy development. *Journal of Applied Developmental Psychology, 27*(1), 31–41. doi:10.1016/j.appdev.2005.12.001

Edwards, P.A. (1995). Connecting African-American families and youth to the school's reading program: Its meaning for school and community literacy. In V.L. Gadsden & D. Wagner (Eds.), *Literacy among African-American youth: Issues in learning, teaching, and schooling* (pp. 263–281). Cresskill, NJ: Hampton.

Epstein, J.L., & Van Voorhis, F.L. (2001). More than minutes: Teachers' roles in designing homework. *Educational Psychologist, 36*(3), 181–193. doi:10.1207/S15326985EP3603_4

Fan, X., & Chen, M. (2001). Parental involvement and students' academic achievement: A meta-analysis. *Educational Psychology Review, 13*(1), 1–22. doi:10.1023/A:1009048817385

González, N., Andrade, R., Civil, M., & Moll, L. (2001). Bridging funds of distributed knowledge: Creating zones of practice in mathematics. *Journal of Education for Students Placed at Risk, 6*(1–2), 115–132. doi:10.1207/S15327671ESPR0601-2_7

Green, C.L., Walker, J.M.T., Hoover-Dempsey, K.V., & Sandler, H.M. (2007). Parents' motivations for involvement in children's education: An empirical test of a theoretical model of parental involvement. *Journal of Educational Psychology, 99*(3), 532–544. doi:10.1037/0022-0663.99.3.532

Hoover-Dempsey, K.V., Bassler, O.C., & Burow, R. (1995). Parents' reported involvement in students' homework: Parameters of reported strategy and practice. *The Elementary School Journal, 95*(5), 435–450. doi:10.1086/461854

Hoover-Dempsey, K.V., Battiato, A.C., Walker, J.M.T., Reed, R.P., DeJong, J.M., & Jones, K.P. (2001). Parental involvement in homework. *Educational Psychologist, 36*(3), 195–210. doi:10.1207/S15326985EP3603_5

Hoover-Dempsey, K.V., Ice, C.L., & Whitaker, M.C. (2009). "We're way past reading together": Why and how parental involvement in adolescence makes sense. In N.E. Hill & R.K. Chao (Eds.), *Families, schools and the adolescent: Connecting research, policy, and practice* (pp. 19–36). New York: Teachers College Press.

Hoover-Dempsey, K.V., & Sandler, H.M. (1995). Parental involvement in children's education: Why does it make a difference? *Teachers College Record, 97*(2), 310–331.

Hoover-Dempsey, K.V., & Sandler, H.M. (1997). Why do parents become involved in their children's education? *Review of Educational Research, 67*(1), 3–42.

Hoover-Dempsey, K.V., & Sandler, H.M. (2005). *Final performance report for OERI Grant # R305T010673: The social context of parental involvement: A path to enhanced achievement.* Presented to Project Monitor, Institute of Education Sciences, U.S. Department of Education, March 22, 2005. Retrieved November 29, 2009, from www.vanderbilt.edu/Peabody/family-school/

Hoover-Dempsey, K.V., Walker, J.M.T., Sandler, H.M., Whetsel, D., Green, C.L., Wilkins, A.S., et al. (2005). Why do parents become involved? Research findings and implications. *The Elementary School Journal, 106*(2), 105–130.

Ivey, G., & Broaddus, K. (2007). A formative experiment investigating literacy engagement among adolescent Latina/o students just beginning to read, write, and speak English. *Reading Research Quarterly, 42*(4), 512–545. doi:10.1598/RRQ.42.4.4

Jeynes, W.H. (2003). A meta-analysis: The effects of parental involvement on minority children's academic achievement. *Education and Urban Society, 35*(2), 202–218. doi:10.1177/0013124502239392

Jeynes, W.H. (2007). The relationship between parental involvement and urban secondary school student academic achievement: A meta-analysis. *Urban Education, 42*(1), 82–110. doi:10.1177/0042085906293818

Lapp, D., Fisher, D., Flood, J., & Moore, K. (2002). "I don't want to teach it wrong:" An investigation of the role families believe they should play in the early literacy development of their children. In D. Shallert, C. Fairbanks, J. Worthy, B. Maloch, & J. Hoffman (Eds.), *The 51st yearbook of the National Reading Conference* (pp. 275–287). Oak Creek, WI: National Reading Conference.

Maccoby, E.E. (1992). The role of parents in the socialization of children: An historical overview. *Developmental Psychology, 28*(6), 1006–1117. doi:10.1037/00121649.28.6.1006

Mapp, K.L., Johnson, V.R., Strickland, C.S., & Meza, C. (2008). High school family centers: Transformative spaces linking schools and families in support of learning. *Marriage & Family Review, 43*(3–4), 338–368. doi:10.1080/01494920802073205

Morrow, L.M., & Young, J. (1997). A family literacy program connecting school and home: Effects on attitude, motivation, and literacy achievement. *Journal of Educational Psychology, 89*(4), 736–742. doi:10.1037/0022-0663.89.4.736

National Council on Family Literacy. (2008). *Family literacy: A catalogue of literature (1995–2007).* Louisville, KY: National Council on Family Literacy.

Patrick, H., Hicks, L., & Ryan, A.M. (1997). Relations of perceived social efficacy and social goal pursuit to self-efficacy for academic work. *The Journal of Early Adolescence, 17*(2), 109–128. doi:10.1177/0272431697017002001

Pintrich, P.R. (2003). A motivational science perspective on the role of student motivation in learning and teaching contexts. *Journal of Educational Psychology, 95*(4), 667–686. doi:10.1037/0022-0663.95.4.667

Pomerantz, E.M., Grolnick, W.S., & Price, C.E. (2005). The role of parents in how children approach achievement: A dynamic process perspective. In A.J. Elliott & C.S. Dweck (Eds.), *Handbook of motivation and competence* (pp. 259–278). New York: Oxford.

Schweinhart, L.J., Montie, J., Xiang, Z., Barnett, W.S., Belfield, C.R., & Nores, M. (2005). *Lifetime effects: The High/Scope Perry preschool study through age 40. Monographs of the High/Scope Educational Research Foundation, 14.* Ypsilanti, MI: High/Scope.

Sénéchal, M., & LeFevre, J. (2002). Parental involvement in the development of children's reading skill: A five-year longitudinal study. *Child Development, 73*(2), 445–460. doi:10.1111/1467-8624.00417

Sonnenschein, S., & Munsterman, K. (2002). The influence of home-based reading interactions on 5-year-olds' reading motivations and early literacy development. *Early Childhood Research Quarterly, 17*(3), 318–337. doi:10.1016/S0885-2006(02)00167-9

Taylor, H.B., Anthony, J.L., Aghara, R., Smith, K.E., & Landry, S.H. (2008). The interaction of early maternal responsiveness and children's cognitive abilities on later decoding and reading comprehension skills. *Early Education and Development, 19*(1), 188–207.

Trevino, R.E. (2004). Against all odds: Lessons from parents of migrant high-achievers. In C. Salinas & M.E. Fránquiz (Eds.), *Scholars in the field: The challenges of migrant education* (pp. 147–161). Charleston, WV: AEL.

Walker, J.M.T., Wilkins, A.S., Dallaire, J., Sandler, H.M., & Hoover-Dempsey, K.V. (2005). Parental involvement: Model revision through scale development. *Elementary School Journal, 106*(2), 86–104.

Wasik, B.H., Dobbins, D.R., & Hermann, S. (2002). Intergenerational family literacy: Concepts, research, and practice. In S. Newman & D. Dickinson (Eds.), *Handbook of early literacy research* (pp. 444–458). New York: Guilford.

Xu, J. (2005). Homework emotion management reported by high school students. *School Community Journal, 15*(2), 21–36.

Zimmerman, B.J., & Martinez-Pons, M.P. (1990). Student differences in self-regulated learning: Relating grade, sex, and giftedness to self-efficacy and strategy use. *Journal of Educational Psychology, 82*(1), 51–59. doi:10.1037/0022-0663.82.1.51

Characteristics of Three Family Literacy Programs That Worked

Lesley Mandel Morrow, Alan L. Mendelsohn,
and Melanie R. Kuhn

Family members who care for children are children's first teachers. They are also children's teachers for the longest time. Beginning at birth, children's experiences affect their success in becoming literate. The success of a school literacy program frequently depends on the literacy environment at home. Family literacy activities must reflect the ethnic, racial, or cultural heritage of the families involved.

The term *family literacy* is a complex concept and has been described in the following ways (Donahue, Finnegan, Lutkus, Allen, & Campbell, 2001; Melzi, Paratore, & Krol-Sinclair, 2000; Morrow, Paratore, & Tracey, 1994):

- Family literacy encompasses the ways families, children, and extended family members use literacy at home and in the community. This includes natural occurrences during daily life, routines to get things done such as making lists, writing messages, keeping records, following written directions, and sharing stories and ideas.

- Family literacy activities may be initiated purposefully by a family member, such as routine bedtime stories or teaching the child the alphabet.

- Family literacy activities may be initiated by the school. These activities are intended for parents to do to support the development of literacy for children and families and include storybook reading, writing notes, and helping with homework.

- Family literacy involves parents coming to school for activities such as back-to-school night, conferences, programs their children are in, observing

From *Bringing Literacy Home* edited by KaiLonnie Dunsmore and Douglas Fisher.
© 2010 by the International Reading Association.

their children's classrooms, and reading to their children's classes or sharing artifacts, hobbies, and professions.

- Family literacy involves parents attending workshops at school to learn about and understand what they can do at home to help their children.
- Family literacy includes teaching adults to read and write at the same time as their children are learning.

In this chapter we describe three projects that began as studies and became family literacy programs: The Family Fluency Program, The Family *Highlights* Program, and the BELLE Project. We review the techniques used in the programs that made them successful. Two of the programs were initiated in school and one, the BELLE Project, was a community program for parents and their children.

Family Literacy Programs Initiated by the School

Involving parents as an integral part of literacy instruction at school is crucial. Parents need to know how they can help at home by supporting the school program. Home–school programs need to be enjoyable and easy to use. Materials and activities sent home should be introduced to children in school first (Morrow, Scoblionko, & Shafer, 1995; Morrow & Young, 1997). In 20 different family intervention studies including 1,583 families, results showed that parent involvement had a positive effect on children's reading acquisition. The most effective technique was training parents to help their children with a reading strategy that the children were working on in school (Darling & Westberg, 2004). Teachers and parents must collaborate, especially in schools with at-risk and diverse students, to contribute to children's literacy growth (Chavkin & Gonzalez, 1995; Wasik, 2004).

The three programs discussed in this chapter are guided by sociocultural theory, which suggests that children develop higher mental processes and gain knowledge through their interactions with adults (Vygotsky, 1978). Sociocognitive theory also suggests that literacy is facilitated as children observe social interactions occurring within the social environment of a culture (Bandura, 1986). The programs we describe involve modeling behavior and social interaction between parent and child in home, school, and community environments.

The Family Literacy Fluency Program

The goal of the Family Literacy Fluency Program (Morrow, Kuhn, & Schwanenflugel, 2006) was to heighten the awareness of parents, children, and teachers concerning the important roles they play in the literacy development of children by helping with the specific skill of fluency initiated at school.

Research reviews of fluent reading suggest that fluency-oriented approaches to literacy instruction are effective at increasing students' automatic word recognition, assisting with comprehension development, and promoting the use of prosody such as stress, pitch, and appropriate phrasing (National Institute of Child Health and Human Development [NICHD], 2000). Studies that have shown promise in enhancing fluency have found that scaffolding the reading of large amounts of connected text and repeated readings of passages are effective strategies (Kuhn & Stahl, 2003; Schreiber, 1991). Other strategies to enhance fluency are partner reading, word reading efficiency (Torgesen, Wagner, & Rashotte, 1999), and listening to good fluent reading by a teacher or on an audio recording (Tan & Nicholson, 1997). Other studies have found that fluency can be enhanced by having teachers model reading texts using appropriate pace, pitch, expression, and phrasing, and then repeating these readings. In addition, teachers should engage children in echo reading and choral reading (Hoffman, 1987; Rasinski, 1990). Although children may decode automatically, they are not necessarily fluent (NICHD, 2000). We have learned that fluency doesn't come naturally to many children. This is a skill that must be taught with the use of specific strategies (Allington, 1983; Reutzel, 1996).

The Family Fluency Program provided fluency strategies for parents to practice with children at home. We wanted to find out if the parents involved in the fluency program did the following:

- Engaged in fluency building activities at home
- Had a heightened awareness about the importance of fluency training in their child's literacy development
- Increased their literacy involvement with their children at home

The Family Fluency Program was part of a larger investigation in school called Fluency Oriented Reading Instruction (FORI). Before discussing the Family Fluency Program further, a brief description of the school fluency program will put it into proper perspective.

The FORI School Study

The purpose of the FORI study was to identify effective procedures for teaching fluency (Kuhn & Stahl, 2003). This national study took place in two school districts in the southeastern United States and one in the northeastern United States. There were 24 second-grade classrooms involved in the large study, with a total of 376 children. The study took place over a period of five years in districts that had large numbers of low-income families. There were significant findings in fluency development in the treatment group over the control group.

In addition to regular reading instruction, the FORI program involved the following:

- On Monday, a 30-minute lesson began with the teacher reading a basal story to the children as they followed along in their own books. Prior to reading, she introduced the vocabulary. The class discussed major concepts and built background knowledge about the text they were about to hear. After reading, discussion about the story continued.
- On Tuesday, a 20-minute lesson consisted of the class echo reading the same basal story. There was discussion about vocabulary, concepts, and relating the story to their life experiences before and after echo reading the story.
- On Wednesday, in a 20-minute lesson, the children choral read the same story with discussion before and after reading. The discussion about the stories became more analytical and inferential with each day.
- On Thursday, a 15-minute session included partner reading of the same story. Students were instructed to discuss the story before and after reading. For the partner reading, one child began by reading one or two pages and his or her partner following by doing the same thing.
- On Friday, teachers did a 20-minute extension activity related to the basal story or read a trade book. The children could then engage in reading and writing about the basal story or the trade book.

The Family Fluency Program That Emerged From the FORI Program Findings

When parents are involved at home as partners in school-related literacy instruction, they learn about the models of learning used and their children's achievement is enhanced (Epstein, 1991). In the Family Fluency Program the basal reader was sent home at least twice a week for parents to read with their children. They read the same story being read in school that week. Parents who could not read English listened to their children read. The children read the story and the parents repeated what their children read. Parents filled out forms to document if they read with their children. There was a space for comments if they had any.

We offered three evening workshops for parents, which took place in October, February, and April. The objectives of the workshops were to heighten awareness about the importance of fluency, describe the school program, and discuss activities that parents could do at home with their children to enhance fluency.

The Parent Workshops. The greatest challenge when creating a family program, especially in a low socioeconomic community, is to get parents to attend. These parents work long hours and they are often uncomfortable coming to school because they are not literate themselves or had a bad experience in school. To help with attendance, we sent home several notes in advance of the meetings and made phone calls to families on the day before the meetings. Teachers helped us by asking the children to remind their parents before and on the day of the meeting. Children were invited to the meeting to participate in a presentation, which helped to get families to attend because the children encouraged their parents to take them. Parents are more likely to come to meetings when their children participate because they enjoy watching them be involved in school activities.

The first training session was successful, with 35 parents and about 50 children attending. The parents brought their second graders as well as some older and younger siblings. For parents who did not attend, we sent home the packet of materials that were given out at the training session. We also made phone calls to explain the program to parents who did not attend.

The meeting began with refreshments. Then the children did a choral reading they had practiced, in which the boys read one part and the girls another. After that the children went to another room where teachers supervised them as they used center materials.

With the children gone, we began the parent workshop by describing the purpose of the school program and the strategies being used. We demonstrated using a short reading selection similar to stories that the children were reading in school. We talked about building a background for the story before it is read and how to connect the story to the lives of the children. We demonstrated echo reading, choral reading, and partner reading. Using the same story, we engaged the parents in a discussion prior to reading. Then we asked the parents to try the fluency strategies with us. We echo read the short story, then we choral read the story, and finally the parents engaged in partner reading. During partner reading, we asked the partners to look at the pictures and discuss what they thought the story might be about. The first reader read one or two pages and the next reader read the next one or two pages until the story was completed. At the end of the story, the partners talked about the parts they liked best and how the story connected to their lives.

We discussed the importance of oral reading and how oral reading as a group provides a sense of community so the teacher or parent can provide a good model for reading as the children follow along. The repetition helps with decoding, learning new vocabulary, understanding the text, and being able to use the correct pace and expression. We provided a handout for the parents, in both English and Spanish, which explained the strategies. (The English version of the handout is shown in Figure 4.1.) We also had a Spanish interpreter for families that spoke Spanish. The interpreter sat in an area where parents could come and sit if they felt they needed to hear the translation. She also helped on a one-to-one basis. We explained to parents who could not read English how

Figure 4.1. Reading Activities to Do With the Books Your Child Brings Home From School

Echo Reading:	You read one line and the child reads the same line after you. Increase the number of lines you read at one time as the child's reading improves. To be sure the child is looking at the words, ask him/her to follow the print with a finger. Try to echo read at least one story each week.
Choral Reading:	You and your child read the same text aloud together. Choral reading should be done at least twice a week.
Partner Reading:	You and your child take turns reading. Start by reading one sentence and asking the child to read the next sentence. As the child's fluency improves, you read a page and he/she reads a page. Partner read about once a week.
Repeated Reading:	Read the same book or story more than once in the same week.
Remember:	Whenever you read with your child, use as much expression as you can so your reading sounds like speaking and the story comes alive.

they could help by listening to their children read and by letting their children echo read to them. They could listen to what the child read and then repeat it. We encouraged them to choral read with stories in their own language as well. We made audio recordings of the stories for families who could not speak English to help them participate. They could echo read, choral read, or partner read these stories.

After our presentation to parents, we invited the children back into the room and this time we worked with another very short story. We talked about the story with the parents and children by looking at the pictures before we began. We talked about new vocabulary and concepts. Then the story was read to the group as a whole. Next, we echo read the story with the parents and children. After echo reading, we all choral read the story. Finally each parent and child partner read the story using the framework for partner reading described earlier. Before the end of the meeting, we reminded parents to read the stories sent home at least twice a week and to complete the forms. We asked them to practice the fluency strategies three times a week. When we finished with the workshop, we socialized while enjoying refreshments.

A second workshop was held mid-year to discuss what parents and children were doing at home. We asked the children and their parents what they liked best: repeating the readings, the discussions, echo reading, choral reading, or partner reading. We asked for their thoughts and feelings about the activities, and we answered questions that they had. We showed video clips of the children in their classrooms participating in echo, choral, and partner reading, which were enjoyed by all. We reviewed the strategies for new families that had not been to the first meeting. Thirty parents and 40 children attended. Most of the parents had attended the first workshop; however, five of them were new and nine from the first did not attend the second workshop.

At the second workshop, we provided the parents and children with an assessment measure for fluency so they were aware of what good fluent reading was. We played recordings of excellent fluent reading, good fluent reading, and fluent reading that needed work. We used the same short story for each of these readings and gave the parents the text so they could follow along. The *Excellent* fluent reading flowed smoothly and at a good pace. All words were decoded properly and expression demonstrated understanding of the text. The *Good* fluent reading was done at a pace that was a little slow, but not choppy, and words were pronounced properly with enough expression to show some understanding. Finally, we evaluated what we called reading that *Needs*

Figure 4.2. Assessing Fluency

1. Record your child reading a short passage.
2. Several months later, record another reading.
3. Play the two recordings to listen for improvement.
4. Evaluate each reading as *Needs Work, Good,* or *Excellent*

- *Needs Work*: Reading is word-by-word, slow, and choppy, with some words missed and not enough expression to show an understanding of the text.
- *Good*: The pace of the reading is slow but not choppy. Most words are pronounced properly with enough expression to show some understanding of the text.
- *Excellent*: Reading flows smoothly at a good pace. All words are decoded properly and expression demonstrates an understanding of what is being read.

Note if there is improvement from the first tape to the second.

Work. This reading was word-by-word, slow, choppy, lacked expression, and contained some words that were read incorrectly. We suggested that parents record their children's reading. A second recording at a later date could be compared with the earlier recording and they could evaluate progress together. Tape recorders and cassettes were provided for parents who did not have them. Parents and children received the handout shown in Figure 4.2 to help them remember the evaluation system.

Thirty-two parents attended the third workshop. Some of the parents had been to all three meetings, whereas others had attended two. None were there for the first time. We again invited the children as well as the parents. We asked parents to bring recordings of their children's reading to determine if they made progress. At this meeting the children performed an echo reading and a choral reading, and two children illustrated a partner reading they had practiced with their teachers in school. Having the children participate in the parent meetings proved to be a good way to get the parents to come and subsequently participate at home. As always, we served refreshments. At the end of the meeting parents received a VIP certificate for being Very Involved Parents.

Results of the Family Fluency Program

We wanted to find out if the parents involved in the fluency workshops did the following:

- Engaged in fluency building activities at home

- Had a heightened awareness about the importance of fluency training in their child's literacy development
- Increased their literacy involvement with their children at home

Teachers' Reports of Parental Involvement. To determine parent participation in their children's schoolwork at home, we asked teachers to report how involved they thought the parents were. Teachers used a scale we provided to rank parents from 1 to 5, with 5 indicating a lot of home involvement and 1 indicating very little home involvement. The average ranking for parents who participated was 3, whereas the average ranking for parents who did not participate was 2. Teacher's rankings were based on forms sent home to parents to report reading with their child. They were also based on teacher perceptions and on informal discussions with parents and children. We believed their responses suggested that our program had had some positive effect.

Parent Surveys. We also administered a survey for parents as a measure of family involvement. The surveys asked parents for the following information:

- How often they were able to help children with homework
- How often they were able to read to or with their children
- How they felt they could help their children to become fluent readers

We received 35 surveys back from the parents who were part of the family program, and 28 back from parents who weren't in the family program.

The nature of the family data is anecdotal, and we also realize that we did not have large numbers of parents involved or responding. In spite of this, the information that was returned was promising. Sixty-nine percent of the parents who participated and who completed surveys said they helped their child with homework five times a week, compared with 45% of parents who did not participate in the home program. Forty-six percent of parents who participated reported reading to or with their children five times a week, 12% read four times a week, and 21% read three times; this represents a total of 79% of those who participated in the program. Of those who did not participate, 9% reported that they were reading to or with their children five times a week, 21% reported reading four times a week, and 28% reported reading three times a week; this represents a total of 58% of the nonparticipating parents. We are aware that this information is based on the parent self-report, but we believe it is strong enough to suggest that the family fluency program made an impact.

Parents who participated in the family program and those who did not were asked how they helped their children become more fluent readers. Parents who participated demonstrated an understanding of how to help children become fluent readers. They listed the strategies that they were taught at the parent sessions and in the materials that were sent home with their children. They also used the vocabulary involved in fluency instruction. For example, they talked about repeated reading, echo reading, choral reading, partner reading, pacing reading, and using expression. These are all activities for developing fluency. The parents who did not participate used these terms to a lesser degree. Those who participated had answers that were more similar to one another. The responses from parents who did not participate were more varied. See Table 4.1 for parents' responses to how they helped develop fluency.

We felt particularly gratified by this survey data because it was open ended and parents came up with responses on their own. The strategies used in fluency development were not common terms at the time and were often unknown to teachers and parents. The survey data shows that many of the parents who participated in the program learned fluency vocabulary and strategies.

Child, Parent, and Teacher Interviews. We interviewed children, parents, and teachers by asking them questions related to the Family Fluency Program. The data was pooled; that is, the answers to all of the questions asked were listed and when an answer occurred more than once, it was not repeated. Children of parents who participated, parents who participated, and teachers were asked, "How do you feel about the home fluency program?"

Children of parents who participated gave the following answers (Morrow, Kuhn, & Schwanenflugel, 2006, pp. 330–331):

> I don't feel alone when I'm reading.
>
> I will know how to help my children when I grow up. I will read the same stories over again with them.
>
> I will partner read, echo read, and choral read with my children.
>
> It is nice to read with your parents. Sometimes you think they don't care about your schoolwork or you, but when they read with you, you know they do.
>
> When I read with my mom I help her with her English.

Parents who participated gave the following answers (Morrow, Kuhn, & Schwanenflugel, 2006, p. 331):

Table 4.1. How to Help My Child Become a Fluent Reader

Parents	Answers	n
Participants	Practice reading by repeating the same story over and over	17
	Choral read	15
	Ask questions about the story	15
	Read to your child, read along with your child, partner read	15
	Sound out words	14
	Help children to read at the right pace, not too fast, not too slow	10
	Read with expression	7
	Encourage and be patient with your child	7
	Echo read	6
	Use computer programs	2
Nonparticipants	Practice phonics	18
	Read to your child often/daily	17
	Have your child read aloud	15
	Work on increasing vocabulary	10
	Read more difficult books	6
	Help with writing	6
	Help with spelling	5
	Provide parental support	5
	Find books of interest to your child	4
	Use easy books	4
	Partner read	3
	Read with expression	2
	Practice the same book over again	2
	Set a good example	2
	Correct mistakes	1
	Encourage children to read alone	1

It was fun to work with my child.

My child looked forward to working with me.

I learned some things about helping my child with reading that I didn't know about before.

I learned some things about reading from my child since my English isn't so good.

I just thought you helped children sound out words; now I know reading the same story over and over is important.

I never knew about reading together; they called it choral reading.

I never knew about partner reading and taking turns.

The activities were easy to do and didn't take much time.

I could see an improvement in my child's reading as a result of the repeated reading that we did.

Teachers gave the following answers (Morrow, Kuhn, & Schwanenflugel, 2006, p. 331):

Parents in the program read with their children more than they had before.

Parents learned the techniques to enhance fluency since they recorded on their forms echo reading, choral reading, and partner reading.

Parents recognized and mentioned the improvement they saw in their children's reading by repeating stories.

I saw improvement in many of my struggling readers as a result of the repeated readings at home. Their decoding and comprehension of repeated stories improved. It also increased their self-esteem.

The Family *Highlights* Program

The Family *Highlights* Program (Morrow & Young, 1997) was similar in format to the Family Fluency Program. It was initiated by the school. The purpose was for parents to work with their children at home to motivate them to want to read and write voluntarily for pleasure and for information. We also wanted children to look at literacy as a social activity to engage in with family members. The treatment group included both a school program and a family literacy component, and the control group used the school program only. The children in this study were evenly and randomly selected from the two first-grade, two second-grade, and two third-grade classrooms. The study took place in an urban district with a diverse population of low and low-middle income families.

The School Program

The school-based program had been put into effect the year before the parent involvement was added. It included the creation of classroom literacy centers with a variety of literacy activities available for children. Featured books were displayed facing out on bookshelves, and books were categorized by topics. There were five to eight books per child at three to four grade levels, and the books represented multiple genres of children's literature. The books could be checked out to take home from the classroom. Pillows, rugs, stuffed animals, and rocking chairs added comfort to the classroom literacy centers. Manipulatives such as felt boards with story characters and recorded stories and headsets were available for the children's use. An "Authors' Spot" was equipped with paper, blank booklets, and writing utensils.

Teachers modeled activities to create interest in reading and writing by involving children in shared read-alouds, telling stories with or without props (such as felt figures and puppets), engaging in journal writing, creating original stories, and listening to stories read with headsets and CDs. Teachers used four selections from the magazine *Highlights for Children* and featured one selection a week. Children could participate in these literacy activities independently or with a friend during literacy center time.

The Family Program

Similar to the Family Fluency Program, the goals and activities done in school were to be participated in at home as well. We were interested in motivating children to want to read and write voluntarily for pleasure and for information. We wanted children to approach literacy as a social activity by engaging in reading and writing with family members. Many of the school activities and materials provided in the school program were available to the parents. We wanted the home program to be familiar for the children so the activities they did with their parents were similar to what they did in school. If parents had limited literacy ability or did not speak English, children could help with the activities. Parents received a felt board and story characters, some puppets, two spiral notebooks for them to keep journals with their children, a few pieces of children's literature, and, monthly, a *Highlights for Children* magazine.

Parents came to meetings throughout the year to learn to use the materials so they could encourage reading and writing at home. They learned new activities at each session. For example, at the first session they learned good dialogic techniques for reading to children and how to do partner journal writing. At the next meeting they practiced telling stories. They also learned to tell stories with props, using felt figures or puppets. At another session we talked about how to make a space for storing books and to have a little literacy center at home. They were also taught to use the *Highlights for Children* magazines that were sent home once a month. There were four activities using *Highlights* for them to do with their children that had already been done in the classroom. The use of *Highlights* was a major activity in the program. It was a shared literacy activity with home and school. The teachers did the featured *Highlights* activities in school with the children. The parents were to repeat them at home. The sections of the magazine featured each week were written in Spanish and in English.

We held three meetings for the parents in the fall and three in the spring. At each meeting we gave parents materials, had children participate in activities with parents, and provided refreshments. Similar to the fluency program, we provided babysitting to supervise children when they were not working with their parents at the meetings. After each strategy was modeled at a meeting, it was reviewed at subsequent meetings. We provided a handbook for the parents listing materials and directions for using them. We were also able to give small stipends to the parents because we were grant funded. We encouraged parents to purchase literacy materials for home with the funding (Morrow, 2003).

Assessments and Results

On all quantitative measures using an analysis of covariance (ANCOVA) with pretest scores as covariates and posttest scores as the dependent variables, children in the groups with the family literacy component tested significantly better than the children in the control group, which had no family literacy component. The quantitative measures were scores from a story retelling, story rewriting, and the California Test of Basic Skills reading section. In addition to quantitative measures, we interviewed children, parents, and teachers to find out if parents were reading and writing and participating in other literacy activities with their children at home.

Child Interviews. Children in the family literacy component group reported that they read or looked at books more than children whose parents did not participate. The children in the family literacy group also asked someone to read to them more often. The interview also found that parents in the family literacy group did read and write more often with their children and chose to do more literacy activities with them in general than parents who did not participate in the family literacy group.

The data were pooled, with answers to all questions listed. When an answer occurred more than once, it was not repeated. The following are the questions asked and answers given by the children interviewed:

What do you like about the family literacy program?
• When I need help someone is there for me.

- It's nice to work with parents. Sometimes you think your parents don't love you, but when they work with you, then you know they do.
- I might not know how to read if they didn't help me.
- It's fun.
- Lots of people help you: grandmas, grandpas, aunts, uncles, big brothers, moms, dads, mom's boyfriend, dad's girlfriend.

When you are a parent how will you help your child?
- I'll read stories to them.
- I'll buy them books to read.
- I'll help them write and spell.
- I'll hold their hand.
- I'll do the same things my parents do.
- I'll go to school to find out how I can help.
- I'll help them make up stories.
- I'll help them pronounce words.

Parent Interviews. We asked parents what they thought was the value of the family program. The following is the pooled information (Morrow & Young, 1997).

What do you think the value of the family program was?
- It is fun to work with your child. It is quality time together.
- It is exciting and you get a wonderful feeling.
- My child looks forward to working with me.
- I learned how to help my child and that I was able to help my child.
- We learn from each other and share ideas.
- I learned about telling stories with felt and drawing stories, which I didn't know about.
- I learned to be more patient with my child.
- I learned that doing fun things is important and that my child will learn that way too.
- When parents help, children will know that school is important.
- When we work together my child teaches me too, since I don't speak English very well.

Teacher Interviews. The information gathered through teacher interviews was handled the same way as the children's data. The following are the questions asked of the teachers and their responses:

What have parents been involved in since the family program?

- Reading to their children
- Encouraging their children to read
- Having children retell stories
- Taking trips to the library
- Working with *Highlights* magazine
- Writing journals
- Participating in activities at the Literacy Center

How have you helped to get them involved?

- I meet with parents to explain the elements of the program.
- I've encouraged them to read and write with their children.
- I keep parents informed as to what we are learning about.
- I invite parents to read to children in school, participate in literacy center time, and help with writing conferences.

The BELLE Project: Bellevue Project for Early Language, Literacy, and Education Success

The BELLE Project family literacy program is very different from the Family Fluency Program and the Family *Highlights* Program. This is a community program initiated by pediatricians from New York University School of Medicine. The goal of this large, randomized research was to determine the impact of mother–child relationship interventions on parenting, language, literacy, and child development. The interventions occur during primary pediatric care appointments for children from birth to age 3 at an urban public hospital that serves ethnically diverse, low socioeconomic status (SES) families, whose children are at risk for not succeeding in school.

This study builds upon similar published research, for example, the Reach Out and Read (ROR) model. In the ROR model, volunteers read to children waiting for the doctor for primary care visits. During the visit the doctor makes an effort to find out about the language and literacy development of the child and what the mothers are doing to help at home. Suggestions for helping are made by the physician, and each parent–child pair receives a book to take home. A large number of studies on ROR have documented a positive impact on a child's language development, resulting from parent–child shared read-alouds (Mendelsohn, 2002; Needlman, Toker, Dreyer, Klass, & Mendelsohn, 2005). The BELLE Project is an extension of ROR and builds on varied interventions to assess what works best for families considered at risk as a result of maternal education level. The program applies research results by Kubicek (1996) and Erickson, Endersbe, and Simon (1999) from the field of child mental health, pediatric primary care, and literacy.

The Program

The inclusion criteria for the 675 mother and child participants in the BELLE Project were that the mother speak English or Spanish as a primary language, planned to have pediatric follow-up at the Bellevue Hospital Center Clinic affiliated with New York University Medical School, had a consistent means of contact, and had children with no significant medical complications. The population was mostly Latino with a small percentage af African Americans. Parents were low income and had limited education.

There are two major components to the program for children in the treatment group. First, all aspects of the ROR program are used: Volunteers read to the children in the waiting room, the doctor makes an effort to find out about the language and literacy development of the child and what the mothers do with the children to enhance language and literacy, the doctor notes the language and literacy development of the child and suggests ways to help the child, and the child is given a toy and a book.

The second component for the treatment group is called the Video Interaction Project (VIP), which applies work done in the field of infant mental health by Kubicek (1996) and Erickson and colleagues (1999) to the pediatric primary care setting. In VIP, mother and child meet with a child development specialist (CDS) at each well-child visit for about 30–45 minutes. The visits take place concurrently with the pediatric well-child visits. The CDS works with the mother to promote interactions and interactive play that facilitate language, literacy, and child development, as documented in research (Hart & Risley, 1995; Morrow, 2009; Tamis-LeMonda, Bornstein, & Baumwell, 2001). The core component of VIP involves video recording the mother and child for 5–7 minutes. The CDS and mother watch the video recording to identify strengths and promote other positive interactions. The CDS gives each parent a toy, a children's book, and a pamphlet about early language, literacy, and child development activities. Research documents the efficacy of VIP with mothers who have limited education (Mendelsohn et al., 2007), with effects on both responsive parenting and child development.

Results

Members of the BELLE Project developed and used the StimQ assessment, which was validated in urban, low SES families. The assessment showed that gains were greatest for the VIP subjects compared with parents who only received the Reach Out and Read program. Mothers with seventh- to eleventh-grade education showed the most helpful language and literacy play interactions with their child. The VIP program does have definite possibilities for use in school. Such school application could include meeting parents of preschoolers about three times a year in school to go over dialogic reading and parenting skills. Also, giving each parent a children's book and a pamphlet about development and review is important. Making a video recording of the parent reading to the child and reviewing it with a CDS would be helpful in giving parents constructive suggestions for improving if necessary. The VIP researchers are beginning work with 3- to 5-year-olds and want to move the treatment into schools.

Challenges and Possibilities

Involving parents in the language and literacy development of their children is very important. There is a great deal of work involved and there can be frustration because of lack of attendance. Because of the responsibilities of work and child care, getting parents to attend and participate is difficult. Many of the families in these programs had only one parent. Often families were being headed by an elderly grandparent. With many obstacles to face, parents find it difficult to take on more responsibilities even though they are sincerely interested in their children.

The Family Fluency Program, the *Highlights* Family Program, and the BELLE Project had similarities and differences, yet they were all successful. The programs heightened parents' awareness about literacy development based on the study they participated in, and the activities enhanced parent involvement in literacy activities at home. Their success was based in part on the following common factors:

- There was transportation if needed.
- The programs provided food for participants.

- There was supervision for children when the trainers wanted to work with the parents alone.
- Children performed for the parents when they came to school.
- To get the parents to participate, program staff made multiple contacts (letters sent home, reminder phone calls, for example).
- There were incentives for the parents; for example, they were given materials and books, received stipends for participating, and they got to see their children perform in front of the group.
- The programs did not require that all modeled tasks had to be done; whatever the parent found practical to do was accepted.
- Tasks were done in school so that the children were familiar with them and could help parents who needed it at home.
- The information and community meetings were culturally sensitive.
- Language interpreters were provided at the meetings.
- Teachers were persistent with families that didn't come; they made repeated phone calls and sent lots of notes and materials home.
- The activities were easy to understand and initiate.
- The activities took a short time to carry out.
- The activities brought about results quickly.

Family literacy programs need to be given as much time and effort as possible both in school and the community. We must spend time on professional development so teachers can learn new strategies to use with children to enhance performance. We must have parent coordinators to put programs into place that include home and school together. Family literacy is one of the missing links to help us close the achievement gap. We can never be completely successful with teaching reading without the help of the home.

REFERENCES

Allington, R.L. (1983). Fluency: The neglected reading goal. *The Reading Teacher*, 36(6), 556–561.

Bandura, A. (1986). *Social foundations of thought and action: A social cognitive theory.* Englewood Cliffs, NJ: Prentice-Hall.

Chavkin, N., & Gonzalez, D.L. (1995). *Forging partnerships between Mexican American parents and the schools.* Washington, DC: Office of Educational Research and Improvement. (ERIC Document Reproduction Service No. ED388489)

Darling, S., & Westberg, L. (2004). Parent involvement in children's acquisition of reading. *The Reading Teacher*, 57(8), 774–776.

Donahue, P.L., Finnegan, R.J., Lutkus, A.D., Allen, N.L., & Campbell, J.R. (2001). *The Nation's report card: Fourth-grade reading 2000*. Washington, DC: U.S. Department of Education, Office of Educational Research and Improvement, National Center for Education Statistics. Retrieved December 13, 2001, from nces.ed.gov/naep3/pdf/main2000/2001499.pdf

Epstein, J.L. (1991). Effects on student achievement of teachers' practices of parent involvement. In S. Silvern (Ed.), *Literacy through family, community, and school interaction* (pp. 261–276). Greenwich, CT: JAI.

Erickson, M., Endersbe, J., & Simon, J. (1999). *Seeing is believing: Videotaping families and using guided self-observation to build parenting skills*. Minneapolis, MN: Regents of the University of Minnesota.

Hart, B., & Risley, T.R. (1995). *Meaningful differences in the everyday experience of young American children*. Baltimore: Paul H. Brookes.

Hoffman, J.V. (1987). Rethinking the role of oral reading. *The Elementary School Journal, 87*(3), 367–373. doi:10.1086/461501

Kubicek, L.F. (1996). Helping young children become competent communicators: The role of relationships. *Zero to Three, 17*(1), 25–30.

Kuhn, M.R., & Stahl, S.A. (2003). Fluency: A review of developmental and remedial strategies. *Journal of Educational Psychology, 95*(1), 3–21. doi:10.1037/00220663.95.1.3

Melzi, G., Paratore, J.R., & Krol-Sinclair, B. (2000). Reading and writing in the daily lives of Latino mothers who participate in a family literacy program. *National Reading Conference Yearbook, 49*, 178–193.

Mendelsohn, A.L. (2002). Promoting language and literacy through reading aloud: The role of the pediatrician. *Current Problems in Pediatric and Adolescent Health Care, 32*(6), 188–210. doi:10.1067/mps.2002.125467

Mendelsohn, A.L., Valdez, P., Flynn, V., Foley, G., Berkule, S., Tomopoulos, S., et al. (2007). Use of videotaped interactions during pediatric well-child care: Impact at 33 months on parenting and child development. *Journal of Developmental and Behavioral Pediatrics, 28*(3), 206–212. doi:10.1097/DBP.0b013e3180324d87

Morrow, L.M. (2003). Motivating lifelong voluntary readers. In J. Flood, D. Lapp, J. Squire, & J. Jensen (Eds.), *Handbook of research on teaching the English language arts* (2nd ed., pp. 857–867). Mahwah, NJ: Erlbaum.

Morrow, L.M. (2009). *Literacy development in the early years: Helping children read and write* (6th ed.). Boston: Allyn & Bacon.

Morrow, L.M., Kuhn, M.R., & Schwanenflugel, P.J. (2006). The family fluency program. *The Reading Teacher, 60*(4), 322–333. doi:10.1598/RT.60.4.2

Morrow, L.M., Paratore, J.R., & Tracey, D.H. (1994). *Family literacy: New perspectives, new opportunities*. Newark, DE: International Reading Association.

Morrow, L.M., Scoblionko, J., & Shafer, D. (1995). The family writing and reading appreciation program. In L.M. Morrow (Ed.), *Family literacy connections in schools and communities* (pp. 70–86). Newark, DE: International Reading Association.

Morrow, L.M., & Young, J. (1997). A family literacy program connecting school and home: Effects on attitude, motivation, and literacy achievement. *Journal of Educational Psychology, 89*(4), 736–742. doi:10.1037/0022-0663.89.4.736

National Institute of Child Health and Human Development. (2000). *Report of the National Reading Panel. Teaching children to read: An evidence-based assessment of the scientific research literature on reading and its implications for reading instruction* (NIH Publication No. 00-4769). Washington, DC: U.S. Government Printing Office.

Needlman, R., Toker, K.H., Dreyer, B.P., Klass, P., & Mendelsohn, A.L. (2005). Effectiveness of a primary care intervention to support reading aloud: A multicenter evaluation. *Ambulatory Pediatrics, 5*(4), 209–215. doi:10.1367/A04110R.1

Rasinski, T.V. (1990). Effects of repeated reading and listening-while-reading on reading fluency. *The Journal of Educational Research, 83*(3), 147–150.

Reutzel, D.R. (1996). Developing at-risk readers' oral reading fluency. In L.R. Putnam

(Ed.), *How to become a better reading teacher: Strategies for assessment and intervention* (pp. 241–254). Englewood Cliffs, NJ: Merrill.

Schreiber, P.A. (1991). Understanding prosody's role in reading acquisition. *Theory Into Practice, 30*(3), 158–164.

Tamis-LeMonda, C.S., Bornstein, M.H., & Baumwell, L. (2001). Maternal responsiveness and children's achievement of language milestones. *Child Development, 72*(3), 748–767. Medline doi:10.1111/1467-8624.00313

Tan, A., & Nicholson, T. (1997). Flashcards revisited: Training poor readers to read words faster improves their comprehension of text. *Journal of Educational Psychology, 89*(2), 276–288. doi:10.1037/0022-0663.89.2.276

Torgesen, J.K., Wagner, R.K., & Rashotte, C.A. (1999). *TOWRE: Test of word reading efficiency.* Austin, TX: Pro-Ed.

Vygotsky, L.S. (1978). *Mind in society: The development of higher psychological processes* (M. Cole, V. John-Steiner, S. Scribner, & E. Souberman, Eds. & Trans.). Cambridge, MA: Harvard University Press.

Wasik, B.H. (2004). *Handbook of family literacy.* Mahwah, NJ: Erlbaum.

CHAPTER 5

Talking Over Books at Home and in School

Nancy Roser

There may be at least three self-evident arguments about children's access to text in the United States today. The first contention concerns sheer numbers: there are *fewer* texts in homes in which families are poor. A corollary of that assertion is that there are also fewer sources from which to purchase or borrow texts in high-poverty communities. The second notion asserts that homes contain different types of texts—with low-income families more likely to gather and preserve "practical" text forms (e.g., records, directions, news) over more school-related forms of print. The third contention, and the one most central to this chapter, is that home texts are referenced and invoked differently in middle- and low-income homes, and that those differences have implications for schooling. I examine each of these assumptions in the following sections, leading toward implications for how well-chosen texts can serve the thought and talk of all children in today's classrooms.

Access to Texts

In a country in which people leave magazines, newspapers, or even books behind on planes, trains, or buses, it is hard to imagine there are children who are not within reach of text. In this chapter, I use the term *text* in recognition that the multimodal world of children includes the texts of videogames, television, cartoons, DVDs, and computers (see Dyson, 2001; Marsh, 2003). Yet, in a study of literacy opportunities across neighborhoods, Neuman and Celano (2001) report that literacy resources are not equally accessible. Examining the print environments of four Philadelphia neighborhoods, the researchers found 10 bookstores in the two high-income communities but none in the two low-income neighborhoods. Although it was possible to purchase print materials for children in the low-income neighborhoods, only four shops stocked texts aimed toward children compared with 24 shops in the high-income neighborhoods. The research team also calculated the ratio of book titles per child in each community. For the high-income neighborhoods, the best case was 13 different available titles per child; but in the two low-income communities, the best case was one title for every 20 children. No middle grade or young adult books at all were available for purchase in the low-income neighborhoods.

Even the public library offerings revealed distinctions, with the two low-income communities holding smaller collections, fewer books per child, and more limited evening hours than high-income communities. Hemmeter (2006) presents findings in agreement, reporting that library use is influenced by distance, income, and availability of relevant material.

When my colleague Jo Worthy and I (Worthy & Roser, 2003) produced a "book flood" for a class of 18 fifth graders learning English as their second language, the flood served to counter the paucity of books in the school neighborhood and to provide titles the students indicated they would like to read if those types of materials had been available (Worthy, Moorman, & Turner, 1999). There was no bookstore of any kind within 10 miles of the children's school, and no nearby library. (In early 2008, a new public library opened less than two miles from the school.) Some children found paperback books for purchase at "that little store, you know, down at the corner" (in a gas station) or received books from a family member—"My uncle he gave it to me" (Worthy & Roser, 2003, p. 186). We interviewed the children, made home visits, and learned that students' personal libraries averaged about eight books, most provided by Reading Is Fundamental, a nonprofit organization that offered book choices three times per year.

The average number of books these children owned aligned with data derived from a 1986 national survey comparing the circumstances of children whose families were recipients of Aid to Families with Dependent Children (AFDC) with those who were not (Zill, Moore, Smith, Stief, & Coiro, 1997). The researchers found that 81% of non-poor children had 10 or more books, compared with 51% for recipients of AFDC. Neither libraries nor bookshops seem accessible to children who are homeless (Noll & Watkins, 2003) or highly mobile (Compton-Lilly, 2003). More recent studies have directly addressed the quantity of texts in low-income homes. In an investigation of home storybook reading in 44 families of low socioeconomic status (SES), Roberts (2008) reports that one third of her informants had no primary-language books in the home, while three quarters had fewer than five books; these findings contrast markedly with published case studies of children in middle class homes. Baghban (1984), for example, studying her daughter's literacy from birth to age 3, listed 74 titles her child owned. White's (1954) reading diary with her daughter, Carol, from ages 2 to 5, referenced 111 titles shared and talked over with her child. In a study of home literacy environments of kindergarten children, Morrow (1983) found significantly more books in the homes of children with high interest in literature, with book presence in all parts of the home, including the kitchen.

It seems possible to conclude that access to texts is not evenly distributed. Even so, Snow and her colleagues (Snow, Barnes, Chandler, Goodman, & Hemphill, 1991) suggest it is misleading to use the number of texts in a home as even a rough indicator of the literacy environment, arguing, as one example, that organized working-class homes may dispose of periodicals, pass along books, or keep print materials out of sight.

Types of Texts in Homes

Nearly 60 years ago, Almy (1949), then a professor at Teachers College, Columbia University, argued that learning to read is related to the number of *responses to literacy opportunities* that children make prior to first grade. Almy interviewed 106 families representing a range of economic levels, asking questions designed to gather parents' specific recollections of their child's experiences with books and stories prior to first grade, for example, "Did he ever use books, magazines, paper or pencil in his play?" (p. 53). Based on the parents' responses, she concluded that successful first graders had requested to be read to and were interested in numbers, letters, and words prior to schooling. Ninety-one percent of the parents reported their children used print materials in their play, including pads, pencils, words, magazines, scrapbooks, blackboards, comics, and coloring books. Parents also reported observing their children drawing, making up stories, and reading pictures in books.

A decade later (in 1958), Durkin (1966), also curious about the factors that marked young readers for success, began the first of two longitudinal studies designed to identify the home-centered literacy opportunities associated with children's early reading. Although Durkin did not set out to document the texts she found in homes, her written report makes it possible to identify the home literacy materials of children who read early. Of the 49 Oakland, California, first graders Durkin identified as "early readers" (representing Asian American, African American, and European American heritages), over half were described as representing lower classes. Through interviews, the children's parents talked about texts borrowed from libraries, those used for playing school, and other written work their children produced during siblings' homework sessions. The majority of parents indicated they had given their child an alphabet book or a picture dictionary (78%). In Durkin's three case studies focusing on children from low-SES homes, parents reported providing alphabet books, picture dictionaries, phonics or handwriting workbooks, storybooks, comics, children's and phonograph records, as well as borrowing books from the library. Durkin noted that in each of the 49 families in which a successful early reader developed, a blackboard was made available (sometimes with alphabet letters on its perimeter), encouraging what she described as the pervasive scribbling of early readers.

Durkin's (1966) second longitudinal study, set in New York City schools, involved 60 families (with 30 early readers and 30 nonearly readers). Approximately one fourth of the interviewed sample was described as low SES. Besides the books owned by children, literacy materials again included blackboards, pencils, and paper. In both groups (early and nonearly readers), parents believed alphabet books played "an especially important role in stimulating early interest in letter names and, sometimes, in letter sounds" (p. 108). Parents also suggested environmental print and the act of *rereading* stories were helpful to their children.

As with Durkin's (1966) studies, it was not Heath's (1983) express purpose in her seminal ethnography, *Ways With Words*, to catalog the specific texts that served two working class mill communities in the Piedmont area of the Carolinas. Rather, she hoped to understand how children learn to use language and literacy within communities. Yet her accounts of literacy environments and events yielded careful descriptions of text types. The home texts in Trackton, a black community with roots in farming, included greeting cards, the drawings of older children, newspapers, car brochures, advertisements, and school information. Every home contained official documents such as birth certificates, tax forms, and loan notes. However, there were few magazines and no books except school texts, the Bible, Sunday School leaflets, and photograph albums. Heath noted, "Expectant mothers [in Trackton] neither buy nor are given...books as gifts" (p. 76). In fact, where books or toys were present, an outsider had typically brought them into the community.

Expectant mothers in Roadville, a white community tenuously clinging to its rapidly vanishing textile mills, might receive gifts of cloth books, often kept on a bookshelf in the baby's room. The majority of the children's books in Roadville homes were not plot driven, but rather nursery rhymes, alphabet, coloring, and label books. Some few, however, were sustained narratives such as "Goldilocks and the Three Bears," realistic fiction, or simplified stories from the Bible (Heath, 1983). Beyond ABC books, according to Heath (1983), books and toys in Roadville were differentiated by gender. Girls received books about "little girls, babies, and baby animals living in a...family-like setting" (p. 133). Boys were offered "books about trucks, ballgames, and boys and their animals" (p. 133). Overall, Roadville children had little exposure to "extended fictive or fanciful stories" (p. 161) before nursery school.

In a long-term project that examined the influence of home background on the literacy development of 24 preschool children from low-income families in San Diego, California (with equal numbers of African American, Anglo American, and Mexican American families), Teale (1986) documented the literacy materials of the homes in his field notes but explained that space limitations prevented him from giving a complete list of those text types in his published account. He found literacy materials to be both wide ranging and varied across homes. Eight of the families, for example, had "numerous printed materials appropriate for and available to" children (p. 178); yet, the remaining homes contained few children's books or text forms specifically for children. In four homes in which one of the parents was a self-professed reader, there were magazines, newspapers, paperbacks, and books borrowed from the library. In the other homes, there were fewer magazines and newspapers. The television guide was pervasive across homes. Five of the children lived in homes with a marked amount of religious materials, and in four homes there was a specially designated place for writing, with accessible paper and pencils. Teale concluded that these data give reason for questioning the assumption that low SES children enter school with "a dearth of literacy experience" (p. 192).

Like Teale, Taylor and Dorsey-Gaines (1988) studied the contributions of home literacy environments, including how families use reading and writing socially. The researchers described the presence of texts in the homes of urban African American children of poverty. Besides pointing toward the functional texts of these homes (e.g., news, notes, forms, the Bible), the researchers observed hand-embellished names, classic texts, formal letters, journals, and market reports. The researchers concluded that middle class observers often operate with fixed and limiting stereotypes of the literate lives in low-income homes.

In an inquiry focused on how parents account for their children's success with literacy in first grade, my colleagues and I (Roser, Hoffman, Kastler, & Sharp, 1994) interviewed the parents of 47 children drawn from 15 different first-grade classrooms. Unlike Durkin's (1966) subjects, these children were selected because they had entered first grade not yet reading conventionally but ended the school year reading at or above grade level. To conduct the interviews, we visited homes (when invited) that crossed economic levels. In one, we watched as chickens walked through the living room; in another, a seating area was completely lined with television sets tuned to different channels. (In that house, the father explained that his child had become a reader through the rolling credits that followed late-night reruns of *Bonanza*.) We invited the parents to talk about the home literacy events that could help to explain the success of their children.

Among the explanatory themes that we developed from parent interviews was one of "making text available" to children. Many of the children proudly showed us a cardboard box (or some other container) filled with their own books (Roser et al, 1994). We noted Dr. Seuss, Little Golden Books, wordless picture books, and children's magazines. Parents also provided (and showed us) the materials and spaces their children used for creating texts—crayons, markers, magnetic letters, paper, and, often, a child-sized table or desk.

Purcell-Gates (1996) describes the range and frequency of literacy practices among 20 families of poverty residing in the Boston metropolitan area. Her research specifically attempted to link the home literacy events that involved each of 24 focal children (ages 4 to 6) with their emergent literacy knowledge. Home literacy events were coded both for the social domain being served (e.g., daily living, storybook time) as well as the texts involved. The families in Purcell-Gates's study relied on print most frequently for entertainment (consulting the television schedule, checking the newspaper for movie times, playing board games that required reading, and reading books and magazines for pleasure). Families also frequently relied on print to accomplish daily tasks (reading coupons, ads, and text on containers).

Later, Duke and Purcell-Gates (2003) revisited and reanalyzed the field notes of Purcell-Gates's (1996) study of home literacy events to identify specifically the genres of text that were present. These data were then compared with data drawn from Duke's (2000a; 2000b) study of print-centered activities in 10 first-grade classrooms, allowing the researchers to account for the genres used in home and school. The comparison data showed the commonality of some texts to both settings (e.g., children's books, signs, labels, magazines, greeting cards), as well as those text forms more common to the home (e.g., Biblical texts, correspondence, coupons, address books) and specific to the school (e.g., worksheets, journals).

Across studies, it is possible to draw a tentative conclusion, as did Teale (1986), that homes vary in the texts they contain, and homes contain variant texts. Taylor (1993) advises that differences in texts between homes of poverty and relative plenty should not lead to a deficit theory of literacy growth. From their within-group observations of literacy environments, Purcell-Gates, L'Allier, and Smith (1995) found that the critical variable is not socioeconomic status, but family literacy practices, maintaining it is as incorrect to argue all low-SES children have impoverished literacy environments as it is to argue all low-SES homes "offer many and varied uses of print in their daily lives" (p. 577). Brooks (2006) provides an additional tenet: Even when children share membership in communities, one cannot assume commonalities in their experiences, knowledge, or interpretations (see also Farver, Xu, Eppe, & Lonigan, 2006).

Texts in Support of Children's Language and Literacy

Ultimately, it may not be the differences in access/quantity or types of texts that mark critical distinctions among literacy environments. Nor is explanation a matter of compiling a list of home activities that involve reading and writing (Barton & Hamilton, 1998; Sonnenschein, Brody, & Munsterman, 1996). Further, accounting for language and literacy is far more complex than regressing parent education, occupation, housing, attitudes toward schooling, experiences, or any of the array of variables that social scientists use to categorize and explain differences. Necessary, perhaps, is a deeper understanding of each child nestled (rather than nested) within a family system that operates within the structures of a social network (Bronfenbrenner, 1979; Edwards & Young, 1992). This section looks toward the ways literate behaviors serve families and the varying beliefs families hold about literacy, as well as evidence in support of the literate practices that involve young children and their caregivers reading and talking together about stories and information books (Paratore, Melzi, & Krol-Sinclair, 2003).

Texts Serve Social and Cultural Purposes

In both communities she studied, Heath (1983) shows how the embedded cultural practices of literacy served purposes, but in different ways and in different degrees. Residents of Roadville and Trackton found the following uses for reading: (a) instrumental (to achieve practical daily tasks), (b) social-interactional (to reach others, make plans), (c) news-related (to learn about distant events), (d) confirmational (to gain support for attitudes and beliefs), and, in Roadville only, for (e) recreational/educational (to entertain or read to preschoolers) purposes.

As an example of how text served young children's literacy, Heath (1983) showed that as Trackton boys were attempting to earn their places on the stage of the public plaza and to enter adult conversations, Trackton preschool girls, seemingly less noted, might be "worked with" by older siblings who sometimes used a book as prop for specific directives or for question asking. She noted that these interactions were short-lived, because Trackton children did not expect questions—especially when it was clear that the questioner already knew the answer.

Acknowledging the varied texts in children's lives, Teale (1986) also develops an explanatory scheme for describing nine domains of family activity mediated by literacy. These practices included literacy related to (1) daily living routines, (2) entertainment, (3) school-related activities, (4) work, (5) religion, (6) interpersonal communication, (7) participation in information networks, (8) storybook time, and (9) literacy for the sake of teaching/learning literacy.

Using Teale's (1986) scheme to analysis the literate practices of four low-income families, Purcell-Gates et al. (1995) found that two of the families (coded as low-literacy) engaged in one literacy event every three hours (e.g., writing a list of ingredients, completing an application, reading a letter concerning a school loan). By contrast, the other two households (high-literacy families) engaged in about 2.5 literacy events per hour, with the most frequent uses found to be for literacy learning and storybook reading.

Numerous studies, too, have pointed toward the consequences when the discourses and purposes that surround literacy at home differ from those at school (Auerbach, 1995; Cairney, 1997; Lapp, Fisher, Flood, & Moore, 2002). It seems essential that the literacy practices and beliefs of nonmainstream parents be well understood as a base for socially, culturally, and historically responsive schooling (Moll, Amanti, Neff, & Gonzalez, 1992; Moll & Greenberg, 1990; Ortiz & Ordoñez-Jasis, 2005). There is decided agreement among studies as to the import of moving beyond the surface features of the literate environment to consider children within families and families within the societal structure and beliefs that envelop them.

Parents' Beliefs About Literacy Learning

When we asked the parents of children who had succeeded in first grade (Kastler, Roser, & Hoffman, 1987) to what they attributed their children's success, the most frequent responses were that the parents themselves had modeled an interest in or a value for reading, and they had read to their children. The parents also credited the efforts of siblings, as well as the personal characteristics of the children themselves ("interested," "curious," "good memory," "verbal," "smart"; p. 91). Interestingly, the parents rarely credited their children's success to schooling, teachers, or programs. Invited to participate because their 6-year-old child who had not been reading conventionally when entering first grade completed first grade reading on grade level, the families crossed the economic spectrum.

In a similar study two decades later, Gillanders and Jiménez (2004) examined the home environments of low-income immigrant Mexican families whose kindergarten-aged children exhibited high levels of literacy compared with their peers. Across their four case descriptions, families consistently implicated the importance of "actively supporting their children's literacy...by engaging them in numerous literacy-related activities" (p. 263). Unlike the findings from low-income parents surveyed by Lapp et al. (2002), these parents did not view literacy support as largely the role of schools and teachers. The researchers indicated that their findings also differ from previous research with Latino parents (e.g., Parra & Henderson, 1982), in which parents reported valuing education but believed academic and intellectual development were the province of the schools.

Teachers, researchers, and theorists seem to agree that families hold different beliefs about literacy, as well as differing understanding of their roles in support of their children's literacy (e.g., DeBaryshe, Binder, & Buell, 2000). Sonnenschein and her colleagues (1996) suggest that the distinct patterns of socialization which can be identified in homes reflect the parents' theories of child development and of parental responsibility; often, the variance in children's school performance can be largely accounted for by the degree to which socialization practices and beliefs mesh with the curriculum and routines of schools.

The research team (Sonnenschein et al., 1997) also investigated differences in parents' views as to the most effective way to help their preschool-aged children learn to read. The researchers coded the parents' responses as representative of either an "entertainment" or a "skills" orientation to literacy development. An entertainment stance was interpreted as parents who approached reading to their children as a way to capture the child's interest and engage playfully with texts. By contrast, parents who subscribed to a skills orientation viewed literacy acquisition as challenging, with the work toward it dependent upon a set of skills that parents could promote, aided by such materials as flashcards or worksheets. The researchers indicated low-income parents were more likely to endorse a skills orientation.

Testing a causal model of the determinants and outcomes of book-reading practices, DeBaryshe (1995) assesses mothers' reading beliefs by asking them to report their expectations for reading aloud to their children. For both samples (predominantly low-income, African American, single mothers), findings indicated that mothers whose views aligned with emergent literacy theories provided more joint picture book sharing and more discussion. That is, mothers with more education and economic resources, as well as stronger literacy orientations, held more "facilitative beliefs" about literacy. These mothers indicated they provided their young children with broader and more frequent reading experiences.

When Weigel, Martin, and Bennett (2006) examined mothers' literacy beliefs over the course of one year, they found role patterns that were described as "facilitative" or "conventional." Mothers who held facilitative roles believed in taking an active role in teaching the children at home and that their efforts would influence their child's vocabulary, general knowledge, and even moral development. Parents holding conventional beliefs assumed schools, more than homes, held responsibility for teaching children. The researchers found that the homes of facilitative mothers had more literacy opportunities, and the children had more print knowledge. Findings seemed to support those of DeBaryshe (1995), although the sample was predominantly Caucasian and middle class.

As further evidence of beliefs in potential collision, Adair and Tobin (2008) draw from interviews they conducted with immigrant parents. The parents expressed opinions about early childhood education different from those held by experts and professional organizations. Immigrant parents wished the schools gave more attention to academic instruction of their young children, "with a stronger emphasis on learning the language of their new country" (p. 147). When photographer Russell Lee recorded sharecroppers' lives in rural Louisiana in the 1930s, he captured an image of a mother teaching her two young boys essentials of literacy (see Figure 5.1). A piece of dark cloth affixed to the wall holds the cursive alphabet, numerals from 1 to 10, and a sentence (The rain are fallin), demonstrating a purpose for learning letters. The children sit erect and attentive, encased by the angle of the walking stick their mother uses to direct attention (and response). Her posture seems to indicate that she is proud of her children and of her own effort. She, too, seems engaged in the task and unaware of the photographer. This mother's beliefs about literacy seem born of skills, and the necessity to help her children recognize and recite, perhaps as she was

Figure 5.1. Louisiana Mother Teaching Her Children, 1939

Note. Farm Security Administration Photo by Russell Lee. Used by permission of the Library of Congress, Prints & Photographs Division, FSA-OWI Collection, Cph 3c18226.

helped. Other print in the room includes the calendar that freezes the moment in time. Newspapers are used as wallcoverings, much like an incident Heath (1983) recorded in Trackton: Miss Bee, visiting her sister, recalled a very practical use for newsprint from her childhood: "I know my *mother*...had put...paper, magazines, 'n patched *up* de house for us to keep *warm,* plastered de house all over wid magazines, to keep us warm" (p. 63).

Most often, it seems, parents of poverty hold a skills emphasis view of literacy and believe that if their children know letters and sounds, they are equipped with the spoils of schooling. Parents with more education and resources interpret the rewards of schooling as enjoyment of reading, as well as satisfaction from having read. Yet, both large-scale and case-study research indicate that poor and working class families "do literacy" (Moll et al., 1992; McTavish, 2007) with their children. In his inspection of survey data, Zill and his colleagues (1997) note considerable diversity in the "welfare population," pointing toward evidence that weighs against stereotypes of urban families. For example, 42% of parents living in poverty claimed to read to their young children three or more times a week, compared with 57% of the non-poor families. In a review of literature on parenting and emerging literacy skills, Landry and Smith (2006) point to the need for more research effort, arguing that although there is evidence of the relation of parents' interactive strategies with children's language development, "less is known about relations between the home literacy environment and aspects of children's early literacy skills other than language" (p. 136).

In one detail-rich account, McTavish (2007) reports the literacy support provided by a working class Canadian family to their 5-year-old daughter. Katie was both initiated and instructed into purpose-filled literacy in her home through such events as helping to record plans on the calendar, making a greeting card, copying a name, and selecting a television show by using the on-screen guide. Katie was read to in the afternoon and at bedtime, with her father the purveyor of information texts, and her mother of fiction. The researcher noted that Katie owned a variety of books, including ones she could recite from memory; further, Katie understood well how print travels across and down the pages of her books, as well as the notion of voice–print matching for each separate word. Katie produced her own lists, and, when marketing, helped her mother read the shopping list, guided by her mother's cueing directives to use sounds associated with the initial letter. Further, Katie was able to appropriate the models of reading that her parents, particularly her mother, provided.

Katie's literacy induction seems what Goodman (2008), addressing the Word Congress in Reading, would describe as "written and oral language occurring simultaneously very early in a child's life," as well as an example of a child "learning to use language because she needed to" (n.p.).

Researchers (Auerbach, 1995; Moll et al., 1992; Taylor, 1993) urge those who would approach to observe and interpret families at work not to dismiss the complex knowledge that is represented and transmitted independently of wealth or schooling. Teale (1986) suggests that to understand the variability it is essential to "'unpackage' terms such as SES and ethnicity and keep at the forefront of our considerations that literacy is a social process and a cultural practice" (p. 193).

What seemed a central conclusion of Heath's (1983) study is that neither "way" with words (neither Trackton's or Roadville's) adequately prepares the child for traditional schooling. Heath's concern about mismatch (and even collision) between home and school is a central thesis of this book. Yet, Hammer, Nimmo, Cohen, Draheim, and Johnson (2005) remind us that solutions are not achieved by distilling beliefs and practices from the mainstream so as to develop intervention programs to "remediate" differences in nonmainstream cultures.

Picture Books, Parents, and Reading With Children

It is the picture book that has provided the most at-the-ready mediator for the inspection of language and the roots of children's literacy. Perhaps because joint book sharing offers a quiet, focused, and relatively contained language event, it is more readily recorded and analyzed than the livelier literacy happenings in a child's day. Thus, the decontextualized conversations that capture and focus children's attention on books and pictures have informed understandings of language and literacy acquisition in many related fields. Based on studies of middle-class parents and their children, book sharing may seem "as much a part of [children's]...routines as brushing their teeth or spilling milk on the kitchen floor" (Sheridan, 1979, p. 11). Yet, in a survey addressing the well-being of American children collected concurrently with U.S. Census data, researchers concluded that 11% of children aged 1–5 had not been read to by a family member in the week prior to the survey (Fields, Smith, Bass, & Lugaila, 2001), a percentage the investigators extrapolated to be 1.6 million young American children. It should be noted that effective family literacy programs, such as the Intergenerational Literacy Project at Boston University, have demonstrated that participants more than doubled their incidence of story reading (Paratore, 2001).

As the number of studies examining the effects of reading to and with children proliferates, so, too, do the claims for the effectiveness of time spent with picture books. Researchers have variantly claimed that book sharing supports children's receptive and expressive vocabularies, print concepts, phonological awareness, general language development, conversational skills, metalinguistic awareness, emergent literacy, reading comprehension, reading achievement, and school success (see, for example, Bus, Van IJzendoorn, & Pellegrini, 1995; Moerk, 1985; Scarborough & Dobrich, 1994; Sénéchal, LeFevre, Thomas, & Daley, 1998; Teale, 1984; Wells, 1985).

In a groundbreaking study, Bruner (1975) points toward the utility of language routines as infants acquire language in the presence of a book and a conversational partner. Ninio and Bruner (1978) then demonstrate how one mother–child dyad produced a ritualized dialogue that supported a child's labeling of pictures (from 8 to 18 months). At the outset, the mother played the roles of both conversants—eliciting labels from the child, accepting the infant's vocalizations and actions as meaningful, and sustaining the dialogue by responding *for* the child, praising, and inviting again. Roadville parents in Heath's (1983) ethnography showed a variant of this structure: "Adults point to the item on the page, name it, provide a simple sentence such as 'That's a lamb.'.... 'What does the lamb say?,'...and answer their own question with 'The lamb says baaaa'" (p. 128).

When Ninio (1980) later compared 40 Israeli mother–child dyads who represented different socioeconomic levels, she found many more similarities than differences in the ways mothers talked over a book with their 19-month-old children. That is, mothers of different cultural backgrounds produced similar labeling routines; further, the labeling talk echoed what she had observed in the earlier study of a middle class dyad (Ninio & Bruner, 1978). Even so, lower SES mothers used fewer words and, as Ninio described them, meager descriptions. Thus, although the researcher observed all of the dyads following labeling routines, she conjectured that the styles of the mothers with less schooling and fewer economic resources were less likely to encourage more complex language as their children developed.

A seeming trend in studies of parents, young children, and books is that lenses have broadened from descriptions of predominantly middle class participants (e.g., Crago, 1993; Hammett, Van Kleeck, & Huberty, 2003) to include diverse samples (e.g., Anderson-Yockel & Haynes, 1994; Hammer et al., 2005; Pellegrini, Perlmutter, Galda, & Brody, 1990; Roberts, 2008). Collectively, studies of parent–child picture book reading give rise to themes of differences in the form and purposes for talk (e.g., the extent to which parents question), as well as the text features, genres, and book familiarity that differentially serve story talk.

Forms and Purposes of Home Storybook Talk. Studies of joint picture book reading have described caregivers who have skillfully adjusted the demands of their talk to their partner, providing necessary scaffolding to allay confusion or to raise the stakes (Pellegrini et al., 1990; Sénéchal, Cornell, & Broda, 1995; Wheeler, 1983). Snow (1977) noted that mother-infant talk is often filled with questions, a device that enables passing the turn to the conversational partner. Yet, in their study of 20 parent–child dyads reading and talking over both familiar and unfamiliar text, Anderson-Yockel and Haynes (1994) found that African American mothers asked fewer questions than did Caucasian mothers (balanced for educational level, income, and occupation). In concert with their parents, Caucasian children also asked more questions, while African American children made more comments. Similarly, in our study of the role adults play in story time, Martinez and I (Roser & Martinez, 1985) found that whether at home or at school, preschoolers talked about books in the ways the adult did.

Heath (1983) has also noted that Trackton parents rarely asked questions. Neither did Trackton children expect adults to ask them questions—especially when it was clear adults already knew the answer. A Trackton grandmother explained: "We don't ask 'em 'bout colors, names, 'n things" (p. 109). Instead, adults used terms themselves with full expectation that children would come to use them, too. Similarly, Trackton children asked "why" questions themselves, but "why" questions were rarely asked of them, so the children did not answer those questions substantively.

Investigating whether changing the level of story time questions would affect language development, Whitehurst and his colleagues (1988) tested a treatment condition in which parents asked their children more open-ended questions during picture book readings (rather than simply inviting children to label and describe). Further, parents were instructed to repeat, recast, and expand their children's responses. The researchers theorized that the latter would allow for children's comparisons of their own language with adults' syntactic strings. Children in the experimental group scored higher on language measures than those in the control group, in which parents read and talked with their children in their customary ways.

Whitehurst and colleagues (1988) work suggests there are questions and then there are questions—talk and then different talk. Parents' initial requests for labels from infants and toddlers must necessarily shift to make room for their children's more elaborated understandings to take shape and find expression (Snow, 1983). For example, Lindfors (1999) explains that an adult's conversational turn can make room for a child's response and elaboration without taking an interrogative form (e.g., An adult might puzzle aloud: "I wonder why that millipede has *all* those legs"). Lindfors labels this kind of talk the language of inquiry. At its best, it is genuine, child-focused, purposeful, and collaborative—opened-ended conjecture not bound by syntax. That is, dialogues need not include interrogatives for ideas to be exchanged or participants to be informed. The rules of conversation speak to turns rather than questions and answers.

Yaden, Smolkin, and Conlon (1989) also encourage parents not to ask questions in their study of preschoolers' questions about books during home storybook reading. Rather, parents were to "receive" children's thoughts in the same way Eeds and Wells (1989) encouraged preservice teachers to minimize questioning in their classroom book discussions so as to achieve "grand conversations." Across two separate longitudinal studies, Yaden and colleagues found most of the questions the children posed focused on the pictures (about 50%), followed by questions about story meaning. The researchers used the children's questions as windows into their sense-making. They posited that parents had laid essential groundwork in book looking, reading, and talking, but it was essential for investigators to listen past parent talk to how children worked toward their own (admittedly socialized) sense of the stories. Because book conversations with infants and toddlers are viewed as joint social and cognitive acts in which parents query so as to elicit labels from their children as they move toward conversations in which *either* partner may offer or ask for information (DeLoache, 1984), it seems important to understand how those initial exchanges become more elaborated.

Books Children Talk About. In many studies of parent–child book sharing, the texts themselves seem secondary to the investigations, at times identified but rarely central to the analysis (e.g., Torr, 2004). That is, books serve as representations of meanings in many studies rather than as a particular art form that serves for objectifying experiences and finding one's stance, as well as a means of induction into one's "literary heritage" (Chambers, 1992; Teale, 1984).

Exceptions include the work of Pellegrini and his colleagues (1990). These researchers hypothesized that text genre and format familiarity would make a difference in the teaching strategies African American mothers used while working with their children who were enrolled in a Head Start program. The researchers offered 13 mother–child pairs informational text in a familiar form (e.g., newspaper ads for toys that had been cut and pasted into booklets), as well as information text in a less familiar form (e.g., information trade books such as *Who Lives in the Zoo?*). Similarly, they provided the dyads both familiar narratives (e.g., cartoon strips) and less familiar narratives (e.g., trade books such as *The Little Red Hen* or *Peter Rabbit*). The researchers found that expository texts (whether in a familiar or traditional trade book form) elicited more parental teaching strategies than did narratives. Similarly, the children participated more frequently in the presence of expository texts (again regardless of form). Notably, the teaching strategies that mothers used were more demanding in the presence of the more familiar forms (newspapers ads). A study with upper middle class preschoolers who were invited to talk with adults about books classified as picture storybooks, information/concept books, and ABC books also pointed toward information books as evoking considerable response (Smolkin, Yaden, Brown, & Hofius, 1992).

A classroom/home study undertaken by Whitehurst and his colleagues (Whitehurst, Arnold, et al., 1994) carefully attended to the books that would be read both at home and at school. The research team indicated that books were selected because of their potential support for vocabulary growth. Further, each book had illustrations that seemed to clarify vocabulary and carry the narrative to a greater extent than did the print. The researchers also excluded any book that was already familiar to children, and supplied a list of trade books that matched criteria (including both expository and narrative titles). What seems useful about such clear descriptions is that a study's findings (in this case, effects on expressive vocabulary) can be interpreted through a more thoroughly described set of text prompts.

Roberts (2008) compares the effects of the native language of texts used for home storybook reading. Preschool children (*n* = 33) from low-SES families whose first language was either Spanish or Hmong were alternately provided read-aloud books in their first or second language across two 6-week sessions. For both groups, Roberts found that reading storybooks at home in the primary language was as effective as reading stories in English for promoting English vocabulary. The researcher provided a listing of 12 pieces of children's literature translated into Hmong and Spanish, arguing that although the texts were not necessarily aligned with children's cultural backgrounds, they provided sequential narrative structures, relevant school vocabulary, and reputations as classic texts.

Anderson-Yockel and Haynes (1994) hypothesize that familiarity with text would affect book talk. In their study of African American and Caucasian mother–child dyads, they asked parents to bring one of the child's favorite and most frequently read books to the taping session. In comparison with experimenter-provided books, when the book was familiar, African American parents asked fewer questions and all caregivers reduced their attentional vocatives, descriptions, and directives/requests. As a result, children talked more, providing more spontaneous verbalizations. In a study of repeated readings during story time, my colleague Martinez and I (Martinez & Roser, 1985), report that when parents (or teachers) read the same story repeatedly, children attended to different aspects than they did on the first reading. Further, we found children talked more (about twice as much) when the story was familiar. Morrow (1988) also reports that 4-year-olds in urban childcare centers made more interpretive responses and produced more talk about print and story structure when a story had become familiar through repeated reading. Seemingly, the book (and its familiarity) affects literate talk.

Talking Over Books at School

Again, it is Heath (1982) who reminds us that the ways we talk over books are as much a part of learned behavior "as are ways of eating, sitting, playing games, and building houses" (p. 49). Snow and Goldfield (1983) intimate that picture book routines are subject to considerable shifts as language develops. That is, the same infants who took their first conversational turns eliciting and supplying labels may eventually partner with adults and peers to produce "considerable discussions of temporal sequencing, motives, consequences, and causes and effects" (p. 554). Even on the first day of school, many young children are already hypothesis-testers, seeking to understand what people mean when they speak (Clark, 1984). Others bring a great deal of understanding about how stories work (Applebee, 1978; Sulzby, 1985), how the written language system serves them (Clay, 1975; Dyson, 1990; Ferreiro & Teberosky, 1982; Teale,

1987), that genres differ (Shine & Roser, 1999), that stories mean something (Dickinson & Smith, 1994; Lehr, 1990), and that they are part of the meaning making (Sipe, 2008). Many children bring those understandings, but not all do (Purcell-Gates, 1995).

Imperatively, the transition from home-based texts to the book conversations of classrooms must make room for the children who have had fewer or different experiences with talking over text. The classrooms and programs that receive young children must also be intent upon providing many and varied literacy experiences within settings rich with uses for text—ensuring that children participate and experiment with written and spoken language in many forms for many real-life purposes. One of the most important invitations that teachers can extend is to join a small community of book talkers and storytellers—people who stretch for language to explain, inquire, or generate ideas. Across grades and genres, children's book talk seems to strengthen with use, depend upon the book and the group for its richness, flourish within a predictable structure, grow more participatory and insightful over time, and rise to the presence of a thoughtful, prepared model (Cochran-Smith, 1984; Eeds & Peterson, 1991; Roser & Martinez, 1995). Book conversations depend upon (among other variables) book choice, community, context, and purpose. It may be worth repeating that well-chosen texts are essential to its purposes (Martinez & Roser, 1995).

As the Trackton grandmother conveyed to Heath (1983), no truly thoughtful discussion begins with asking a question to which one already knows the answer. At times, as Eeds and Wells (1989) suggest, classrooms can become territories for gentle inquisitions. These researchers contend "almost all of children's experiences with literature in elementary schools today are in this inquisition mode" (p. 4). To offset the trend, Eeds and Wells asked teacher education candidates not to approach literature discussions with sets of prepared questions that lead toward a critic's central tenets, but rather to allow meanings to emerge from the group, as conversants construct, examine, support, and shift their interpretations.

If schools are—as Eeds and Wells (1989) suggest—places where questions run amok, my son, Jay, caught on quickly. In February of his kindergarten year, I overheard him "playing school" with his sister, Erin, aged 3. Erin was sitting on a staircase with other "kids"—several stuffed animals. Jay stood authoritatively before his class. Although I was writing furiously, neither child could see me.

Jay: What kind of tree did George Washington cut down?

Erin: [No answer.]

Jay: Cherry!

Erin: A tree with cherries on it?

Jay: Right!

Erin: What happened to the cherries?

Jay: I don't know. Was Abraham Lincoln important or mean?

Erin: Important.

Jay: Right! What does communication mean? [He pronounced it *kuh-moo-nuh-ka-shun*.]

Erin: I don't know.

Jay: Communication means when people talk to each other. What does transportation mean?

Erin: I don't know.

Jay: Transportation means people can move. OK. This is the hardest question. What letter person starts with the last letter in the alphabet?

Erin: Me!

Jay: No, you're wrong.

Erin: Can I go?

Jay had already interpreted the culture of schooling as the asking of questions, the gathering and evaluation of response, and the provision of answers (Cazden, 1988). Erin hadn't yet gone to school; news about a chopped tree with cherries on it seemed worth pursuing. She hadn't yet learned that student questions ("What happened to the cherries?") were not part of this language routine. Yet, her "teacher's" answer to her question ("I don't know") provided Erin with a useful situationally embedded phrase to rely upon through a steady bombardment of subsequent questions. Equipped with "I don't know," she no longer needed to sit silently (as she had after the first question). When Jay asked a narrower question with an either/or answer ("Was Abraham Lincoln important or mean?"), she grasped at a time-honored student strategy (guess), and answered, "Important." Finally, Jay's questions became altogether too remote from her life experiences. Even an attempt to reinsert herself into the dialogue (shouting enthusiastically, "Me!" in the vague hope she was a "Letter People") didn't work. She was "wrong," and schooling was no longer worthwhile ("Can I go?"). The segment may be analogous to the classroom inquisitions that Eeds and Wells (1989) decry.

Wells (1985) determines that even though most children entered school communicating freely and effectively with the people in their environment, school instantly spreads the sample, partly as a result of teachers' attempts to secure answers to questions they judge to be self-evident—what Wells terms "requests for display" (p. 230). First-grade teacher and teacher-researcher, Compton-Lilly (2003), believes one of her central efforts is to remember "that the alternative discourses children bring to school reflect useful, powerful, and productive ways of being and making sense of the world" (p. 28). Perhaps, in the best of classrooms, the routines closely mesh with what Mason (1990) describes: "A protective umbrella of explanations, interpretations, and clarifications is provided by adults who know what their children know, and how to connect story information with their children's background experiences" (p. 2).

Author and essayist Chambers (1996) describes the beginning of book conversations as reissuing the invitation to notice, and then to "Tell us...." There would seem to be no threat or surprise to children in the invitation to "notice." If language researchers are accurate, children have been asked to notice from their first encounters with books. Everyone notices something. Art curators ask it of patrons gazing at paintings, giving time and a forum for the noticings. Effective book conversations begin with the collection and winnowing of the noticings within any group. Chambers's second invitation to book talk also seems nearly ontogenetic in that participants are invited to "puzzle" over events and circumstances. Everyone wonders (e.g., "What happened to the cherries?"), or can be led to wonder in the presence of relevant books, experiences, and good demonstration. The third of Chambers's invitations to book talkers is the invitation to "connect" with books—through identifying, remembering, or invoking other stories and experiences that link the text to the fabric of human existence (Dworin, 2006). Across the three invitations, there seems to be close alignment with the ripples of a child's developing talk that Snow and Ninio (1986) describe.

Such, too, are the conversations that Cochran-Smith (1984) describes in her work with preschoolers' book conversations. Children's ways of making sense of stories included readying themselves for reading, making life connections with the text, and making text connections with their lives. Cochran-Smith noted that the majority of story reading episodes produced interactions of all three types in no particular sequence. Sipe (2002) also describes classrooms in which young children are able to respond actively, but purposefully, to the text—to talk back to stories, to step into the action, and even to take over the story. In his grounded theory of children's literary understanding, he speaks to the power of text to draw in young readers such that the barrier between story and life become permeable, and the children's talk readily flits between the two. Sipe also identifies performative responses, in which children creatively and playfully enact, elaborate, and manipulate the text.

In addition to texts that are accessible, relevant, varied, manageable, and of quality, story time for children who speak a language other than English must involve texts and contexts that are interpretable. Battle's (1995) description of the way one teacher ensured collaborative story talk in a bilingual kindergarten demonstrates the dexterity with which the teacher invited children to freely use either language in response to books read aloud in either English or Spanish. In interviews, the teacher indicated she gave special attention to selecting books for read-aloud so as to engage her students and encourage thoughtful talk. She believed her classroom must be a safe place to try out one's second language with the assurance that it is the message rather than the form that will be responded to; that children must be encouraged to both ask and share opinions during story talk; and that no child should be required to talk until he or she just can't help talking. Similarly, in describing the texts she selected to support inquiry groups in a second-grade bilingual class, Martínez-Roldán (2005) chose titles students could "potentially connect to, think about, and/or talk about, whether the books were read aloud to them or read with others" (p. 29).

In addition to story time and book discussions, there appear to be additional instructional supports that undergird children's thoughtful processing and reflection on text. Holdaway's (1979) extrapolation from the value of picture book reading in homes meant making stories "big," because using Big Books in classrooms could allow for approximations of the close conversations that children have with parents about texts—the sharing of reading. Overall, studies in Head Start programs, preschools, and kindergarten have noted effects of shared reading for children's vocabulary, comprehension, phonological awareness, print concepts, and engagement with literature (Dickinson, 1989; Dickinson & Smith, 1994; McGee & Schickedanz, 2007; Wasik & Bond, 2001; Whitehurst, Arnold et al., 1994; Whitehurst, Epstein, et al., 1994). The procedures for shared reading involve children in attending to, listening, conjecturing, reading, discussing, and revisiting stories together. Sharing the reading also allows for discoveries and instruction in how books and print work.

The best Big Books are enlargements of the best pieces of literature across genres, giving children and teachers openings for their best thinking. To support thoughtful talk in the presence of well-selected books, McGee (1992) guides fledgling book talkers to critical inferences through the careful planning and judicious placement (after conversation subsided) of a single, central inferential question. Lehr (1990) contends that even the youngest of readers talked thoughtfully about thematic elements when the texts were well matched with children's experiences. Short (1992, 1993) shows the results of children's insightful talk while drawing together related books in thematic units. In our own work with literature unit explorations (with kindergarten through second-grade children whose first language was not English), we added evidence that children's discoveries of connections across texts and with their own experiences stoke their drawings, talk, reading, and writing, as well as their book familiarity (Roser, Hoffman, & Farest, 1990; Roser, Hoffman, Labbo, & Farest, 1992). Similarly, Sipe and Bauer (2001) report that a great deal of urban kindergartners' talk (about 75%) was reflective of their thoughtful analysis of stories. Children talked over the significance of format, language, illustrations, plot meanings, and character relations.

Hickman's (1981) pioneering work on children's responses to books showed that classrooms can provide a range of outlets for meaning making, including movement, drama, art, and other media that support and encourage thought and talk. Like Sipe (2001), she found that 5- and 6-year-olds responded to literature through body movements such as dance and applause, by sharing discoveries in books, through actions and drama, and by making representations based on literature.

Others have pointed to the role that teachers play in helping children say what they have to say in book discussions (e.g., Maloch, 2002, 2008; Roser, Martinez, Fuhrken, & McDonnold, 2007). In a comparison of the storybook reading styles of parents reading to preschoolers with teachers reading to the same-aged children, Martinez and I (Roser & Martinez, 1985) identify three roles teachers and parents seemed to take: (1) co-responder, (2) informer, and (3) director. As a co-responder, the adult entered the conversation as a participant and modeled literary meaning making and response. As the informer, the adult interpreted aspects of the story and guided children through the process of constructing meaning. The director role was one of assuring children followed procedures and routines typically unrelated to story understanding. In a study of the storybook read-aloud styles of six kindergarten teachers, Martinez and Teale (1993) document differences in three facets of the teachers' read-aloud style: (1) the focus of their talk, (2) the type of information talked about, and (3) their instructional strategies. They conclude that each teacher presented a distinctive profile. Sipe (2008), too, describes roles that teachers play as they scaffold young readers during story time, including tour guide, fellow wonderer, and extender/refiner of texts. In a cluster analysis of book talk in 25 preschool classrooms, Dickinson and Smith (1994) also find three patterns: (1) co-constructive, involving cognitively challenging conversations, (2) didactic-interactional, in which students produce recitations in response to factual questions, and (3) performance-oriented, which involves extended discussions. It seems logical to conclude that children must be offered varying ways to make meaning, including a way with words.

Researchers have observed the potential of book conversations to seed language, internalize skills and concepts, evoke complex thought, encourage interest, promote literacy, collect and fund knowledge, fuel writing, and provide reason for turns and socialization in preparation for lifelong reading. It is, as Meek (1988) showed, that texts teach what readers learn. The evidence pool is now too extensive to summarize fully in one chapter (see Cairney, 2003, for a comprehensive treatment of literacy within young children's families). Further, the pool of evidence is not without theories that conflict, confusing nomenclature, policies that impinge, and a need for additional answers. There is also a need for more teacher/researcher knowledge of the world of children's texts—so as to get the right texts into the right hands. Necessary, too, are thoughtful displays of evidence so that schools and teachers who seek guidance find reasoned summaries to aid decisions about language and literacy instruction.

Making Room for Book Talk

Edwards (1995) describes how a group of low-income parents expressed their frustrations and confusions when asked to read aloud to their children. As one parent told her, "I wish somebody would tell me what to do, because I am fed up with teachers saying, 'Read to your child'" (p. 56). Another parent stated, "I try to read, but I guess I am not doing it right. My child becomes bored, not interested in the book, so I quit trying to read" (p. 56).

Yet, I recently watched a high-income, highly educated first-time parent reading to her infant. She held the board book awkwardly, pronounced each of the words carefully, and read each page. When she had finished, she raised the same questions: "What does it mean to read to a baby? Why am I repeatedly told to do this when the baby isn't paying attention, doesn't know what I'm saying, and is too young to understand this book? What's expected here?" Teachers and parents ask valid questions.

What's expected (many think) is that children can be initiated into literacy as they are initiated into language through highly satisfying, and increasingly representational, social experiences (Snow, 1983). Long before they can read for themselves, children gain a sense of the sounds, structures, organization, and purposes of written language when parents and caregivers read to them. They learn that pictures symbolize reality, and perhaps lay the groundwork for their later understandings of the symbolic system of written language. They are learning to use a powerful tool (language) to objectify and organize life.

Of course, babies first like books that provide satisfying sounds (their parent imitating an animal, for example), books that bounce a bit, have chewable edges, and end quickly. But soon they are toddlers, and their fingers point. "Whazzat?" they often ask, as someone has asked them, and book conversations are in play. As Snow and Goldfield (1983) attest, "The social context of language acquisition is not a separate topic...it is central to an understanding of language learning" (p. 552). The differences for children may not lie in the variant ways their adults initiate labeling, but rather the opportunities to engage in more extended conversations as children mature. The continuity of the conversation may help to offset the effects Chall, Jacobs, and Baldwin (1990) describe as the "slump." That is, children who get off to successful, language-filled starts ought to find conversational partners to help them stay on that path. The widely cited vocabulary study of Hart and Risley (1995) documents that children in middle-class homes hear many more different words than children living in poverty and are spoken to much more frequently. Subsequently, the children varied markedly in the trajectory of their vocabulary growth.

Ultimately, whether young children talk, draw, scribble, enact, build, listen to, or connect with narrative and information, it may be that time in schools in which they are invited to express their own meanings of events (including the meanings of books) is the fledgling nest from which the more abstract conversations of schooling eventually take wing. When we who work with children and their teachers think about the language of book discussions—discussions in which children are invited to the pages to play their roles, speak their minds, and join the dialogue on the themes and issues that link and distinguish us— we can't help railing against the possibility that beginning language users, so curious, intent, and purposeful, ever lapse into silence or share only safe talk in safe ways in response to questions and texts no one really cares about.

REFERENCES

Adair, J., & Tobin, J. (2008). Listening to the voices of immigrant parents. In C. Genishi & A.L. Goodwin (Eds.), *Diversities in early childhood education: Rethinking and doing* (pp. 137–150). New York: Routledge.

Almy, M.C. (1949). *Children's experiences prior to first grade and success in beginning reading.* New York: Teachers College, Columbia University.

Anderson-Yockel, J., & Haynes, W.O. (1994). Joint book-reading strategies in working-class African American and white mother–toddler dyads. *Journal of Speech and Hearing Research, 37*(3), 583–593.

Applebee, A.N. (1978). *The child's concept of story: Ages two to seventeen.* Chicago: University of Chicago Press.

Auerbach, E. (1995). Deconstructing the discourse of strengths in family literacy. *Journal of Reading Behavior, 27*(4), 643–661.

Baghban, M. (1984). *Our daughter learns to read and write: A case study from birth to three.* Newark, DE: International Reading Association.

Barton, D., & Hamilton, M. (1998). *Local literacy: Reading and writing in one community.* London: Routledge.

Battle, J. (1995). Collaborative story talk in a bilingual kindergarten. In N.L. Roser & M.G. Martinez (Eds.), *Book talk and beyond: Children and teachers respond to literature* (pp. 157–167). Newark, DE: International Reading Association.

Bronfenbrenner, U. (1979). *The ecology of human development: Experiments by nature and design.* Cambridge, MA: Harvard University Press.

Brooks, W. (2006). Reading representations of themselves: Urban youth use culture and African American textual features to develop literary understandings. *Reading Research Quarterly, 41*(3), 372–392. doi:10.1598/RRQ. 41.3.4

Bruner, J.S. (1975). The ontogenesis of speech acts. *Journal of Child Language, 2*(1), 1–21. doi:10. 1017/S0305000900000866

Bus, A., Van IJzendoorn, M., & Pellegrini, A. (1995). Joint book reading makes for success in learning to read: A meta-analysis on inter-generational transmission of literacy. *Review of Educational Research, 65*(1), 1–21.

Cairney, T.H. (1997). Acknowledging diversity in home literacy practices: Moving towards partnership with parents. *Early Child Development and Care, 127*(1), 61–73. doi:10. 1080/0300443971270106

Cairney, T.H. (2003). Literacy within family life. In N. Hall, J. Larson, & J. Marsh (Eds.), *Handbook of early childhood literacy* (pp. 85–111). London: Sage.

Cazden, C.B. (1988). *Classroom discourse: The language of teaching and learning.* Portsmouth, NH: Heinemann.

Chall, J.S., Jacobs, V.A., & Baldwin, L.E. (1990). *The reading crisis: Why poor children fall behind.* Cambridge, MA: Harvard University Press.

Chambers, A. (1992). And they lived badly ever after. In K. Kimberly, M. Meek, & J. Miller (Eds.), *New readings: Contributions to an understanding of literacy* (pp. 157–167). London: A & C Black.

Chambers, A. (1996). *Tell me: Children, reading, and talk.* York, ME: Stenhouse.

Clark, M.M. (1984). Literacy at home and at school: Insights from a study of young fluent readers. In H. Goelman, A. Oberg, & F. Smith (Eds.), *Awakening to literacy* (pp. 122–130). Exeter, NH: Heinemann.

Clay, M.M. (1975). *What did I write? Beginning writing behaviour.* Exeter, NH: Heinemann.

Cochran-Smith, M. (1984). *The making of a reader.* Norwood, NJ: Ablex.

Compton-Lilly, C. (2003). *Reading families: The literate lives of urban children.* New York: Teachers College Press.

Crago, M. (1993). Creating and comprehending the fantastic: A case study of a child from twenty to thirty-five months. *Children's Literature in Education, 24*(3), 209–222. doi:10.1007/BF01134175

DeBaryshe, B.D. (1995). Maternal belief systems: Linchpin in the home reading process. *Journal of Applied Developmental Psychology, 16*(1), 1–20. doi:10.1016/01933973(95)90013-6

DeBaryshe, B.D., Binder, J.C., & Buell, M.J. (2000). Mothers' implicit theories of early literacy instruction: Implications for children's reading and writing. *Early Child Development and Care, 160*(1), 119–131. doi:10.1080/0030443001 600111

DeLoache, J.S. (1984, April). *What's this? Maternal questions in joint picture book reading with toddlers.* Paper presented at the annual meeting of the American Educational Research Association, New York. (ERIC Document Reproduction Service No. ED251176)

Dickinson, D.K. (1989). Effects of a shared reading program on one Head Start language and literacy environment. In J. Allen & J.M. Mason (Eds.), *Risk makers, risk takers, risk breakers: Reducing the risks for young literacy learners* (pp. 125–151). Portsmouth, NH: Heinemann.

Dickinson, D.K., & Smith, M.W. (1994). Long-term effects of preschool teachers' book readings on low-income children's vocabulary and story comprehension. *Reading Research Quarterly, 29*(2), 104–122. doi:10.2307/747807

Duke, N.K. (2000a). 3.6 minutes per day: The scarcity of informational texts in first grade. *Reading Research Quarterly, 35*(2), 202–224. doi:10.1598/RRQ.35.2.1

Duke, N.K. (2000b). For the rich it's richer: Print experiences and environments offered to children in very low- and very high-socioeconomic status first-grade classrooms. *American Educational Research Journal, 37*(2), 441–478.

Duke, N.K., & Purcell-Gates, V. (2003). Genres at home and at school: Bridging the known to the new. *The Reading Teacher, 57*(1), 30–37. doi:10.1598/RT.57.1.4

Durkin, D. (1966). *Children who read early: Two longitudinal studies.* New York: Teachers College Press.

Dworin, J.E. (2006). The family stories project: Using funds of knowledge for writing. *The Reading Teacher, 59*(6), 510–520. doi:10.1598/RT.59.6.1

Dyson, A.H. (1990). Symbol makers, symbol weavers: How children link play, pictures, and print. *Young Children, 45*(2), 50–57.

Dyson, A.H. (2001). Donkey Kong in Little Bear country: A first grader's composing development in the media spotlight. *The Elementary School Journal, 101*(4), 417–433. doi:10.1086/499679

Edwards, P.A. (1995). Combing parents' and teachers' thoughts about storybook reading at home and school. In L.M. Morrow (Ed.), *Family literacy: Connections in schools and communities* (pp. 54–69). Newark, DE: International Reading Association.

Edwards, P.A., & Young, L.S.J. (1992). Beyond parents: Family, community, and school involvement. *Phi Delta Kappan, 74*(1), 72, 74, 76, 78, 80.

Eeds, M., & Peterson, R. (1991). Teacher as curator: Learning to talk about literature. *The Reading Teacher, 45*(2), 118–126.

Eeds, M., & Wells, D. (1989). Grand conversations: An exploration of meaning construction in literature study groups. *Research in the Teaching of English, 23*(1), 4–29.

Farver, J., Xu, Y., Eppe, S., & Lonigan, C. (2006). Home environments and young Latino children's school readiness. *Early Childhood Research Quarterly, 21*(2), 196–212. doi:10.1016/j.ecresq.2006.04.008

Ferreiro, E., & Teberosky, A. (1982). *Literacy before schooling.* Portsmouth, NH: Heinemann.

Fields, J.M., Smith, K., Bass, L.E., & Lugaila, T. (2001). A child's day: Home, school, and play (Selected indicators of child well-being, P70-68). Current Population Reports. Washington, DC: US Census Bureau.

Gillanders, C., & Jiménez, R.T. (2004). Reaching for success: A close-up of Mexican immigrant parents in the USA who foster literacy success for their kindergarten children. *Journal of Early Childhood Literacy, 4*(3), 243–269. doi:10.1177/1468798404044513

Goodman, Y. (2008, July 31). *Learning to read by reading to learn.* Keynote address, World

Congress on Reading, International Reading Association, Costa Rica.

Hammer, C.S., Nimmo, D., Cohen, R., Draheim, H.C., & Johnson, A.A. (2005). Book reading interactions between African American and Puerto Rican Head Start children and their mothers. *Journal of Early Childhood Literacy, 5*(3), 195–227. doi:10.1177/1468798405058683

Hammett, L.A., Van Kleeck, A., & Huberty, C.J. (2003). Patterns of parents' extratextual interactions during book sharing with preschool children: A cluster analysis study. *Reading Research Quarterly, 38*(4), 442–468. doi:10.1598/RRQ.38.4.2

Hart, B., & Risley, T.R. (1995). *Meaningful differences in the everyday experience of young American children.* Baltimore: Paul H. Brookes.

Heath, S.B. (1982). What no bedtime story means: Narrative skill at home and school. *Language in Society, 11*(1), 49–76. doi:10.1017/S0047404500009039

Heath, S.B. (1983). *Ways with words: Language, life, and work in communities and classrooms.* Cambridge, England: Cambridge University Press.

Hemmeter, J.A. (2006). Household use of public libraries and large bookstores. *Library & Information Science Research, 28*(4), 595–616. doi:10.1016/j.lisr.2006.05.008

Hickman, J. (1981). A new perspective on response to literature: Research in an elementary school setting. *Research in the Teaching of English, 15*(4), 343–354.

Holdaway, D. (1979). *The foundations of literacy.* New York: Ashton Scholastic.

Kastler, L.A., Roser, N.L., & Hoffman, J.V. (1987). Understandings of the forms and functions of written language: Insights from children and parents. In J. Readence, & R.S. Baldwin (Eds.), *Research in literacy: Merging perspectives* (36th yearbook of the National Reading Conference, pp. 85–92). Rochester, NY: National Reading Conference.

Landry, S.H., & Smith, K.E. (2006). The influence of parenting on emerging literacy skills. In D.K. Dickinson & S.B. Neuman (Eds.), *Handbook of early literacy research* (Vol. 2, pp. 135–148). New York: Guilford.

Lapp, D., Fisher, D., Flood, J., & Moore, K. (2002). "I don't want to teach it wrong": An investigation of the role families believe they should play in the early literacy development of their children. In D. Schallert, C. Fairbanks, J. Worthy, B. Maloch, & J. Hoffman (Eds.), *51st yearbook of the National Reading Conference* (pp. 275–286). Oak Creek, WI: National Reading Conference.

Lehr, S. (1990). Literature and the construction of meaning: The preschool child's developing sense of theme. *Journal of Research in Childhood Education, 5*(1), 37–46.

Lindfors, J.W. (1999). *Children's inquiry: Using language to make sense of the world.* New York: Teachers College Press.

Maloch, B. (2002). Scaffolding student talk: One teacher's role in literature discussion groups. *Reading Research Quarterly, 37*(1), 94–112. doi:10.1598/RRQ.37.1.4

Maloch, B. (2008). Beyond exposure: The uses of informational texts in a second grade classroom. *Research in the Teaching of English, 42*(3), 315–362.

Marsh, J. (2003). Early childhood literacy and popular culture. In N. Hall, J. Larson, & J. Marsh (Eds.), *Handbook of early childhood literacy* (pp. 112–125). London: Sage.

Martinez, M.G., & Roser, N.L. (1985). Read it again: The value of repeated readings during storytime. *The Reading Teacher, 38*(8), 782–786.

Martinez, M.G., & Roser, N.L. (1995). The books make a difference in story talk. In N.L. Roser & M.G. Martinez (Eds.), *Book talk and beyond: Children and teachers respond to literature* (pp. 32–41). Newark, DE: International Reading Association.

Martinez, M.G., & Teale, W.H. (1993). Teachers' storybook reading style: A comparison of six teachers. *Research in the Teaching of English, 27*(2), 175–199.

Martínez-Roldán, C.M. (2005). The inquiry acts of bilingual children in literature discussions. *Language Arts, 83*(1), 22–32.

Mason, J. (1990). *Reading stories to preliterate children: A proposed connection to reading* (Tech. Rep. No. 510). Washington, DC: Office of Educational Research and Improvement,

University of Illinois Center for the Study of Reading.

McGee, L.M. (1992). An exploration of meaning construction in first graders' grand conversations. In C.K. Kinzer & D.J. Leu (Eds.), *Literacy research, theory, and practice: Views from many perspectives* (41st yearbook of the National Reading Conference, pp. 177–186). Chicago: National Reading Conference.

McGee, L.M., & Schickedanz, J.A. (2007). Repeated interactive read-alouds in preschool and kindergarten. *The Reading Teacher, 60*(8), 742–751. doi:10.1598/RT.60.8.4

McTavish, M. (2007). Constructing the big picture: A working class family supports their daughter's pathways to literacy. *The Reading Teacher, 60*(5), 476–485. doi:10.1598/RT.60.5.7

Meek, M.M. (1988). *How texts teach what readers learn*. Stroud, England: Thimble.

Moerk, E.L. (1985). Picture-book reading by mothers and young children and its impact upon language development. *Journal of Pragmatics, 9*(4), 547–566. doi:10.1016/03782166(85)90021-9

Moll, L., Amanti, C., Neff, D., & González, N. (1992). Funds of knowledge for teaching: Using a qualitative approach to connect homes and classrooms. *Theory Into Practice, 31*(2), 132–141.

Moll, L.C., & Greenberg, J.B. (1990). Creating zones of possibilities: Combining social contexts for instruction. In L.C. Moll (Ed.), *Vygotsky and education: Instructional implications and applications of sociohistorical psychology* (pp. 319–348). Cambridge, England: Cambridge University Press.

Morrow, L.M. (1983). Home and school correlates of early interest in literature. *The Journal of Educational Research, 76*(4), 221–230.

Morrow, L.M. (1988). Young children's responses to one-to-one story readings in school settings. *Reading Research Quarterly, 23*(1), 89–107. doi:10.2307/747906

Neuman, S.B., & Celano, D. (2001). Access to print in low-income and middle-income communities: An ecological study of four neighborhoods. *Reading Research Quarterly, 36*(1), 8–26. doi:10.1598/RRQ.36.1.1

Ninio, A. (1980). Picture-book reading in mother–infant dyads belonging to two subgroups in Israel. *Child Development, 51*(2), 587–590. doi:10.2307/1129299

Ninio, A., & Bruner, J.S. (1978). The achievement and antecedents of labeling. *Journal of Child Language, 5*(1), 1–15. doi:10.1017/S0305000900001896

Noll, E., & Watkins, R. (2003). The impact of homelessness on children's literacy experiences. *The Reading Teacher, 57*(4), 362–371.

Ortiz, R.W., & Ordoñez-Jasis, R. (2005). Leyendo juntos (reading together): New directions for Latino parents' early literacy involvement. *The Reading Teacher, 59*(2), 110–121. doi:10.1598/RT.59.2.1

Paratore, J.R. (2001). *Opening doors, opening opportunities: Family literacy in an urban community*. Boston: Allyn & Bacon.

Paratore, J.R., Melzi, G., & Krol-Sinclair, B. (2003). Learning about the literate lives of Latino families. In D.M. Barone & L.M. Morrow (Eds.), *Literacy and young children: Research-based practices* (pp. 101–118). New York: Guilford.

Parra, E., & Henderson, R.W. (1982). Mexican-American perceptions of parent and teacher roles in child development. In J.A. Fishman & G.D. Keller (Eds.), *Bilingual education for Hispanic students in the United States* (pp. 289–302). New York: Teachers College Press.

Pellegrini, A.D., Perlmutter, J.C., Galda, L., & Brody, G.H. (1990). Joint reading between black Head Start children and their mothers. *Child Development, 61*(2), 443–453. doi:10.2307/1131106

Purcell-Gates, V. (1995). *Other people's words: The cycle of low literacy*. Cambridge, MA: Harvard University Press.

Purcell-Gates, V. (1996). Stories, coupons, and the TV Guide: Relationships between home literacy experiences and emergent literacy knowledge. *Reading Research Quarterly, 31*(4), 406–429. doi:10.1598/RRQ.31.4.4

Purcell-Gates, V., L'Allier, S., & Smith, D. (1995). Literacy at the Harts' and the Larsons': Diversity among poor, innercity families. *The Reading Teacher, 48*(7), 572–578.

Roberts, T.A. (2008). Home storybook reading in primary or second language with preschool children: Evidence of equal effectiveness for second-language acquisition. *Reading Research Quarterly, 43*(2), 103–130. doi:10.1598/RRQ.43.2.1

Roser, N., Martinez, M., Fuhrken, C., & McDonnold, K. (2007). Characters as guides to meaning. *The Reading Teacher, 60*(6), 548–559. doi:10.1598/RT.60.6.5

Roser, N.L., Hoffman, J.V., & Farest, C. (1990). Language, literature, and at-risk children. *The Reading Teacher, 43*(8), 554–559.

Roser, N.L., Hoffman, J.V., Kastler, L., & Sharp, C. (1994). What parents tell us about children's emerging literacy. In S. Reifel (Ed.), *Advances in early education and day care: Topics in early literacy, teacher preparation, and international perspectives on early care* (Vol. 6, pp. 61–82). Greenwich, CT: JAI.

Roser, N.L., Hoffman, J.V., Labbo, L.D., & Farest, C. (1992). Language charts: A record of story time talk. *Language Arts, 69*(1), 44–52.

Roser, N.L., & Martinez, M.G. (1985). Roles adults play in preschoolers' response to literature. *Language Arts, 62*(5), 485–495.

Roser, N.L., & Martinez, M.G. (Eds.). (1995). *Book talk and beyond: Children and teachers respond to literature.* Newark, DE: International Reading Association.

Scarborough, H.S., & Dobrich, W. (1994). On the efficacy of reading to preschoolers. *Developmental Review, 14*(3), 245–302. doi:10.1006/drev.1994.1010

Sénéchal, M., Cornell, E.H., & Broda, L.S. (1995). Age-related differences in the organization of parent-infant interactions during picture-book reading. *Early Childhood Research Quarterly, 10*(3), 317–337. doi:10.1016/0885-2006(95)90010-1

Sénéchal, M., LeFevre, J., Thomas, E., & Daley, K. (1998). Differential effects of home literacy experiences on the development of oral and written language. *Reading Research Quarterly, 33*(1), 96–116. doi:10.1598/RRQ.33.1.5

Sheridan, D. (1979). "Flopsy, Mopsy, and Tooth": The storytelling of preschoolers. *Language Arts, 56*(1), 10–15.

Shine, S., & Roser, N.L. (1999). The role of genre in preschooolers' response to picture books. *Research in the Teaching of English, 34*(2), 197–254.

Short, K.G. (1992). Intertextuality: Searching for patterns that connect. In C.K. Kinzer & D.J. Leu (Eds.), *Literacy research, theory, and practice: Views from many perspectives* (41st yearbook of the National Reading Conference, pp. 187–197). Chicago: National Reading Conference.

Short, K.G. (1993). Making connections across literature and life. In K.E. Holland, R.A. Hungerford, & S.B. Ernst (Eds.), *Journeying: Children responding to literature* (pp. 284–301). Portsmouth, NH: Heinemann.

Sipe, L.R. (2002). Talking back and taking over: Young children's expressive engagement during storybook read-alouds. *The Reading Teacher, 55*(5), 476–483.

Sipe, L.R. (2008). *Storytime: Young children's literary understanding in the classroom.* New York: Teachers College Press.

Sipe, L.R., & Bauer, J.T. (2001). Urban kindergartners' literary understanding of picture storybooks. *The New Advocate, 14*(4), 329–342.

Smolkin, L.B., Yaden, D.B., Brown, L., & Hofius, B. (1992). The effects of genre, visual design choices, and discourse structure on preschoolers' responses to picture books during parent-child read-alouds. In C.K. Kinzer & D.J. Leu (Eds.), *Literacy research, theory, and practice* (41st yearbook of the National Reading Conference, pp. 291–301). Chicago: National Reading Conference.

Snow, C.E. (1977). The development of conversation between mothers and babies. *Journal of Child Language, 4*(1), 1–22. doi:10.1017/S0305000900000453

Snow, C.E. (1983). Literacy and language: Relationships during the preschool years. *Harvard Educational Review, 53*(2), 165–189.

Snow, C.E., Barnes, W.S., Chandler, J., Goodman, I.F., & Hemphill, L. (1991). *Unfulfilled expectations: Home and school influences on literacy.* Cambridge, MA: Harvard University Press.

Snow, C.E., & Goldfield, B.A. (1983). Turn the page please: Situation-specific language acquisition. *Journal of Child Language, 10*(3), 551–569. doi:10.1017/S0305000900005365

Snow, C.E., & Ninio, A. (1986). The contracts of literacy: What children learn from learning to read books. In W.H. Teale & E. Sulzby

(Eds.), *Emergent literacy: Writing and reading* (pp. 116–138). Norwood, NJ: Ablex.

Sonnenschein, S., Baker, L., Serpell, R., Scher, D., Goddard-Truitt, V., & Munsterman, K. (1997). Potential beliefs about ways to help children learn to read: The impact of an entertainment or a skills perspective. *Early Child Development and Care, 127*(1), 111–118. doi:10.1080/0300443971270109

Sonnenschein, S., Brody, G., & Munsterman, K. (1996). The influence of family beliefs and practices on children's reading development. In L. Baker, P. Afflerbach, & D. Reinking (Eds.), *Developing engaged readers in school and home communities* (pp. 3–20). Mahwah, NJ: Erlbaum.

Sulzby, E. (1985). Children's emergent reading of favorite storybooks: A developmental study. *Reading Research Quarterly, 20*(4), 458–481. doi:10.1598/RRQ.20.4.4

Taylor, D. (1993). Family literacy: Resisting deficit models. *TESOL Quarterly, 27*(3), 550–553. doi:10.2307/3587487

Taylor, D., & Dorsey-Gaines, C. (1988). *Growing up literate: Learning from inner-city families.* Portsmouth: Heinemann.

Teale, W.H. (1984). Reading to young children: Its significance for literacy development. In H. Goelman, A. Oberg, & F. Smith (Eds.), *Awakening to literacy* (pp. 110–121). Exeter, NH: Heinemann.

Teale, W.H. (1986). Home background and young children's literacy development. In W.H. Teale & E. Sulzby (Eds.), *Emergent literacy: Writing and reading* (pp. 173–206). Norwood, NJ: Ablex.

Teale, W.H. (1987). Emergent literacy: Reading and writing development in early childhood. In J. Readence & R.S. Baldwin (Eds.), *Research in literacy: Merging perspectives* (36th yearbook of the National Reading Conference, pp. 45–74). Rochester, NY: National Reading Conference.

Torr, J. (2004). Talking about picture books: The influence of maternal education on four-year-old children's talk with mothers and pre-school teachers. *Journal of Early Childhood Literacy, 4*(2), 181–210. doi:10.1177/1468798404044515

Wasik, B.A., & Bond, M.A. (2001). Beyond the pages of a book: Interactive book reading and language development in preschool classrooms. *Journal of Educational Psychology, 93*(2), 243–250. doi:10.1037/0022-0663.93.2.243

Weigel, D.J., Martin, S.S., & Bennett, K.K. (2006). Mothers' literacy beliefs: Connections with the home literacy environment and pre-school children's literacy development. *Journal of Early Childhood Literacy, 6*(2), 191–211. doi:10.1177/1468798406066444

Wells, G. (1985). Preschool literacy-related activities and success in school. In D.R. Olson, N. Torrance, & A. Hildyard (Eds.), *Literacy, language, and learning: The nature and consequences of reading and writing* (pp. 229–255). Cambridge, England: Cambridge University Press.

Wheeler, M.P. (1983). Context-related age changes in mothers' speech: Joint book reading. *Journal of Child Language, 10*(1), 259–263. doi:10.1017/S0305000900005304

White, D. (1954). *Books before five.* Portsmouth, NH: Heinemann.

Whitehurst, G.J., Arnold, D.S., Epstein, J.N., Angell, A.L., Smith, M., & Fischel, J.E. (1994). A picture book reading intervention in day care and home for children from low-income families. *Developmental Psychology, 30*(5), 679–689. doi:10.1037/00121649.30.5.679

Whitehurst, G.J., Epstein, J.N., Angell, A.L., Payne, A.C., Crone, D.A., & Fischel, J.E. (1994). Outcomes of an emergent literacy intervention in Head Start. *Journal of Educational Psychology, 86*(4), 542–555. doi:10.1037/0022-0663.86.4.542

Whitehurst, G.J., Falco, F.L., Lonigan, C.J., Fischel, J.E., DeBaryshe, B.D., Valdez-Menchaca, M.C., et al. (1988). Accelerating language development through picture book reading. *Developmental Psychology, 24*(4), 552–559. doi:10.1037/00121649.24.4.552

Worthy, J., Moorman, M., & Turner, M. (1999). What Johnny likes to read is hard to find in schools. *Reading Research Quarterly, 34*(1), 12–27. doi:10.1598/RRQ.34.1.2

Worthy, J., & Roser, N.L. (2003). Flood ensurance: When children have books they can and want to read. In D. Lapp, C. Block, E. Cooper, J. Flood, N. Roser, & J. Tinajero

(Eds.), *Teaching all the children: Strategies for developing literacy in an urban setting* (pp. 179–192). New York: Guilford.

Yaden, D.B., Jr., Smolkin, L.B., & Conlon, A. (1989). Preschoolers' questions about pictures, print conventions, and story text during reading aloud at home. *Reading Research Quarterly*, 24(2), 188–214. doi:10.2307/747864

Zill, N., Moore, K.A., Smith, E.W., Stief, T., & Coiro, M.J. (1997). The life circumstances and development of children in welfare families: A profile based on national survey data. In P.L. Chase-Lansdale & J. Brooks-Gunn (Eds.), *Escape from poverty: What makes a difference?* (pp. 38–62). Cambridge, England: Cambridge University Press.

CHAPTER 6

Stories, Facts, and Possibilities: Bridging the Home and School Worlds for Students Acquiring a School Discourse

Diane Lapp

In *Re-Reading Families: The Literate Lives of Urban Children, Four Years Later*, Compton-Lilly (2007) continues the story of several urban children and their families who she first introduced to us four years earlier. The majority of the parents she portrays hold views similar to those of one, Ms. Rodriguez, who talks about the potential for children to slip through the cracks of school unless they have parents who "show up at school meetings and talk to the teachers" (p. 5).

Insights from parents and family members like Ms. Rodriguez characterize a personal vision of parenting as being the bridge between the learning that occurs for their children at home and at school. These views parallel those from well-executed studies conducted over the last 60 years that conclude that children who have parents with knowledge about how schools function have a greater chance for success because their parents offer home learning experiences that are similar to, as well as supportive of, those occurring at school (Almy, 1949; Hart & Risley, 1995; McMillon & Edwards, 2008). Aware that schools experience higher academic success among their students when the parents and faculty share a high degree of communication about how to foster children's literacy, educators continually strive to develop these authentic relationships (Caspe, Lopez, & Wolos, 2007).

In fact, the significance of the home–school relationship was established years ago from the findings of a 1966 federal study that was conducted by Coleman and a team of researchers (Coleman et al., 1966) to determine the

---

From *Bringing Literacy Home* edited by KaiLonnie Dunsmore and Douglas Fisher.

relationship between student achievement and school spending. They found that how well students do in school is dependent primarily on their home environments and secondarily on their peer groups. The significance of the home environment in a child's literacy development was also identified by Guthrie and Greaney (1991) as a factor of significance that correlated with students' independent reading habits. Notice as you read the following quote the importance of the family as a major factor in what most would view as very positive independent literacy practice.

> The amount of independent reading for both boys and girls is positively correlated with the availability of printed material, ownership of a library card, reading achievement level, methods of reading instruction, recreational interests, language/literacy interactions, and *parental example and home values*. Children's self-generated purposes for reading have been classified as utilitarian, diversionary, and enjoyment. The amount of reading for enjoyment is influenced by achievement level. (p. 90, emphasis added)

More specifically, findings from bodies of research support the conclusion that students who most frequently succeed in school have parents who (a) actively support their children's school participation by helping with homework; (b) attend PTA meetings, parent's night, and other school and classroom functions; and (c) consistently communicate with the teachers in an attempt to craft a shared plan for success. They are also very often from more prosperous homes that can provide them with simple but significant opportunities like Internet connections, books, and travel experiences (Goldin & Katz, 2008) while also exposing them to beliefs that bathe them in examples of the power of the development of one's human capital. In short, these parents act as the child's first teacher by preparing them with funds of knowledge that guarantee them a successful school trajectory and then act as their partners on their school journeys.

Children in these homes are growing up in what Gee (1996, 1999) calls *mainstream homes*, where there exist similarities between home and school social practices. Gee refers to these social practices as discourses. These discursive social practices (with their underlying norms, values, beliefs, and attitudes) are primarily acquired through enculturation or apprenticeship. His distinction between discourse (with a little *d*) and Discourse (with a big *D*) is helpful when we consider the families who are school savvy and those who are not.

For Gee (1999), discourse (with a little *d*) refers to language in use, or the ways in which people use language in oral or written encounters. Language in use involves much more than just language, however. It is melded integrally with nonlanguage "stuff," such as behaviors, values, ways of thinking, clothes, food, customs, and perspectives that are used by members of a group, to enact specific identities and activities. When this melding occurs, big-D Discourses are involved. Therefore, Discourse characterizes such things as "one's body language, clothes, gestures, actions, interactions, ways of thinking, symbols, tools, technologies (be they guns or graphs), values, attitudes, beliefs, and emotions." (p. 7). One's Discourse then provides a profile of one's ways of using language as well as symbolic expressions and artifacts of thinking, feeling, believing, valuing, and acting that connect the members of a social group.

Because the momentous role that families play in the early and continuing literacy development of children has been well documented (Purcell-Gates, 1995; Sonnenschein, Brody, & Munsterman, 1996; Sulzby & Teale, 1991), the focus of this chapter is instead on the children of parents who do not have within their "figured worlds" (Holland, Lachicotte, Skinner, & Cain, 1998) a view of themselves as having responsibility for their children's early literacy learning. As depicted by the one family in focus, many of these parents, although well intentioned, are not aware that children are well on their way to succeeding in literacy when they have the opportunity to learn its functional uses through authentic daily family life experiences (Flood, 1975; Goodman, 1986; McTavish, 2007; Taylor, 1997). If parents do have this understanding, many are unsure of the exact role they should play (Lapp, Fisher, Flood, & Moore, 2002; Neuman, Caperelli, & Kee, 1998). This view is often arrived at as a result of socialization within their Discourse community, uncertainties about exactly what this role would constitute, insecurities about their personal knowledge base, limited schedules, overwhelming responsibilities, and beliefs about the roles of the school and teachers.

Unfortunately, teachers often view this lack of knowing as a sign of disinterest and are therefore unsure of how to establish a bridge to connect the child's home and school experiences (Lee, 2007, 2008). Because of this difference in beliefs and perceived roles, these parents are often at odds with their children's teachers about what characterizes appropriate parenting, effective parental involvement, and suitable at-home literacy experiences (Edwards & Turner, 2009; Paratore, 2001).

In this chapter, while acknowledging the power of the home as the foundational support for a child's school experiences, I first discuss why such support cannot be a pronouncement of failure for those children without these early experiences. I then offer suggestions that use the wide variability among families as a rich context in which successful learning experiences can be built universally, one child at a time, in one classroom at a time, by one teacher at a time. When all forces in a child's life unite to support their success, we will truly realize the meaning of the African proverb, "When spider webs unite, they can tie a lion."

Situationally Framed

The family story I tell in this chapter is situated in a sociocultural perspective of literacy that is much broader than an individual's personal home and school reading and writing events. Rather, it spotlights one's identity kit (Gee, 1990), which tells the story of each person's personal view of self within a family or community as well as the perceptions others hold about the individual or group (Lave & Wenger, 1991). Within each community there are behaviors, expectations, and processes that characterize the group's shared literacy events as well as the values placed on these events (Heath, 1983). Because each individual's literacies are well developed within these community contexts, children come to school with literacy practices and resources that reflect those of their home, their first community (Moll & Greenberg, 1990). This scenario works well for those children whose early literacy practices validate the prescribed literacy practices they are about to meet in the world of school.

Knoblauch and Brannon (1993) note that the literacy practices of school are often characterized as those designed to transmit a segment of cultural values that are depicted through the canons of Western society's literature and religion (Hirsch, 1987). It is a belief of many that success in acquiring this canonical knowledge of western society is rewarded through monetary gains played out by one's opportunity to use this informational base to function in a larger capitalist society (Hollingsworth & Boyer, 2008). Unfortunately, many students who are not the recipients of these rewards have not been exposed to the beliefs or the entitlement of capitalism by older members of their cultural groups. These elders historically have been physically and financially enslaved by others and more recently by a lack of their own mental emancipation (Garvey, 1986; Regosin, 2002; Wertsch, 1998), caused by labels and stereotypes being placed upon them (Ladson-Billings, 1994) when they have attempted to remonstrate against these inequities.

Different Is Different—Not More or Less, Just Different

Lareau (2003) believes, as a result of insights gained from her studies shadowing a range of parents from those who were less financially wealthy to those who were very financially wealthy, that wealthier parents fill their children's time with activities and conversation that make them comfortable with adults, authority, and the academic language they will meet at school. She notes that even when events like visiting libraries and museums are free, less economically wealthy parents do not take advantage of these experiences. For many reasons, including schedules, lack of transportation, and unfamiliarity with these cultural events, it is not part of their parenting repertoires. Children from less financially wealthy homes do not view school experiences and language as familiar, unlike wealthier children who from the time of their birth view school success as a shared responsibility.

What happens when the children from these less financially wealthy homes get to school and meet their teachers who have preconceived notions, as a result of their own experiences, about what the children have or should have been doing during their first five years of life? The unfortunate results of this incompatibility of beliefs, experiences, and expectations is borne out by data from the California Department of Education (2008) during the 2006–2007 school year, which notes that one of every four students drops out of high school. Who are the students in this crisis situation? What are their profiles? By ethnicity, 40.2% are African American, 35.4% are Latino, 20.1% are Caucasian, and 13.4% are Asian. The majority of them are economically impoverished; many speak English as their second language, and academic English, which is school talk, is an unfamiliar discourse.

As Lansberg and Bume (2008) report about the situation, "These statistics highlight a problem that is getting worse in California. Even using the old system of measurement the number of dropouts has grown by 83% over five years while the number of high school graduates has gone up only 9%" (p. 1). This crisis will likely expand, because growing numbers of English-language learners are pursuing an education in American classrooms (National Center for Education Statistics, 2002, 2005). Thomas and Collier (2001) estimate that by the year 2040, 40% of the students in American public schools will speak a first language other than English. This is already true in California, where more than 50% of the students in public schools currently speak a first language other than English (Garcia & Montavon, 2007).

Why This Mismatch?

Lansberg and Bume (2008) identify three primary reasons for this dropout trend: "an increase in Latino immigrants, who are one of the groups most likely to drop out; the raising of academic standards; and insufficient funding for public education" (p. 18). Are you wondering why immigrants who come to a new country to pursue a "better" life would be one of the primary groups considered the most likely to drop out? This seems to be a conundrum. Do these new immigrants not see education as the ticket to success? Or is it that, as I have earlier noted, our educational system after all of these years is still unable to adjust to student and family differences? Are the stories of these families who are new to the United States different from those of the socially and economically less privileged African American and European American students from families who have lived in America for centuries? Could it be that literacy differences of all of these students are really seen as literacy deficits by their teachers (Taylor, 1991; Taylor & Dorsey-Gaines, 1988)? Are these educators not being prepared to help children from economically insecure groups build new Discourses as extensions of their cultural knowledge and existing literacies (Moll & Gonzalez, 1994)? If so, then "we must arm teachers with the knowledge and cultural appreciation and then give them the autonomy, authority, and freedom to teach each and every child" (Purcell-Gates, 1995, p. 196).

In actuality, teachers need experiences that enable them to more fully understand and value the familial practices, language, hopes, and fears of nonmainstream, less financially mobile students (Delpit, 1995). Armed with such knowledge, they will be able to support these students as they validate their culture in all its diversity and use it to move toward self-actualization by developing an expanded vision of personal, social, and financial opportunities (Tembo, 2000). Teachers will also be able to initiate home–school partnerships that acknowledge all parents as the first teachers of their children as well as value the cultures of the homes and the experiences occurring within them.

As a teacher educator, I am filled with hope by the work of Yang and Gustafsson (2004), who found that family economics and opportunities were not as significant a predictor of success as was the child's cultural capital in the family. If we can use this finding as a thematic starting point from which to draw inferences and build a school climate that also supports venues of success, then we will ensure that there will no longer be a cultural mismatch between schools and some of the children they purport to serve. This is more than an extrapolation bathed in idealism, because I have personally seen the in-school successes achieved by students who have become graduates of programs like Achievement Via Individual Determination (AVID; Swanson, 2005). Within AVID, students are treated as having high cultural capital by their teachers.

While AVID is often described as a college-prep program for students who are from homes with no college graduates, it does much more than teach skills like meeting deadlines and taking notes, which are associated with school and professional success (Nelson, 2007). It also connects students with teachers who believe they will succeed both academically and socially. The teacher assumes the role of a cheerleader who encourages, supports, and models in many cases life-expanding behaviors. Experiences of this type must be made available to all students if we ever hope to reverse the devastating dropout rate among nonmainstream children, especially children of color.

The remainder of this chapter will build this hope into a construction of reality by considering stories, facts, and possibilities that eliminate barriers between teachers and their African American Vernacular English (AAVE)–speaking students who are one segment of this nonmainstream school population and the focal population of this chapter. I have no intention now or ever of imposing a white intellectual conversation on a black experience. Rather, I am highly motivated to continue to get to know more fully this cultural group, because these are the families of the students I mentor and teach.

Stories: Getting to Know One Family by Joining Them

To promote early learning, many parent education programs have been designed to introduce parents to ways to support their children's literacy development experiences. These have met success nationally for those parents who have had the good fortune to attend. Critical relationships between families and teachers that have been established through these linkages have served as the stepping-stones toward future literacy success for many children. When families and teachers are involved in these mutually supportive programs as a community, they bond in the understanding that they are jointly supporting the child's learning experiences (Comer, 1998). They work as a collaborative team, with trust and respect for one another in a harmonious partnership that has been well documented as a contributing factor to children's school success (Epstein & Salinas, 2004; International Reading Association, 2002; Neuman &

Celano, 2001; Purcell-Gates, 1993, 1995, 2000; Taylor & Dorsey-Gaines, 1988; Tutwiler, 2005; Yaden & Paratore, 2002).

Rodgers and Hammerstein's well-known 1950s tune "Getting to know you, getting to know all about you. Getting to like you, getting to hope you like me..." should be the underlying theme of parent and teacher interactions. This isn't always the case when parents and teachers come from different cultures and economic levels and have not gained an understanding and a respect for one another's cultures, experiences, and home language. Fortunately, this song is the reoccurring chorus of an experience a family and I have shared for the last 11 years.

A Lived Partnership

The importance of family–school partnerships became all too clear to me in 1998 when I decided to spend my sabbatical team-teaching in a first-grade classroom. Early in the year, my host teacher colleague, Kelly Moore, and I were planning for the September back-to-school night. I was hoping to meet the parent of Anthony, a child I had been working with extensively. From my conversations with Kelly I knew that Anthony's mom had been hesitant to participate in any previous early school literacy parent programs for her older children. But before I continue telling you about the back-to-school night, let me digress and tell you a little about Anthony.

Anthony, Also Known as Bossman

Adorable Anthony came to first grade without having attended preschool or kindergarten, because in California kindergarten is not mandatory. When we teachers hear something like this we lean toward believing this borders on neglect, because we know how much is learned during these early years and also how much first-grade teachers rely on this early acquired body of knowledge to scaffold the new instruction.

Although we talk much about the importance of differentiating instruction to meet the needs of children, we also understand that being able to do so is complex, especially when the instruction being planned is for a child like Anthony, whose literacy base is not what is expected by teachers of first graders. Anthony didn't understand the concept of a last name. He thought his last name was his nickname, Bossman. He could count to 10 and he knew his colors but not any letters of the alphabet. In literacy language, he was not phonemically aware.

Unfortunately, the school trajectory isn't very positive for children, like Anthony, who enter first grade with this less-than-anticipated academic knowledge base. Fortunately for Kelly and me, he came to our classroom, and we had the opportunity to practice the instruction we preach about in the methods courses we teach.

During Anthony's first year at school, he worked almost exclusively with either Kelly or me in individual and small-group settings. We also referred him to Reading Recovery, but his performance was so poor that he was dropped from the program. Through our interactions we were able to support his literacy learning and his belief that he was a very able learner. We have chronicled the functioning of this classroom in an article (Lapp, Flood, & Goss, 2000) and a handbook chapter (Lapp, Flood, & Moore, 2008). During the following year Kelly taught a first/second grade combination class and was fortunate to have Anthony once again as a member of this learning community. She continued to differentiate instruction in ways that positively acknowledged his home language register of AAVE and home learning experiences while supporting his academic learning.

Together we have guided his classroom placements for the last 11 years. His path has not been continually uphill because his shy personality is often seen as aloof and antiestablishment. At this time, Anthony is an eleventh grader in a charter high school where, because of the quality of the administration and teaching staff, he is well respected for who he is. Kelly continues to be one of his teachers. He finds much humor as well as security in this fact. Even after all of these years, he needs continual encouragement and nudging. Because of the support he has received from all of his teachers and the love of his family, he is succeeding at school and has career plans to be an ambulance driver, a paramedic, or, as of late, a nurse.

The Other Half of Anthony's Story: What About Angul?

Anthony is one of seven siblings who are growing up in a home with their mom, their aunt, and three cousins. Anthony is the twin of a girl named Angul who was in the first grade next door with a teacher with 20 years of experience. Angul had the same early literacy experiences as Anthony and therefore had also been dropped from Reading Recovery.

Unfortunately for Angul, her first-grade teacher did not use a method to teach reading that supported literacy learning for Angul. The teacher read wonderful stories to the children, but this was not enough for Angul. Learning to read happened for all of the children who were being supported in their reading at home. This, however, was not the case for Angul, who by the end of first grade could not read but did enjoy being read to. This enjoyment of listening to good literature is proof of the adage "children do learn what they are taught."

Angul's teacher came to Kelly crying and said she hadn't known how to teach Angul to read. She didn't want to retain her but instead wanted Kelly to have her placed in the first/second-grade combo that Kelly was preparing to teach. While Kelly was very willing, the administrative policy did not allow siblings in the same class. So Angul went to a second-grade class with a teacher who had 12 years of experience but also didn't teach reading in a way that would benefit Angul. In fact, he suggested to the principal during the third week of the school year that Angul was not smart enough to learn to read.

Many economically poor children like Angul are incorrectly evaluated and labeled and are ineffectually taught because of a similar lack of understanding and knowledge on the part of their teachers. Both of her teachers likely had been raised in worlds very different from Angul's—worlds where everyone spoke a close approximation of academic English. The teacher preparation programs and the professional development sessions they had attended had apparently not prepared them to teach Angul and other children like her (Kunjufu, 2002). Given their life experiences and professional backgrounds, it is not surprising that teachers like these, teachers with a correctionist view (Birch, 2001) of literacy instruction, are ineffective for children like Angul—children who come to school speaking a language register other than the one their teachers understand or find acceptable (Christenbury, 2000). Teacher education programs must continue to attempt to help teachers expand their pedagogical repertoires so that children like Angul do not suffer.

Fortunately for Angul, her mom and I had become friends, so I suggested putting Angul in a classroom of a first-year teacher who had just finished her teaching credential in a program that was designed to prepare teachers to teach children who come to school with the strengths exhibited by Angul and Anthony. This teacher believed that Angul had language and experiences of value that she could draw from to teach her to read. By the end of the second grade, Angul, who was by then reading like a first grader and feeling great success in doing so, asked if she could stay longer with this teacher. All agreed, and Angul spent her third school year in this safe, caring environment where, similar to what was happening for Anthony, her school experiences were differentiated to meet her literacy development. At the time of this writing, Angul is a tenth grader, maintains a B average, and says that she likes school so much that she wants to be a teacher.

Like many parents who have not succeeded at school themselves, Anthony and Angul's mom didn't come to the first parent meeting and still only feels comfortable doing so when I attend with her. She refers to me as her kids' "school Mom" and, indeed, all of her children look to me for help with their academic decisions. I have learned to look at many school experiences from multiple and contradictory perspectives as I have guided the academic experiences of Anthony, Angul, and their siblings. Hopefully these varied and often conflicting perspectives have helped me to be a better teacher educator.

For example, I was initially very excited that the San Diego Unified School district has a voluntary integration system, Voluntary Enrollment Exchange Program (VEEP), which allows children from low-performing schools in the less affluent areas to attend schools "across town" in neighborhoods that have a larger financial base. These more affluent neighborhoods can spend much more money to provide the children in the schools with additional opportunities, including music resource teachers, which are paid for by the PTA. The district also provides transportation to these VEEP children. After sharing this information with Anthony and Angul's mom, we agreed that this excellent opportunity, which neither she nor any of her friends had known about, would be terrific for her children. I completed the appropriate paperwork and off the children went to the new school. All seemed to be going well in the elementary grades, even when the homework assignments were often beyond the scope of Mom's finances or academic base. Realizing this, Jim Flood, Doug Fisher, and I built into our preservice courses experiences that took future teachers into the homes of children, including Anthony and Angul, for at-home evening tutoring. These experiences offered the children homework support while enabling the future teachers to realize that, although most children need homework help, they do not all have equal access to it or to the supplies to complete it. They also realized that although the homework being assigned is often viewed by the classroom teacher as an extension of what was introduced during the school day, in reality it often includes just enough new facts to make it unfamiliar to the children and their families.

A second contradictory experience happened for me when Anthony and Angul entered middle school and the infamous genre studies program that was touted as the program that would provide additional support to children who were not yet reading and writing at grade level. On the surface this sounded like the perfect answer to the need for differentiated instruction. But when I visited the genre classes, I saw that all of the children participating were the VEEP children. They spent all morning in these tracked remedial literacy classes while other children who were at grade level experienced electives and advanced study. From my conversations with the teachers and administrators, I realized that they could not understand that in this environment of discrimination, there would be little hope that the VEEP children would ever reach grade level literacy proficiency.

Fortunately, the genre studies program was dropped when the literacy scores of the VEEP children didn't advance. When I hear this program discussed among educators, two reasons that are often cited for the program's inability to raise test scores are the lack of motivation on the part of the VEEP children and the lack of school involvement by their parents. When I discussed the segregation that existed in the genre studies program with one of my friends, a principal in one of the schools across town in an affluent neighborhood, he confirmed many of the ideas about the class divide in American schools noted by Sacks (2007), when he said that many of the neighborhood parents who hadn't yet put their children in private schools would have done so if they had thought their children were being slowed down by having the VEEP children in their classes. The genre studies program allowed the school to accommodate the neighborhood families while appearing to look integrated and supportive of the academic differences among students.

A third multiperspective experience I have encountered is the insider's view of the Individual Education Plan (IEP) meeting. When Anthony and Angul's mom and I used to arrive at IEP meetings to discuss Ashley, an older sibling who in first grade had been placed in a special day class for children with "mental handicaps," the room was always filled with early arrival educators who were often already in conversation about Ashley. After this happened to us a couple of times, I asked my colleague Nancy Frey, who in her earlier career had been a special education teacher and support provider and who knew all of the state rules, to attend with us. With Nancy as our advocate, we were on equal ground.

Through the years I have moved to the sidelines in all teacher–parent meetings, because Anthony and Angul's mom now feels freer to chat with the teachers about her children. I realized in the early years that when we sat side by side the teachers often only addressed me and never looked at her. After the meetings she and I always discuss everything that was said about her children, some of which she accepts. She has told me that before we became friends she chose not to go to the parent meetings because she believed that all she would hear were negative things about her children. She felt the teachers didn't really know her children because when they called they never told her anything positive about them. She said this hadn't changed since her own childhood, when her mother got calls from teachers who always said negative things about her siblings and her, such as "They are too quiet" or "They didn't finish their homework." She says she didn't finish her homework because she often didn't know how to do it and her mother couldn't help her after about fourth grade.

I believe that all parents who are not well versed in the workings of special education should never attend an IEP meeting without a knowledgeable advocate. I am convinced that Anthony and Angul and all of their younger siblings would have had unchanged, negative school experiences if my colleagues and I had not entered into a school partnership with them and their mom. Ashley, an older sister, went to school with the same experiential base as had Anthony and Angul and had encountered teachers similar to those of Angul who had suggested special education for her when they didn't know how to teach her to read. Unfortunately, Ashley's teacher was successful in placing her in a special day classroom and in blaming Ashley for not learning.

Blaming the child rather than learning how to teach the child who has arrived in one's classroom seems to be the behavioral norm for about 20% of teachers, those who make about 80% of the referrals to special education (U.S. Census Bureau, 2001). Fortunately for Ashley, her life took a more positive turn once Nancy Frey became her advocate. But what about others and the fact that while African American children account for 17% of the student population, almost half of all of the children placed in special education are African American (U.S. Census Bureau, 2001)? I wonder how much more of a crisis will have to occur in the lives of African American students before it becomes obvious that even though there exists a mismatch between the home and school experiences of these children, the burden for their success or failure can no longer be relegated to them, their families, and their early home experiences. It must be the responsibility of the school community.

A major mismatch that has occurred for Angul and Anthony, their siblings, and their mother before them is that their home discourse/language and the discourse that is expected from them outside of the home are very different. With the support of very knowledgeable teachers, the oldest child of the family successfully learned to code-switch from home language to school language and therefore, unlike many of her peers and siblings, was never stigmatized, relegated to special education testing, or placed in low-paying jobs as an adult (Richardson, 2003).

Anthony, who has not fully mastered code-switching, uses silence as a linguistic response. Unfortunately, silence is a dangerous literacy practice that is often interpreted negatively by teachers as insolence or opposition (Fine, 1995), which results in permanent identity damage. Anthony has come from a family and a neighborhood where

> people speak other languages or variant, non-prestigious forms of English and...while [he] has doubtless been sensitive to the differences between [his] way of speaking and [his] teachers', [he has] never been able to sort out or develop attitudes toward the differences that do not put [him] in conflict, one way or another, with the key academic tasks of learning to read and write and talk in standard English. (Shaughnessy, 1977, p. 179)

Because of Anthony's placement in a school with teachers who are very knowledge about language, he is being encouraged through modeling, effective instruction, and continual conversation to expand the nuances of his school language in an attempt to eliminate this cultural problem, a problem that will exist as long as African American discourse and the dominant European American discourse of school are entwined and compared (Wheeler & Swords, 2006). He loves to read and write poetry and is very willing to share his voice through his poetry journal. Thank heavens for his teachers who support and encourage multiple ways of knowing and sharing.

Facts: Getting to Know the Children and Their Parents

I started getting to know Anthony and Angul's mom because I really liked her children and wanted to take them to a movie that was popular among the other first graders. She trusted me and has since told me that she felt that I respected her children, her, and their home and that I knew she knew more about her children than I did. She felt, however, that I knew more about the workings of school than she did and so she believed I would offer her children these educational experiences. This was and continues to be a relationship built upon trust and respect. This isn't always the case between teachers and families; and this is why many school–home relationships fail.

Ladson-Billings (1994) notes that throughout the history of education,

> even when the goal was to improve both student and teacher effectiveness, the use of such terms as "culturally deprived and disadvantaged" contributed to a perception of African American students as deprived, deficient, and deviant. Educational interventions, in the form of compensatory education (to compensate for the deprivation and disadvantage assumed to be inherent in African American homes and communities), often were based on a view of African American children as deficient white children. (p. 8)

Ladson-Billings (1994) further states that according to Cuban (1989), the term "at-risk" is now the replacement term being "used to describe certain students and their families in much the same way that they had been described for almost two hundred years" (as cited in Ladson-Billings, p. 9). With a resistance to address or investigate the "possibilities of distinct cultural characteristics (requiring some specific attention) or the detrimental impact of systemic racism" the two most popular explanations for low academic achievement of at-risk children are frequently identified as "social and environmental," which then supports "[locating] the problem in the children themselves or in their families" (p. 9). Is it any wonder then that the American view that has been historically perpetuated with satisfaction and a lack of responsibility about nonmainstream children is that poverty and its consequence, "a lack of opportunity are the only plausible reasons for poor performance" (Ladson-Billings, 1994, p. 9)?

A few years ago in an effort to more fully know families like Anthony's, who are living below the poverty level, my colleagues and I (Lapp, Fisher, Flood, & Moore, 2002) decided to investigate the role that these parents believed they should play in the early literacy development of their children as well as their rationale for these beliefs. We wanted to better understand the families who are often labeled as invisible or considered difficult to reach because they infrequently attend school activities. Because their thoughts and beliefs are often unknown within the school community, they are frequently mischaracterized as having a lack of involvement by faculties attempting to draw from their funds of knowledge to interpret what they perceive (Deschenes, Cuban,

& Tyack, 2001). A brief review of what we found adds to the discussion being shared in this chapter.

To begin, the 341 adults participating in our study were the parents or primary caregivers of 120 kindergarten and 120 first graders from 12 public school classrooms in which we worked as part of a university–public school collaborative. Of these families, approximately 70% lived in subsidized (Section 8) housing and their children received free or reduced-price lunch. One hundred forty-four (58%) of the children lived in a family configuration other than two parents; some lived with one parent, aunts and uncles, or a parent and grandparent. The ethnicity of the children, which represented that of the school area, included 45% African Americans, 21% Latinos, 18% Asian-Pacific Islanders, and 16% Caucasian.

The parent group was surveyed, and a random sample of 24 was also interviewed. The surveys, which included a stamped addressed envelope, were first distributed to the children by their teachers. Additional copies were also provided to the director of the community-based parent center, who maintained strong connections with many of the families and with other family center directors. He distributed these to the parents who had not returned the original surveys. A third attempt was made to collect the survey information from nonrespondents via the U.S. postal service. This final copy of the survey also contained a letter encouraging the families to return the survey to the school or the community center.

When parents did not feel comfortable reading the survey, responses were collected orally and recorded by the teachers and director. Following these three data collection events, 174 (72.5%) of the surveys were returned. Of those returned, 63 (36%) were returned to the teacher, 96 (55%) were obtained by the director of the community center, and 15 (9%) were returned in the U.S. mail. In addition, we interviewed at least one family member from a random selection of 24 families at locations convenient for them, including their homes, the parent center, and on the sidewalk outside the school building before or after school. All of the interviews and the questionnaires focused on identifying the following:

- How the parent or family defined literacy
- What they saw as the home and school responsibilities for literacy development
- How they had learned skills to develop their children's literacy

- Differences in perceived responsibilities by income level

To briefly summarize, we overwhelmingly found that not every parent was aware that children who learn the functional uses of literacy through their daily family life experiences are well on their way to succeeding in school literacy events (Taylor, 1997). We also found that while many families had a very positive attitude about school and learning, they did not necessarily believe they had the skills, knowledge, or means to develop their children's early literacy awareness. They placed their trust in the schools. We found this to be very surprising, because many of these adults shared that as students they had not had positive school experiences because school personnel had devalued their cultural capital. Despite this past experience, these adults were placing confidence as well as their children's intellectual lives in the hands of their children's schools.

Through insights gained from our conversations with these families, we realized we were witnessing an example of what seemed to us to be an illogical Catch-22 situation in which parents who had been so devalued in their own school experiences also seemed conditioned or predisposed to believe that if they stayed away and didn't rock the school boat their children might have a better chance to succeed. Through the subsequent years as we have used knowledge acquired from this study to build school programs and curriculum for students from families in this community, we have come to more fully understand that one of the reasons for our being perplexed at the time was that different cultural groups have different norms, values, beliefs, behaviors, and ways of acting and interacting (Au, 2005).

Because we know our own cultures so well, our cultural norms are often tacit and taken for granted; many of us are not aware of the norms that constitute others' cultural ways of being because we are all steeped in our own cultures. Reflection has made very clear to us that, although we believed that we were coming to know these families, we had instead been blindsided by our experiences as we entered into a culture that to us had unfamiliar rules and norms about how to behave and converse in schools and with educators.

However, one major finding of significance to the discussion being posited in this chapter is that there were significant differences between the perceptions of parents who were poor and those who were very poor about their role in their child's early literacy development. More specifically, although 70% of the students in this study attended schools where 70% of the student population received free or reduced-price lunch, 30% of the students attended schools with less than 20% of the students receiving free or reduced-price lunch. Parents were asked to identify who should assume the responsibility for tasks ranging from praying to academic tasks like saying and identifying alphabet letters and name writing. The more academic the task became, the more often the less wealthy of these parents looked to the school for their children's literacy instruction, with two notable exceptions—teaching reading and writing numbers. In both of these cases, the responsibility was clearly seen by all as that of the school. Here again the families placed their hopes with the teachers in the schools. Families clearly placed the responsibility for teaching their children to read with the teachers.

One additional finding of major significance that continues to guide our work with the parents of the students we teach is that the majority of the families in this study were very willing to be involved in their children's literacy development. Unfortunately, they were often unsure about what they should do as literacy supporters. While the majority of respondents acknowledged the importance of reading, they believed that learning to read begins in first grade with the teacher. They did not have an understanding of the importance schools place on a certain set of early (birth to first grade) literacy events.

We have also realized from continuing conversations with these parents that school faculties do not realize all of their missed opportunities to take advantage of shared at-home family experiences. These experiences include watching television, listening to music, or creating performances that should at least be acknowledged as significant and at best be propelled into early experiences that count at school. Instead, educators and many national leaders and celebrities—including Bill Cosby, Jesse Jackson, and Barack Obama (Sweet, 2008)—say that families must turn off their TVs. We disagree.

Because we have found from our research and experiences that these media-centered experiences are the constant shared activities of the parents and children we continue to teach (Lapp, Fisher, Flood, & Moore, 2002), we believe, as do many of our colleagues (Padak & Rasinski, 2006), that we must begin with what is family reality. We therefore propose that capitalizing on the television and movie media events families are sharing at home means respecting these language and literacy experiences by inviting students to bring them to school and using them as the foundation for expanded school dialogue and literacy development. By doing so we will provide opportunities and avenues for our students to communicate and critically evaluate "the knowledge, beliefs, practices, and roots of the cultures in [their] environments through their oral and written discourse" (Severino, Guerra, & Butler, 1997, p. 106); as we come to know each other better no one will be discredited (Morrison, 1984) or labeled as lesser. Instead, each of us will be provided with opportunities to continually expand our cultural lenses and Discourse communities.

Possibility: Partnerships of Equality = True Partnerships

The experiences shared in this chapter are very much in sync with the findings and suggestions of Henderson and Mapp (2002), who analyzed 51 studies addressing the influence of school–family–community relationships on academic achievement. The studies spanned diverse cultures and populations and the full range of K–12 grade levels. A major finding was that a key feature of effective school–family involvement programs is that they are *linked to learning*, and that information and messages about how parents can support their children at home should be woven into the existing family and community activities and events. As suggested by the African proverb "He who does not know one thing knows another," all participants have much to share and therefore all voices should be heard in establishing and maintaining a partnership. To this end, Mapp reaffirmed in a recent interview (Fusaro, 2008) the importance of parent–school relationships that recognize that all parents regardless of income, education, or cultural background can in some way be involved in their children's learning, because they all want their children to succeed.

Given that so many differences do exist among families we must do the following:

- Craft new home–school relationships that build on what exists rather than lamenting that which has not happened for so many children when they are being compared with children from economically well-to-do English-speaking families.
- Build from what is, from what exists as the "credible history, culture, and language that all families hold" (Whitmore & Norton-Meier, 2008, p. 450) if we are intent on creating home–school relationships where children are validated rather than castigated because of their uniqueness— where children as individuals or as groups are not discussed as a referent to any other group (O'Connor, Lewis, & Mueller, 2007).

- Look into the homes of the students we teach and honor what we see as the basis of a partnership that supports continued learning for all members of the partnership.

Finally, we must share our insights with future teachers by taking them into the real worlds of the children they will meet in their classrooms who have grown up in homes that are dissimilar from theirs. With this knowledge begins each teacher's power to teach the children in their classrooms and to forge partnerships with their families who, while different from them, are certainly not deficient.

REFERENCES

Almy, M.C. (1949). *Children's experiences prior to first grade and success in beginning reading.* New York: Bureau of Publications, Teachers College, Columbia University.

Au, K.H. (2005). *Literacy instruction in multicultural settings.* Fort Worth, TX: Holt, Rinehart & Winston.

Birch, B. (2001). Grammar standards: It's all in your attitude. *Language Arts, 78*(6), 535–542.

California Department of Education. (2008). *High school drop out rate (2006–2007).* Retrieved July 16, 2008, from dq.cde.ca.gov/dataquest

Caspe, M., Lopez, M.E., & Wolos, C. (2007). *Family involvement in elementary school children's education.* Cambridge, MA: Harvard Family Research Project. Retrieved November 15, 2008, from www.hfrp.org/publications-resources/browse-our-publications/family-involvement-in-elementary-school-childrens-education

Christenbury, L. (2000). *Making the journey: Being and becoming a teacher of English language arts* (2nd ed.). Portsmouth, NH: Boynton/Cook.

Coleman, J.S., Campbell, E.Q., Hoson, C.J., McPartland, J., Mood, A.M., Weinfeld, F.D., et al. (1966). *Equality of educational opportunity.* Cambridge, MA: Harvard University Press.

Comer, J.P. (1998). *Waiting for a miracle: Why schools can't solve our problems—and how we can.* New York: Penguin.

Compton-Lilly, C. (2007). *Re-reading families: The literate lives of urban children, four years later.* New York: Teachers College Press.

Cuban, L. (1989). The 'at-risk' label and the problem of urban school reform. *Phi Delta Kappan, 70*(10), 780–784, 799–801.

Delpit, L. (1995). *Other people's children: Cultural conflict in the classroom.* New York: New Press.

Deschenes, S., Cuban, L., & Tyack, D. (2001). Mismatch: Historical perspectives on schools and students who don't fit them. *Teachers College Record, 103*(4), 525–547. doi:10.1111/0161-4681.00126

Edwards, P.A., & Turner, J.D. (2009). Family literacy and reading comprehension. In S.E. Israel & G.G. Duffy (Eds.), *Handbook of research on reading comprehension* (pp.622–641). Mahwah, NJ: Erlbaum.

Epstein, J.L., & Salinas, K.C. (2004). Partnering with families and communities. *Schools as Learning Communities, 61*(8), 12–18.

Fine, M. (1995). Silencing and literacy. In V.L. Gadsden & D.A. Wagner (Eds.), *Literacy among African-American youth: Issues in learning, teaching, and schooling* (pp. 201–222). Cresskill, NJ: Hampton.

Flood, J. (1975). *Predictor of reading achievement: An investigation of selected antecedents to reading.* Unpublished doctoral dissertation, Stanford University, Stanford, CA.

Fusaro, M. (2008). *Popping the question: How can schools engage families in education?* Retrieved October 19, 2009, from www

.uknow.gse.harvard.edu/community/CF5-3-207.html

Garcia, G.G., & Montavon, M.V. (2007). Making content-area instruction comprehensible for English language learners. In D. Lapp, J. Flood, & N. Farnan (Eds.), Content area reading and learning: Instructional strategies (3rd ed., pp. 157–174). Mahwah, NJ: Erlbaum.

Garvey, A.J. (1986). The philosophy and opinions of Marcus Garvey, or, Africa for the Africans. Dover, MA: Majority Press.

Gee, J.P. (1990). Social linguistics and literacies: Ideology in discourses. New York: Falmer.

Gee, J.P. (1996). Social linguistics and literacies: Ideology in discourses (2nd ed.). London: Taylor & Francis.

Gee, J.P. (1999). An introduction to discourse analysis: Theory and method. New York: Routledge.

Goldin, C.D., & Katz, L.F. (2008). The race between education and technology. Cambridge, MA: Belknap Press/Harvard University Press.

Goodman, Y.M. (1986). Children coming to know literacy. In W.H. Teale & E. Sulzby (Eds.), Emergent literacy: Writing and reading (pp. 1–14). Norwood, NJ: Ablex.

Guthrie, J.T., & Greaney, V. (1991). Literacy acts. In R. Barr, M.L. Kamil, P. Mosenthal, & P.D. Pearson (Eds.), Handbook of reading research (Vol. 2, pp. 68–96). Mahwah, NJ: Erlbaum.

Hart, B., & Risley, T.R. (1995). Meaningful differences in the everyday experience of young American children. Baltimore: Paul H. Brookes.

Heath, S.B. (1983). Ways with words: Language, life, and work in communities and classrooms. Cambridge: Cambridge University Press.

Henderson, A.T, & Mapp, K.L. (2002). A new wave of evidence: The impact of school, family, and community connections on student achievement. Retrieved October 19, 2009, from www.sedl.org/connections/resources/evidence.pdf

Hirsch, E.D., Jr. (1987). Cultural literacy: What every American needs to know. Boston: Houghton Mifflin.

Holland, D., Lachicotte, W., Jr., Skinner, D., & Cain, C. (1998). Identity and agency in cultural worlds. Cambridge, MA: Harvard University Press.

Hollingsworth, J.R., & Boyer, R. (Eds.). (2008). Contemporary capitalism: The embeddedness of institutions. Cambridge, England: Cambridge University Press.

International Reading Association. (2002, April/May). Position statement points way to stronger, better family–school partnerships. Reading Today, 19(5), 48.

Knoblauch, C.H., & Brannon, L. (1993). Critical teaching and the idea of literacy. Portsmouth, NH: Boynton/Cook.

Kunjufu, J. (2002). Black students: Middle class teachers. Chicago: African American Images.

Ladson-Billings, G. (1994). The Dreamkeepers: Successful teachers of African American children. San Francisco: Jossey-Bass.

Lansberg, M., & Bume, H., (2008, July 17). 1 in 4 quit high school in California. Los Angeles Times, pp.1, 18.

Lapp, D., Fisher, D., Flood, J., & Moore, K. (2002) "I don't want to teach it wrong": An investigation of the role families believe they should play in the early literacy development of their children. In D. Schallert, C. Fairbanks, J. Worthy, B. Maloch, & J. Hoffman (Eds.), 51st yearbook of the National Reading Conference (pp. 275–287). Oak Creek, WI: National Reading Conference.

Lapp, D., Flood, J., & Goss, K. (2000). Desks don't move—students do: In effective classroom environments. The Reading Teacher, 54(1), 31–36.

Lapp, D., Flood, J., & Moore, K. (2008). Differentiating visual, communicative, and performance arts instruction in well-managed classrooms. In J. Flood, S.B. Heath, & D. Lapp (Eds.), Handbook of research on teaching literacy through the communicative and visual arts (Vol. 2, pp. 537–544). Mahwah, NJ: Erlbaum.

Lareau, A. (2003). Unequal childhoods: Class, race, and family life. Berkeley: University of California Press.

Lave, J., & Wenger, E. (1991). Situated learning: Legitimate peripheral participation. New York: Cambridge University Press.

Lee, C.D. (2007). Culture, literacy, and learning: Taking bloom in the midst of the whirlwind. New York: Teachers College Press.

156   Lapp

Lee, C.D. (2008). The centrality of culture to the scientific study of learning and development: How an ecological framework in education research facilitates civic responsibility. *Educational Researcher, 37*(5), 267–297. doi:10.3102/0013189X08322683

McMillon, G.M.T., & Edwards, P.A. (2008). Examining shared domains of literacy in the home, church and school of African American children. In J. Flood, S.B. Heath, & D. Lapp (Eds.), *Handbook of research on teaching literacy through the communicative and visual arts* (Vol. 2, pp. 319–328). New York: Erlbaum.

McTavish, M. (2007). Constructing the big picture: A working class family supports their daughter's pathways to literacy. *The Reading Teacher, 60*(5), 476–485. doi:10.1598/RT.60.5.7

Moll, L.C., & Gonzalez, N. (1994). Lessons from research with language-minority children. *Journal of Reading Behavior, 26*(4), 439–456.

Moll, L.C., & Greenberg, J.B. (1990). Creating zones of possibilities: Combining social contexts for instruction. In L.C. Moll (Ed.), *Vygotsky and education: Instructional implications and applications of sociohistorical psychology* (pp.319–348). New York: Cambridge University Press.

Morrison, T. (1984). Rootedness: The Ancestor as foundation, an interview with Mari Evans. In M. Evans (Ed.), *Black women writers 1950–1980: A critical evaluation* (pp. 339–345). Garden City, NY: Anchor.

National Center for Education Statistics. (2002). *Public school student, staff, and graduate counts by state: School year 2000–01 (NCEAS Pub. 2003-348-313).* Washington, DC: Author.

National Center for Education Statistics. (2005). *Digest of education statistics.* Washington, DC: U.S. Government Printing Office.

Nelson, J. (2007). AVIDly seeking success. *Educational Leadership, 64*(7), 72–74.

Neuman, S.B., Caperelli, B.J., & Kee, C. (1998). Literacy learning: A family matter. *The Reading Teacher, 52*(3), 244–252.

Neuman, S.B., & Celano, D. (2001). Access to print in low-income and middle-income communities: An ecological study of four neighborhoods. *Reading Research Quarterly, 36*(1), 8–26. doi:10.1598/RRQ.36.1.1

O'Connor, C., Lewis, A., & Mueller, J. (2007). Researching "black" educational experiences and outcomes: Theoretical and methodological considerations. *Educational Researcher, 36*(9), 541–552. doi:10.3102/0013189X07312661

Padak, N., & Rasinski, T. (2006). Home–school partnerships in literacy education: From rhetoric to reality. *The Reading Teacher, 60*(3), 292–296. doi:10.1598/RT.60.3.11

Paratore, J.R. (2001). *Opening doors, opening opportunities: Family literacy in an urban community.* Boston: Allyn & Bacon.

Purcell-Gates, V. (1993). Issues for family literacy research: Voices from the trenches. *Language Arts, 70*(8), 670–677.

Purcell-Gates, V. (1995). *Other people's words: The cycle of low literacy.* Cambridge, MA: Harvard University Press.

Purcell-Gates, V. (2000). Family literacy. In M.L. Kamil, P.B. Mosenthal, P.D. Pearson, & R. Barr (Eds.), *Handbook of reading research* (Vol. 3, pp. 853–870). Mahwah, NJ: Erlbaum.

Regosin, E.A. (2002). *Freedom's promise: Ex-slave families and citizenship in the age of emancipation.* Charlottesville, VA: University of Virginia Press.

Richardson, E.B. (2003). *African American literacies.* New York: Routledge.

Sacks, P. (2007). *Tearing down the gates: Confronting the class divide in American education.* Berkeley: University of California Press.

Severino, C., Guerra, J.C., & Butler, J.E. (1997). *Writing in multicultural settings.* New York: Modern Language Association of America.

Shaughnessy, M.P. (1977). *Errors and expectations: A guide for the teacher of basic writing.* New York: Oxford University Press.

Sonnenschein, S., Brody, G., & Munsterman, K. (1996). The influence of family beliefs and practices on children's early reading development. In L. Baker, P. Afflerbach, & D. Reinking (Eds.), *Developing engaged readers in school and home communities* (pp. 3–20). Mahwah, NJ: Erlbaum.

Sulzby, E., & Teale, W.H. (1991). Emergent literacy. In R. Barr, M.L. Kamil, P. Mosenthal, & P.D. Pearson (Eds.), *Handbook of reading research* (Vol. 2, pp. 727–757). White Plains, NY: Longman.

Swanson, M.C. (2005). *An interview with Mary Catherine Swanson: About (AVID) Advancement Via Individual Determination.* Retrieved October 20, 2009, from www.avidonline .org/content/pdf/2048.pdf

Sweet, L. (2008). *Obama tells blacks: Shape up.* Retrieved October 19, 2009, from www.sun times.com/news/sweet/819177,CST-NWS-sweet29.article

Taylor, C. (1991). *The malaise of modernity.* Toronto, Canada: Anansi.

Taylor, D. (Ed.). (1997). *Many families, many literacies: An international declaration of principles.* Portsmouth, NH: Heinemann.

Taylor, D., & Dorsey-Gaines, C. (1988). *Growing up literate: Learning from inner-city families.* Portsmouth, NH: Heinemann.

Tembo, M.S. (2000). *Breaking out of racial mental bondage is a radical perspective.* www.bridge water.edu/~mtembo/RacialLiberationJan28 2000.htm

Thomas, W.P., & Collier, V.P. (2001). *A national study of school effectiveness for language minority students' long-term academic achievement.* Washington, DC: Center for Research on Education, Diversity, and Excellence/Center for Applied Linguistics.

Tutwiler, S.W. (2005). *Teachers as collaborative partners: Working with diverse families and communities.* New York: Routledge.

U.S. Census Bureau. (2001). *Statistical abstract of the United States.* Washington, DC: Author.

Wertsch, J.V. (1998). *Mind as action.* New York: Oxford University Press.

Wheeler, R.S., & Swords, R. (2006). *Code-switching: Teaching standard English in urban classrooms.* Urbana, IL: National Council of Teachers of English.

Whitmore, K.F., & Norton-Meier, L.A. (2008). Pearl and Ronda: Revaluing mothers' literate lives to imagine new relationships between homes and elementary schools. *Journal of Adolescent & Adult Literacy, 51*(6), 450–461. doi:10.1598/JAAL.51.6.2

Yaden, D.B., & Paratore, J.R. (2002). Family literacy at the turn of the millennium: The costly future of maintaining the status quo. In J. Flood, D. Lapp, J. Jensen, & J. Squire (Eds.), *Handbook of research on teaching the English language arts* (pp. 532–545). Mahwah, NJ: Erlbaum.

Yang, Y., & Gustafsson, J.-E. (2004). Measuring socioeconomic status at individual and collective levels. *Educational Research and Evaluation, 10*(3), 259–288. doi:10.1076/edre .10.3.259.30268

Connecting School With Home Culture

CHAPTER 7

Teaching Literacy
in Cultural Context

Geneva Gay

It is well within the realm of possibility that conventional approaches to the study and implementation of literacy programs overlook some power potentialities embedded in literacy as practiced among different ethnic groups within their own cultural traditions, communities, contexts, and family interactions. These possibilities need to be conceded and examined thoroughly in efforts to transform literacy learning opportunities and outcomes for African, Asian, Native, Latino, and European American students and recent immigrants, especially if they are poor and not performing well in schools. In the discussions that follow, literacies are conceived broadly, but grouped into two large categories. One is academic, or school-based, knowledge and skills, and the other is cultural competencies based in different ethnic groups, cultures, families, and communities.

The intent is to explain the potential of using cultural knowledge and skills practiced in different families and communities of color for teaching academic literacies more effectively to underachieving marginalized students of color (a term used interchangeably with *ethnically diverse students* to refer to the collective of Asian, African, Latino, and Native Americans), and to make an appeal for adding cultural competence to the host of literacies that all students should acquire. The need for this dual approach to literacy is examined from the perspective of both teaching and learning with the argument being that teachers need to develop more cultural competencies about African, Asian, Native, and Latino Americans to help students from these groups perform better in school, and to be more knowledgeable about their own, one another's, and mainstream U.S. cultural heritages. Examples of some actual practices in these endeavors are included to amplify general ideas and to serve as motivators and models from

From *Bringing Literacy Home* edited by KaiLonnie Dunsmore and Douglas Fisher.

which other educators can extrapolate techniques that can be used in their own teaching of literacy in cultural context for ethnically diverse students.

Literacy Practices in Ethnically Diverse Families and Cultural Contexts

Moll and his colleagues (Moll & González, 2004; González, Moll, & Amanti, 2005) provide some powerful examples of literacy skills Mexican and Mexican American youths practice in everyday interactions within their families and cultural communities, and the academic potential of these household skills and knowledge. They note that the low-income families they studied are not social and intellectual wastelands. Instead, the adults and children routinely use reading, writing, mathematics, complex thinking, and problem solving and negotiate social relationships on the basis of their lived experiences.

Another graphic example of how culturally embedded literacy practices are often overlooked or misunderstood by school personnel involves young, poor, African American students. They are often thought to have difficulty mastering early school literacy skills (especially reading) because their homes are not print-rich, and they receive little if any reading stimulation or academically useful literacy socialization prior to coming to school as kindergartners. According to Lee (2005), it is very unlikely in the media-rich era in which we live that these students "do not have meaningful emergent literacy constructs that are useful resources for learning to read" (p. 61). Although they may begin formal schooling not knowing their letters or colors, they are quite skilled in family relationships, social interactions, and age-appropriate practices within their own cultures, and know a great deal about commercialized popular mainstream culture. Many have memorized the lyrics of popular songs; can reproduce advertising jingles with ease; know the relationships and profiles of characters in television programs of interest to them; recognize symbols associated with commercial enterprises, such as the golden arches of McDonald's and Target's bull's-eye; tell coherent, well-developed stories about rather complex interactions; and can operate electronic technology (such as video games, computers, and DVD players) easily with few instructions from older, more advanced users. The absence of word reading from books is compensated by visual and signal reading of people, situations, and signs, and by listening to and telling very inventive, exciting, and entertaining stories about events and interactions in everyday life.

In her studies of the routine talk of African American adolescent speakers of Ebonics (or African American Vernacular English), Lee (2005) observed similar social and cultural competencies that can be viable foundations for teaching academic literacies, such as reading, writing, and oral communication. She noted that these students are skillful in using a wide variety of verbal techniques such as rhythm, rhyme, alliteration, metaphor, irony, and satire.

Two other compelling examples of cultural and family literacies, or funds of knowledge, that teachers can use to better culturally contextualize their classroom instruction for ethnically diverse students involve Native Americans. One is an "Open Letter to a Non-Indian Teacher," written by "An Indian Mother" (Seale & Stapin, 2005). In it the mother explains:

> My child's [family] experiences have been as intense and meaningful to him as any child's.... He does not speak standard English but he is in no way "linguistically handicapped." If you will take the time and courtesy to listen and observe carefully, you will see that he and the other Indian children communicate very well, both among themselves and with other Indians. They speak functional English, very effectively augmented by fluency in the silent language...of facial expressions, gestures, body movements, and the use of personal space.... They will know your feelings and attitudes with unerring precision, no matter how careful you arrange your smile or modulate your voice. (pp. 8–9)

The second Native American example comes from "An Indian Father's Plea," written by Medicine Grizzlybear (Lake, 1990). In it he tries to make sense of why his 5-year-old son, Wind-Wolf, was declared a "slow learner" shortly after entering kindergarten in a mainstream school. The father explains that since birth Wind-Wolf had been immersed in rich culturally textured literacy (although nonprint) environments and relationships, and by the standards of his cultural group he is quite accomplished for a 5-year-old. His accomplishments included being constantly engaged in learning situations provided by both women and men that were "very colorful, complicated, sensitive, and diverse," and allowed for the functional integrating of "the physical and spiritual, matter and energy, conscious and unconscious, individual and social" (p. 50). Grizzlybear supported these general conclusions with a number of specific cultural skills Wind-Wolf had mastered by the time he began kindergarten:

> [Having] been in more than 20 different sacred sweat-lodge rituals...since he was 3 years old...[being] taught his numbers while [his mother, grandmothers, and aunts] sorted out the complex materials used to make the abstract designs in native baskets...beaded belts and necklaces...by helping his father count and sort the rocks to

be used in the sweat lodges...[and] by counting the sticks we use in our traditional native hand games.... If you ask him how many months in a year, he will probably tell you 13...because he has been taught by our traditional people that there are 13 full moons in a year according to the native tribal calendar.... He may have trouble writing his name on a piece of paper, but he knows how to say it and many other things in several different languages. (pp. 50–51)

The Native American mother and father in these narratives also noted that their children are trained early and thoroughly in morality, respect, courtesy, spirituality, observation, reflection, introspection, and connectedness. They concluded their statements by reminding teachers that Native American children are culturally different, not deprived, and are differently literate, not illiterate. How teachers respond to their accomplishments, what they say and do in the classroom, or don't say or do, have profound effects on whether schooling for these children will be a success or failure (Lake, 1990; Seale & Stapin, 2005).

Cultural Competence as Literacy and as Conduit for Academic Learning

Another critical dimension of literacy in cultural context is teaching students about and respect for the histories, experiences, and heritages of different ethnic groups. In explaining this point about studying Native American cultures, Medicine Grizzlybear (Lake, 1990) made some comments that are apropos for other ethnic groups as well:

My Indian child has a constitutional right to learn, retain, and maintain his heritage and culture. By the same token...non-Indian children also have a constitutional right to learn about Native American heritage and culture, because Indians play a significant part in the history of Western society. (p. 52)

Part of this literacy dimension is teaching students more accurate, inclusive, and comprehensive versions of the historical and cultural developments of the United States.

These skills are necessary for effective membership in culturally, ethnically, racially, socially, and linguistically pluralistic societies such as the United States, as well as for the academic achievement and personal well-being of individual students. Simply put, we do not know as much as we need to know about ourselves and one another as members of various ethnic and cultural groups.

Schools, families, and communities are morally obligated to ensure that children and youth are taught knowledge and skills to counteract cultural ignorance, racial oppression, and cultural hegemony. Because the United States is becoming more culturally, ethnically, and linguistically diverse, it is imperative that preparation for meeting the demands of this diversity is as much a part of literacy learning as are reading, writing, and mathematics.

Another part of this mandate is ensuring that the cultural heritages and identities of ethnically diverse students are not compromised in the process of teaching them academic literacy skills. Students should never be placed in a situation, even inadvertently, where they feel they must separate themselves from their ethnicity and culture or feel apologetic for or ashamed of who they are as they pursue school learning. Instead, academic and cultural literacies should be complementary and reciprocal; one should facilitate the accomplishment of the other. Thus, students should be learning to read, write, think, and act as they study culturally diverse issues and events. For example, knowledge of African, Asian, Latino, and Native Americans should be woven routinely into scientific, technological, aesthetic, and interpersonal literacies, just as students should be practicing problem solving, critical thinking, reading comprehension, mathematical skills, and oral and written communication as they examine such ethnically specific issues as immigration and resettlement, civil rights, racial profiling, employment trends, and various forms of culturally conscious art, music, and literature. This reciprocity between academic and cultural literacies comprises what is sometimes called *scaffolding*, *biculturalism*, or *cultural hybridity*. Whatever the preferred nomenclature, it is a desirable literacy for people to be able to function effectively in different cultural contexts, without compromising the integrity of their indigenous cultures, languages, and identities.

Research, theory, and practice attest to the positive correlation that exists among cultural knowledge, ethnic self-concepts, and academic, career, and social success. People who have a strong sense of cultural pride and self-acceptance of their ethnic identities tend to perform better in their various role functions. Part of this personal agency and empowerment occurs because such individuals are less concerned about conducting themselves according to standards imposed on them by cultural norms of others, apologizing for their identities and heritages, or dispelling racial stereotypes. They are not insensitive to and disrespectful of ethnic others or mainstream social norms, but they do not try to be someone they are not, such as by mimicking middle class European Americans, or acting white. This self-acceptance allows students of color to spend more intellectual and psycho-emotional time, energy, and effort on academic task performance. Personally, I have often said that I did not become intelligent until I became Black, meaning genuine and conscious acceptance of my ethnicity coincided with higher levels and a better quality of academic engagement and achievement.

Many other individuals of color tell similar stories about the relationship between ethnic pride and task performance. For example, Holliday (1999) recorded the stories of 38 African Americans who tell about grappling with insidious racial inequities, as well as their persistence and creativity in learning how to transmute these injustices. One of the contributors captures the message and spirit of most of the others. She said, "I came to understand that to be black in America was to live in two worlds, to experience two selves, to play two sets of roles, and to struggle to preserve sanity and certainty when those two realities collided" (Holliday, 1999, p. 1). This person is not alone in having to deal with a dual identity, nor is dual identity limited to adults, the past, or only one ethnic group of color. Unfortunately, it is too often a common occurrence that transcends age, generation, gender, social class, and ethnicity. These realities and related skills should be major parts of the broad landscape of literacy learning in families, communities, and schools.

Edwards and Polite (1992) studied 41 high-achieving African American professionals to create a profile of African American success. The results revealed that the most successful individuals were

> not just competent or even intellectually and academically gifted, but practical, shrewd, and flexible. They operate out of a heightened sense of consciousness which gives them a finely tuned sense of control—an ability to assess a situation, make critical judgments, and take action. (p. 349)

They have a positive sense of their personal and ethnic selves, which allows them to embrace who they are unapologetically and to deal with various life and work situations without losing their personal integrity. Their ability to

> not just overcome but to triumph in the face of obstacles, to make a way out of what appears to be no way, to wrest destiny from the seemingly arbitrary hands of fate, constitutes power that is transcendent, freedom that is supreme. (Edwards & Polite, 1992, p. 274)

Surely, the kind of understandings and coping devices that Holliday's (1999) contributors and the individuals in Edwards's and Polite's (1992) study cultivated deserve to be part of any literacy agenda for today's students, both in schools and in other learning situations. These transformations of identities and racial inequities, and their associated efficacy, require more than the mere acquisition of cultural knowledge; its acceptance, internalization, and actualization in behavior are imperative, too. A similar mandate applies to other forms of literacy as well. Simply because individuals know the rules of grammar and good writing does not mean they will be good writers. Knowing how to read does not ensure that people will be readers or that they can read different kinds of materials with the same levels of effectiveness. Knowing factual information that does not affirm racial biases does not prevent racial prejudices nor does knowledge of the legal and moral edicts about equality, justice, and human dignity stop racism and other forms of oppression, or ethnic disparities in opportunities, power, and privilege, from occurring. Therefore, it is helpful in assessing and improving students' competencies to distinguish between *acquisition* and *application* literacies.

Culturally Responsive Literacy Teaching in Practice

Three specific cases are presented here to illustrate how teaching culturally responsive literacy is actualized in elementary and secondary schools, colleges, and teacher education. The cases are not all-inclusive but do include dimensions of both academic and cultural literacy. Nor are the cases specifically named culturally responsive teaching, but they are in intent and substance. Their inclusion in this discussion acknowledges that concerns about cultural responsiveness in educating ethnically diverse students has a long history (for some advocates), that literacy has many manifestations, and that useful lessons can be learned from historical precedents. These practices also demonstrate that sometimes teachers are actively engaged in culturally responsive literacy teaching without realizing it and that their efforts should be praised.

Developing Critical Cultural Consciousness Among Teachers

Teachers need to be taught culturally responsive content knowledge and pedagogical skills in ways that are sensitive to who they are culturally, racially, and ethnically, and to where they are in their career matriculation. This might be called *culturally responsive professional literacy*. Space limitations do not allow for a comprehensive discussion of this here. The focus is on only one dimension, *developing critical cultural consciousness*. Other aspects are equally important, such as cultural knowledge specific to different ethnic groups; knowledge of contributions of different ethnic groups and individuals to various disciplines; designing culturally responsive curricula, pedagogy, and assessment procedures; creating learning communities among ethnically diverse students; building caring and respectful relationships with culturally different students; and cultivating welcoming and inclusive climates for cultural, ethnic, and racial diversity in classrooms. But, developing critical cultural consciousness is a place to begin the process of becoming culturally responsive because of the importance of teachers' beliefs in determining their instructional behaviors and the role that teachers play in shaping classroom dynamics and discourse. According to Gay (2000) and Gay and Kirkland (2003), critical cultural consciousness encompasses knowledge, attitudes, and actions. Culturally conscious teachers critique and carefully monitor their personal beliefs about cultural diversity and their instructional behaviors toward ethnically different students; have a deep knowledge of their own and their students' cultures, families, and communities; and routinely incorporate more positive and varied cultural content about ethnically diverse groups into their curriculum and instruction. Specific professional development opportunities should be provided for pre- and inservice teachers to develop these competencies.

I remind my teacher-education students that culturally responsive knowledge and skills develop over time. They do not have to wait until they achieve full mastery of knowledge about ethnic and cultural diversity, or guarantees of success, before doing any culturally responsive teaching. A more reasonable approach is to acquire some solid cultural knowledge and pedagogical foundations and then build on them as they engage in teaching. Sometimes, the process begins with my students taking inventories of and reflecting on their own cultures and ethnicities. One activity used to facilitate this is having teacher-education students pack a metaphorical suitcase of things that that they will take on their multicultural education journeys. This exercise is an opportunity for them to become conscious of cultural attitudes, values, and beliefs embedded in their thinking about teaching to, for, and about diversity, and to model teaching techniques that can be used with K–12 students with some age-appropriate modifications. At the end of the class, students are asked to repack their suitcases for subsequent trips and to leave messages for others who will come after them. Here is a chance for them to reflect on their emerging multicultural literacy and to demonstrate how it is affecting their instructional perceptions and behaviors.

A wide variety of things are placed in these suitcases, including prior knowledge, academic and social experiences, family members and memories, values and attitudes, friendships, travels, questions, fears, racial and ethnic identities and traditions, personal dispositions, personality traits, and memorable books, films, and insights gleaned from these memories and reflections. Occasionally, some individuals pack empty spaces in their suitcases, either because they cannot give name to what they are taking along, or because they don't want to take so much cultural baggage that there is no room to add anything new to their repertoires of cultural knowledge, attitudes, beliefs, and behaviors. The students are encouraged to use different expressive genres in describing the contents of their suitcases, such as letters, short stories, poems, dialogues, essays, interviews, arts, and photography. These suitcases help preservice teachers understand how academic and cultural literacies function in conjunction with each other. They also begin to realize that writing and speaking are more than technical crafts and understand that what people say and write are statements about who they are. Personal experiences with an unusual and sometimes unnerving expressive genre (such as poetic, visual, and metaphorical representations of ideas) help aspiring teachers gain some empathetic insights into how immigrant students may feel trying to learn while coping with the strangeness of U.S. mainstream culture and the English language.

Two excerpts from teacher-education students' work illustrate the specific types of items students place in their suitcases (names used throughout are pseudonyms). Michelle's suitcase was filled with apprehensions related to "entering a personally uncharted territory," but excitement about what she would find there. She attributed these apparent contradictions to the following:

> My own lack of an ethnic or noticeably cultural identity. As a white, middle-class American, non-religious female I've spent a great deal of my life feeling generic and "mass-produced...." My family regularly celebrated Hanukkah with close family friends, and while I spun the dreidel and lit the candles with my Jewish "cousins," I felt that I was an imposter in the activities.... Can I be an effective multicultural educator when I feel like I don't have anything to offer culturally? What I lack in culture, I do feel I can compensate for with curiosity. For as long as I can remember—and perhaps due to my own feelings of inadequacy in the culture department—I've been fascinated with other cultures and have made efforts to travel widely and explore new places. Nothing makes you think more closely about who you are and what

beliefs you hold than visiting a place that challenges those notions through different individual, environmental, and governmental beliefs.

In reflecting on the experience as she repacked her suitcase at the end of the class. Toya explained,

> I initially wrote that my journey into multicultural education would be packed with a hope for equality and a sense of curiosity [about different cultures and ethnic groups]. This remains true. However, I now know that it will take much more.... I now throw in a lot of "elbow grease" and perseverance. Hope and curiosities are nice if I plan to stand on the sidelines and watch. If I'm going to take an active role in promoting multicultural education it will require much hard work and will take dogged determination.... I have a lot of work to do to better figure out where I fit into the picture of culture and ethnicity. Simply writing my-self off as of white mixed background with little sense of ethnicity will not do.

My preservice teacher candidates also are asked to symbolize, in nontraditional communicative formats, their understandings of important information studied about the cultural experiences and educational needs of ethnically diverse students. The intent of this expectation is for them to become sensitized to the potentials and challenges of different styles of communicating that may be exhibited by the students they teach. In one assignment, for example, I ask my students to write an "I am" poem after examining characteristics of culture, ethnicity, individuality, education, and interactions among them. The activity also provides prospective teachers an opportunity to articulate their understanding of these concepts as they apply to themselves personally and the professional roles they want to play as advocates of cultural diversity. The poems are written in metaphorical voice to encourage higher order thinking, and they have four different parts to generate multiple perspectives and comprehensive analyses: (1) ancestral origins, (2) family backgrounds, (3) individual personality attributes, and (4) aspirations for teaching cultural diversity. These parameters and goals for writing the poems are common expectations in teaching cultural diversity. Therefore, this learning activity allows prospective teachers to practice ways of learning similar to those they will expect of the students they teach. I wrote the following poem as a sample of what I wanted my teacher education students to do:

> I began in a distant land far from Western shores
> In a place of maybes and possibilities
> Since history offers no particulars and certainties

And personal memories are too short to reach across gaping holes left by centuries
    of unknowns
I was born of minds, bodies, souls, and spirits that had to be incredibly strong
Because they weren't supposed to continue to procreate beyond castration

I come from weekdays of hoping for rain to bring a little reprieve
When a drink of ice water was as delicious as an ice cream cone
Where the big events were the church anniversary, revival meetings, once-in-a-while
    county fairs, and relatives coming home
A time when store bought toys were fanciful dreams
Compensated for with creative imagination and daring schemes
Of wondering what it would be like to ride a bus to school
And read a book once in a while that no one else had used before me

I am a curious mind in constant motion
Always wondering as I wander
What makes us do the things we do the way we do them
And how can we be better than what we currently are
I am joy in the most inane things
That causes others to not even bother to ponder
I am an aberration in the midst of my normalcy

I want to be a moral code in the face of immorality
I want to be the sane voice that counters insanity
I want to be a courageous stance in the presence of cowardice
I want to be change against conformity
I want to be sincerity and dignity
I want to be the promise of democracy
I want to be diversity!

Another critical consciousness exercise I use with my teacher-education students is having them create visual art and technology presentations to demonstrate their understanding of major conceptual and philosophical ideas about educating underachieving students of color. The latest version of this activity required them to collectively create a "Cultural Diversity Talking Quilt." The class was divided into five small study groups, and each group was responsible for producing a section of the quilt (which was, in fact, a stand-alone mini quilt). Each group chose a theme to represent, such as E pluribus unum, cultural connections, or crossing cultural borders. Their artistic images were to "speak" or exemplify the selected theme. Each group was expected to assume the primary responsibility for making and composing the quilt pieces (as paper art constructions), but they could solicit contributions from elementary-age students at the community organizations where they were participating in field experiences. The teacher education students had to collaborate with one another to ensure that their selected themes and visual images complemented one another, because the separate sections of the quilt had to be arranged to form a coherent whole.

It was a rather bold and daring step to take in having an art and technology project replace the more conventional research papers or unit planning as the culminating activity in a teacher education course. Novelty and unconventionality are sometimes essential to effective culturally responsive literacy teaching and learning. Yet, the students' cognitive knowledge development and practice of pedagogical skills were not compromised. To complete their quilts they had to engage in many of the same academic and intellectual challenges that writing a research paper involves as well as apply some different literacies and performance modes. All were consistent with the ideological principles of culturally responsive literacy introduced earlier in this discussion. They had to conduct general academic research as well as collect and communicate information from and for specific cultural contexts; convert knowledge from one form to another; document, present, and interpret information; and find ways to entice elementary school students to work with them in completing the tasks. Therefore, in creating the quilts my teacher-education students were practicing multiple literacies simultaneously (e.g., intellectual, aesthetic, artistic, cultural, communicative, critical thinking and problem solving, shared responsibility, community building), and experiencing alternative teaching techniques that could be used with their own students to develop similar competencies.

The Foxfire Approach

The Foxfire approach of culturally responsive literacy in practice involved Appalachian students in Rabun Country, Georgia, learning communication and language arts skills while conducting cultural ethnographies and developing cultural pride. Called Foxfire, the project reached its pinnacle between 1967 and 1984, but continued into the early 1990s. The Foxfire project grew out of creator Eliot Wigginton's determination to make English instruction more meaningful for his 9th- and 10th-grade Appalachian students. It eventually expanded into an academic program of 16 courses, a series of *Foxfire* magazines, nine published books compiled from the oral history research of the participating students, community development initiatives; teacher networks for professional development, recordings and videotapes, lecture series in which students were copresenters, student exchange programs, the creation of a Foxfire Center composed of authentic replicas of Appalachian log cabins, the inspiration for a Broadway play based on the first three Foxfire books, and being a prototype for more than 200 similar projects throughout the United States and in other countries (Knapp, 1993; Puckett, 1989; Wigginton, 1985, 1989, 1991). Students played pivotal roles in most of these activities, including providing the primary content and being decision makers and leaders. For example, they were speakers in the lecture series and served as consultants to the authors of the Broadway play and producers of the films about their learning projects.

In a letter written to a friend soon after the school year began in 1966, Wigginton (1985) described the attitudes and behaviors of his students that prompted him to pursue alternative approaches to teaching English and language arts. His descriptions sound very much like the laments of many teachers today working in urban and rural schools populated by high percentages of poor underachieving African, Latino, Native, Asian, and European American students and recent immigrant students. Wigginton described most of his students as alienated, disinterested, and unmotivated by school and his attempts to teach them. His first inclination was to respond to these attitudes and behaviors with intimidation, threat, punishment, and reasserting teacher authority. Fortunately, he reconsidered the wisdom of these choices, found them wanting, and sought other, nontraditional interventions. These included collaborating and sharing responsibility with students in deciding what to teach and how to learn and tapping into the talent potential and cultural funds of knowledge offered by the Appalachian communities surrounding the school.

Wigginton (1985) did not achieve instantaneous success. But he was determined and persistent in his efforts to make his teaching more relevant and effective. He also had a strong belief in the right and ability of students to help construct their own educational destinies, and that every student should be actively engaged in useful, productive, positive, rewarding, stimulating, and exciting learning. Today these teacher attitudes, expectations, and behaviors would be seen as a signal of caring pedagogy. Pursuing these objectives lead to instructional techniques that came to be known as *cultural journalism* (Puckett, 1989; Wigginton, 1985, 1989, 1991) and initially embodied in form as *Foxfire*, a student-produced magazine. Its major features were collections and reporting of local Appalachian culture, history, folklore, customs, and traditions. In other words, the students researched, cataloged, codified, and disseminated their own family, cultural, and community competencies, or funds of knowledge.

A host of culturally responsive literacies were embedded in the Foxfire project. Among them were developing cultural knowledge and self-study; legitimizing the family and community funds of knowledge of culturally diverse students; contextualizing academic learning in the lived experiences of diverse students; recognizing situated competencies; using community cultural resources and students' prior social experiences as conduits for classroom teaching; honoring the cultural heritages and experiences of ethnically, racially, and socially diverse students; teaching academic and cultural competencies simultaneously; and partnering students and teachers genuinely in the learning process. Some of these were beautifully illustrated by Wigginton (1985) in his reflections on learning about a local custom of locating and transplanting wild ginseng seedlings, taught to him by a ninth grader who was not a very good student in school. Yet, in his own cultural and environmental domains this student was very skillful and an accomplished teacher. He was well informed about the woods, growing cycles, and the times and locations for planting to obtain the best results. The student presented this information without rancor or joy over the teacher's lack of knowledge about something he himself had mastered as a small child. He simply shared his world and knowledge with an outsider who was respectful of them, wanted to know more, and acknowledged his ability to satisfy these needs—that is, to teach. The lessons were conducted with the ease, quality, confidence, and assurance that come naturally with competence.

The Foxfire project also is a graphic example of the positive benefits for ethnically diverse students when academic and cultural knowledge and skills are integrated in teaching. The students learned standard English and language arts skills in the process of collecting and reporting data on their cultural communities, customs, and artifacts. They were taught units on grammar, formal letter writing, poetry, interviewing, superstitions, writing for clarity, and magazine and newspaper production. Some of the first products published in the *Foxfire* magazine and books resulted from homework assignments associated with these units. Wigginton (1985) also gave the students the Georgia state language arts learning objectives (i.e., standards). He then asked them to determine where these existed in the real world and how people used them on a daily basis. The students used their transcriptions of the oral histories they collected from local residents to practice the academic language arts standards. In the following statement, Wigginton explains how the students developed

English skills as they documented their cultural attributes, traditions, beliefs, and practices:

> English, in its simplest definition, is communication—reaching out and touching people with words, sounds, and visual images.... In their work with photography,... text (which must be grammatically correct except in the use of pure dialect from tapes that they transcribe), lay-out, make-up, [correspondence], art and cover design, and selection of manuscripts from [outside] poets and writers...my students learn more about English than from any other curriculum I could devise. (p. 13)

Furthermore, Foxfire actualized the culturally responsive teaching principle of helping ethnically diverse students develop knowledge, appreciation, and pride in their own cultural heritages. This was lacking in many of the participating students, as is the case with some members of other ethnic groups (especially those of color and poverty) today. Often cultural ignorance is accompanied by shame, embarrassment, and prejudice toward self and others. Wigginton thought studying their own cultures would counteract these attitudes for his Appalachian students by accommodating the interests and abilities of individuals with different skills, turning a positive spotlight onto their cultural backgrounds, making them active procurers and conservationists of their own culture, and prompting self-reflection. He assumed that out of these experiences would come

> a genuine appreciation for roots and heritage and family.... [The] kind of resonance that comes—and vibrates in one's soul like a guitar string—with an understanding of *family*—who I am and where I'm from and the fact that I'm part of a long continuum of hope and prayer and celebration of life that I must carry forward. (Wigginton, 1985, p. 75)

All students need to know thoroughly and embrace genuinely these kinds of cultural history and affinity for their own ethnic groups. They are necessary foundations for extending similar courtesies to other groups, strong antidotes (although not total panaceas) to prejudices and biases toward those who are culturally different, and powerful stimulants for school-based learning.

The *Foxfire* magazines and books that the students produced encompassed very laudable literacy achievements, but they were not the most profound in Wigginton's (1985) estimation. Even greater accomplishments were the overall effects of the experiences on the students. Their performance on a multitude of high-order academic skills increased radically (including mastery of English mechanics and writing skills, community-based data collection, decision making, and collaborative leadership and accountability); their self-confidence, and cultural pride soared; truancy and school nonattendance virtually disappeared; and the students became a "collection of reasonably whole human beings working and sharing and learning together" (p. 115). Although the students who participated in Foxfire were not academically gifted and talented, they learned the meaning of community and embraced their societal obligations to themselves, others, and the community as a whole. They also could do what employers desire—that is, analyze situations coherently, with depth and clarity, maneuver around obstacles, be self-motivated and show initiative, and work with others to advance the common good (Knapp, 1993).

Culturally Responsive Literacy Through Ethnically Specific Institutions

Teaching culturally responsive literacy is not restricted to individual families and classroom teachers. It also can occur at the institutional level, both within the educational enterprise and various ethnic communities (such as social services, child care, or religious and cultural agencies). Prominent examples are schools, colleges, universities, and programs of study in the United States established for the express purpose of meeting the educational needs of particular ethnic groups (such as Native Americans and African Americans). Illustrative of K–12 institutions designed for particular ethnic groups (hence, *ethnic heritage programs and schools*) are Rock Point and Rough Rock Community demonstration schools of the Navajo Nation; Afrocentric programs and schools such as the Afrocentric Educational Academy in Minneapolis, the Meadows-Livingston School in San Francisco, and the Malcolm X Academy in Detroit; the Kamehameha Early Education Program (KEEP), a language arts intervention for Native Hawaiians; and the el Puente Academy for Peace and Justice for Latinos in Brooklyn. Community colleges in ethnically diverse, densely populated areas routinely exhibit some elements of culturally responsive teaching. These are apparent in the design and delivery of relevant curriculum, instruction, and support services for various ethnic constituencies from underrepresented groups, linguistically diverse backgrounds, recent immigration experiences, and individuals who were academically challenged in or dropped out of high school.

Two examples of culturally responsive literacy development in higher education are included here as reminders that this need and intervention are not limited to K–12 schools. The first case describes two Native American heritage colleges—Haskell Indian Nations University in Kansas and Dine College on the Navajo Reservation. Haskell is a four-year intertribal institution and one of the 34 federally recognized tribal colleges and universities (TCUs) located in 13 states (mostly Midwestern U.S.) that serve over 30,000 students. Haskell enrolls students from 160 tribal groups and is committed to empowering Native American and Native Alaskan scholars for leadership and service to native communities and the world. This is accomplished by promoting sovereignty and self-determination through culturally based holistic learning environments and programs that uphold traditional American Indian and Alaskan Native cultural values of respect, cooperation, honesty, and communal responsibility (www .haskell.edu; McCarty, 2002). The programs of study offered at Haskell combine "the intellectual, physical, social, emotional, and spiritual components of American Indian life into a unique university experience" (www.haskell.edu, n.p.). Part of this uniqueness is requiring all students to take courses in American Indian/Native Alaskan citizenship and contemporary issues, along with general liberal arts and the requirements of specific degree specializations (education, business, sociology, psychology, computer science, etc.) typically taught by universities. Some of the cultural citizenship courses are Environmental Protection in Indian Country; Indian Law and Legislation; Indian Real Estate and Land Management; Fundamentals of Tribal Sovereignty; Tribal Resources and Economic Development; Cherokee and Choctaw Languages; as well as American Indian poetry, painting, film, history, rhetoric, literature, and educational philosophy courses (www.haskell.edu).

Similar missions and programs exist at Dine College of the Navajo Nation. It offers a Dine Culture Curriculum that teaches cultural heritage and a wide range of language literacy skills such as Navajo as a second language; Navajo literature, legends, and stories; Navajo linguistics; and Navajo public speaking. The philosophy of the institution is to offer learning experiences that foster social responsibility, community service, and scholarly research that contribute to the social, economic, and cultural well-being of the Navajo Nation (www.dine college.edu). The programs of study are designed to exemplify Dine cultural values and beliefs that "place human life in harmony with the natural universe," with the expected outcome for students being "efficacy, self-confidence, responsibility, critical thinking, and courage to act" (Duval, 2005, p. 5). The hope is that this teaching will develop a stronger sense of kinship, a deeper respect and more genuine pride among students for their own cultures and those of other clans within the Navajo Nation. These values and expected outcomes are considered *essential cultural literacy* for members, and for others who wish to understand Navajo culture.

The second institutional case of culturally responsive literacy development in higher education includes Historically Black Colleges and Universities (HBCUs). They have a long legacy and impressive record of successfully teaching a wide variety of literacies for African Americans, including academic, disciplinary, cultural, civic responsibility, leadership, modeling and mentoring, and personal caring. There are now approximately 100 of these institutions across 20 states, Washington, D.C., and the Virgin Islands. I asked 10 graduates of HBCUs to explain why these institutions are successful in educating African Americans. They had attended a wide range of colleges in different states at different times, and focused on different areas of study. However, there were some common themes across institutional, temporal, and individual contexts. The stories these HBCU alumni tell are too extensive to include here in their entirety, so only a few short excerpts are provided.

All 10 individuals agreed that HBCUs are diligent about meeting the *multidimensional needs* of students by promoting positive growth in intellectual functioning, personal self-esteem, psychosocial development, cultural competence, and economic productivity (Fleming, 1984). These achievements occur because HBCUs are committed to educating the whole person. One student recalled that she and her peers at Tougaloo College were repeatedly reminded by their teachers that they were intellectually the cream of the crop (i.e., the academic vanguard) and, as such they were expected to contribute to the betterment of the local, state, and national African American communities and causes. They were taught that responsibilities come with their intellectual and educational privilege as college students. These involved doing something to help less fortunate African Americans—such as volunteer community service—and participating in political activism. The moral edict underlying this teaching, according to students at Tougaloo and Spelman College can be summarized in the adage, "To whom much is given, much is required."

Swygert (1995), the President of Howard University, shared some insights about what happens on HBCU campuses that facilitates these kinds of achievements and accomplishments:

> It is at these institutions that our [African Americans'] identity as a people and our ancestors' achievements are illuminated, where we explore the "self" and the "other," where...we begin the arduous journey in preparing ourselves for survival in a society which is "ours" and, yet, not "ours," where we impart to students the moral

imperatives which will sustain and guide them in times of despair and reflection, where we prepare students not only for professions and careers, but to be caring and informed men and women. (p. v)

Another student did not take any specific courses on African American history and culture at Grambling State University, but she was immersed in an environment where African Americans were visible and their contributions celebrated. Learning in a culturally rich and validating environment improved her ethnic pride and personal self-acceptance, which, in turn, had positive effects on her academic achievement. This was a critical form of cultural literacy for this young woman because she arrived at college with ambivalent feelings about her ethnicity and limited formal cultural knowledge of African Americans. Her experience at Grambling pulled her out of these feelings of ambiguity, uncertainty, and ignorance, and "hooked her up" with her own culture, ethnicity, and other African Americans as she learned the knowledge required for her selected area of academic study.

Students' cultural literacy was more explicit at Tougaloo, where African American heritage and contributions to the state of Mississippi and the national Civil Rights movement were stressed. All students were required to take courses in African American history and culture. Students at Spelman received overt instructions in African American culture as well. One student recalled a yearlong required course on "African Diaspora in the World." It included examinations of interactions between Black men and women, cultural knowledge, and a variety of readings about African and African American histories, cultures, experiences, and societies. This learning experience validated this student's ethnic and cultural identities and helped her develop a strong sense of self, which relieved her from the burden of feeling she always had to shield her racial and ethnic identity from derogatory attacks from mainstream society.

Another student did not experience that particular course at Spelman (having attended several years before it was instituted), but African American culture was still a vital and pervasive feature of her education. She remembered learning about Black women in the Bible, historical individuals who were strong social activists, and being reminded to always be ladylike because high-profile dignitaries and visitors were frequently on campus. The students at Spelman were expected to follow the example of their predecessors by making significant accomplishments and carrying on the legacy of success. A male student had similar expectations, teachings, and encounters at Morehouse College. Being a "Morehouse Man" was a badge of honor and everyone was taught to give the identity the respect it deserved by demonstrating high-quality academic accomplishment, social decorum, impeccable public persona, and active political engagement. Another male student also remembered fondly Southern University socializing him and other students to look, behave, and dress in a manner becoming African American college men and women.

The comments of these alumni speak powerfully to Davis's (1998) contention that HBCUs are sites for explicitly teaching African American cultural and social capital, because the students acquire cultural knowledge and establish cultural and community connections along with academic achievement. Their programs of study, teaching styles, and learning environments include various strategies from "the more explicit, direct instruction of proper etiquette and public social behavior, to the less obvious integration of African American literature and history in the curriculum" (p. 149). Consequently, HBCUs are compelling examples of culturally responsive literacy teaching praxis.

Infinite Possibilities

The discussions in this chapter view literacy broadly as being of many different kinds and as operating on multiple levels of competence and complexity. One of these categories of literacy is cultural competence in its own right and as a complement to academic and subject-specific knowledge and skills. Another conception argues that all literacies are easier and more effectively learned by ethnically and racially diverse students when they are taught within different cultural contexts. In other words, literacy learning is strongly influenced by the sociocultural ecology in which it occurs. The conceptual principles and practices presented are only a few samples of the many variations of culturally responsive literacy development. They demonstrate that academic (i.e., reading, writing, critical thing, problem solving) and cultural (i.e., knowledge, pride, respect, heritage) literacies can be taught in concert. When this is done, the achievement of students is better in both.

Several practical messages about teaching academic and cultural literacy to ethnically diverse students of color in PreK–college education are worth underscoring:

- Both students and teachers should acquire more knowledge about the cultures, histories, and contributions of the ethnic groups of which the United States is comprised.

- Teachers should use culturally and ethnically diverse examples, materials, experiences, and perspectives as contexts for teaching and as embodiments of academic or school-based literacies.

- Teachers should apply academic literacies in the process of teaching and learning about cultural diversity.

- Teachers should actively engage ethnically diverse students in constructing and directing their own learning, including identifying literacy needs and factors that obstruct and facilitate learning them.

- Teachers should use multiple techniques that are informed by knowledge of *specific* ethnic and cultural differences to teach all kinds of literacy skills.

- Teachers should teach skills needed to modify, select, or identify academic and cultural literacies appropriate for different contexts, purposes, audiences, and interactions.

- Teachers should serve as collaborators, resources, facilitators, and cultural brokers for ethnically diverse students, not merely repositories of academic knowledge.

- Teachers should create learning communities in which the progress of each ethnically, racially, and culturally diverse student is the concern and responsibility of every student as well as the teacher.

- Teachers should always model or demonstrate for students what various academic and cultural literacies look like in actual practice independently and in conjunction with one another.

- Teachers should teach ethnically diverse students of color skills for crossing borders among different cultural systems (such as families, schools, and communities) without compromising their own indigenous cultures.

- Teachers should learn how to access the cultural literacies, or funds of knowledge, taught in ethnically and culturally diverse families and communities and should use them as scaffolds in teaching school-based literacies.

To accomplish these goals, teachers need to know and accept African, Asian, European, Latino, and Native ancestry students as specific cultural beings and should use this knowledge to guide the design and implementation of literacy programs and practices for them. Knowledge of subject matter, the laws of learning, and skills for teaching school literacies are givens, but they alone will not guarantee successful literacy learning (or other aspects of education) for culturally, ethnically, and socially diverse students. Cultural competence on the part of both students and teachers, and about self and others, is imperative, too. Teachers must be diligent, creative, and transformative in these pursuits. As Ayers (2004) explains,

> A primary challenge to teachers is to see each student as a three-dimensional creature, a person much like themselves, with hopes, dreams, aspirations, skills, and capabilities;...with experience, history, a past, several possible pathways, a future. This...requires patience, curiosity, wonder, awe, humility. It demands sustained focus, intelligent judgment, inquiry and investigation..... This, then, is an intellectual task of serious and huge proportions. (p. 3)

When cultural competence is added to academic knowledge and skills, the literacy learning for ethnically diverse students grows exponentially. All educators should understand these relationships and benefits and their instructional implications for making literacy learning more enticing and empowering for Asian, African, Latino, Native, and European American students from a wide range of experiential backgrounds, varying degrees of ethnic and cultural affiliation, and different levels of intellectual ability. Once this is done, the possibilities for teaching and learning what, how, and for whom are infinite.

REFERENCES

Ayers, W. (2004). *Teaching the personal and the political: Essays on hope and justice*. New York: Teachers College Press.

Davis, J.E. (1998). Cultural capital and the role of historically Black colleges and universities in educational reproduction. In K. Freeman (Ed.), *African American culture and heritage in higher education research and practice* (pp. 143–153). Westport, CT: Praeger.

Duval, C.A. (2005). Navajo bilingual and cultural education programs: Will the Navajo be able to revitalize and maintain their language and culture? *Journal of the Faculty of International Studies, 15*(2), 77–89.

Edwards, A., & Polite, C.K. (1992). *Children of the dream: The psychology of Black success*. New York: Doubleday.

Fleming, J. (1984). *Blacks in college: A comparative study of students' success in Black and White institutions*. San Francisco: Jossey-Bass.

Gay, G. (2000). *Culturally responsive teaching: Theory, research, and practice*. New York: Teachers College Press.

Gay, G., & Kirkland, K. (2003). Developing cultural critical consciousness and self-reflection in preservice teacher education. *Theory Into Practice, 42*(3), 181–187.

González, N., Moll, L.C., & Amanti C. (Eds.). (2005). *Funds of knowledge: Theorizing practices in households, communities, and classrooms*. Mahwah, NJ: Erlbaum.

Holliday, L. (1999). *Children of the dream: Our own stories of growing up black in America*. New York: Pocket.

Knapp, C.E. (1993). An interview with Eliot Wigginton: Reflecting on the Foxfire approach. *Phi Delta Kappan, 74*(10), 779–782.

Lake, R. (1990). An Indian father's plea. *Teacher Magazine, 2*(1), 48–53.

Lee, C.D. (2005). Intervention research based on current views of cognition and learning. In J.E. King (Ed.), *Black education: A transformative research and action agenda for the new century* (pp. 73–114). Mahwah, NJ: Erlbaum.

McCarty, T.L. (2002). *A place to be Navajo: Rough Rock and the struggle for self-determination in indigenous schooling.* Mahwah, NJ: Erlbaum.

Moll, L.C., & González, N. (2004). Engaging life: A funds-of-knowledge approach to multicultural education. In J.A. Banks & C.A. McGee Banks (Eds.), *Handbook of research on multicultural education* (2nd ed., pp. 699–715). San Francisco: Jossey-Bass.

Puckett, J.L. (1989). *Foxfire reconsidered: A twenty-year experiment in progressive education.* Urbana: University of Illinois Press.

Seale, D., & Stapin, B. (Eds.). (2005). *A broken flute: The native experience in books for children.* Walnut Creek, CA: AltaMira.

Swygert, H.P. (1995). Foreword. In *White House Initiative on Historically Black Colleges and Universities* (pp. v–vi). New York: Arco.

Wigginton, E. (1985). *Sometimes a shining moment: The Foxfire experience.* New York: Doubleday.

Wigginton, E. (1989). Foxfire grows up. *Harvard Educational Review, 59*(1), 24–49.

Wigginton, E. (1991). *Foxfire: 25 years.* New York: Doubleday.

CHAPTER 8

The Role of Family Literacy Programs in the School Success or Failure of African American Families and Children

Patricia A. Edwards

Two African American leaders made poignant statements about the importance of literacy: "Once you learn to read, you will be forever free" (Frederick Douglass) and "If you can't read, it's going to be hard to realize dreams" (Booker T. Washington). For many African Americans, the freedom and dreams to which Douglass and Washington refer have not been realized as a result of their failure in school as children. Nevertheless, Gadsden (1993) states that "literacy and education are valued and valuable possessions that African American families have respected, revered, and sought as a means to personal freedom and communal hope, from enslavement to the present" (p. 29). And few would disagree that education is the key to success and parents are educators' greatest allies (Edwards, 2004, 2009a; Epstein, 2001; Lawrence-Lightfoot, 2003). Irvine (1991) argues that for African American parents, their role as teachers in the home is "crucial" and is the one role directly related to the achievement of African American students. Unfortunately, the role of culturally and linguistically diverse parents in their children's education in family literacy programs is a source of conflict and controversy (Edwards & Turner, 2009). In this chapter, I illuminate the fact that some poor African American parents know how to help their children and others do not. I begin by providing an overview of the literature on the importance of parents' reading to their children. I raise questions as to what should be done in cases where poor African American parents do not know how to read to their children. Next, I challenge

From *Bringing Literacy Home* edited by KaiLonnie Dunsmore and Douglas Fisher.
© 2010 by the International Reading Association.

the critics of family literacy programs that "educate" parents, especially poor African American parents, on how to read to their children. Following this, I highlight the voices of poor African American parents who participated in a family literacy program. I conclude by offering a new dialogic discourse, a model of change called *pedagogy of cultural reciprocity*, which suggests that different practices, values, traditions, understandings, and ideologies are reconfigured and acquired by both school and home agencies. This model of change provides the mechanism for schools and families to assume shared responsibilities for the socialization and education of children. This model also assumes that teachers and parents will share common goals for their children that are achieved most effectively when teachers and parents work together.

Not All Poor African American Parents Are the Same

The school, according to Comer (1993), is an instrument of the mainstream culture. Indeed, schools—public schools at least—not only inculcate the middle class, middle income culture but they are also designed to shape and mold students to fit that culture. Yet, many poor families are not really a part of that culture; as a result, they send children to school ill-prepared to learn within the cultural model of learning the school employs. The children lack the values, attitudes, beliefs, and communicative styles upon which the school is built and which the school uses to teach the child. Such children are often hopelessly behind when they start school. However, I know that this is not the case for all poor African American school children. Sampson (2004) is quick to point out that "some poor Blacks...appear to be middle class and do many of the things that seem to be important for good academic performance for their children, while others are not and do not" (p. 12).

Clark (1983) makes detailed observations on the quality of home life, noting how family habits and interactions affect school success and which characteristics of family life provide children with school survival skills, a complex set of behaviors, attitudes, and knowledge that are the essential elements in academic success. Corno (1989) describes these school survival skills as becoming literate about classrooms. Of course, the parents of these students can and should assist them with the process of developing these school survival skills, which leads their children to becoming literate about classrooms. Corno notes,

The term *classroom literacy* can be used to denote a state of being literate about classrooms. Just as we can be literate about subject matter such as science, art, or history, so we can be literate about events, people, and places like classrooms. Being literate about classrooms means being able to read classrooms as texts. As with any text, the text of a classroom may be read at many levels. Students who are literate about classrooms will "read" them at a higher semantic level than those who are not. (p. 29)

Clark's (1983) research is an excellent example of how parents helped their children develop school survival skills and become literate about classrooms. He reports that high achieving African American students had parents who did the following:

- Were assertive in their parent involvement efforts
- Kept abreast of their children's school progress
- Were optimistic and tended to perceive themselves as having effective coping mechanisms and strategies
- Set high and realistic expectations for their children
- Held positive achievement orientations and supported tenets of the achievement ideology
- Set clear, explicit achievement-oriented norm
- Established clear, specific role boundaries
- Deliberately engaged in experiences and behaviors designed to promote achievement
- Had positive parent-child relations characterized by nurturance, support, respect, trust, and open communication

Conversely, underachieving African American students had parents who were less optimistic and expressed feelings of helplessness and hopelessness, were less assertive and involved in their children's education, set unrealistic and unclear expectations for their children, and were less confident in terms of their parenting skills. Sampson (2002) concurs with Clark (1983) by saying that "differences in family dynamics and/or home environment account for the differences in school performance" (p. vii).

Taylor, Pearson, Clark, and Walpole (2000) report in their work with low-income schools that beat the odds that a large number of African American parents were involved in their children's literacy lives. They further reported that teachers in the most effective schools realized that good communication and collaboration, found among the staff, must also extend to the parents of the children in their schools. However, when African American parents are not involved, I believe that schools should create an opportunity for them to participate and support their opportunity to do so. Family literacy training provides that opportunity for some poor African American parents to learn how to help their children, especially with how to read to them.

Over 15 years ago, I provided such a type of validated and flexible solution. I assisted parents at Donaldsonville Elementary School in Louisiana in learning how to participate in effective book-reading interactions with their children. The program involved defining for parents the participatory skills and behaviors found in effective parent–child reading interactions. I gave the parents the opportunity to reinforce important learning concepts and skills at home. More important, what I learned from these parents was how uncomfortable they felt when teachers asked them to read to their children. The comments that follow represent the feelings and emotions of the Donaldsonville Elementary School parents.

> I'm embarrassed, scared, angry, and feel completely helpless because I can't read. I do care 'bout my children and I want them to do well in school. Why don't them teachers believe me when I say I want the best for my children? I know that my children ain't done well in kindergarten and first grade and had to repeat them grades. My older children are in the lowest sections, in Title 1, and are struggling in their subjects. My children are frustrated, and I am frustrated, too. I don't know how to help them especially when the teacher wants me to read to them. These teachers think that reading to children is so easy and simple, but it's hard if you don't know how to read yourself. (Edwards, 1995a, p. 54)

The Importance of Parent–Child Book Reading: An Overview

Despite the fact that educators and researchers have spent more than 30 years trying to explain why African American children continue to lag behind Caucasian children in reading achievement, the enigma persists—why are large numbers of African American children not learning to read? Several educators and researchers have suggested that the problem may lie in the fact that many economically and educationally disadvantaged children enter school with little or no knowledge of books. In response to this claim, reading educators have suggested that one way to help these children is by encouraging their parents to read aloud to them.

In *Becoming a Nation of Readers: The Report of the Commission on Reading*, the authors state that "parents play roles of inestimable importance in laying the foundations for learning to read" (Anderson, Hiebert, Scott, & Wilkinson, 1985, p. 57). Adams (1990), in her extensive review, identifies reading aloud to children as one of the most important activities for building the skills necessary for early reading. She also estimates that children who are read to for approximately 30 minutes each night will have acquired 1,000 hours of print exposure when they begin kindergarten. This extensive print exposure is seen as an important prerequisite for children to begin to understand the phonemic structure of language and to readily identify letters. Mahoney and Wilcox (1985) conclude,

> If a child comes from a reading family where books are a shared source of pleasure, he or she will have an understanding of the language of the literacy world and respond to the use of books in a classroom as a natural expansion of pleasant home experiences. (p. ix)

Few would question the importance of reading aloud to children, but a number of researchers have questioned the feasibility of teachers requesting that parents read to their children when the parents themselves are unable to read. The simple request made by the teacher, "Read to your child," can be a nightmare to parents who cannot read—invoking feelings of despair, inadequacy, frustration, and fear (Edwards, 1995a, 1995b). According to Chall, Heron, and Hilferty (1987), 27 million Americans cannot read a bedtime story to a child. They describe functional illiteracy as an epidemic having reached 1 out of 5 Americans: Illiteracy "robs them of a decent living...of the simplest of human pleasures, like reading a fairy tale to a child" (p. 90). France and Meeks (1987) also argue that

> parents who do have basic literacy skills are greatly handicapped in meeting the challenge of creating a "curriculum of the home" to prepare their children to succeed in school. Furthermore, they can't help their children build a foundation for literacy because they are unable to read to them. (p. 222)

If it has taken researchers more than 30 years to try to explain why African American children continue to lag behind Caucasian children in reading achievement, one can reasonably assume that those children who were subjects in the early studies are now parents and grandparents. One could also argue that if the parents' experiences with school were unsuccessful, there is a strong possibility that their children's experiences with school will be unsuccessful. Consequently, the question raised by France and Meeks (1987) is extremely important: What, then, can be done to help illiterate and semiliterate parents give their children the support they need to be successful readers? My response to this question is the development of family literacy programs. However, I have a second question: Why has it been so difficult for educators to include illiterate and semiliterate parents in the educational process?

A Possible Explanation

Educators have heard many conflicting messages about how to work with families, especially related to family literacy programs. Gadsden (1994) summarizes some of the tensions surrounding family literacy and examines the disagreement and dissension that characterizes work in family literacy as emerging from two seriously conflicting premises: one that perceives the family's lack of school-like literacy as a barrier to learning, and the other that sees the home literacy practices that are already present—however different they may be from school-based literacy—as a bridge to new learning. Rather than choosing sides in the debate, however, Gadsden argues that both premises may be useful. She suggests that educators might adopt a reciprocal approach, predicated on an understanding that teachers need to instruct parents in school-based literacy and also seek to learn about parents' existing knowledge and resources to integrate those into school curricula.

While Gadsden (1994) outlines many of the tensions in the field of family literacy, I believe it is necessary to highlight some of the frameworks that researchers have proposed with regard to working with families. I have found three research-based courses of actions, which I have categorized (see Edwards, 2003) by drawing upon the framework of Wiley (1996): *accommodation, incorporation,* and *adaptation.*

> *Accommodation* requires teachers, supervisors, personnel officers, and gatekeepers to have a better understanding of the communicative styles and literacy practices of their students. (p. 148)
>
> *Incorporation* requires researchers to study community practices that have not been valued previously by the schools, and to incorporate them into the curriculum. It also means surrendering a privileged position by acknowledging that something can be learned from other ethnic groups. (pp. 148–149)

Adaptation involves the expectation that children and adults who are held to have substandard knowledge and skills will acculturate or learn to match or measure up to the norms of those who control the schools, institutions, and workplace. (p. 147)

As one would expect, there is strong research support for each of these courses of action. Supporters of accommodation argue that "literacy learning begins in the home, not the school, and that instruction should build on the foundation for literacy learning established in the home" (Au, 1993, p. 35). Research has shown that even in conditions of extreme poverty, homes can be rich in print, and family members may engage in literacy activities of many kinds on a daily basis (Anderson & Stokes, 1984; Heath, 1983; Purcell-Gates, 1996; Taylor & Dorsey-Gaines, 1988; Teale, 1986).

Over the past few years, teacher educators have developed strategies to prepare preservice teachers to accommodate students and families. These preparatory strategies include autobiographies (Florio-Ruane, 2001), personal life stories (Fry & McKinney, 1997); cultural self-analysis (Schmidt, 1998), photos of local knowledge sources (Allen & Labbo, 2001), and early field experiences (Jones & Blendinger, 1994; Lazar & Weisberg, 1996). In my opinion, the accommodation course of action seems extremely one-sided—it offers few resources to parents and seems to be built upon the naïve assumption that culturally sensitized teachers will be able to make up for learning experiences, opportunities, and resources that may be missing in the lives of some children. This may lead to early disillusionment for many new and experienced teachers when they realize that, despite their sensitivity, their students still don't achieve at the level of middle class counterparts.

The second course of action, incorporation, has been well supported by the research community. It is argued, for example, that "teachers and parents need to understand the way each defines, values, and uses literacy as part of cultural practices. Such mutual understanding offers the potential for schooling to be adjusted to meet the needs of families" (Cairney, 1997, p. 70). It also has been advocated that

as educators we must not assume that we can only teach the families how to do school, but that we can learn valuable lessons by coming to know the families, and by taking the time to establish the social relationships necessary to create personal links between households and classrooms. (Moll, 1999, p. xiii)

According to Wiley (1996), "surrendering a privileged position by acknowledging that something can be learned from other groups need not be taken as a retreat from high standards nor as imposing a hardship on the children of the middle-class" (p. 149). However, he warns, "In order for incorporation to occur, teachers need knowledge of the language, communication styles, and literacy practices of their students" (p. 149). He admits that schools encounter logistical challenges in using incorporation and that Heath's (1983) suggestion of turning teachers into learners and students into ethnographers "is no simple task; Heath's own efforts involved years of community and school ethnographic work" (Wiley, p. 150). While schools and classroom teachers might agree that it would be beneficial to have knowledge of the language, communication, styles and literacy practices of *all* their students, in reality it would be nearly impossible to gain this much needed knowledge during a nine-month school year.

From the last course of action, adaptation, has emerged controversy and conflict concerning how families should be involved in their children's literacy development and what they need to know to be effective partners in literacy. Supporters of adaptation claim that many poor, minority, and immigrant parents want to give their children linguistic, social, and cultural capital to deal in the marketplace of schools (Gallimore, Weisner, Kaufman, & Bernheimer, 1989; Super & Harkness, 1986). They also have suggested that "when schools fail to provide parents with factual, empowering information and strategies for supporting their child's learning, the parents are even more likely to feel ambivalence as educators [of their own children]" (Clark, 1988, p. 95).

Supporters of the adaptation approach recognize that there are multiple activities in addition to reading aloud that help children become better readers and successful students; telling stories and singing songs also may encourage the acquisition of literacy skills (Glazer, 1989; Moss & Fawcett, 1995; National Education Goals Panel, 1997; Sonnenschein, Brody, & Munsterman, 1996). Key adaptation studies, however, have focused on ways of showing parents how to read to their children or assist them with school-like literacy events (Darling & Hayes, 1988; Edwards, 1993; Handel, 1992; Rodriguez-Brown, Li, & Albom, 1999; Winter & Rouse, 1990). This group of researchers recognizes that while the importance of parent–child book reading has been chronicled in reading research (Andersonet al., 1985; Doake, 1986; Gallimore & Goldenberg, 1989; Huey, 1908; Teale, 1981), an extensive body of research also exists describing the difficulties lower socioeconomic status (SES) parents have in sharing books with their young children (Farran, 1982; Heath, 1982a, 1982b, 1986; Heath,

Branscombe, & Thomas, 1985; Heath & Thomas, 1984; McCormick & Mason, 1986; Ninio, 1980; Snow & Ninio, 1986).

What I found in my 1989 study titled "Supporting Lower SES Mothers' Attempts to Provide Scaffolding for Book Reading" is that book reading is a very simple teacher directive but a very complex and difficult task for some parents (see Edwards, 1989). I put forth the argument that to simply inform parents of the importance of reading to their children is not sufficient. Instead, we must go beyond *telling* to *showing* lower socioeconomic parents how to participate in parent–child book-reading interactions with their children and support their attempts to do.

The adaptation approach has lead to the creation of family literacy programs that train parents how to read to their children while creating controversy over the nature of that training. Some researchers have warned that there is a danger that this approach leads to "blaming the victim" (Cairney, 1997; García, 1994; Nieto, 1992; Shockley, 1994; Street, 1995). Another claim is that this approach communicates a deficit model of learning development and ignores that literacy is embedded in home life (Anderson & Stokes, 1984; Erickson, 1989; Hearron, 1992; Taylor & Dorsey-Gaines, 1988). It also has been suggested that family literacy educational programs imply that the homes of poor, minority, and immigrant children are lacking in literacy (Anderson & Stokes, 1984; Auerbach, 1989; Chall & Snow, 1982; Delgado-Gaitán, 1987; Erickson, 1989; Goldenberg, 1984), or that these programs fail to recognize that "literacy is not something which can be pasted on to family life, it is deeply embedded within it" (Macleod, 1996, p. 130). Another criticism is that parent training programs "have perpetuated the 'we know, you don't know' dichotomy" (Shockley, 1994, p. 500).

As an African American scholar who developed a family literacy program embedded within an adaptation perspective and who has trained parents to read to their children, I question the criticisms raised by these researchers:

> Where have researchers' fears, doubts, reservations come from? What do researchers think these parents are being "forced" to read? Does evidence exist where researchers have interviewed parents who have attended these family literacy programs? Is it fair for researchers to insert their own personal feelings about parents participating in family literacy programs without highlighting parents' voices, perceptions, and evaluations? Are researchers' fears, doubts, and reservations justified? (Edwards, 1995c, p. 562)

Further, I would argue that these criticisms are not justified because children have to understand how to function within the "culture of power" to do well in school (Delpit, 1988). Auerbach (1989) agrees that "authority is vested in those belonging to the mainstream culture, the literacy practices of the mainstream become the norm and have higher status in school contexts" (p. 173). Children in academic families are familiar with cultural capital and the culture of literacy, making it easier for them to adapt to the literacy environment of school:

> They already know, or acquire implicitly as they develop, the varying registers of written language with the accompanying "ways of meaning" and "ways of saying," the vocabulary, the syntax, the intentionality. This makes learning the "new" so much easier. (Purcell-Gates, 1996, pp. 182–183)

I recognize that elementary and secondary education alone cannot solve the problems of educating the nation's youngsters for the 21st century. Also, I recognize that the critical role of the home and family must be addressed to break the cycle of illiteracy and improve economic circumstances for youngsters. At the 1996 annual meeting of the International Reading Association, former U.S. Secretary of Education Richard W. Riley echoed my thoughts when he issued this challenge in his keynote address:

> My friends, it's time to get serious. The dumbing down of American education must end. If children need extra help to measure up, they should get it. Let's provide tutors, and call in the families, or keep the schools open late and open in the summer, too, if we must. But whatever we do, let's end this tyranny of low expectation once and for all. Illiteracy is the ball and chain that ties us to poverty. We must smash it forever.

My way of smashing illiteracy was to develop two family literacy programs: *Parents as Partners in Reading: A Family Literacy Training Program* (see Edwards, 1990a, 1993) and *Talking Your Way to Literacy: A Program to Help Nonreading Parents Prepare Their Children for Reading* (see Edwards, 1990b). I had no idea, however, that my work—which exposed poor parents and children to trade books as well as to school-like interaction styles, such as labeling pictures and labeling letters—would receive such a strong reaction from the research community. In short, because my work took a decidedly adaptive approach, I was criticized for implying that something was wrong, or deficient, with the ways in which parents socialize their children (Pellegrini, 1991).

As an African American researcher, I am amazed that there has been such a heated debate over the issue of whether parents, and especially poor, African American parents, should receive assistance in how to participate in one-on-one interactions with their children. Researchers agree that parents are their children's first teachers, especially with respect to reading (Edwards, 2004; Taylor & Strickland, 1986), that book reading is the parent involvement activity most frequently requested by teachers (Edwards, 2004; Vukelich, 1984), that parents needs to understand that storybook reading is the cornerstone of reading instruction in the early grades (Adams, 1990; Edwards, 2003; Edwards & Garcia, 1991; Taylor & Strickland, 1986), and that

> parents, [especially poor African American parents] have the right to know that sharing books with their children may be the most powerful and significant predictor of school achievement. Not only do they have the right to know, they have the right to receive assistance in how to participate in book reading interactions with their young children. (Edwards, 1991, p. 211)

Due to the fact that there is overwhelming evidence that one-on-one parent–child interactions are correlated with school success for middle class children, we should assist poor African American parents and children in participating in successful one-one-one book-reading interactions. Researchers who are uncomfortable with family literacy programs that train poor African American parents how to share books with their children should respect the fact that some minority researchers are just as nervous and upset when researchers insist on neither informing nor assisting poor African American parents in how to share books with their children. Further, the present-day achievement gap between African American and Caucasian children that places African American children educationally at risk dictates that something must be done to assure improved educational outcomes for those children (Hale-Benson, 1990).

Reflecting on critiques of my work, I thought of historian and civil rights activist DuBois (1990), who wrote of the plight of African Americans prior to desegregation. He commented that a European American need only be conscious of what it was like to be white, a life without restrictions based on race. However, African American men and women needed to have what he called a "double-consciousness," to know what it was to be black and know the associated limitations, but also to know the life of white people as different and less limiting than their own.

I believe in the adaptation approach, because children who live outside the mainstream of American life are precious human cargo and do not have time to wait until researchers find plausible answers about accommodating and incorporating their literacy practices into the school curriculum. While we patiently wait for answers from the research community, these families and children are forced to develop a "double consciousness" of how to negotiate the borders between home and school.

Personally speaking, in my journey of developing a "double consciousness," I did not perceive that my home was lacking literacy. I did not feel inferior. In fact, I felt empowered when I could move successfully between the black and white worlds. I was already succeeding at home, but my parents wanted me to succeed in school, too. African Americans have historically wanted "to ensure that school provides their children with discourse patterns, interactional styles, and spoken and written languages codes that will allow them success in the larger society" (Delpit, 1995, p. 29).

I argue that Delpit's comments have implications for helping African American families to participate in school-like literacy events. Her message also has implications for other ethnic minorities who want their children to succeed in mainstream schools (Delgado-Gaitán, 1987; Jiménez, Moll, Rodriguez-Brown, & Barrera, 1999; Purcell-Gates, 1996). The research and practitioner communities need to be sensitive to this perspective.

Parents Have Their "Say" About the Parents As Partners in Reading Family Literacy Program

The parents who participated in the family literacy program I developed at Donaldsonville Elementary School in Louisiana argued that the program served as a lifeline between their children's success and failure in school. Comments that parents shared with me during our parent–child book-reading sessions also echoed this point:

> I was so tired of teachers telling me to read to my child and assuming that I knew how to do it. The Parents as Partners in Reading program showed me how to read to my child and I feel like I'm making a difference in my child's education.

> I stopped pretending that I knew how to read to my child. I admitted to myself that I needed to take the time to participate in this program so that I could learn how to do what teachers expected me to do which is "read to my child." This program made me feel that I was my child's first teacher and now I feel more comfortable in this role.

> I've always loved to read, but I didn't read as effectively to my child as I should have. But now I know it; now I'm always reading a child's book, and I'm enjoying it because of what I've learned.

These parents appreciated that fact that the Parents as Partners in Reading program acknowledged that understanding how to read to one's children is not an innate skill. These parents' expressions reflect their relief at not having to pretend that they knew how to read or maintain a facade of what teachers imagined as at-home literacy. Instead, with the teachers in the family literacy program, these parents were discovering for themselves the joys of reading, coming to feel empowered as readers and parents, and realizing their own potentials as teachers.

Pedagogy of Cultural Reciprocity

Li (2006) builds on Winters's (1993) notion of "reciprocal enculturation" to propose a new dialogic discourse, a model of change that she calls a *pedagogy of cultural reciprocity*. In this model, Li suggests that different practices, values, traditions, understandings, and ideologies are reconfigured and acquired by both school and home agencies.

I employed the pedagogy of cultural reciprocity and helped the parents of Donaldsonville Elementary School develop "school survival skills" and become literate about classrooms. In particular, I showed them how to share books with their children and assisted them in helping their children develop word knowledge, understand the meaning of print, and increase their awareness of written letters and words. I also used Raphael's (1982) Question Answer Relationships (QAR) strategy as a way to help the Louisiana parents understand how to ask school-based questions. The book-reading strategies coupled with the QAR strategy made the schooling process for the parents culturally transparent. In another project, Dail, McGee, and I introduced a community book club to parents and teachers in a rural Mississippi community as a way to help parents become literate about classrooms (see Dail, McGee, & Edwards, 2009).

The pedagogy of cultural reciprocity has the potential to prevent comments like the one below from teachers who are frustrated with parents that they feel don't help their children, especially by sharing books with them. I often heard comments like the following about poor African American parents:

> Each year when we see parents at the beginning of the school year we tell them the same old thing, "Please read to your child at least two to three times per week. It will make a world of difference in how well your child does in school." We know the parents hear what we are saying, but we don't think they have read or plan to read one *single* book to their children. We, as kindergarten and first-grade teachers, cannot

solve all of these children's literacy problems by ourselves. The parents must help us. (Edwards, 1995c, p. 55)

Attaining Access to Cultural Capital, Freedom, and Dreams

If parents' ways of preparing children for school are significantly inconsistent with school-based literacy practices, it can create problems for children when they enter the school environment. I believe we should ask ourselves two questions if and when this situation occurs: (1) Should educators simply acknowledge that an inconsistency between home and school exists? (2) Should we attempt to develop programs to bridge the gap between home- and school-based literacy practices? I suggest the latter approach. Over 30 years ago, Leichter (1973) supported this approach:

> Cultural distance in education values between parents and teachers should be examined in two directions, asking by what processes the school reinforces, complements, contradicts, or inhibits the efforts of the family and community and by what processes the family and community reinforce, contradict, or inhibit the efforts of the school. (p. 73)

Blaming parents or schools for failure in students' literacy achievement wastes time and energy; we should support parents and teachers by helping them become familiar with school-based literacy practices—sharing books with children is one of the practices. Doing this provides parents with "the opportunity to engage the multiple references that construct different cultural codes, experiences, and histories" (Giroux, 1991, p. xiv).

The parents who participated in the family literacy programs I developed shared what they had learned in the book-reading sessions with their friends, neighbors, church members, and relatives. The program had worked itself into the daily lives of these parents and children as well as the larger community. One parent wrote an article for the local newspaper entitled "How I Can Make a Difference." An excerpt from the article follows:

> It is said that children imitate what they see, so it's up to us to show them that we, the parents, are effective teachers, in a way that provides our children with the best training possible to read. In essence a way in which I can make a difference is by taking the time out to help my daughter understand that reading is a fundamental part of our lives. (Richardson, 1988, p. 6)

The Parents as Partners in Reading program linked book reading with the contexts of families' daily lives. Parents became "sufficiently aware of their impact on their children's reading" (Pflaum, 1986, p. 10). The book-reading program became a program of empowerment rather than acculturation for these poor African American parents and children. Through the program, these parents learned what was expected of their children in school. They also became aware of what their children were capable of doing with appropriate guidance. Their own confidence in their reading ability and their ability to help their children with school activities increased. More importantly, when these parents learned to read and share books with their children, they moved closer to attaining access to the cultural capital, freedom, and dreams Frederick Douglass and Booker T. Washington spoke of.

The Parents as Partners in Reading program serves as a successful example to teachers and administrators of the importance of creating a structure for involving poor parents in their children's schooling process, especially in their development as readers and writers. Epstein (1987) asserts, "Parent involvement is everybody's job but nobody's job until a structure is put in place to support it" (p. 10). As I note, "History has shown that Blacks had to fight to become literate in this country" (Edwards, 2009b, p. 295). The Parents as Partners in Reading family literacy program provided the structure for these poor African American parents to fight to become literate for themselves and their children.

REFERENCES

Adams, M.J. (1990). *Beginning to read: Thinking and learning about print.* Cambridge, MA: MIT Press.

Allen, J., & Labbo, L. (2001). Giving it a second thought: Making culturally engaged teaching culturally engaging. *Language Arts, 79*(1), 40–52.

Anderson, A.B., & Stokes, S.J. (1984). Social and institutional influences on the development and practice of literacy. In H. Goelman, A. Oberg, & F. Smith (Eds.), *Awakening to literacy* (pp. 24–37). Exeter, NH: Heinemann.

Anderson, R.C., Hiebert, E., Scott, J.A., & Wilkinson, I.A.G. (1985). *Becoming a nation of readers: The report of the Commission on Reading.* Washington, DC: The National Institute of Education.

Au, K.H. (1993). *Literacy instruction in multicultural settings.* Forth Worth, TX: Harcourt Brace College.

Auerbach, E.R. (1989). Toward a social-contextual approach to family literacy. *Harvard Educational Review, 59*(2), 165–181.

Cairney, T.H. (1997). Acknowledging diversity in home literacy practices: Moving towards partnership with parents. *Early Child Development and Care, 127*(1), 61–73. doi:10.1080/0300443971270106

Chall, J.S., Heron, E., & Hilferty, A. (1987). Adult literacy: New and enduring problems. *Phi Delta Kappan, 69*(3), 190–196.

Chall, J.S., & Snow, C. (1982). *Families and literacy: The contribution of out-of-school experiences to children's acquisition of literacy. A final report to the National Institute of Education.*

Cambridge, MA: Harvard Graduate School of Education.

Clark, R.M. (1983). *Family life and school achievement: Why poor black children succeed or fail.* Chicago: The University of Chicago Press.

Clark, R.M. (1988). Parents as providers of linguistic and social capital. *Educational Horizons, 66*(2), 93–95.

Comer, J.P. (1993). *School power: Implications of an intervention project.* New York: Free Press.

Corno, L. (1989). What it means to be literate about classrooms. In D. Bloome (Ed.), *Classroom and literacy* (pp. 29–52). Norwood, NJ: Ablex.

Dail, A.R., McGee, L. M., & Edwards, P.A. (2009). The role of community book club in changing literacy practices. *Literacy Teaching and Learning, 13*(1–2), 25–56.

Darling, S., & Hayes, A.E. (1988). *Breaking the cycle of illiteracy: The Kenan family literacy model program.* Louisville, KY: National Center for Family Literacy.

Delgado-Gaitán, C. (1987). Mexican adult literacy: New directions for immigrants. In S.R. Goldman & H.T. Trueba (Eds.), *Becoming literate in English as a second language* (pp. 9–32). Norwood, NJ: Ablex.

Delpit, L. (1988). The silenced dialogue: Power and pedagogy in educating other people's children. *Harvard Educational Review, 58*(3), 280–298.

Delpit, L. (1995). *Other people's children: Cultural conflict in the classroom.* New York: New Press.

Doake, D.B. (1986). Learning to read: It starts in the home. In D.R. Tovey & J.E. Kerber (Eds.), *Roles in literacy learning: A new perspective* (pp. 2–9). Newark, DE: International Reading Association.

DuBois, W.E.B. (1990). *The souls of black folk.* New York: Vintage.

Edwards, P.A. (1989). Supporting lower SES mothers' attempts to provide scaffolding for bookreading. In J. Allen & J.M. Mason (Eds.), *Risk makers, risk takers, risk breakers: Reducing the risks for young literacy learners* (pp. 222–250). Portsmouth, NH: Heinemann.

Edwards, P.A. (1990a). *Parents as partners in reading: A family literacy training program.* Chicago: Children's Press.

Edwards, P.A. (1990b). *Talking your way to literacy: A program to help nonreading parents prepare their children for reading.* Chicago: Children's Press.

Edwards, P.A. (1991). Fostering early literacy through parent coaching. In E.H. Hiebert (Ed.), *Literacy for a diverse society: Perspectives, practices, and policies* (pp. 199–213). New York: Teachers College Press.

Edwards, P.A. (1993). *Parents as partners in reading: A family literacy training program* (2nd ed.). Chicago: Children's Press.

Edwards, P.A. (1995a). Combining parents' and teachers' thoughts about storybook reading at home and school. In L.M. Morrow (Ed.), *Family literacy: Connections in schools and communities* (pp. 54–60). Newark, DE: International Reading Association.

Edwards, P.A. (1995b). Connecting African-American families and youth to the school's reading program: Its meaning for school and community literacy. In V.L. Gadsden & D.A. Wagner (Eds.), *Literacy among African-American youth: Issues in learning, teaching and schooling* (pp. 263–281). Cresskill, NJ: Hampton.

Edwards, P.A. (1995c). Empowering low-income mothers and fathers to share books with young children. *The Reading Teacher, 48*(7), 558–564.

Edwards, P.A. (2003). The impact of family on literacy development: Convergence, controversy, and instructional implications. In J.V. Hoffman, D.L. Shallert, C.M. Fairbanks, J. Worthy, & B. Maloch (Eds.), *52nd yearbook of the National Reading Conference* (pp. 92–103). Milwaukee, WI: National Reading Conference.

Edwards, P.A. (2004). *Children literacy development: Making it happen through school, family, and community involvement.* Boston: Allyn & Bacon.

Edwards, P.A. (2009a). *Tapping the potential of parents: A strategic guide to boosting student achievement through family involvement.* New York: Scholastic.

Edwards, P.A. (2009b). *The education of African American students: Voicing, the debates, controversies, and solutions.* In D.W. Rowe, R. Jimenez, D. Compton, D. Dickinson, Y.

Kim, K. Leander, et al. (Eds.), *57th year-book of the National Reading Conference* (pp. 294–323). Milwaukee, WI: National Reading Conference.

Edwards, P.A., & Garcia, G.E. (1991). Parental involvement in mainstream schools. In M. Foster (Ed.), *Readings on equal education: Qualitative investigations into schools and schooling* (pp. 167–187). New York: AMS.

Edwards, P.A., & Turner, J.D. (2009). Family literacy and reading comprehension. In S.E. Israel & G.G. Duffy (Eds.), *Handbook of research on reading comprehension* (pp.622–641). Mahwah, NJ: Erlbaum.

Epstein, J.L. (1987). Parent involvement: State education agencies should lead the way. *Community Education Journal, 14*(4), 4–10.

Epstein, J.L. (2001). *School, family, and community partnerships: Preparing educators and improving schools.* Boulder, CO: Westview.

Erickson, F. (1989). Foreword. Literacy risks for students, parents, and teachers. In J. Allen & J. Mason (Eds.), *Risk makers, risk takers, risk breakers: Reducing the risks for your literacy learners* (pp. xiii–xvi). Portsmouth, NH: Heinemann.

Farran, D.C. (1982). Mother-child interaction, language development and the school performance of poverty children. In L. Feagans & D.C. Farran (Eds.), *Language of children reared in poverty: Implications for evaluation and intervention* (pp. 19–52). New York: Academic.

Florio-Ruane, S. (2001). *Teacher education and the cultural imagination: Autobiography, conversation, and narrative.* Mahwah, NJ: Erlbaum.

France, M.G., & Meeks, J.W. (1987). Parents who can't read: What the schools can do. *Journal of Reading, 31*(3), 222–227.

Fry, P.G., & McKinney, L.J. (1997). A qualitative study of preservice teachers' early field experiences in an urban, culturally different school. *Urban Education, 32*(2), 184–201. doi:10.1177/0042085997032002002

Gadsden, V.L. (1993). Literacy, education, and identity among African-Americans: The communal nature of learning. *Urban Education, 27*(4), 352–369. doi:10.1177/004208599302 7004003

Gadsden, V.L. (1994). Understanding family literacy: Conceptual issues facing the field. *Teachers College Record, 96*(1), 58–86.

Gallimore, R., & Goldenberg, C.N. (1989, March). *School effects on emergent literacy experiences in families of Spanish-speaking children.* Paper prepared for a symposium on Vygotsky and education at the annual meeting of the American Educational Research Association, San Francisco, CA.

Gallimore, R., Weisner, T.S., Kaufman, S.Z., & Bernheimer, L.P. (1989). The social construction of ecocultural niches: Family accommodation of developmentally delayed children. *American Journal of Mental Retardation, 94*(3), 216–230.

García, E.E. (1994). *Understanding and meeting the challenge of student cultural diversity.* Boston: Houghton Mifflin.

Giroux, H.A. (1991). Series introduction: Literacy, difference, and the politics of border crossing. In C. Mitchell & K. Weiler (Eds.), *Rewriting literacy: Culture and the discourse of the other* (pp. ix–xvi). New York: Bergin & Garvey.

Glazer, S. (1989). Oral language and literacy. In D.S. Strickland & L.M. Morrow (Eds.), *Emerging literacy: Young children learn to read and write* (pp. 16–26). Newark, DE: International Reading Association.

Goldenberg, C.N. (1984, October). *Low-income Hispanic parents' contributions to the reading achievement of their first-grade children.* Paper presented at the meeting of the Evaluation Network/Evaluation Research Society, San Francisco, CA.

Hale-Benson, J. (1990). Achieving equal educational outcomes for black children. In A. Barona & E.E. Garcia (Eds.), *Children at risk: Poverty, minority status, and others issues in educational equity* (pp. 201–215). Washington, DC: National Association of School Psychologists.

Handel, R.E. (1992). The partnership for family reading: Benefits for families and schools. *The Reading Teacher, 46*(2), 116–126.

Hearron, P.F. (1992). *Kindergarten homework in nonmainstream families: The school–family interace in the ecology of emergent literacy.*

Unpublished doctoral dissertation, Michigan State University, East Lansing, MI.

Heath, S.B. (1982a). Questioning at home and at school: A comparative study. In G. Spindler (Ed.), *Doing the ethnography of schooling: Education anthropology in action* (pp. 102–129). New York: Holt, Rinehart and Winston.

Heath, S.B. (1982b). What no bedtime story means: Narrative skills at home and school. *Language in Society, 11*(1), 49–76. doi:10.1017/S0047404500009039

Heath, S.B. (1983). *Ways with words: Language, life, and work in communities and classrooms.* New York: Cambridge University Press.

Heath, S.B. (1986). Separating "things of the imagination" from life: Learning to read and write. In W.H. Teale & E. Sulzby (Eds.), *Emergent literacy: Writing and reading* (pp. 156–172). Norwood, NJ: Ablex.

Heath, S.B., Branscombe, A., & Thomas, C. (1985). The book as narrative prop in language acquisition. In B. Schieiffelin & P. Gilmore (Eds.), *The acquisition of literacy: Ethnographic perspectives* (pp. 16–34). Norwood, NJ: Ablex.

Heath, S.B., & Thomas, C. (1984). The achievement of preschool literacy for mother and child. In H. Goelman, A. Oberg, & F. Smith (Eds.), *Awakening to literacy* (pp. 51–72). Portsmouth, NH: Heinemann.

Huey, E.B. (1908). *The psychology and pedagogy of reading.* New York: Macmillan.

Irvine, J.J. (1991). *Black students and school failure: Policies, practices, and prescriptions.* New York: Praeger.

Jiménez, R.T., Moll, L.C., Rodriguez-Brown, F.V., & Barrera, R.B. (1999). Latina and Latino researchers interact on issues related to literacy learning. *Reading Research Quarterly, 34*(2), 217–230. doi:10.1598/RRQ.34.2.5

Jones, L.T., & Blendinger, J. (1994). New beginnings: Preparing future teachers to work with diverse families. *Action in Teacher Education, 16*(3), 79–86.

Lawrence-Lightfoot, S. (2003). *The essential conversation: What parents and teachers can learn from each other.* New York: Random House.

Lazar, A.M., & Weisberg, R. (1996). Inviting parents' perspectives: Building home-school partnerships to support children who

struggle with literacy. *The Reading Teacher, 50*(3), 228–237.

Leichter, H.J. (1973). The concept of educative style. *Teachers College Record, 75*(2), 239–250.

Li, G. (2006). *Culturally contested pedagogy: Battles of literacy and schooling between mainstream teachers and Asian immigrant parents.* Albany, NY: SUNY Press.

Macleod, F. (1996). Integrating home and school resources to raise literacy levels of parents and children. *Early Child Development and Care, 117*(1), 123–132. doi:10.1080/0300443961170109

Mahoney, E., & Wilcox, L. (1985). *Ready, set, read: Best books to prepare preschoolers.* Metuchen, NJ: Scarecrow.

McCormick, C.E., & Mason, J.M. (1986). Intervention procedures for increasing preschool children's interest in and knowledge about reading. In W.H. Teale & E. Sulzby (Eds.), *Emergent literacy: Writing and reading* (pp. 90–115). Norwood, NJ: Ablex.

Moll, L.C. (1999). Foreword. In J. Paratore, G. Melzei, & B. Krol-Sinclair (Eds.), *What should we expect of family literacy? Experiences of Latino children whose parents participate in an intergenerational literacy project* (pp. x–xii). Newark, DE: International Reading Association.

Moss, B., & Fawcett, G. (1995). Bringing the curriculum of the world of the home to the school. *Reading & Writing Quarterly: Overcoming Learning Difficulties, 11*(3), 247–256.

National Education Goals Panel. (1997). *Special early literacy report, 1997.* Washington, DC: U.S. Government Printing Office.

Nieto, S. (1992). *Affirming diversity: The sociopolitical context of multicultural education.* New York: Longman.

Ninio, A. (1980). Ostensive definition in vocabulary teaching. *Journal of Child Language, 7*(3), 565–573. doi:10.1017/S0305000900002853

Pellegrini, A.D. (1991). A critique of the concept of at risk as applied to emergent literacy. *Language Arts, 68*(5), 380–385.

Pflaum, S.W. (1986). *The development of language and literacy in young children* (3rd ed.). Columbus, OH: Merrill.

Purcell-Gates, V. (1996). Stories, coupons, and the *TV Guide*: Relationships between home literacy experiences and emergent literacy knowledge. *Reading Research Quarterly, 31*(4), 406–428. doi:10.1598/RRQ.31.4.4

Raphael, T.E. (1982). Question-answering strategies for children. *The Reading Teacher, 36*(2), 186–190.

Richardson, J. (1988, April 10). How can I make a difference. *The Donaldsonville Chief,* p. 6.

Rodriguez-Brown, F.V., Li, R.F., & Albom, J.B. (1999). Hispanic parents' awareness and use of literacy-rich environments at home and in the community. *Education and Urban Society, 32*(1), 41–57. doi:10.1177/0013124599032001003

Sampson, W.A. (2002). *Black student achievement: How much do family and school really matter?* Lanham, MD: Scarecrow.

Sampson, W.A. (2004). *Black and brown: Race, ethnicity, and school preparation.* Lanham, MD: Scarecrow.

Schmidt, P.R. (1998). The ABC's of cultural understanding and communication. *Equity & Excellence in Education, 31*(2), 28–38. doi:10.1080/1066568980310204

Shockley, B. (1994). Extending the literate community: Home-to-school and school-to-home. *The Reading Teacher, 47*(6), 500–502.

Snow, C.E., & Ninio, A. (1986). The contracts of literacy: What children learn from learning to read books. In W.H. Teale & E. Sulzby (Eds.), *Emergent literacy: Writing and reading* (pp. 116–138). Norwood, NJ: Ablex.

Sonnenschein, S., Brody, G., & Munsterman, K. (1996). The influence of family beliefs and practices on children's early reading development. In L. Baker, P. Afflerbach, & D. Reinking (Eds.), *Developing engaged readers in school and home communities* (pp. 3–20). Mahwah, NJ: Erlbaum.

Street, B.V. (1995). *Social literacies: Critical approaches to literacy in development, ethnography, and education.* London: Longman.

Super, C.M., & Harkness, S. (1986). The developmental niche: A conceptualization at the interface of child and culture. *International Journal of Behavioral Development, 9*(4), 545–569.

Taylor, B.M., Pearson, P.D., Clark, K., & Walpole, S. (2000). Effective schools and accomplished teachers: Lessons about primary-grade reading instruction in low-income schools. *The Elementary School Journal, 101*(2), 121–165. doi:10.1086/499662

Taylor, D., & Dorsey-Gaines, C. (1988). *Growing up literate: Learning from inner-city families.* Portsmouth, NH: Heinemann.

Taylor, D., & Strickland, D.S. (1986). *Family storybook reading.* Portsmouth, NH: Heinemann.

Teale, W.H. (1981). Parents reading to their children: What we know and need to know. *Language Arts, 58*(8), 902–911.

Teale, W.H. (1986). Home background and literacy development. In W.H. Teale & E. Sulzby (Eds.), *Emergent literacy: Writing and reading* (pp. 173–204). Norwood, NJ: Ablex.

Vukelich, C. (1984). Parents' role in the reading process: A review of practical suggestions and ways to communicate with parents. *The Reading Teacher, 37*(6), 472–477.

Wiley, T.G. (1996). *Literacy and language diversity in sociocultural contexts, literacy and language diversity in the Unites States.* (Language in Education: Theory and Practice, 87). Washington, DC: Center for Applied Linguistics; McHenry, IL: Delta Systems.

Winter, M., & Rouse, J. (1990). Fostering intergenerational literacy: The Missouri parents as teachers program. *The Reading Teacher, 43*(6), 382–386.

Winters, W.G. (1993). *African American mothers and urban schools: The power of participation.* New York: Lexington.

CHAPTER 9

Latino Culture and Schooling: Reflections on Family Literacy With a Culturally and Linguistically Different Community

Flora V. Rodríguez-Brown

Research on parental involvement suggests that cultural and socioeconomic status (SES) determine how parents define their role in their children's education (Laureau, 1989; Valdés, 1996). Latino families must cope with values and expectations of at least two different cultures as they participate in the process of educating their children in schools in the United States. This chapter discusses cultural differences that might affect the way Latino parents see their role as teachers and some barriers that Latino families have to overcome to be successful in supporting their children's learning at school. The chapter also reports on successful practices that support these families as they try to understand the expectations of U.S. schools and become involved in their children's education. The way that educational institutions respond to and teach these children has an impact not only on their families but also on the whole country's economy and well-being.

Latinos in the United States

The term *Latino* in this chapter refers to individuals who have emigrated from or are descendants of immigrants from different Latin American countries, mostly Mexico. In the United States, these individuals differ in terms of SES, levels of education, years of residence here, and degrees of bilingualism, as well as other

From *Bringing Literacy Home* edited by KaiLonnie Dunsmore and Douglas Fisher.
© 2010 by the International Reading Association.

factors. The term *Latino* masks cultural, linguistic, national, religious, and other differences that account for within-group variation, which might be as significant as across-group variation.

Children of immigrants make up one out of five K–12 students in the United States (Capps, et al., 2005). Latinos are the largest culturally and linguistically different population in that group. Data from *The Condition of Education* (U.S. Department of Education, 2007) indicate that the number of U.S. children who speak a language other than English at home more than doubled between 1979 and 2005, and the majority of these children (over 80%) speak Spanish at home. They attend schools all over the United States, but the largest concentration of children who speak Spanish at home live and attend school in New Mexico, Texas, California, Arizona, Nevada, Colorado, Florida, New York, New Jersey, and Illinois. According to Fry (2006), the enrollment in U.S. public schools has increased mainly due to the 64% increase in the Hispanic population between 1994 and 2003.

In general, Latinos have positive attitudes toward their local schools and report that they are involved in their children's education (The Pew Hispanic Center & the Kaiser Family Foundation, 2004). The same report explains that Latino parents believe that their children do not do as well in school as other populations because of a disconnection between home and school and the lack of a bridge between parents and teachers and between the schools and the community. In contrast to the Caucasian population, Latinos are in favor of improving the schools where they live rather than moving their children to different schools.

Data from The Pew Hispanic Center (2006) show that Hispanics (both immigrant and natives) endorse the importance of the English language "regardless of income, party affiliation, fluency in English, or how long they have been living in the United States" (p. 1). As a result of immigration, the number of Spanish-speaking adult Latinos is greater than those who are bilingual or English dominant, but second-generation Latinos are more English than Spanish dominant (The Pew Hispanic Center & the Kaiser Family Foundation, 2004).

Current statistical data on Latinos show that they are the least educated population in the United States, due mostly to continuous immigration of adults with little education from Latin America. Data show that 73% of native-born Latinos finish high school, compared with 89% of Caucasians. When the Latino population data (native-born and immigrant) are not disaggregated, only 57% of immigrant Latinos finish high school. The data also show that 66% of Latino children attend predominantly minority schools in comparison to only 9% of

Caucasian children. In California alone, 16% of the teachers in predominantly minority school districts do not have the proper credentials, while only 9% do not have the proper credentials in schools attended mostly by Caucasian students. These factors result in differences in the quality of education received by Latino children when compared with Caucasian students.

Because the Latino population in the United States is so culturally and linguistically diverse (The Pew Hispanic Center, 2006), schools must address the needs of an even more diverse group than described thus far. According to Zentella (2005), "In addition to national origin and linguistic distinctions, class and race account for telling intragroup differences" (p. 21) among Latinos, which might explain why some individuals accommodate better than others to new situations.

Cultural Differences and Parental Involvement

If school districts and teachers were aware of cultural and linguistic aspects of the Latino culture that influence values and beliefs, especially about schooling, it could help teachers understand and accept the particularities of these families.

Several concepts that are central to the Latino culture affect the way that parents define their role in the education of their children. If not understood by the educational system, these concepts can act as barriers to parental involvement. The first is the concept of *familia* or family, which is central to life for Latinos (Abi-Nader, 1991). *Familia* provides individuals with a sense of belonging and interdependence; it implies, even requires, loyalty and obligation. In the Latino culture, *familia* includes not only parents and children, but the extended families and their networks. The *familia* shares responsibility for a child's success or failure. When evaluating parental involvement, schools and teachers have to understand that the extended family, rather than just the parents, is involved in supporting the children as they learn and develop (de la Vega, 2007). This means that there are many more resources available within the family than might be evident if only the education and skills of the parents are considered.

Another concept involves the distinction between the terms *educate* and *teach*. Several researchers (e.g., Goldenberg, 1989; Goldenberg & Gallimore, 1995; Reese, Balzano, Gallimore, & Goldenberg, 1995; Rodríguez-Brown, 2001; Valdés, 1996, among others) have found and discussed salient concepts of Latino parents' roles in their children's education. Many of these researchers have described a dichotomy, particularly for new immigrants. These parents define their role or responsibility to educate (*educar*) their children by teaching them morals, manners, and values. Children are taught to be respectful, obedient, and reserved. When one asks Latino parents what and how they support their children's learning at home, they explain that they teach their children to be *bien educados* (well educated). Delgado-Gaitán and Trueba (1991) found the Latino parents' expectation is that their children have *buena educación* (a good education). If Latino parents are asked directly about whether they teach their children to read and write at home, they react with surprise. They believe that it is the role of the school to teach (*enseñar*) such things as reading, writing, and math. Carrasquillo and London (1993) describe how Latino parents in their study believed that the school had the responsibility for their children's academic development.

Latino parents always find it surprising when a teacher in a U.S. school expects them to teach their children the letters and numbers and read often to their children before they get to school. Many Latino parents explain that they do not have the education to teach their children school-related subjects. They also believe that their lack of English proficiency precludes them from supporting their children's learning at home. These two beliefs can become barriers to their involvement in their children's education. When told that they can teach their children in Spanish, they are surprised. They also feel proud and validated when a teacher explains that not all knowledge comes from schooling, and that they have a lot of knowledge that they could share with their children to support their learning at school.

Latino parents also believe that it is disrespectful to interfere with the teachers' role. Latinos show great *respeto* (respect) for teachers and schools. The concept of *respeto* is discussed widely in Valdés (1996). According to Saracho and Hancock (1986), Latino culture includes "hierarchical regard," or respect toward elders or those in power and positions of authority within the home, school, state, and church. Teachers are highly respected in the Latino culture. Latino parents believe that teachers have more knowledge than they or than others in the community have. Teachers are more educated, and they have special ways and knowledge to teach children. Therefore Latino parents view the school and the teacher with *respeto* and feel they should not interfere with the ways the school teaches their children (Flores, Cousin, & Diaz, 1991).

Despite parents' belief that they are not qualified to help their children with school work, findings from a longitudinal study by Reese and Gallimore (2000) show that Latino parents are willing and able to follow a teacher's explicit request for them to read to their children at home as part of the daily homework. This request had a positive effect on the families' behaviors and on their view of their role as teachers in their children's literacy development. Although parents in this study showed specific cultural ways of learning and teaching which were different from those of the school, they were able to learn and use new strategies and activities so long as their values and morals were not compromised.

Delgado-Gaitán (1987) and Shannon (1996), among others, argue that teachers and schools do not have accurate perceptions about Latino immigrant families in relation to schooling because of these cultural differences. Many schools expect parents to serve as an extension of the school in support of the children's learning; however, as explained above, Latino parents believe it is the responsibility of the school to teach their children and support their academic development (Carrasquillo & London, 1993). Valdés (1996) believes that schools do not understand the possibility of differences across diverse families. These differing expectations between teachers and parents can produce misunderstandings that interfere with the development of relationships between Latino immigrant families and the schools.

It is important, then, for teachers to get to know the parents of the children in their classroom and to develop relationships with those parents and the community to create some continuity between learning at home and learning at school. According to Zentella (2005), successful connections between "educators and Latino families must be based on mutual respect for our cultural differences, without exaggerating them to the point that they obscure our shared humanity and dreams" (p. 29). This mutual respect is what de la Vega (2007) calls *confianza* (mutual trust) and explains that an understanding of it is central to developing relationships with Latino parents and to working with the Latino community. It is through social networks that one develops trust with the parents (de la Vega; Moll, 1992). Trust then leads to a sense of *confianza*, which allows for better communication between parents and teachers. Teachers and schools can then be more effective in conveying to the Latino parents the school's expectations for parents' involvement in school learning.

Parental involvement can be viewed in a number of ways (Epstein, 1995). These categories are defined as parenting, communicating, volunteering, learning at home, decision making, and collaborating with the community. De la Vega (2007) views Epstein's categories of parental involvement as problematic because they are based on what middle class parents usually do. She believes that it is more important to examine why parents get involved and how culturally and linguistically different parents use personal resources and knowledge to support their children's learning. My work (Rodríguez-Brown, 2004, 2009) is based on Epstein's (1995) category of Learning at Home. I believe that educators can learn how parents see their role as teachers through an awareness of cultural learning models used at home to support children's learning. I also stress the importance of knowing what Latino parents do with their children at home, how they support their children's learning, and whether there is congruency between ways of learning at home and at school. The issue of congruency, or bridging home–school learning, is critical to the education of culturally and linguistically different children, particularly Latino children. Teachers need to learn about the knowledge that exists in the community and the homes of the children in their classrooms and to see the relevance of knowledge, cultural ways, and discourses of the home. Teachers can use that knowledge as stepping-stones to new knowledge. This can enhance continuity between home and school and allow teachers to become partners with the families in their children's education.

Cultural misunderstandings of specific cultural beliefs and practices can have effects far beyond the individual parent–teacher or parent–school relationship. Family literacy programs that are created according to what the school thinks the parents need to know to support their children are not very successful. I call programs planned without parent and community input "functional" (Rodríguez-Brown, 2004, 2009). Programs that take into account and respect parents' knowledge, cultural ways, and discourse differences are more effective with culturally and linguistically different parents. These programs accept what parents bring to the learning situation and share with them new activities that can be used within the parents' cultural ways as they share knowledge with their children. School programs and activities that are developed for and support Latino parents' involvement in their children's learning as expected in U.S. schools need to be based on principles of *respeto* (respect) and *confianza* (mutual trust). Vásquez, Pease-Alvarez, and Shannon (1994) found that parents were interested in supporting their children's literacy learning when the activities taught in the program were relevant to their cultural beliefs.

Delgado-Gaitán and Trueba (1991) believe the success or failure of a school intervention or program for Latino parents depends on whether there is collaboration with the parents or the community in the development of the program. Delgado-Gaitán (1996) found that Mexican parents who participated in her project and were part of Comité de Padres Latinos (Latino Parents' Committee; COPLA) were very committed and interested in the literacy activities taught through the program because they participated in the creation of the program. COPLA was a parent leadership group described by Delgado-Gaitán (2001) in her longitudinal ethnographic study of Latinos in Carpintería, California. The committee was a community structure created by parents to teach Latino families how to communicate better with the school and also how to support their children's learning at home. COPLA helped new immigrant families' transition to a new culture by using their cultural values and traditions as strengths, which helped them build positive links among parents, children, families, and the schools.

The community and the school should work together in creating participatory structures in schools that are appropriate for different types of parents. Delgado-Gaitán and Trueba (1991) found that when systematic linkages between teachers and Latino parents existed, the interventions or programs were co-constructed in a mutual and respectful manner. Programs for Latino families should be directed to the development of knowledge that leads to self-efficacy for parents. In this way, Latino parents will become partners with the school in creating continuity in learning at home and school and thus support their children's academic success.

Research on Schooling and Latino Families

Research on schooling with Latino families has shown that parents have high expectations for their children, but they are not sure how they can help or foster school success (Delgado-Gaitán, 1992; Goldenberg & Gallimore, 1991). Goldenberg, Gallimore, Reese, and Garnier (2001) found that although educational aspirations of Latino parents are high through their children's elementary years, their expectations fluctuate according to their children's school performance. Reese and Gallimore (2000) found that Latino families are willing to learn and use new ways to share literacy with their children. Goldenberg (1987) and Goldenberg and Gallimore (1991) found that teachers who give specific instructions on ways to help children with homework are more effective in involving parents in their children's school learning.

The issue of discontinuity between home and school has been widely discussed in research on the schooling of Latino and other linguistically and culturally different children (Gallimore, Boggs, & Jordan, 1974; Moll, 1994; Reese

& Gallimore, 2000; Trueba, Jacobs, & Kirton, 1990; Valdés, 1996), but not everyone shares the discontinuity perspective. Weisner, Gallimore, and Jordan (1988) criticize discontinuity explanations about why linguistically and culturally different children do not perform well in U.S. schools. They raise the issue of within-group variability among people from the same ethnic group. Other critics (Chandler, Argyris, Barnes, Goodman, & Snow, 1985) have found variability among people in different cultural groups in the ways they adapt to change and new circumstances. Issues of discontinuity are further clouded by a contrasting and deficit perspective, in which cultural ways of nonmainstream groups are seen as inadequate rather than different. Other researchers, such as Weisner (1997) and Gutiérrez and Rogoff (2003) believe that there is a problem with studying issues of discontinuity between home and school under the presumptions that culture is static and categorical, and that differences can be defined as traits. The issues of discontinuity, individual variability, group traits, and cultural ways of learning have been studied from a variety of perspectives and with various approaches or models. Each perspective colors the analysis of the data and thus the results and interpretation of the researchers.

One such perspective is that of cultural models, which includes the cultural and social resources that individuals or groups of individuals bring to their understanding of social situations (Rogers, 2001). Gee (1999) describes cultural models as "story lines," or scripts that people have in their mind when they engage in meaning-making activities. When literacy is involved in the meaning making, the cultural models can refer to resources that people use to interpret or to produce texts (Fairclough, 1992). In regard to families and their participation in their children's schooling, cultural models influence not only what parents teach their children at home but also how they teach it.

Viewing culture as flexible and dynamic, Reese and Gallimore (2000) studied changes in beliefs and literacy practices at home with immigrant Mexican families. They used a cultural model approach to studying learning at home, specifically early literacy development in children (Weisner, 1997).

Reese and Gallimore (2000) describe the effects that Mexican and Mexican American parents' views and beliefs about literacy have on the way they structure activities that support literacy learning at home. One belief these parents have is that children learn to read through repeated practice once they start school. Reese and Gallimore feel that this belief, or cultural model, is derived from the experiences of previous generations in rural ranchos where there was little formal schooling. This Latino cultural model, brought by Latino immigrants to the United States, guides what they do with their children in support of their literacy learning here.

Reese and Gallimore (2000) found variability and flexibility in that Mexican and Mexican American parents in their study were willing to modify or adapt their cultural ways or models to support their children's learning according to expectations from U.S. schools, so long as the adaptations did not compromise their morals and values. The parents saw their beliefs about literacy learning as flexible and adaptable to new circumstances. According to Reese and Gallimore, changes in the Mexican parents' cultural model for literacy development recommended by the school teachers were not seen as threats to their traditional values. For example, although the parents in the study did not see themselves as teachers, once they learned that reading to children at home supported literacy learning at school, they complied with teachers' explicit assignments and suggestions.

In this situation, continuity between home and school was created in response to teachers' requests and not just from parents' observations in the new environment. Perhaps the viewpoint that cultural models are flexible helps to explain why new immigrant parents are willing to modify and adapt their cultural ways in a new context in response to teachers' requests.

This case shows what can be accomplished with Latino families through parent training, particularly in situations where parents' cultural ways are accepted and new practices are taught and discussed with them as they become more involved with their children's education and as they learn more about school expectations. These kinds of acceptance and training are required for the process of adaptation to be effective with Latino families (Rodríguez-Brown, 2004, 2009).

Because of the flexible nature of the Mexican parents' cultural model, Reese and Gallimore (2000) found that continuities and discontinuities co-exist in home–school literacy interactions. This finding contrasts with discontinuity explanations from previous research (Goldenberg & Gallimore, 1995), which describe discontinuities and no commonalities between learning at home and school, as Latino immigrant parents adapt to their new context.

Another theoretical construct used to explain discontinuity are the discourse differences between the home and the community, schools, and other social institutions (Gee, 1996; Moll, Amanti, Neff, & Gonzalez, 1992; Purcell-Gates, 1995). Differences in discourse are described by Gee (1999), who makes a distinction between discourse (with a lowercase *d*), which relates to linguistic aspects of language defined as "language-in-use or stretches of language (like conversations or stories)" (p. 17), and Discourse (with a capital *D*), which includes linguistic aspects of language and also beliefs, sociocultural issues, political issues related to language, symbols, objects, tools, and places related to a particular identity.

According to Gee (1996), children acquire their primary discourse at home and in the community by exposure, immersion, and practice. Children must learn a secondary discourse when they come in contact with social institutions such as schools. Purcell-Gates (1995) and Teale (1986), among others, believe that children whose primary discourse is similar to the school discourse, usually mainstream children, are able to adjust to school easier and faster and can be more successful than children whose primary discourse is very different from the discourse of school.

However, children from culturally and linguistically diverse families, many of them Latino, have primary discourses that are different from the mainstream. Learning the secondary discourse of school is more tenuous for those children, and they have the most trouble in the transition between home and school.

In summary, there are several points that teachers, school personnel, and program directors and developers should keep in mind when working with diverse parents and communities, and specifically in Latino communities. First of all, it is necessary to accept and respect the language and knowledge that children bring to school. In Latino communities, it is necessary for teachers to gain *confianza* with the parents by participating in existing networks. Interventions or programs that support Latino parents' learning about schools in the United States are more effective when the programs are created in consultation with parents. These programs should recognize and accept the linguistic characteristics, cultural practices, and knowledge that families bring to the learning situation and add new practices that would enhance the connection between learning at home and at school. In working with Latino families, it is important for schools and teachers to let parents know that their contributions to their children's learning are important and wanted. Educators should encourage parents to use the language they know better to support their children's learning.

The Research in Practice: Project FLAME

As their young children's first teachers, parents play a vital role in their children's lives and in their preparation for formal schooling. It is important that schools, especially those with large populations of culturally and linguistically diverse children, view parents, the home, and community as resources in support of children's transition to and success in the school setting.

Parents should feel that the ways they encourage, teach, and share knowledge with their children at home and their efforts to support what their children learn at school are valuable, and that these ways of learning at home are recognized as such by the school. In order for that to happen, parents need to feel welcomed, respected, important, and validated by the school and teachers. In the following sections, I use Project FLAME (Family Literacy: Aprendiendo, Mejorando, Educando [Learning, Improving, Educating]; Rodríguez-Brown & Shanahan, 1989) as context to explain how a research-based program developed by university professors can be adapted to a specific community when the design is supported by a sociocultural framework that makes the program relevant to the target community. (More in-depth information about the FLAME model and its sociocultural framework can be found in Rodríguez-Brown, 2004, 2009.)

Project FLAME was developed in response to the need for Latino parents to get more involved in their children's learning at home and the need to reduce discontinuities between home and school. In creating an acronym for the program, we decided to include words in both Spanish and English to represent the value we place on bilingualism. FLAME is considered a comprehensive family literacy model because it includes activities that deal not only with literacy but also with the home–school connection by providing activities that allow parents and teachers to talk and work together to facilitate the children's transition between home and school. The program is intended for Latino families who have children between the ages of 3 and 9.

The original FLAME program (Rodriguez-Brown & Shanahan, 1989) was funded by the U.S. Department of Education. The purpose of the program was to enhance the literacy learning opportunities of a mostly Latino new immigrant population. Several beliefs about literacy learning guided the development of the original program design:

- Literacy learning is a more culturally bound activity than other aspects of school learning, and, as such, it is more influenced by parental and home factors.
- The literacy culture of the home is more likely to diverge from the literacy culture of the school when children come from homes where English is a second language or where English is not used at all.

- Communication styles, views of literacy, and the nature of literacy interactions at home differ from those at school, and this difference has an impact on Latino children's literacy development.

The Project FLAME context for program activities is the *familia*, because the concept is central to cultural descriptions of Latinos (Abi-Nader, 1991). More specifically, meeting the needs of the family is one of the greatest motivations for Latino parents to support their children's learning and school success (Delgado-Gaitán, 1992; Quintero & Huerta-Macías, 1992). Because of their view about family, Latino parents prefer to participate in activities or interventions that benefit not only the parents, but also the whole family (Rodríguez-Brown & Meehan, 1998). Therefore, family literacy is the vehicle used to increase opportunities for families to learn their roles as teachers, find new ways to support their children's literacy learning, and understand how to reduce discontinuities between home and school. Based on these beliefs about literacy development and knowledge about Latino family cultural preferences, the program seeks to train parents to become good literacy models and to support the literacy development of their children in the language they know better.

Program Assumptions and Theoretical Design

The design of Project FLAME is based on four assumptions:

1. A supportive home environment is essential to literacy development.
2. Parents can have a positive effect on their children's learning.
3. Parents who are confident and successful learners themselves will be the most effective teachers for their children.
4. Literacy is the school subject most likely to be influenced by the social and cultural contexts of the family.

The program has four objectives:

1. To increase parents' ability to act as positive literacy models for their children
2. To increase parents' ability to provide literacy opportunities for their children
3. To improve parents' literacy skills so they can more efficiently initiate, encourage, support, and extend their children's learning

4. To increase and improve the relationship between parents and the schools

To meet these objectives, the program design includes four components, which are supported by research in literacy learning: literacy modeling, literacy opportunity, literacy interaction, and home–school connection. (A discussion of the research base for these components can be found in Rodríguez-Brown, 2009.) The content of each component is explained here.

Literacy Modeling. For the purposes of the program, a literacy model is defined as a significant person in the child's environment who uses literacy in an open and obvious manner. In FLAME, the primary vehicle for helping parents become positive literacy models is ESL or basic skills classes. Parents are encouraged to increase their own literacy and language use, to use reading and writing in the company of children, and to draw their children's attention to subtle uses of reading and writing.

Literacy Opportunity. Parents learn how to locate and select appropriate books, magazines, and other literacy materials for their children. Moreover, parents learn to use public libraries to increase the availability of literacy materials appropriate for their children at home. Parents also learn to develop a literacy center at home where young children can use items such as pencils, paper, markers, scissors, books, and other materials in support of their early literacy learning; older children can read books and do homework in the literacy center.

Literacy Interaction. Parents participate in activities that prepare them for reading more effectively to their children. They learn how to talk with their children about books. In addition, parents learn the value of songs, games, and other activities that support their children's phonemic awareness. They also learn about community resources that they can share with their children as a way to support their children's literacy learning.

Home–School Connection. Parents learn about the role of teachers in their children's education. Classroom visits are organized for parents to observe teachers. This activity helps parents establish early communication with teachers. The visits also increase home–school collaboration with teachers. Through these classroom visits and informal talks with teachers, good relations and mutual respect develop between parents and schools.

Although the theoretical design for FLAME has four components, they are not taught separately. Rather, program activities are planned so that each one can contribute to more than one objective or component of the design. This approach is an effort to deal with the complexity of creating a home literacy culture that reflects the parents' cultural practices and also supports and connects with ways in which their children learn at school. The program activities recognize and reflect these subtle intricacies.

Instructional Program

The instructional design of the program includes two main modules, or integrated sets of activities—Parents as Teachers, and Parents as Learners.

Parents as Teachers. The Parents as Teachers module comprises what is actually the family literacy program. It consists of bimonthly workshops with a focus on the four objectives for home literacy as described in the theoretical design of the program. Sessions are conducted in the language that parents know better. They focus on literacy opportunity, literacy modeling, literacy interaction. and the home–school connection. For example, one of the workshops is on sharing books with children, another teaches parents how to teach the ABCs through culturally relevant activities, and a third one teaches parents how to observe classrooms.

Workshops are organized around a common parallel structure, which usually includes the following components.

Introductory activity—This includes an introduction to the topic and questions for brainstorming so that parents bring up what they know about the topic and what is relevant to them. If parents do not offer enough input, they are provided with prompts that allow them to connect with the topic.

Discussion—Questions are raised that allow parents to talk about the topic in more detail. Usually questions are provided, but parents are also encouraged to bring their own questions into the discussion. The questions might lead parents to develop categories or more specific topics to cover. Parents usually participate actively in this discussion.

Role-playing—Participants present ideas about how they work with their children at home on issues related to the topic of the workshop. Often they develop role-playing activities that lead to a discussion about various approaches to teaching or supporting children's learning in ways that are congruent with the home discourse patterns and the parents' cultural ways of teaching and learning.

Wrap-up—During this time parents discuss what they have learned in the workshop and ways in which they plan to support their children's learning at home using what they have learned. To support the parents' discussions, sessions start with one or two preplanned questions and then parents are asked to offer their own questions. In every discussion there is an opportunity for participants to bring new questions and concerns to the attention of the group.

Follow-up and homework—Parents are asked to practice what they have learned with their children at home. They are asked to keep notes or remember what happens with their children and to be ready to discuss their experience and ask more questions before the next workshop.

This format is used by parent trainers and the university staff to plan the actual lessons specific to each site. Through participation in various activities of the FLAME program, parents are expected to learn the following:

- How to create a home literacy center
- How to select children's books that are appropriate and enjoyable
- How to share books with children and talk about books when their own literacy is limited
- How to use library resources
- How to teach the ABCs through language games, songs, and language experience activities
- How to encourage young children to write at home
- How to find literacy uses with their children while at home, at the market, and during other daily activities in the community
- How their children are taught in schools through classroom observations
- How to discuss their children's education with teachers and principals
- How to help their children understand numbers and arithmetic through games and activities
- How to monitor and help with their children's homework even when they do not know the subject areas themselves

To make the activities relevant for parents, Project FLAME involves parents in the planning of the workshops. Also, the cultural ways and discourses present in their homes are used in the activities as parents learn about more specific ways to support the home–school connection.

Parents as Learners. The Parents as Learners module includes instruction in basic skills, general educational development, or English as a Second Language (ESL), according to the needs of the project participants. Sessions takes place twice a week for 2 hours each for 28 weeks during the school year. The purpose of the module is to support the role of parents as learners and as models of literacy learning. Actually, these classes have also served as a hook or recruitment tool to attract parents to the program.

The topics of the twice-weekly Parents as Learners sessions are chosen based on the specific literacy learning needs of the parents at a particular site. For ESL instruction, FLAME uses a communicative competence perspective and a participatory approach, which is based on ideas from Auerbach (1989). First, parents choose the specific topics for the lessons. Examples of topics are using the phone to call the school, the teacher, or the doctor's office; shopping for food or cosmetic products; and applying for a job. Topics might vary from site to site and from year to year.

Once the ESL topics are chosen, lesson plans are developed in collaboration with the parents. Lessons are specific to the site and to the English language proficiency of parents in the program. The emphasis is on oral communication in contexts in which program participants use English. When parents realize that they can use the English they are practicing in class, they begin inquiring about the proper way to say things, which provides authentic contexts and motivation for grammar lessons.

Eventually, participants learn about different functions of writing and are given opportunities to practice different genres of writing. Parents often become interested in the role of written language and the value of keeping journals and doing creative writing. Each year an anthology of participants' writing is published. Writing can be in Spanish, English, or a combination of both (hybrid language), because some parents do not feel comfortable writing in English. When the parents are preparing their writing for the anthology, all FLAME writers participate in editing. At this time, they are introduced to grammatical concepts in a contextualized and relevant manner. Topics in the anthology vary by program site and school year. Participants have written about their homes, keeping up a house, their children, their families in Mexico and Chicago, and their experiences coming to the United States, among other topics.

Parents as Learners sessions are usually connected to Parents as Teachers sessions. For example, parents might write and make books for their children during the ESL class, an activity that increases home literacy opportunities and that is emphasized in several of the Parents as Teachers workshops.

Other FLAME Activities

The basic FLAME program as it was originally designed has been described here. However, once the program was initiated, other modules were developed to complement the original program and to make it more relevant to the communities that it served. The following modules are now a part of the FLAME program.

Parents as Leaders. During literacy workshops, parents consistently raised issues that, although not related to literacy, were relevant to the families' daily lives. To meet this need and still keep the focus of the program on literacy, a beyond-literacy module was developed that is called Parents as Leaders. This module takes place as a summer leadership institute. During the year, each site keeps a record of community issues that arise during ESL class discussions. Typically, toward the end of the school year, parents from all program sites decide on issues of interest to the family or the community that they would like to learn more about and better understand. Then, outside speakers are brought in to talk about those issues. Sessions are presented in the language that the parents know better. Some of the topics covered in recent summer institutes have included discipline at home, parents' rights, immigration, banks and their role in the community, and the use of hospital services. These topics also served to shape the content and procedures of other project activities.

Training of Trainers. Another module that was developed in response to participants' concerns and needs is called Training of Trainers. The goal of the module is to train people in the community who will be qualified to offer the program when the university is not available to provide services. Parents who have graduated from FLAME have the opportunity to further develop their literacy leadership activities in the community. Participants are parents who have completed two years in the basic FLAME program and show promise as literacy leaders. Training is provided for planning and implementing FLAME workshops. During the first year, trainees serve as aides to university staff who implement the lessons. During the second year, FLAME trainees are in charge of the workshops, with the assistance of the university staff. After two years, they receive a diploma stating that they have completed the training to become FLAME trainers. Several graduates have been hired to provide family literacy training in schools in Chicago.

Parents as Volunteers. FLAME parents' desire to volunteer in their children's schools and teachers' uneasiness in allowing parents to serve as teachers in their classrooms led to the development of the Parents as Volunteers module. It has been instituted successfully at one school. Parents sign up in the principal's office to volunteer in classrooms. Then, the principal asks teachers if they need trained parent volunteers. Teachers who are interested give the FLAME program staff pertinent information, books, and any materials a parent might need, along with the days and times they would like a parent in their classroom. Parents are trained to present the lessons, and then they go to the classrooms and teach as planned.

Child Care. As part of program activities, FLAME graduates are hired to provide child care for parents while they attend sessions and workshops. These graduates learn various educational activities that they can use with the children and also get paid for their services.

Functional or Critical Literacy Program

The original program design (content and activities) was developed according to what we (Rodríguez-Brown & Shanahan, 1989) believed parents needed to know and do to support their children's literacy learning at home. This is referred to as a "functional" perspective program design (Rodríguez-Brown & Mulhern, 1993), because the program developers were outsiders to the community for which the program was intended. Also, the community did not have any input regarding areas of need or relevance to their concerns and interests as the program was developed.

The experience of working with Latino families in a community context made us aware of the need to listen to their voices and their concerns. This was necessary to keep the program relevant to the cultural group and to allow participants to use the information critically in their lives. The critical use of information refers to parents understanding the concepts presented to them, taking ownership of new knowledge acquired through the program, adapting it to their needs, and allowing that knowledge to support not only the sharing of literacy with their children but also literacy in their everyday lives. The need for participants to feel ownership of their new knowledge and their awareness of how this knowledge can enrich their lives is one of the reasons why we added some modules to the original framework. This addition converted the FLAME program model from a functional to a critical model of family literacy.

Family literacy programs designed from a functional perspective tend to disappear fast or become irrelevant to the intended audience unless they become critical to the participants' lives. To establish a critical perspective in programs involving adult learners (parents) and in dealing with adults who are culturally and linguistically different, it is necessary to acknowledge and connect with the knowledge that adult learners bring to the learning situation. The program should support participants in finding ways to fit new learning into an already existing repertoire of cultural ways of learning.

While working with families through Project FLAME, it became apparent that these families brought a lot of knowledge to the program. We decided that we needed to recognize this knowledge and use it in the planning of program activities. We looked for support from current research that could justify and explain the need for programs that are directed toward linguistic minorities or other marginalized groups to acknowledge and respect the existing knowledge, ways of learning, discourses, and learning repertoires that these communities already possess. The work of Gee (1999), Gutiérrez and Rogoff (2003), Reese and Gallimore (2000), Rogers (2001, 2002), and The New London Group (1996), among others, led to and became the basis for the development of a sociocultural framework to further support our work with Latino families through Project FLAME. The sociocultural framework that we developed informs and underlies all program activities, and it has made the program more relevant to the communities it serves. It also situates the program within a critical rather than functional perspective.

A Sociocultural Framework for Family Literacy Programs in Diverse Communities

There are several points that inform our practice and that we believe are useful for teachers, school personnel, and program directors when planning or working with diverse parents and communities.

- Let families know that their contributions to their children's learning are important and wanted.
- Allow parents to use the language they know better in all project activities and encourage them to use that language at home to support their children's learning.
- Accept all knowledge that participants bring to the learning situation.
- Use families' cultural ways of learning/teaching as stepping-stones to new learning.
- Connect with the knowledge that participants bring to a learning situation to make new knowledge more relevant for participants.
- Add, rather than subtract, new knowledge and interactions to already existing practices in families and the community.
- Use funds of knowledge and cultural ways already existent in the community to structure program activities to enhance the program effectiveness.
- Expose program participants to multiple pedagogies as they learn how to provide their children with knowledge that supports their transition from learning at home to learning at school.

In creating family literacy programs for Latinos and other minority groups, it is important for the participants to whom the program is directed to have a voice in, and, to some degree, to have ownership of the program. With linguistic minority populations, issues of cultural and linguistic differences have to be acknowledged and understood by program designers. This will facilitate the creation of activities that are relevant to the purposes of the program and also to the population served.

The impact of a family literacy program, defined as parents and children sharing literacy, for Latino families would be greater if the parents were to share literacy with their children in the language they know best. We want parents to be good models of literacy for their children, and they can ask better questions, extend stories, sing songs, and give explanations in their native language. At the same time, parents can become models for their children while they learn English and their children see them reading and writing. It is important to remember that what makes a good family literacy program for Latino and other linguistic minority parents is the respect and acceptance of the families' contributions to their children's learning as stepping-stones to new learning and new literacy repertoires. What good ways to create bridges between learning at home and at school and to support children's learning.

REFERENCES

Abi-Nader, J. (1991, April). *Family values and the motivation of Hispanic youth*. Paper presented at the annual meeting of the American Educational Research Association, Chicago, IL.

Auerbach, E.R. (1989). Toward a social-contextual approach to family literacy. *Harvard Educational Review, 59*(3), 165–181.

Capps, R., Fix, M.E., Murray, J., Ost, J., Passel, J.S., & Hernandez, S.H. (2005). *The new demography of America's schools: Immigration and No Child Left Behind Act*. Washington, DC: Urban Institute.

Carrasquillo, A.L., & London, C.B.G. (1993). *Parents and schools: A source book*. New York: Garland.

Chandler, J., Argyris, D., Barnes, W., Goodman, I., & Snow, C. (1985). Parents as teachers: Observations of low-income parents and children in a homework-like task. In B. Schieffelin & P. Gilmore (Eds.), *The acquisition of literacy: Ethnographic perspectives* (pp. 171–187). Norwood, NJ: Ablex.

de la Vega, E. (2007, April). *Culture, confianza, and caring: A key to connections between Mexicana/Latina mothers and schools*. Paper presented at the annual meeting of the American Educational Research Association, Chicago, Illinois.

Delgado-Gaitán, C. (1987). Mexican adult literacy: New directions for immigrants. In S.R. Goldman & H. Trueba (Eds.), *Becoming literate in English as a second language* (pp. 9–32). Norwood, NJ: Ablex.

Delgado-Gaitán, C. (1992). School matters in the Mexican-American home: Socializing children to education. *American Educational Research Journal, 29*(3), 495–513.

Delgado-Gaitán, C. (1996). *Protean literacy: Extending the discourse on empowerment*. Washington, DC: Farmer Press.

Delgado-Gaitán, C. (2001). *The power of community: Mobilizing for family and schooling*. Lanham, MD: Rowman & Littlefield.

Delgado-Gaitán, C., & Trueba, H. (1991). *Crossing cultural borders: Education for immigrant families in America*. London: Farmer.

Epstein, J.L. (1995). School/family/community partnerships: Caring for the children we share. *Phi Delta Kappan, 76*(9), 701–712.

Fairclough, N. (1992). *Discourse and social change*. Cambridge, England: Polity Press.

Flores, B., Cousin, P.T., & Diaz, E. (1991). Transforming deficit myths about learning, language, and culture. *Language Arts, 68*(5), 369–379.

Fry, R. (2006). *The changing landscape of American public education: New students, new schools*. Washington, DC: The Pew Hispanic Center.

Gallimore, R., Boggs, J.W., & Jordan, C. (1974). *Culture, behavior and education: A study of Hawaiian-Americans*. Beverly Hills, CA: Sage.

Gee, J.P. (1996). *Social linguistics and literacies: Ideologies in discourses*. London: Farmer Press.

Gee, J.P. (1999). *An introduction to discourse analysis: Theory and method*. New York: Routledge.

Goldenberg, C., Gallimore, R., Reese, L., & Garnier, H. (2001). Cause or effect? A longitudinal study of immigrant Latino parents' aspirations and expectations, and their children's school performance. *American Educational Research Journal, 38*(3), 547–582. doi:10.3102/00028312038003547

Goldenberg, C.N. (1987). Low-income Hispanic parents' contributions to their first-grade children's word recognition skills. *Anthropology & Education Quarterly, 18*(3), 149–179. doi:10.1525/aeq.1987.18.3.05x1130l

Goldenberg, C.N. (1989). Parents' effects on academic grouping for reading: Three case studies. *American Educational Research Journal, 26*(3), 329–352.

Goldenberg, C.N., & Gallimore, R. (1991). Local knowledge, research knowledge, and educational change: A case study of early Spanish reading improvement. *Educational Researcher, 20*(8), 2–14.

Goldenberg, C.N., & Gallimore, R. (1995). Immigrant Latino parents' values and beliefs about their children's education: Continuities and discontinuities across cultures and generations. In P. Pintrich & M. Maehr (Eds.), *Advances in motivation and achievement: Culture, ethnicity, and motivation* (Vol. 9, pp. 183–228). Greenwich, CT: Ablex.

Gutiérrez, K.D., & Rogoff, B. (2003). Cultural ways of learning: Individual traits or repertoires of practice. *Educational Researcher, 32*(5), 19–25. doi:10.3102/0013189X032005019

Laureau, A. (1989). *Home advantage: Social class and parental intervention in elementary education.* Philadelphia: Falmer Press.

Moll, L.C. (1992). Bilingual classroom studies and community analysis: Some recent trends. *Educational Researcher, 21*(2), 20–24.

Moll, L.C. (1994). Literacy research in community and classrooms: A sociocultural approach. In R.B. Ruddell, M.R. Ruddell, & H. Singer (Eds.), *Theoretical models and processes of reading* (4th ed., pp. 179–207). Newark, DE: International Reading Association.

Moll, L.C., Amanti, C., Neff, D., & González, N. (1992). Funds of knowledge for teaching: Using a qualitative approach to connect homes and classrooms. *Theory Into Practice, 31*(1), 132–141.

Purcell-Gates, V. (1995). *Other people's words: The cycle of low literacy.* Cambridge, MA: Harvard University Press.

Quintero, E., & Huerta-Macías, A. (1992). Learning together: Issues for language minority parents and their children. *Journal of Educational Issues of Language Minority Students, 10*, 41–56.

Reese, L., Balzano, S., Gallimore, R., & Goldenberg, C. (1995). The concept of "educación": Latino family values and American schooling. *International Journal of Educational Research, 23*(1), 57–81. doi:10.1016/0883-0355(95)93535-4

Reese, L., & Gallimore, R. (2000, February). Immigrant Latinos' cultural models of literacy development: An alternative perspective on home-school discontinuities.

American Journal of Education, 108, 103–134. doi:10.1086/444236

Rodríguez-Brown, F.V. (2001). Home–school collaboration: Successful models in the Hispanic community. In P.B. Mosenthal & P.R. Schmitt (Eds.), *Reconceptualizing literacy in the new age of multiculturalism and pluralism* (pp. 273–288). Greenwich, CT: Information Age.

Rodríguez-Brown, F.V. (2004). Project FLAME: A parent support family literacy model. In B. Wasik (Ed.), *Handbook of family literacy* (pp. 213–229). Mahwah, NJ: Erlbaum.

Rodríguez-Brown, F.V. (2009). *The home–school connection: Lessons learned in a culturally and linguistically diverse community.* New York: Routledge.

Rodríguez-Brown, F.V., & Meehan, M.A. (1998). Family literacy and adult education: Project FLAME. In C. Smith (Ed.), *Literacy for the twentieth-first century: Research, policy, practices, and the National Adult Literacy Survey* (pp. 176–193). Westport, CT: Praeger.

Rodríguez-Brown, F.V., & Mulhern, M.M. (1993). Fostering critical literacy through family literacy: A study of families in a Mexican-immigrant community. *Bilingual Research Journal, 17*(3/4), 1–16.

Rodríguez-Brown, F.V., & Shanahan, T. (1989). *Literacy for the limited English proficient child: A family approach.* (Proposal submitted to OBEMLA/USDE, under the Title VII ESEA Family Literacy Program.) Unpublished manuscript, University of Illinois at Chicago.

Rogers, R. (2001). Family literacy and cultural models. In J.V. Hoffman, D.L. Schallert, C.M. Fairbanks, J. Worthy, & B. Maloch (Eds.), *50th yearbook of the National Reading Conference* (pp. 96–114). Chicago: National Reading Conference.

Rogers, R. (2002). Between contexts: A critical analysis of family literacy, discursive practices, and literate subjectivities. *Reading Research Quarterly, 37*(3), 248–277. doi:10.1598/RRQ.37.3.1

Saracho, O.N., & Hancock, F.M. (1986). Mexican-American culture. In O.N. Saracho & B. Spodek (Eds.), *Understanding the multicultural experience in early childhood education* (pp. 3–15). Washington, DC: National

Association for the Education of Young Children.

Shannon, S.M. (1996). Minority parent involvement: A Mexican's mother's experience and a teacher's interpretation. *Education and Urban Society, 29*(1), 71–84. doi:10.1177/0013124596029001006

Teale, W.H. (1986). Home background and young children's literacy development. In W.H. Teale & E. Sulsby (Eds.), *Emergent literacy: Writing and reading* (pp. 173–206). Norwood, NJ: Ablex.

The New London Group. (1996). A pedagogy of multiliteracies: Designing social futures. *Harvard Educational Review, 66*(1), 60–62.

The Pew Hispanic Center. (2006, June). *Hispanics' attitudes toward learning English: Fact sheet.* Washington, DC: Author.

The Pew Hispanic Center & the Kaiser Family Foundation. (2004). *National survey of Latinos.* Washington, DC: Pew Hispanic Center. Retrieved June 24, 2007, from pewhispanic.org/reports/report.php?ReportID=25

Trueba, H., Jacobs, L., & Kirton, E. (1990). *Cultural conflict and adaptation: The case of Hmong children in American society.* New York: Falmer Press.

U.S. Department of Education. (2007). *The condition of education, 2007* (NCES 2007-064). Washington, DC: U.S. Government Printing Office.

Valdés, G. (1996). *Con respeto: Bridging the differences between culturally diverse families and schools: An ethnographic portrait.* New York: Teachers College Press.

Vásquez, O.A., Pease-Alvarez, L., & Shannon, S.M. (1994). *Pushing boundaries: Language and culture in a Mexicano community.* New York: Cambridge University Press.

Weisner, T.S. (1997). The ecocultural project of human development: Why ethnography and its findings matter. *Ethos, 25*(2), 177–190. doi:10.1525/eth.1997.25.2.177

Weisner, T.S., Gallimore, R., & Jordan, C. (1988). Unpacking cultural effects on classroom learning: Native Hawaiian peer assistance and child-generated activity. *Anthropology & Education Quarterly, 19*(4), 327–353. doi:10.1525/aeq.1988.19.4.05x0915e

Zentella, A.C. (Ed.). (2005). *Building on strength: Language and literacy in Latino families and communities.* New York: Teachers College Press.

CHAPTER 10

Making the Book Talk: Literacy in Successful Urban Classrooms and Communities

Gloria Ladson-Billings

R ecent reports from the National Assessment of Educational Progress (NAEP; Lee, Grigg, & Donahue, 2007) indicate that African American students continue to lag behind their Caucasian counterparts in reading and mathematics. This chapter focuses on reading, or more broadly literacy, and details some of the successes that can happen in classrooms where teachers understand the relationships between and among students' historical, sociocultural, and community identities and experiences. In particular, the chapter describes how teachers can leverage family literacy practices to improve literacy performance.

The following quotation comes from the 1770 narrative of an enslaved African named James Albert Gronniosaw, who was fascinated by the entire notion of literacy:

> My master used to read prayers in public to the ship's crew every Sabbath day; and when I first saw him read, I was never so surprised in my life, as when I saw the book talk to my master, for I thought it did.... I opened it, and put my ear down close upon it, in great hope that it would say something to me; but I became very sorry, and greatly disappointed, when I found it would not speak. (Gronniosaw, cited in Cornelius, 1991, p. 194)

Mr. Gronniosaw, during his enslavement, saw his master reading the Bible and presumed that the book "talked" to his master and that his master merely repeated what the book said to him. In many ways Mr. Gronniosaw was right. Texts do "talk," and those who are literate are able to interpret and make meaning from those texts. However, the achievement data indicate that African American students regularly fail to develop proficiency in literacy—particularly reading and writing. In this chapter, I set a historical context that suggests this failure to learn to read is paradoxical, and then I describe instances where teachers have successfully helped African American students acquire the necessary skills to become literate. The data for this discussion come from three studies—one from expert teachers of African American students, one from novice teachers who commit to teaching students from cultural backgrounds different from their own, and a third from veteran Caucasian teachers who previously struggled to teach African American students successfully.

Family literacy in African American culture rarely is situated solely in nuclear families. Rather "family" literacy practices encompass the reading, writing, speaking, and listening practices of church (and other religious institutions), extended family, local services (e.g., barbers and beauticians), and cultural forms (including national magazines like *Ebony*, *Essence*, and *Jet* that circulate throughout the community many times regardless of official subscription numbers). Thus, in this chapter, I share school-based practices that may complement these family/community/cultural literacy practices.

Read and Die

Historically, African Americans have had a paradoxical relationship with literacy. Literacy held both the keys to life (or liberation) and to death. Frederick Douglass's (1960) oft-cited narrative describes his quest to learn to read. Initially his master's wife sought to teach him to read because she found young Frederick to be so clever. When she was found out by her husband, she was reprimanded sternly and forced to stop instructing her young slave. Because of his interest in learning to read, Frederick tricks a group of young Caucasian boys into teaching him additional reading skills.

The fear of allowing an enslaved person to read was linked to the fact that a literate African American could write his or her own manumission papers and be knowledgeable about what was transpiring in the society regarding changing thoughts about slavery. A literate African American could participate, even if vicariously, in the ongoing abolition debate and the changing tenor of sentiment toward war, secession, and slavery. On a more personal level, the literate enslaved African American could find out vital information about local policy and practices involving slavery. For example, it was important to know who was about to be bought or sold; who was being pursued by slave hunters; or what farms and plantations experienced slave rebellions and revolts.

A literate slave was seen as so dangerous to slave owners and defenders of slavery that those who taught slaves to read could be put to death. Certainly, a slave who read could be put to death. Despite the danger of learning to read, the historical record documents a variety of attempts by slaves to establish their own schools (Lerner, 1972). An enslaved woman, Mila Granson, ran a midnight school to which slaves stole away late at night after a full day of working the fields (Lerner, 1972). By candlelight in her little slave shack, Granson instructed her charges.

If we fast forward to the 20th-century modern Civil Rights movement, we realize that an important strategic move is to ramp up the literacy of African Americans in the South (Morris, 1986). Earlier federal adult literacy projects had failed dismally because they treated the students like children and focused primarily on the individual benefits of knowing how to read. On the other hand, civil rights strategists used Citizenship Schools (Clark & Brown, 1990; Morris, 1986).

The federal government strategy had been to recruit adults each evening into classrooms that children had used in the mornings and attempt to teach them to read using the very same methods used for children. The adults were greeted with lessons that sounded like, "A is for *apple*; B is for *ball*." Not surprisingly, adults regularly washed out of the literacy programs. When Myles Horton (Horton, Kohl, & Kohl, 1998) and Septima Clark (Clark & Brown, 1990) decided to initiate Citizenship Schools throughout the South, they decided on a very different course from that of the federal government. First, Clark insisted that the teachers not be professionals. Rather, she felt that certified teachers would merely replicate what the federal literacy teachers did. She believed that adults new to teaching would be willing to try different strategies for teaching.

With the help of Esau Jenkins (who served as a bus driver; Morris, 1986) and other local people—clerks, hairdressers, and laborers—Clark (Clark & Brown, 1990) set up a school where students were asked to first identify their reasons for learning to read. Many participants indicated that they wanted to learn to read the Bible while others were more interested in practical knowledge that might help them find employment. Clark and her associates wanted to make sure that their students were prepared to vote and participate actively in the Civil Rights movement.

The work of the Citizenship Schools spread throughout the rural South. Activists such as Septima Clark, Esau Jenkins, and Fannie Lou Hamer had their political awakening as a result of these schools. Each graduate of the Citizenship Schools was charged with developing another Citizenship School as a way of spreading literacy and political awareness. This approach to literacy was similarly replicated in a number of developing nations under Freire (1993) and others who understood that literacy was much more than reading words on a page. The "family" in this case is an extended group of individuals who were using literacy to fight for larger social and civic goals.

What It Means to Be Literate

Being literate is much more than being able to decode words and comprehend text. It includes the ability to make meaning, draw inferences and conclusions, establish one's identity in relation to text, and read "between the lines and beyond the pages" (Ladson-Billings, 1992).

Many of the instructional and assessment strategies we use in schools miss the mark when it comes to helping students to become literate. Students may be able to read short passages and decode words but are they really literate? Are their literacy skills transferable across disciplines and contexts? Do they understand literacy as an important tool for making sense of their world? Do teachers who are under incredible pressure to produce high test scores on standardized tests have the skills, time, and opportunity to teach in ways that ensure the literacy of their students?

In my own work, I have examined what I think of as "authentic" literacy—the kind of literacy that empowers students to read accurately and critically. In the subsequent sections, I describe what that kind of literacy teaching looks like in the work of a number of other literacy scholars and in three of my own research projects.

Three Studies of "Real" Literacy

Over the past 20 years, I have been studying teachers who are successful with African American students (Ladson-Billings, 1994). Many have read my work incorrectly as a demand for some special treatment for African American students. However, my work has always been aimed at finding ways to improve education for all students. The fact that I chose to route that improvement through those who were most disenfranchised seemed to disturb some but reflects an important epistemological turn in the research—to study success from the bottom up. Scholars such as Lee (2007), Willis (2008), and Gadsden (1999) have looked carefully at the literacy teaching and learning of African American students. Their work also incorporates a perspective of extended family as central to literacy in African American communities.

Lee's (2007) work explores the notion of cultural modeling as a strategy for getting African American adolescents to read complex texts such as Shakespeare's *King Lear* and Toni Morrison's *Beloved*. Lee serves as both researcher and teacher in her project, where she moves students attending the poorest-performing high school in a major city from barely being able to decode words to developing sophisticated analyses of texts. Lee moves the students from the rap music and videos they regularly engaged with in a family setting to a vocabulary about texts that includes concepts such as unreliable narrators, metaphors, similes, and positioning of the reader. Her model contends that students already possess many of the skills that teachers require of them in English classes. However, the teachers cannot articulate how they learned these skills themselves. The challenge for students is how to take the skills out of the contexts in which they best understand them (e.g., raps, videos, popular songs, movies, and youth language) and transfer them to unfamiliar, yet canonical texts.

Willis (2008) uses the family experiences of her sons and their literacy learning to inform her preparation of teachers in a predominately Caucasian university setting. Despite their excellent preparation and home life, Willis learned that her sons lacked confidence that the things they cared about mattered to their teachers and their Caucasian classmates. Willis found that her sons were constantly judging themselves against what they thought was a superior standard—that of their Caucasian peers. Willis's sons did not believe that the family and community stories they so readily shared had any currency in the classroom. Her youngest son refused to enter a literary contest because he thought his stories were not "good enough." Willis's work demonstrates the ways that students' perceptions of how they are received impacts their participation in the literacy classroom.

Gadsden's (1999) work looks at the intergenerational family nature of literacy learning. In a complex research design, she traced three generations of African American families from Charleston, South Carolina, to Washington, DC, to New York and Philadelphia. Her participants ranged in age from their early adolescence to mid to late 80s. She learned that despite the commonly accepted notion that African Americans were not particularly interested in learning (and in this case learning to read) generations of African Americans had developed elaborate rituals and strategies for keeping literacy traditions alive. Bible reading, hymn singing, recitations, and family oral histories all contributed to a rich set of literacy practices that kept reading, writing, and speaking alive within families.

In the following sections, I give brief synopses of three studies I conducted between 1989 and 2001. The first study is within the larger study I called the Dreamkeepers (Ladson-Billings, 1994). It is a comparison of the reading practices of two teachers who were matched on a variety of variables—age, gender, experiences—but who chose radically different approaches to literacy teaching. The second study (Ladson-Billings, 2001) looks at a group of novice teachers who begin by making a commitment to teaching in schools serving students different from them racially, ethnically, and linguistically. Through a complex series of questioning and reflection, these teachers learn what it means to really teach students to read. The third study (Ladson-Billings & Gomez, 2001) examines inservice teachers who know they need help to become better literacy teachers for African American students (particularly African American male students). Their stories are less stories of triumph than stories of persistence and negotiation. However, in some ways their stories best reflect what we expect of most teachers—struggles, small victories, and the willingness to keep trying.

Literacy Is the Key

In the classrooms of two teachers—Ann Lewis and Julia Devereaux (pseudonyms)—I learned what it means to insist that students become literate (Ladson-Billings, 1994). Ann was a walking advertisement for what is commonly called the whole language (WL) movement in literacy (Goodman, 1996). WL is contested and controversial on several fronts. Its detractors insist that learning skills first is fundamental to learning to read. Its adherents insist that those learning to read should not learn skills in isolation and that the many irregularities of the English language make phonics an unreliable strategy for ensuring that children learn to read. According to WL proponents, the important task of reading is making meaning from text. If the only thing students can do is call out words that they decode, they are not actually reading.

Ann Lewis's classroom is a study in progressive approaches to literacy. Her sixth-grade students were used to following specific rules about reading and writing, but in her class they were given freedom to allow their ideas to direct their thinking and literacy. During one of the extended periods I spent in her class, Ann posed the question, "Is violence ever justified?" Initially her students responded with a quick, "No." However, Ann continued to challenge them. "What about you, Pedro? Do you think violence is ever justified?" Ann knew that Pedro's family had fled violence in Nicaragua and his family had fought valiantly against right-wing militias. Pedro sat up in his seat and said, "Yeah, sometimes you have to fight back!" Ann then asked, "And what about you, Calvin? Is violence ever justified?" She asked this question fully aware that Calvin had a family member who had been gunned down by a rival gang. Calvin's older brother seemed obsessed with getting even. "Damn straight it's justified," replied Calvin.

Ann's probing of the question was designed not to encourage violence but to make her students complicate their thinking and to use their family/community experiences to lay the groundwork for a unit of study that would revolve around the violence question. She had assembled a selection of books that would force the students to debate this question many times. They would read, write, and speak about this question and simultaneously improve their thinking and their literacy skills. This dual mission was especially important to Ann. She was not merely creating readers; she was helping to create thinkers who were able to read.

To Ann, focusing solely on the mechanics of reading was like the work of the federal literacy projects previously discussed. The students might learn some minimum skills and develop some functionality in manipulating words and text, but they were unlikely to learn to read deeply and critically. In fact, she believed that using only a skills-based approach to reading might mean that her students would not read at all outside of the demands of the classroom. So, similar to the way students learned at home, Ann placed the literacy in social, historical, and cultural contexts.

In a nearby school in this same district, I was also observing an excellent literacy teacher named Julia Devereaux. Ann and Julia were longtime friends. Both had grown up in the very community in which they were teaching. They had attended grade school together and were both active in the teachers' union. Ann had been the teachers' association president and Julia was the president at the time of my study. I was in their classrooms as part of a larger study of effective teachers of African American students. Ann and Julia were a kind of microstudy of literacy. I chose them because despite their similarities, they were different in two ways. Ann was Caucasian and Julia was African American. More important, Ann was committed to WL instruction and Julia was equally committed to a phonics-based approach to literacy learning.

"Students must learn the basics before they can master more difficult reading tasks," said Julia during one of our early interviews. Julia's philosophy about teaching African American students to read mirrored that of urban education scholar Delpit (1996). Julia had been selected as one of five teachers to go to Chicago and receive training at Marva Collins's Westside Preparatory Academy (Collins & Tamarkin, 1990). What Julia learned in Chicago fit perfectly with the district's mandate regarding reading. The approved textbook in the district was from the much-maligned Open Court series. Julia was pleased with the series and was able to document tremendous growth among her students while using it.

I sat in Julia's fourth-grade class during the reading block with some degree of skepticism. I had spent considerable time in Ann Lewis's class and witnessed the way her students interacted with text. They could think and reason, pose questions, and challenge authors. They knew how to master texts and were facile with words and ideas. I had seen WL work with students with whom others argued it could not work. I was convinced it was the way. When I arrived in Julia Devereaux's classroom, I settled in to document what, if anything, a phonics-based approach had to offer.

To be fair, what Julia Devereaux did in the classroom may not be seen by all as a strictly phonics-based approach to teaching reading. She did begin with the students going through a phonics drill which Collins (Collins & Tamarkin, 1990) had conducted with students. Each day one of Julia's students stood at the front of the room with a pointer and went through the consonant sounds in the English alphabet. The other students followed the leader's direction and made the sounds indicated by the letters. "/K/-/k/-/k/ *kaleidoscope*, /l/-/l/-/l/ *limitation*, /m/-/m/-/m/ *magnificent*." I admit I was impressed. Rather than the simplistic, "*A* is for *apple*" that was characteristic of the federal literacy project schools, Julia's fourth-grade students were at least learning some sophisticated words. Was it merely the same strategy shrouded in a more complex vocabulary, or was Julia demanding something more of her students?

After the phonics drill Julia began a guided reading lesson with the students. The story in the basal was an adaptation of a classic tale and started by introducing a princess. Quickly going "off script," Julia asked the students to describe what they thought the princess looked like. "She's has long blonde hair and blue eyes," came the response.

"What!" exclaimed Julia. "Where did you get the idea that the princess has blonde hair and blue eyes?"

"All princesses have blonde hair and blue eyes," remarked one of the girls.

"You really believe that?" asked Julia.

"Well every princess I ever saw did," said one of the boys. At that moment Julia grabbed John Steptoe's book, *Mufaro's Beautiful Daughters*, from a nearby bookshelf. She read a few pages establishing that the black girls in the story were soon to be princesses. For the next 15–20 minutes Julia and her students discussed standards of beauty and how we come to determine what looks are desirable. I realized in the midst of that lesson that the methodological wars being waged in the pages of scholarly journals were not at all what was happening in the classrooms I was observing. Methodology was being mediated by pedagogical expertise.

Watching Ann Lewis and Julia Deveraux helped to underscore for me the centrality of pedagogy in ensuring student achievement. While the scholarly world was embroiled in what seemed to be a never-ending debate about which was better—phonics or whole language—Ann and Julia had settled the debate for their classrooms. Their decisions were linked to their own perspectives on pedagogy and learning, but more important, their decisions were linked to the results they were seeing in the classroom. In each of these classrooms, children were becoming literate and being challenged to read beyond the pages—to read the world.

Learning to Be Literate

From the 1994–1995 to the 1996–1997 academic years, my colleagues and I in the Department of Curriculum and Instruction at the University of Wisconsin–Madison implemented a post-baccalaureate elementary teacher education program for teacher candidates who had expressed a desire to teach in diverse schools and communities. The people selected for this program needed to demonstrate through academic attainment, desire, and life experience that they were well suited for what would be an intensive and challenging 15-month program called Teach for Diversity (TFD). They would be asked to be flexible and reflective practitioners (Zeichner & Liston, 1996). Rather than the typical performance model of novice practice, in which student teachers work hard to perfect a few lessons to perform in front of the critical eyes of a university-based supervisor who visits sporadically, the model for TFD was more akin to an apprenticeship. Participants also needed to demonstrate that they could engage families and communities in their practice.

We sent the novice teachers into the field with little more than sets of questions to ask of their cooperating teachers and the children in their classrooms. The students were constantly asking questions such as, Why did you select this method? How did you decide on that strategy? How do you know this is appropriate for these children? What made you use this type of classroom management? What are the families' perceptions of what you do? The cooperating teachers grew weary of the constant questions but admitted that the questions were forcing them to examine their own practice and that as they answered the student teachers' questions, they clarified their own thinking about their pedagogy. A description of the entire TFD program is beyond the scope of this chapter, but I do want to home in on the literacy practice of one of the teachers as an example of how new teachers also can promote success in African American learners.

Kyla (pseudonym) may have seemed an odd choice for the TFD program. On the surface she looked a lot like the students that were a part of the regular undergraduate program. She was Caucasian, monolingual English, and Midwestern. However, what we read about her on paper made her a good candidate. She had graduated from another Midwestern U.S. university in sociology. She had been active in campus politics and applied to TFD after having been a graduate student in social work in one of the nation's more prestigious east coast universities.

Kyla described her experience in the large East Coast city as disastrous. By her own admission she was woefully unprepared to advise poor families of color.

> Here I am this young, white girl from Normal, Illinois, standing in an SRO [single room occupancy] hotel with a mother and her 4 kids. The mom is HIV positive and homeless. What do I have to say to her? I felt like a failure and a fool.

However, this experience taught Kyla that rather than quit, she needed to learn more and she needed to learn it in different ways. She decided not to pursue the social work degree and got involved with community organizing.

She learned with community members who were following Alinsky's (1989) ideas about organizing and changing society. Through this experience, Kyla learned an important lesson about teaching—that real teaching always involves learning. She brought this perspective into the TFD program and the classroom to which she was assigned.

Kyla's cooperating teacher had a background in comparative literature and came of age as a part of the Civil Rights and Women's movements. She believed that students, regardless of age, were entitled to be treated with respect and that their schooling experiences should combine intellectual rigor with social consciousness. This was an excellent fit for Kyla, and their compatibility is evident in the fact that more than 10 years after her participation in TFD Kyla and her cooperating teacher remain close colleagues and continue to collaborate on curriculum and instructional planning (even though they work in different schools in the district). Kyla's early social work experience has helped her connect with students' families in deep and meaningful ways. She seemed particularly successful with African American male students.

What I saw in Kyla's teaching was what I later called a demand for success (Ladson-Billings, 2002). While she was empathetic to young students' (grades 2 and 3) frustration with learning to read, she held true to her responsibility as a teacher to hold them to high standards. In far too many classes, African American boys are seen as angry, defiant, withdrawn, and disinterested in intellectual pursuits. As a consequence they are more likely to be identified for placement in special education (Harry & Klingner, 2006; Kunjufu, 2005; Losen & Orfield, 2002).

In our discussions about the progress of one of her African American boys who was a struggling reader, Kyla indicated that her strategy with the student was grounded in her understanding of the need for students to develop some sense of agency and power in the classroom. She knew the easier course might have been to find something less challenging for him to read, but she felt that tack would undermine the message that he was both capable and accountable. Clearly, Kyla did not want to hold the student to a lower standard, but she knew she had to do some scaffolding to keep him from being defeated by the text. As she sat close by, she let him know that he had some support and that he was expected to stay on task. The learning was slow and Kyla showed incredible patience. She admitted that her lessons in community organizing and working closely with families were instrumental in developing her patience.

She was willing to show her students some empathy, but she also had a responsibility to challenge them beyond where many others might. This gentle but insistent pushing is something many African American students never experience. Haberman (1997) argues that many urban school students are encouraged to strike a poor bargain in the classroom: "You be quiet and don't cause trouble and I won't ask you to do any work." Thus, we see classroom upon classroom of urban students, particularly African American boys, who sit in classrooms sleeping with their heads on their desks. They are bored and lack the skills to do the tasks the teacher requires, and the teacher is either afraid or not interested enough to demand any real work from them. Kyla's engagement with students and their families worked against that norm.

It Does Not Matter Where They Start

My final example comes from a study of teachers who knew they were not succeeding with all students. Originally, their discourse was about how "some" students struggled to learn and how their families did not contribute to their literacy learning. The teachers would never voice that the "some" they were referring to were African American students, particularly African American boys. This study involved a group of seven primary teachers in grades K–2. The study was advertised as a small learning community designed to help ensure that all students achieved in literacy. Participation was voluntary. Teachers had to agree to allow us (myself, my co-investigator, and two graduate assistants) to observe their classrooms 3–5 times each week and to participate in a monthly group meeting. In our first meeting we asked the teachers to bring along their class rosters and tell us which students they believed would struggle to learn to read.

As the teachers gave us the students' names a disturbing pattern emerged. Almost all of the students listed were African American or immigrants. My colleague and I said nothing, knowing that any comment about race this early in the rapport building process would probably derail the project. In fact, it took the teachers almost eight months before they acknowledged the racial aspect of their pedagogical struggles. This was an important acknowledgment, because when the teachers decided to own this issue it made it clear that it was on their agenda and not ours.

Another self-revelation occurred when we asked the teachers to bring in the results of an early diagnostic test the students had taken. As the teachers looked at the data, they discovered that almost all of the students they identified failed to score well on the items identified as "phonemic awareness." One of the teachers blurted out, "Well we don't really teach that!" Again, my co-investigator and

I said nothing. However, another one of the teachers said, "Apparently, we need to start teaching it!" This straightforward assertion indicated that the teachers were willing to look at their own practice rather than blame the students.

As the data session drew to a close another teacher remarked, "This is so frustrating. Our focus students are just so low." Again, without prompting another teacher stated, "It doesn't matter where they start out. It's where they end up that's our responsibility." This statement sustained us through the three years of the project, because in a number of instances we saw some really awful things happen to African American students in the classroom, such as regularly sending students out of class for minor infractions like not having a pencil and permitting children to do nothing for long stretches of time. However, as our collective eyes were able to document these things and speak about them without blaming the teachers, we started to see some encouraging changes.

During one of our monthly sessions we asked the teachers to tell us what they had taught in reading the previous week. The discussion started out with teachers sharing a list of activities: "We read *Frog and Toad*"; "The children wrote in their journals about our neighborhood field trip"; "I read the children a story." My co-investigator and I decided to probe a little deeper: "You told us what activities you had the students participate in, but we didn't hear what you taught." Only one teacher, who was regarded as "a bit too structured" by her peers, was able to tell us what she taught.

> We are working on sequencing events in a text. Students have to provide a rationale for why they believe something comes next in a story. We started with simple beginning, middle, and end events and worked our way up to five to seven events in a sequence. The students got really good by the third day.

During one of my classroom observations in this project I witnessed a literacy lesson in a K–1 classroom that began with the teacher gathering the children on the rug and asking what fun, interesting, or exciting thing they had done over the weekend. Clearly, the teacher was attempting to engage the students' at-home activities in the classroom literacy practices. The children were eager to share stories of going to visit relatives, going to the park, going to the movies, playing with friends, or having a family game night. The teacher built upon the students' enthusiasm by directing them to go back to their assigned tables and share their weekend stories with their tablemates. "After everyone has shared, your table needs to pick the experiences of one of the people at your table and write a sentence about it," said the teacher. Most of the children eagerly set about the task, but one African American girl I will call Shannon was clearly unenthusiastic about doing what the teacher asked. She argued with her table-mates about regularly excluding her from activities and finally insisted that she did not want to share because they never pick her ideas anyway. The children at Shannon's table agreed on a sentence offered by a Caucasian boy and as the children set about trying to write his sentence, "I went to my grandmother's house this weekend," Shannon sat sulking.

Eventually the teacher made her way to Shannon's table and asked her what she was writing. Shannon replied, "I ain't writin' nuttin'!" The teacher looked at her with sympathetic eyes and said, "That's OK. Maybe you'll feel like writing something tomorrow." I was incredulous. Why was Shannon not being held to the same standard as the other students? This issue was compounded when, on several subsequent visits, I saw Shannon continue in this pattern of not writing and the teacher agreeing that "maybe you will feel like writing tomorrow." I called this behavior on the part of the teacher "permission to fail" (Ladson-Billings, 2002) and I contrasted it with what teachers do for Caucasian, middle class students, which is to demand success.

At another meeting, the teachers came prepared to share the results of an assignment we had given them. We asked the teachers to interview their focus students and ask them three questions: "What does it mean to be a good reader in this classroom? Who do you think is a good reader in our classroom? Are you a good reader?" One unexpected response to this activity was that in most classrooms all of the students wanted to participate and the teachers agreed to interview them all. The second unexpected response was that over and over the response to the question, "What does it mean to be a good reader in this class-room?" was, "Be quiet and keep your hands, feet, and other objects to yourself." The teachers were shocked but again, to their credit, they acknowledged that students felt this way because it must be exactly what they were conveying to them. Again, the "too structured" teacher had a different set of responses. Her students said things like, A good reader is someone who can sound out the words. A good reader is someone who looks at the picture if he can't figure out what the words say. A good reader is someone who looks at the other words in the sentence to see if they can figure out what a word is. A good reader asks other good readers for help if they can't figure it out for themselves.

This time the teacher's colleagues turned to her and began to ask her what sorts of things she did in her literacy lessons. They also asked if they could visit her classroom. She somewhat reluctantly agreed and began to accept this new status as a more accomplished literacy teacher. Her colleagues began to talk about how their own commitments to ideology over student achievement were not serving them well. Finally, a teacher blurted out, "Let's face it. We're doing a terrible job with black boys!" Someone was finally acknowledging the elephant we had been dragging around for months. This breakthrough created an environment where we could begin to ask hard questions and the teachers could place their own practice under intense scrutiny.

The good news about this project was that by the end of our three years with this group of teachers, all of the students who were initially identified as unlikely to learn to read passed the state's third-grade reading assessment. This was the first time this had happened in this school, and it was cause for celebration. The principal ordered a special cake and made an announcement over the school's public address system. Where these students ended up was indeed credited to this group of teachers. One of the key features that grew out of the teachers' work was a family literacy night that hardly got off the ground the first year but, by the end of the third year, involved more than 75 eagerly participating families in a low-income African American community.

Lessons Learned

Despite the fact that this research was done in three separate environments with teachers at different points in their careers, the research did allow for comparisons across sites and there are some themes that show up across all three projects. All three projects demonstrate the importance of immersing students in text-rich environments, providing access to reading and writing meaningful texts, and linking literacy to the lives of students.

Text-Rich Environments

In each instance where I have seen African American students thrive as readers, I observed that their learning took place in what I am calling "text-rich environments." These are the kinds of classrooms where it is almost impossible to *not* learn to read. Teachers in these classrooms surround students with books and print materials of all sorts. In Ann Lewis's class, the texts included a wide assortment of trade books, magazines, comic books, graphic novels, posters, and journals. In Julia Devereaux's class, despite the use of a fairly traditional basal,

Julia regularly supplemented literacy instruction with trade books. Students had regular exposure to the word wall and the phonetic alphabet chart.

In the case of Kyla, the novice teacher who worked with the struggling reader, texts were at the core of her interaction with him. Originally, the student felt that the assigned text was too difficult, but Kyla did not relent. The book had the power to make or break his identity as a reader. Kyla's determination to have the student see himself as a reader required her to saturate his classroom experiences with texts. She was not interested in merely telling the student what a smart boy he was; she knew he had to discover that for himself, and the text was at the center of his self-discovery.

In the case of our team of teachers, they were less successful when they withheld text from students. Although most of the teachers felt they were inducting students into a text-rich environment, the students' own notions of literacy revealed that they believed reading to be about following the rules and behaving well. They were not making a connection between texts and thinking or between words and ideas. Students seemed to think if they sat still enough and were quiet enough they would eventually learn to read.

Providing Access to Meaningful Reading and Writing

In addition to surrounding students with text-rich environments, teachers facilitate the literacy learning of African American students when they allow them to read and write that which they find meaningful. For Ann Lewis, providing students with a provocative question (e.g., "Is violence ever necessary?") forced students to search for meaning in the texts they read and the journal entries they wrote. For Julia Devereaux, the presence of a discrepant event—a princess who was not blonde haired and blue eyed—forced the students to search for deeper meaning in a standard textbook.

Kyla's work with her struggling student made him more aware of the importance of reading as an intellectual activity. The teacher's investment in his literacy learning forced him to find meaning in what he was doing and to make the text a personal challenge that he had to conquer. The student's satisfaction with reading what he thought was too hard helped him to establish himself in the classroom, and having access to that text, rather than an easier, less challenging one, gave him a new sense of himself as a learner.

The teachers in our group study began to understand the importance of meaningful texts and meaningful writing opportunities when they discovered for themselves that they actually were not teaching their students. They were filling the literacy block with activities, but there was no meaningful learning taking place. Students were occupied but not engaged. The reflective process of looking at the substance of their teaching forced the teachers to reconsider what it meant to be a literacy teacher.

Linking Literacy to the Family Lives of Students

The final theme that emerges from the three studies is one that reminds us that without understanding how literacy affects their lives and their families, students are unlikely to understand its importance. In Ann Lewis's and Julia Devereaux's classes, students learned that reading and writing were valuable skills that opened their worlds and challenged their minds. Like the slave in the quote at the beginning of this chapter, the students were learning to make books talk so they could unlock their secrets.

In novice teacher Kyla's classroom, her student's attempt to learn to read was central to his understanding of himself as a learner. Kyla had to make reading meaningful for him or risk losing him into that long list of unfortunate statistics about African American boys. For the student, reading was going to be almost an educational life or death situation, and Kyla was taking no chances. She was tough because she needed to help him understand that learning to read well was serious business.

In the case of the cohort of teachers in the professional development research, linking literacy to the lives of African American students was not something that had occurred to them. They presumed that all children would want to read and write because it is such a normal desire. However, they had not considered that when some students see themselves falling behind they begin to disengage and feel alienated from reading. When one teacher in their group was achieving success, their initial response was derision. However, as she continued to demonstrate that her strategies worked with African American learners, they became more willing to listen to her. She talked about how she helped the students connect what she was teaching them with their family lives. She used familiar experiences and events to draw them into reading and then she taught them the skills and strategies to tackle unfamiliar texts and become more competent readers and writers.

For too long we have insisted that teaching African American students to read is about choosing the correct method. However, over the past 20 years I have observed many instances of successful literacy practices that use a variety of instructional strategies to ensure students' success. Whether students receive strong phonics instruction, WL, or some combination of both, it appears that teachers' commitment to student learning, rather than any one method, is the more critical determinant of whether African American children learn to "make the book talk."

REFERENCES

Alinsky, S. (1989). *Rules for radicals: A practical primer for realistic radicals.* New York: Vintage Books.

Clark, S.P., & Brown, C.S. (1990). *Ready from within: Septima Clark and the civil rights movement: A first-person narrative.* Trenton, NJ: Africa World Press.

Collins, M., & Tamarkin, C. (1990). *Marva Collins' way* (2nd ed.). Los Angeles: Jeremy P. Tarcher/Putnam.

Cornelius, J.D. (1991). *When I can read my title clear: Literacy, slavery, and religion in the antebellum south.* Columbia: University of South Carolina Press.

Delpit, L. (1996). *Other people's children: Cultural conflict in the classroom.* New York: New Press.

Douglass, F. (1960). *Narrative of the life of Frederick Douglass.* Cambridge, MA: Belknap Press of Harvard University. (Original work published in 1845)

Freire, P. (1993). *Pedagogy of the oppressed* (M.B. Ramos, Trans.). New York: Continuum.

Gadsden, V.L. (1999). Intergenerational literacy within families. In M. Kamil, P.B. Mosenthal, P.D. Pearson, & R. Barr (Eds.), *Handbook of reading research* (Vol. 3, pp. 871–887). New York: Longman.

Goodman, K. (1996). *On reading.* New York: Heinemann.

Haberman, M. (1997). Unemployment training: The ideology of non work learned in urban schools. *Phi Delta Kappan, 78*(7), 499–503.

Harry, B., & Klingner, J. (2006). *Why are so many minority students in special education? Understanding race & disability in schools.* New York: Teachers College Press.

Horton, M., Kohl, H., & Kohl, J. (1998). *The long haul: An autobiography.* New York: Teachers College Press.

Kunjufu, J. (2005). *Keeping black boys out of special education.* Chicago: African American Images.

Ladson-Billings, G. (1992). Reading between the lines and beyond the pages: A culturally relevant approach to literacy teaching. *Theory Into Practice, 31*(4), 312–320.

Ladson-Billings, G. (1994). *The dreamkeepers: Successful teachers of African American children.* San Francisco: Jossey-Bass.

Ladson-Billings, G. (2001). *Crossing over to Canaan: The journey of new teachers in diverse classrooms.* San Francisco: Jossey-Bass.

Ladson-Billings, G. (2002). "I ain't writin' nuttin'." Permissions to fail and demands to succeed in urban classrooms. In L. Delpit & J. Dowdy (Eds.), *The skin that we speak: Thoughts on language and culture in the classroom* (pp. 107–120). New York: The Free Press.

Ladson-Billings, G., & Gomez, M.L. (2001). Just showing up: Supporting early literacy through teachers' professional communities. *Phi Delta Kappan, 82*(9), 675–680.

Lee, C.D. (2007). *Culture, literacy and learning: Taking bloom in the midst of the whirlwind.* New York: Teachers College Press.

Lee, J., Grigg, W.S., & Donahue, P.L. (2007). *The nation's report card: Reading 2007* (NCES 2007-496). Washington, DC: National Center for Education Statistics, Institute of Education Sciences, U.S. Department of Education.

Lerner, G. (Ed.). (1972). *Black women in white America: A documentary history.* New York: Vintage Books.

Losen, D.J., & Orfield, G. (Eds.). (2002). *Racial inequality in special education.* Cambridge, MA: Harvard Education Publishing Group.

Morris, A.D. (1986). *Origins of the Civil Rights Movement: Black communities organizing for change.* New York: The Free Press.

Willis, A.I. (2008). *Reading comprehension research and testing in the US: Undercurrents of race, class, and power in the struggle for meaning.* Mahwah, NJ: Erlbaum.

Zeichner, K.M., & Liston, D.P. (1996). *Reflective teaching: An introduction.* Mahwah, NJ: Erlbaum.

CHAPTER 11

Making Up for Lost Time: Connecting Inexperienced Teenage Readers With Books

Gay Ivey

W hen I was first asked to write a chapter about the connection between family literacy and adolescent literacy, I wondered, What do I know about family literacy? After all, most of the professional literature in literacy I had read that focused on families targeted very young children. Plus, my research has centered on secondary classroom instruction, and although I have known the families of many students who participated in studies I conducted, I had never explored the roles of those families and their influence on literacy development and practices. As it turns out, neither had many other adolescent literacy researchers.

But the need for families, communities, schools, and the worlds of teacher education, research, and policy to come together to develop a common vision for improving the literate lives of adolescents is clear. In this chapter, I will not report on any shovel-ready projects for families and adolescents, per se, but instead I'll describe what I have learned about adolescent literacy development that is worth considering as we begin to envision a concerted effort to transform the literacy education experiences of older students still working to become proficient readers and writers.

The Status of Adolescent Literacy

Despite a surge of interest in adolescent literacy during the past decade and expensive initiatives aimed at secondary schools (e.g., see the Striving Readers Program at www.ed.gov/programs/strivingreaders), there is little evidence of improvement. The National Assessment of Educational Progress reveals no significant progress in reducing the numbers of low-achieving readers, with roughly one quarter of all eighth graders scoring below the basic level of competence consistently from 1992 to 2007 (Lee, Grigg, & Donahue, 2007). Fourth graders demonstrated no major strides in literacy from 2001 to 2006 (Mullis, Martin, Kennedy, & Foy, 2007).

Not coincidentally, perhaps, there is little evidence that literacy instruction and the reading and writing experiences students receive in middle and high school has evolved much either. English classrooms operate much as they did 50 years ago, still maintaining a dual emphasis on whole-class reading in the literary canon and traditional writing instruction (Applebee, 1993; Scherff & Piazza, 2005; Yagelski, 2005). Most programs appear to be aimed at preparing all students to be English literature scholars or high school English teachers rather than competent and critical readers and writers of a wide range of texts that allow them to be personally and professionally fulfilled individuals who can participate in their communities and society in meaningful ways (Slater, 2004). This unrelenting focus on classic novels, or even more recent award-winning young adult novels assigned to the whole class, is clearly at odds both with students' needs and with most state-level English language arts curriculum standards (Fisher & Ivey, 2007). Likewise, literacy experiences across school subjects continue to center on reading textbooks for factual information (Bean, 2000), and often with no instruction or support for how to read and write critically beyond the upper elementary grades.

This stagnation of adolescent literacy achievement and instruction has been duly noted by professional organizations and policy advocates. During the past decade, both the National Council of Teachers of English (National Council of Teachers of English Commission on Reading, 2004) and the International Reading Association (Moore, Bean, Birdyshaw, & Rycik, 1999) have published compelling statements about what older struggling readers need to develop and flourish in their literate lives. Common across conversations are suggestions about the need for practices such as wide independent reading in diverse, self-selected texts; instruction in how to read thoughtfully and strategically; opportunities to think critically about texts; and participation in authentic discussions. Other organizations have suggested very specific guidelines for what should be taught in secondary reading programs. For instance, the Alliance for Excellence in Education named 15 elements of instruction (e.g., direct instruction in reading comprehension) for inclusion in secondary reading programs (Biancarosa & Snow, 2004).

Although we are no longer short on documents advocating for more attention to adolescent literacy, it is difficult to identify data-driven studies that combine these evidence-based suggestions, much less those that offer useable models to show how these practices take shape in a real classroom. A plethora of commercially available programs purport to raise literacy achievement, but we know of none that have demonstrated through independent research studies that they make much of a difference for adolescents. In a recent meta-analysis of reading programs for middle and high schools, Slavin, Cheung, Groff, and Lake (2008) fail to identify even one study that demonstrated strong effectiveness. For purposes of the review, the programs were divided into four categories: (1) reading curricula (e.g., textbook or packaged materials), (2) mixed methods (i.e., combined small-group and whole-class instruction with computer-based materials and other activities), (3) computer-assisted instruction, and (4) instructional process approaches that involve extensive professional development to implement specific methods. Initially, over 100 programs were considered, but there were only 33 research studies that met the criteria of (a) randomized samples or matched control groups, (b) treatment duration of more than 12 weeks, and (c) valid measures that were independent of the treatment.

Despite the popularity of reading curricula programs, Slavin and his colleagues (2008) could not identify even one program linked to research studies that qualified for the meta-analysis. Of all other kinds of programs with qualifying research studies, only four were found to be even moderately effective, and two of these four were developed by Slavin, who authored the meta-analysis. An even closer look at all the studies that were considered reveals that only a few of them were published in highly selective peer-reviewed research journals.

We find an equally insufficient body of evidence for the components of instruction often included in these programs, for instance, fluency practice, word-level work, and vocabulary lessons. The results of a meta-analysis of specific reading interventions conducted by Scammacca et al. (2007) offers little confidence that focusing on specific components of the reading process would benefit older students' reading comprehension. An examination across studies revealed, not surprisingly, that interventions aimed at increasing proficiency at a particular characteristic of skilled reading, such as fluency, word-level knowledge, or vocabulary, yield a small effect on that particular feature, but not on reading comprehension, and in particular, not when standardized measures independent of the treatment are used. In addition, specific interventions tend to lose their effectiveness when implemented by classroom teachers rather than the researchers who designed the interventions.

No doubt the rising popularity of skills-based instruction in secondary reading programs, despite the lack of research base, emanates from recent trends in early reading instruction, originating in large part from the findings disseminated by the National Reading Panel (National Institute of Child Health and Human Development, 2000), which were applied to early literacy funding initiatives such as Reading First and perpetuated by the marketplace for instructional materials linked to these initiatives. Besides the fact that early criticisms of the National Reading Panel's report (e.g., Allington, 2002; Cunningham, 2001) are now playing out in the failure of Reading First to show substantial progress for young students (Gamse, Bloom, Kemple, & Jacob, 2008), there is no reason to believe that any of these recommendations should ever have been applied to older readers (Ivey, 2008; Ivey & Baker, 2004).

So, in setting the stage for what families, communities, schools, researchers, and policymakers need to know about the status of instruction for struggling adolescent readers, some common understandings are in order. First, traditional instruction and literacy experiences in English classrooms and content area classrooms have not evolved along with our understandings of what inexperienced readers and writers need, and thus likely fail to accelerate their literacy achievement and motivation. Second, there is insufficient evidence for the effectiveness of most existing reading programs aimed at middle and high school students. Third, there is little reason to believe that a basic-skills approach is the answer for older struggling readers.

On the surface, possibilities for inexperienced adolescent readers and writers appear bleak, but only if we perpetuate the status quo. In the remainder of this chapter, I will argue for refocusing research and instructional priorities for middle and high school students who are still learning to read and write. First, I will make the case that literacy engagement should be our main instructional goal in secondary reading programs. Second, I will discuss the formative experiment (Jacob, 1992) as a pragmatic research model. Third, I will describe two examples of formative experiments aimed at increasing literacy engagement for older inexperienced readers. I will conclude with a discussion of how findings from these studies provide useful guidelines for initiatives to promote adolescent reading improvement in homes, communities, and schools.

Engagement First in Creating Literacy-Rich Contexts for Adolescents

In making the case for engagement as a pedagogical goal in working with older readers, I borrow the notion of engagement offered by Guthrie and Wigfield (2000): "Engaged readers in the classroom or elsewhere coordinate their strategies and knowledge (cognition) within a community of literacy (social) in order to fulfill their personal goals, desires, and intentions (motivation)" (p. 404). Engagement, or voluntary, self-regulated critical reading, can be juxtaposed with noncompliance in reading and with mere compliance, that is, reading just to complete the task or to avoid the consequences associated with noncompliance. In common terms, engaged readers would participate in literacy activities even if not required to do so because it satisfies an intrinsic desire to know or experience something worthwhile.

Engaged reading is a beneficial goal for inexperienced readers from a range of backgrounds because of its link to literacy achievement. International assessments of adolescents' reading have indicated that reading engagement has a stronger correlation with achievement than any other student factor, including socioeconomic background, gender, or time spent doing homework (Kirsch et al., 2002). Volume of reading experiences is also a strong predictor on national assessments of progress in literacy (Guthrie, Schafer, & Huang, 2001). Perhaps the most compelling connection between engaged reading and achievement is its potential for reducing the gap between subgroups of students from differing backgrounds. Highly engaged readers from low-income households achieve better in reading than weakly engaged readers from medium- to high-income households (Kirsch et al., 2002).

Unfortunately, there is limited evidence that schools contribute significantly to building adolescents' reading engagement. For instance, a secondary analysis of the Programme for International Student Assessment (PISA) 2000 data (Organisation for Economic Co-operation and Development, 2001) for 15-year-old students from England revealed that one year of schooling had no significant impact on reading engagement (Luyten, Peschar, & Coe, 2008). Surveys of adolescents conducted in the United States also point to the failure of schools to provide the reading materials and time necessary to create a motivating context for reading (e.g., Ivey & Broaddus, 2001; Worthy, Moorman, & Turner, 1999).

A host of correlational studies support the connection between time spent reading and competence with reading (Allington, 2005); in particular, students who read more outside of school are the higher achieving readers (Anderson, Wilson, & Fielding, 1988). Students who participate in voluntary reading programs in school are more likely to read on their own outside of school (Pilgreen & Krashen, 1993). It stands to reason that what happens in the school day should motivate and enable students to read outside of school. But in addition to the fact that skills-focused interventions do not currently have a supportive and compelling evidence base, it is hard to see how school time spent working on isolated word-level tasks or fluency drills, for instance, would inspire a student to read when reading is not required.

A primary focus on engagement does not, of course, completely nullify the need for instruction in reading processes, but it certainly may lessen it. Time spent reading builds vocabulary perhaps more than vocabulary instruction (Nagy, Anderson, & Herman, 1987), and fluency can be improved from much engagement with readable texts (Allington, 2005). Even the need for comprehension instruction, arguably a top priority in middle and high school reading programs lately, may seem considerably less urgent when students are reading more. In studying the impact of Concept-Oriented Reading Instruction (CORI), Guthrie and his colleagues (1996) reported that, when students are engaged in reading high-interest texts to answer questions they pose related to scientific phenomena, they demonstrate all of the characteristics of expert, strategic readers, and they do so independently of instruction on strategic processes. In summary, creating engagement in reading appears to play a crucial role in building literacy competence for older readers from a variety of backgrounds, but the potential of engaged reading has not been realized in secondary schools.

Bridging Research and Practice in Adolescent Literacy Through Formative Experiments

Existing research provides only a limited understanding of what constitutes an effective literacy intervention for older, inexperienced readers (Alvermann, 2002b). Most of what we know about the learning of struggling adolescent readers comes from either traditional experiments, which aim to determine what is most effective, what causes particular behaviors, and what results from certain kinds of instruction, or from a range of qualitative studies that were set up to describe specific contexts or phenomena. Fundamentally, both of these approaches focus on interventions or practices that already exist. The problem, as established earlier in this chapter, is that we need to create new contexts for engagement rather than evaluate or describe what is currently in place. Alternatively, formative experiments (Jacob, 1992) make sense when the intention of the study is to create a new workable instructional program. Formative experiments allow researchers to design interventions that are responsive to the needs of particular students and to adapt them when necessary.

Formative experiments can be understood best through the six guiding questions offered by Reinking and Bradley (2008):

1. What is the pedagogical goal to be investigated, why is that goal valued and important, and what theory and previous empirical work speak to accomplishing that goal instructionally?

2. What intervention, consistent with a guided theory, has the potential to achieve the pedagogical goal and why?

3. What factors enhance or inhibit the effectiveness, efficiency, and appeal of the intervention in regard to achieving the set pedagogical goal?

4. How can the intervention be modified to achieve the pedagogical goal more effectively and efficiently and in a way that is appealing and engaging to all stakeholders?

5. What unanticipated positive and negative effects does the intervention produce?

6. Has the instructional environment changed as a result of the intervention?

In short, the formative experiment approach allows researchers and teachers to identify a worthwhile goal for instruction, design an initial instructional plan based on the best available theoretically sound advice on what works, and then tinker with the intervention until all students reach the goal. Bonuses of this approach are potential larger changes in the context surrounding students' experiences.

The ability to fine-tune an intervention for a specific population or for individual readers within a formative experiment is key for older struggling readers. Their needs are multifaceted and often difficult to label or typify. Buly and Valencia (2002) underscored this phenomenon when they created rich profiles of fourth graders who had failed state reading assessments. In short, they were able to demonstrate how simplistic scores from standardized tests fail to capture the variation across students and the complexities within students that were more evident from a series of informal assessments. Likewise, reading programs that categorize students, presuppose and standardize teaching topics (e.g., separate blocks of time for fluency instruction, vocabulary learning, and comprehension instruction every day), or homogenize teaching would likely miss the mark for older struggling readers whose literacy identities are not so simplistic (e.g., Alvermann, 2002a). This is particularly the case for adolescent English-language learners (ELLs; Ivey & Broaddus, 2007; Rubenstein-Ávila, 2003). Creating interventions that engage students from diverse backgrounds and with varied experiences in reading would require the flexibility and adaptability afforded by a formative experiment.

Two Engagement-Focused Adolescent Literacy Interventions

Here I describe adolescent literacy interventions derived from formative experiments. The first example involves a group of middle grades ELLs, and the second example, from a current and ongoing experiment, takes place in diverse middle and high school English and reading classrooms in two states.

An Engagement-Focused Intervention for Middle School ELLs

This first model emanated from a study completed in a seventh- and eighth-grade language arts classroom for recent immigrants in a school-based English as a second language instructional program (Ivey & Broaddus, 2007). The needs of the 14 students involved in this project were substantial and diverse. Although students had come to the United States from seven different countries, all students spoke Spanish as a first language and all were at the beginning stages of learning to read, write, speak, and understand English. First-language literacy experiences ranged from strong to extremely limited.

Several theoretical issues drove the initial model for intervention; these issues were based on a collective analysis of research on early literacy acquisition, second-language literacy acquisition, and adolescent literacy. First, it was evident that certain practices effective for early literacy acquisition in general would be appropriate for second-language literacy acquisition. Second, it was unclear how existing assessments would inform instruction to foster literacy engagement for these students. Third, cultural and academic complexity within individuals would likely influence their motivation and skill to read and write.

Fourth, students' personal knowledge and personal uses of literacy might play a part in literacy engagement. Fifth, interesting content and concepts, rather than skills-driven instruction, would most likely engage students in reading and writing.

The initial instruction plan consisted of two basic parts: (1) student self-selected reading and (2) teacher-directed reading and writing activities. The context for both parts included a significant focus on reading materials that were both accessible and culturally relevant. Thus, in daily self-selected reading times, students could select from a range of texts including bilingual books, beginning reading texts in English, easy informational texts on topics such as skeletons and animals, and trade books that highlighted Latino cultures. The teacher-directed small-group and whole-class activities typically included either a teacher read-aloud or guided reading of a text that pertained to students' cultural or personal experiences (e.g., moving to a new country) or to topics generally appealing to middle school students (e.g., spiders, bats). These experiences with texts were generally followed by either the prompt for students to write a personal response or to create a log of new information or vocabulary learned from the text.

As we observed and worked with students under this initial plan, it was clear that certain adjustments were necessary if we were to see all students engaged in reading and writing regularly. Three important changes were as follows. First, we had to greatly expand the volume and diversity of texts in the classroom to meet students' needs. Second, we realized the need for more scaffolding for students to access the more difficult, high-interest texts that appealed to them. Third, we needed to scaffold writing experiences for many students.

The resulting intervention—in other words, what it took to engage all students in reading and writing—highlighted very specific considerations not only regarding the need to account for individual complexity but also regarding the instructional roles of the teacher. The two basic components of the initial intervention—self-selected reading and whole-class/small-group teacher-directed reading and writing activities—were modified and extended in several ways.

Self-Selected Reading. Making reading time count for individual students in this classroom required, first of all, a closer look at reading materials. At the beginning of the intervention, we included four basic categories of books: (1) books written entirely in Spanish; (2) bilingual picture books; (3) easy English picture book narratives on friends and family; and (4) high-interest, easy-to-read informational books in English. To increase engagement in reading for all students, we had to take a more deliberate approach to matching students with texts by considering individual experiences and interests. We also had to further expand the range of materials to take into account that different texts were required for different instructional purposes. In the end, we found that the following categories of materials were necessary for this population of students:

- Emergent literacy content books
- Emergent literacy concept books
- Word-play books
- Wordless picture books
- Simpler bilingual books
- Picture books with repetitive patterns
- Picture books that highlighted familiar spoken language
- Digital resources
- Other materials from outside of school including menus, greeting cards, and letters

But just bringing this wider range of materials into the classroom was insufficient to get students engaged during self-selected reading times. We adapted the original schedule to include a short teacher read-aloud and book talk time just before each self-selected reading time. As we learned from middle school students in a previous study (Ivey & Broaddus, 2001), students valued these introductions to books as a way to identify texts that made sense and mattered to them. We also realized the need to support individual students more proactively during self-selected reading times to help clear up confusion associated with language and to model fluent reading. The one-to-one instruction that evolved during self-selected reading was all focused on the goal of helping individual students become engaged and continue reading on their own.

Teacher-Directed Reading/Writing Activities. At the onset of the intervention, whole-class and small-group literacy experiences consisted mainly of either a teacher read-aloud or small-group guided reading followed by the expectation that students would respond in writing by connecting to a personal experience or documenting new information. Few students were engaged in these activities, and for the most part, they were confused about what to do. Students who attempted to write in English often struggled with spelling, syntax, and vocabulary. It became clear that students' engagement in writing and improvement in writing would remain halted in this context.

Two modifications were necessary to make it possible for students to use writing to think, learn, and communicate in English. First, the Language Experience Approach (Stauffer, 1970) became a mainstay of writing support in the classroom. In short, students selected interesting images from wordless picture books and websites and dictated captions and stories to accompany these images. Students found these images both comprehensible and personally meaningful, and they were able to focus on meanings of words they wanted to include in their dictations. Notably, students were able to use both their first language and English words they knew as starting points for their dictations. Because they were initially freed from the physical act of writing and were given the opportunity to think through and talk about their ideas first, they could focus on meaning. Whereas assignments to "write on your own" in response to a text often masked what students knew, the Language Experience Approach capitalized on their true capabilities.

Second, we began to provide models for format when students wrote on their own. Patterned texts gave students sentence structures to use so that they could focus on content. Although writing from a pattern may be typically associated with younger emergent readers, the information students were able to apply to their writing when given the support of a framework allowed them to work with age-appropriate and culturally relevant subject matters.

An Engagement-Focused Intervention for Inexperienced Adolescent Readers

The second adolescent literacy intervention (Ivey & Heubach, 2009) is being derived from an ongoing formative experiment in four secondary schools. The goal of this study is to determine the texts, contexts, and instruction that work to increase engaged reading for students in two middle school language arts classrooms and three high school remedial reading classrooms. Although this study is currently underway, I will describe the initial intervention and some preliminary findings.

The framework for this intervention is includes four related components: (1) regular, substantial blocks of time for self-selected independent reading in texts connected by topic but varying in levels of difficulty to address individual needs, (2) regular whole-class lessons on strategic comprehension processes, (3) regular one-to-one instruction on individual reading needs during self-selected reading, and (4) once-weekly opportunities to share new understandings gained from reading through writing, reading performance, or discussion.

Each component of our plan is supported by existing theories. First, older students understand the importance of time set aside for reading self-selected texts during the school day (Ivey & Broaddus, 2001; Stewart, Paradis, Ross, & Lewis, 1996; Worthy & McKool, 1996). In addition, we know that students are motivated to read when they can address broad conceptual questions and have available to them diverse, readable texts for exploring these relevant issues (Guthrie et al., 1996). Thus, the core of our intervention is self-selected reading around specific concepts of high interest to adolescents. Each class receives expansive rotating collections of books we refer to as concept boxes. A concept box (approximately 150 books per box) has been developed for the topics of personal struggle and perseverance, other worlds (fantasy and science fiction), justice, relationships, and obsessions (informational high-interest texts). The collections of books in each concept box span difficulty levels, formats, and genres. The majority of intervention time is devoted to time spent reading within these concepts, and students read multiple titles within one concept box over several weeks before the class proceeds to a new concept box.

Second, because the development of comprehension is a long-term, multidimensional process (RAND Reading Study Group, 2002), and because students must face an increasingly varied and complex set of texts for learning, attention to comprehension in a wide range of reading materials is appropriate for all students. Duffy (2003) proposes that specific aspects of reading can and should be explained to students. Each teacher presents a series of lessons that include teacher explanation, then teacher modeling, then teacher-guided practice for students, and finally, independent student application during self-selected reading. Within this framework, we expect that students will come to understand the critical processes of good readers (e.g., inferring, evaluating, monitoring comprehension), but with a recurring consideration of three essential questions that lead to productive reading: (1) What do I already know that helps me understand the text? (2) Does the reading make sense to me, and if not, what can I do about it? and (3) What does the author want me to know?

Third, having opportunities for the teacher to understand individual needs in reading is an essential component of the intervention. Because the teacher is in the best position for understanding student strengths and needs (Johnston, 1987), it is necessary to spend time with students and join them in their self-selected reading. This involves not just monitoring students per se, but allows teachers to model engagement in the text themselves and to offer specific advice about reading. For instance, when a teacher notices that a student is not engaged during reading time, he or she joins the student for a conversation about the book to determine the barriers to connection. This allows the teacher and student to either work together to clear up whatever is causing confusion in the text or to search for another text the student finds engaging.

Finally, the element of sharing is essential to establishing a motivating and enabling context for reading. Writing about literature and sharing the writing with an audience of peers helps students extend their understanding of the texts they read and develop a better sense of what it means to read thoughtfully (Kirby, Kirby, & Liner, 2004). Furthermore, talking with peers about a text helps students to become more interested in what they are reading and to anticipate what will happen next (Schallert & Reed, 1997). Likewise, reading performance of texts for peers can result in notable changes in attitudes about reading (Wolf, 1998). We suspect that capitalizing on the social aspects of these three kinds of experiences will increase student engagement during self-selected reading.

Preliminary results indicate three major considerations as we tinker with the initial intervention. First, given access to books and the time to read in school, most students—even those who had not read much previously—have begun to read with great fervor, many choosing to do so outside of school and other times when reading is not required. Second, to ensure that every student is engaged, we need an even larger quantity of books spanning reading levels and topics than we initially planned. Students at the lowest reading levels, who require the greatest access to books, have the fewest choices. The quantity of easy-to-read books with content and concepts that match the personal knowledge and interests of adolescents is extremely limited. Thus, alternative means of getting readable, engaging texts to the least experienced readers has necessitated the creation of texts using methods such as the Language Experience Approach, particularly using digital images (Ivey & Broaddus, 2007). Third, the teachers who have read more books from the concept boxes have been more successful at getting students engaged in reading than teachers who know fewer books.

Implications for Additional Adolescent Literacy Interventions

I began this chapter by describing the lack of progress in both literacy achievement and classroom instruction for older students still learning to read and write over the past several decades. Furthermore, I argued that we know of few existing reading programs for adolescents that are supported by a strong evidence base. I pointed out that although the evidence for teaching specific reading skills as a way to accelerate reading achievement is scarce, the goal of focusing on increased engagement in reading has considerable empirical support. Finally, I described the formative experiment as a viable method for creating effective adolescent literacy interventions, and I described two examples of two such interventions centered on increasing engaged reading.

These types of interventions offer some useful principles for creating home, community, and school-based programs to increase adolescents' participation in literacy. Successful and appealing programs, particularly for youths who are still inexperienced as readers and writers, ought to be inspired and informed by the following understandings:

- *Books matter to adolescents.* Programs intended to increase reading activity absolutely must prioritize the acquisition of lots of current, high-quality trade books that resound with the interests and experiences of youth. The satisfaction of connecting with stories and information is key to motivating students to read, but currently, many students do not have access to readable, alluring books either in or out of school. Furthermore, the collections of books provided to adolescents need to be updated and constantly changing to match both the rapid evolution of youth culture and the developing social, emotional, and cognitive maturities of individual teens.

- *Engaged reading requires time and space.* Ideally, all students would be provided with regular sustained periods during the school day to become involved in self-selected reading when also freed from common practices such as book reports, comprehension questions, worksheets, and projects that may actually detract from engaged reading. For inexperienced readers in particular, school needs to be a springboard for what happens outside of school. It is hard to imagine how a day spent filled with low-level skills work or assigned, difficult reading would inspire students to then read on their own at home. Communities interested in promoting literacy engagement for teens might consider creating spaces and times that welcome the reading, discussion, and sharing of the texts that adolescents like to read, with an eye toward issues important to youth, such as relationships, justice, personal struggles, and making difficult choices.

- *Inexperienced adolescent readers need others to connect them to books.* Facilitators of reading programs for adolescents must be knowledgeable of a wide range of texts, and in particular the high-interest texts that matter to adolescents. In most cases, these will differ drastically from the more traditional texts students encounter in school English and reading classrooms. Facilitators and those who work directly with adolescent readers must also seek to find reading materials that resonate with the experiences and curiosities of individual teens. In addition, teens need opportunities to exchange responses to reading with peers. An ideal program for inspiring engaged reading would be led by an adult who clearly has strong knowledge of adolescents and either strong knowledge of young adult literature or the willingness and desire to become immersed in the texts important to young people. A capable facilitator could provide good models for talk about books that could be used by adolescents as they inspire each other to read more.

REFERENCES

Allington, R.L. (2002). *Big brother and the national reading curriculum: How ideology trumped evidence.* Portsmouth, NH: Heinemann.

Allington, R.L. (2005). *What really matters for struggling readers: Designing research-based programs* (2nd ed.). Boston: Pearson/Allyn & Bacon.

Alvermann, D.E. (2002a). Reading adolescents' reading identities: Looking back to see ahead. *Journal of Adolescent & Adult Literacy,* 44(8), 676–690.

Alvermann, D.E. (2002b). Effective literacy instruction for adolescents. *Journal of Literacy Research,* 34(2), 189–208.

Anderson, R.C., Wilson, P.T., & Fielding, L.G. (1988). Growth in reading and how children spend their time outside of school. *Reading Research Quarterly,* 23(3), 285–303.

Applebee, A.N. (1993). *Literature in the secondary school: Studies of curriculum and instruction in the United States.* Urbana, IL: National Council of Teachers of English.

Bean, T.W. (2000). Reading in the content areas: Social constructivist dimensions. In M.L. Kamil, P.B. Mosenthal, P.D. Pearson, & R. Barr (Eds.), *Handbook of reading research* (Vol. 3, pp. 629–644). Mahwah, NJ: Erlbaum.

Biancarosa, G., & Snow, C.E. (2004). *Reading Next—A vision for action and research in middle and high school literacy: A Report to Carnegie Corporation of New York.* Washington, DC: Alliance for Excellence in Education.

Buly, M.R., & Valencia, S.W. (2002). Below the bar: Profiles of students who fail state reading assessments. *Educational Evaluation and Policy Analysis,* 24(3), 219–239. doi:10.3102/01623737024003219

Cunningham, J.W. (2001). The National Reading Panel Report. *Reading Research Quarterly,* 36(3), 326–335. doi:10.1598/RRQ.36.3.5

Duffy, G.G. (2003). *Explaining reading: A resource for teaching concepts, skills, and strategies.* New York: Guilford.

Fisher, D., & Ivey, G. (2007). Farewell to *A Farewell to Arms*: Deemphasizing the whole-class novel. *Phi Delta Kappan, 88*(7), 494–497.

Gamse, B.C., Bloom, H.S., Kemple, J.J., & Jacob, R.T. (2008). *Reading First Impact Study: Interim Report* (NCEE 2008-4016). Washington, DC: National Center for Education Evaluation and Regional Assistance, Institute of Education Sciences, U.S. Department of Education.

Guthrie, J.T., Schafer, W.D., & Huang, C.W. (2001). Benefits of opportunity to read and balanced instruction on the NAEP. *The Journal of Educational Research, 94*(3), 145–162.

Guthrie, J.T., Van Meter, P., McCann, A.D., Wigfield, A., Bennett, L., Poundstone, C.C., et al. (1996). Growth of literacy engagement: Changes in motivations and strategies during concept-oriented reading instruction. *Reading Research Quarterly, 31*(3), 306–332. doi:10.1598/RRQ.31.3.5

Guthrie, J.T., & Wigfield, A. (2000). Engagement and motivation in reading. In M.L. Kamil, P.B. Mosenthal, P.D. Pearson, & R. Barr (Eds.), *Handbook of reading research* (Vol. 3, pp. 403–422). Mahwah, NJ: Erlbaum.

Ivey, G. (2008). Intervening when older youth struggle with reading. In K.A. Hinchman & H.K. Sheridan-Thomas (Eds.), *Best practices in adolescent literacy instruction* (pp. 247–261). New York: Guilford.

Ivey, G., & Baker, M.I. (2004). Phonics instruction for older students? Just say no. *Educational Leadership, 61*(6), 35–39.

Ivey, G., & Broaddus, K. (2001). "Just plain reading": A survey of what makes students want to read in middle school classrooms. *Reading Research Quarterly, 36*(4), 350–377. doi:10.1598/RRQ.36.4.2

Ivey, G., & Broaddus, K. (2007). A formative experiment investigating literacy engagement among adolescent Latina/o students just beginning to read, write, and speak English. *Reading Research Quarterly, 42*(4), 512–545. doi:10.1598/RRQ.42.4.4

Ivey, G., & Heubach, K. (2009). *Designing wide reading-focused interventions for inexperienced adolescent readers.* Paper presented at the annual convention of the International Reading Association, Minneapolis, MN.

Jacob, E. (1992). Culture, context, and cognition. In M.D. Lecompte, W.L. Millroy, & J. Preissle (Eds.), *The handbook of qualitative research in education* (pp. 293–335). San Diego, CA: Academic.

Johnston, P.H. (1987). Teachers as evaluation experts. *The Reading Teacher, 40*(8), 744–748.

Kirby, D., Kirby, D.L., & Liner, T. (2004). *Inside out: Strategies for teaching writing* (3rd ed.). Portsmouth, NH: Heinemann.

Kirsch, I., de Jong, J., Lafontaine, D., McQueen, J., Mendelovits, J., & Monseur, C. (2002). *Reading for change: Performance and engagement across countries: Results from PISA 2000.* Paris: Organisation for Economic Co-operation and Development.

Lee, J., Grigg, W.S., & Donahue, P.L. (2007). *The nation's report card: Reading 2007* (NCES 2007-496). Washington, DC: National Center for Education Statistics, Institute of Education Sciences, U.S. Department of Education.

Luyten, H., Peschar, J., & Coe, R. (2008). Effects of schooling on reading performance, reading engagement, and reading activities of 15-year-olds in England. *American Educational Research Journal, 45*(2), 319–342. doi:10.3102/0002831207313345

Moore, D.W., Bean, T.W., Birdyshaw, D., & Rycik, J.A. (1999). *Adolescent literacy: A position statement for the Commission on Adolescent Literacy of the International Reading Association.* Newark, DE: International Reading Association.

Mullis, I.V.S., Martin, M.O., Kennedy, A.M., & Foy, P. (2007). *IEA's Progress in International Reading Literacy Study in primary schools in 40 countries.* Chestnut Hill, MA: TIMSS & PIRLS International Study Center, Boston College.

Nagy, W., Anderson, R.C., & Herman, P.A. (1987). Learning word meanings from context during normal reading. *American Educational Research Journal, 24*(2), 237–270.

National Council of Teachers of English Commission on Reading. (2004). *A call to action: What we know about adolescent literacy and ways to support teachers in meeting students' needs.* Urbana, IL: National Council of Teachers of English.

National Institute of Child Health and Human Development. (2000). *Report of the National Reading Panel. Teaching children to read: An evidence-based assessment of the scientific research literature on reading and its implications for reading instruction* (NIH Publication No. 00-4769). Washington, DC: U.S. Government Printing Office.

Organisation for Economic Co-operation and Development. (2001). *Knowledge and skills for life: First results from the OECD Programme for International Student Assessment (PISA) 2000.* Paris: Author.

Pilgreen, J., & Krashen, S. (1993). Sustained silent reading with English as a second language high school students: Impact on reading comprehension, reading frequency, and reading enjoyment. *School Library Media Quarterly, 22*(1), 21–23.

RAND Reading Study Group. (2002). *Reading for understanding: Toward an R&D program in reading comprehension.* Santa Monica, CA: RAND.

Reinking, D., & Bradley, B. (2008). *On formative and design experiments: Approaches to language and literacy research.* New York: Teachers College Press.

Rubenstein-Ávila, E. (2003). Conversing with Miguel: An adolescent English language learner struggling with later literacy development. *Journal of Adolescent & Adult Literacy, 47*(4), 290–301.

Scammacca, N., Roberts, G., Vaughn, S., Edmonds, M., Wexler, J., Reutebuch, C.K., et al. (2007). *Interventions for struggling adolescent readers: A meta-analysis with implications for practice.* Portsmouth, NH: RMC Research Corporation, Center on Instruction.

Schallert, D.L., & Reed, J.H. (1997). The pull of the text and the process of involvement in reading. In J.T. Guthrie & A. Wigfield (Eds.), *Reading engagement: Motivating readers through integrated instruction* (pp. 68–85). Newark, DE: International Reading Association.

Scherff, L., & Piazza, C. (2005). The more things change, the more they stay the same: A survey of high school students' writing experiences. *Research in the Teaching of English, 39*(3), 271–304.

Slater, W. (2004). Teaching English from a literacy perspective: The goal of high literacy for all students. In T.L. Jetton & J.A. Dole (Eds.), *Adolescent literacy research and practice* (pp. 40–58). New York: Guilford.

Slavin, R.E., Cheung, A., Groff, C., & Lake, C. (2008). Effective reading programs for middle and high schools: A best-evidence synthesis. *Reading Research Quarterly, 43*(3), 290–322. doi:10.1598/RRQ.43.3.4

Stauffer, R.G. (1970). *The language-experience approach to the teaching of reading.* New York: Harper & Row.

Stewart, R., Paradis, E.E., Ross, B., & Lewis, M.J. (1996). Student voices: What works in literature-based developmental reading. *Journal of Adolescent & Adult Literacy, 39*(6), 468–478.

Wolf, S.A. (1998). The flight of reading: Shifts in instruction, orchestration, and attitudes through classroom theatre. *Reading Research Quarterly, 33*(4), 382–415. doi:10.1598/RRQ.33.4.3

Worthy, J., & McKool, S. (1996). Students who say they hate to read: The importance of opportunity, choice, and access. In D.J. Leu, Jr., C.K. Kinzer, & K.A. Hinchman (Eds.), *Literacies for the 21st century: Research and practice* (45th yearbook of the National Reading Conference, pp. 245–256). Chicago: National Reading Conference.

Worthy, J., Moorman, M., & Turner, M. (1999). What Johnny likes to read is hard to find in school. *Reading Research Quarterly, 34*(1), 12–27. doi:10.1598/RRQ.34.1.2

Yagelski, R.P. (2005). Stasis and change: English education and the crisis of sustainability. *English Education, 37*(4), 262–271.

Implications for Family Literacy Research and Scholarship

CHAPTER 12

Writing the Next Chapter in Family Literacy: Clues to Long-Term Effects

Jeanne R. Paratore, Barbara Krol-Sinclair,
Brooke David, and Adina Schick

The work reported in this chapter began as a fairly straightforward investigation. We set out to discover if parents' participation in a family literacy program had long-term effects on their children's school success. To do so, we collected the type of evidence you would expect: school attendance rates, grades, test scores, high school graduation rates, and so forth. But, like so much work with families, as we knocked on doors to speak with parents and children who had long ago left the program, we found that our deepest understandings evolved not only from the numbers we collected and crunched but also from listening to the stories that were told. Here, we share both types of evidence as we strive to understand the worthiness of the time we spend with parents and their children. We begin with a brief summary of our understanding of the theoretical and research foundation for the work we are doing.

Rationale

The role that parents play in their children's education has long been a focus of study by educators and policymakers, particularly in relation to efforts to understand high rates of failure among some groups of children. Evidence documenting the relationship between children's early reading success and parents' own reading behaviors has led many educators to seek educational interventions that address the family unit rather than the child alone. Sticht and McDonald

(1989) were among the earliest to refer to such programs as "intergenerational literacy programs," and subsequently others have referred to them variously as "two-generation programs" (e.g., St. Pierre, Layzer, & Barnes, 1998) and, more commonly, as "family literacy" programs (e.g., Morrow, Paratore, Gaber, Harrison, & Tracey, 1993).

Justification for the importance of such programs is generally grounded in research related to two parent-related factors: parental education and home literacy practices. The importance of the first factor, parental education, is underscored by results from the National Assessment of Educational Progress (e.g., Denton & West, 2002), which has repeatedly shown that children who have higher rates of performance on reading achievement tests also have parents with higher levels of education. Evidence of this relationship continues to grow, with several recent studies yielding similar findings (e.g., Davis-Kean, 2005; Downer & Pianta, 2006; Lee & Bowen, 2006; Magnuson, 2007; Mantzicopoulos, 2003). The importance of the second factor, home literacy practices, became a particular focus in 1966 with the publication of Durkin's (1966) oft-cited study of children who read early, in which she reported that children whose parents read to them, wrote with them, answered questions about print, and modeled their own interest in books and reading were more likely to meet with success in the first grade. In the years since Durkin's study, the idea that parent–child literacy interactions at home are influential in children's literacy learning at school has received substantial support from numerous other investigations (e.g., Baker, Mackler, Sonnenschein, & Serpell, 2001; Clark, 1976; deJong & Leseman, 2001; Sénéchal & LeFevre, 2002; Sénéchal, LeFevre, & Thomas, 1998; Sénéchal & Young, 2008). Studies consistently support a relationship between children's success in early reading and parents' own reading and interest in books, parent–child storybook reading, parents' explicit teaching of literacy skills and abilities, and parents' general interactions with their children around print.

In response to evidence such as this, administrators and teachers often spend a substantial amount of time and resources on programs that support parent involvement in general and family literacy in particular. One could argue that this is positive—that common sense dictates that any program that emphasizes parent involvement in children's learning is bound to have positive effects. However, this wouldn't be entirely accurate. There are some studies (e.g., Mattingly, Prislan, McKenzie, Rodriguez, & Kayzar, 2002) that have found that only certain types of parent involvement and family literacy interventions are associated with academic gains for children. In 2009, Even Start, the largest federally funded family literacy intervention program in the United States, was recommended for defunding because of lack of evidence of effectiveness (McCallion, 2006; Office of Management and Budget, 2009). In a time of dwindling resources, it is critically important that we have a clear understanding of the types of programs that make a difference, and, in turn, that we promote programs and practices that we can predict with a high degree of certainty will make an important difference in children's learning success.

At present, the body of knowledge relevant to understanding the effects of family literacy interventions has been criticized as being limited by both the number of studies—too few—and the nature of studies—generally nonexperimental and focused on short-term effects (Gadsden, 2000; Purcell-Gates, 2000; Yaden & Paratore, 2002). The work we report in this chapter represents one attempt to address the need for long-term evidence. As we reviewed evidence related to the Intergenerational Literacy Program (ILP), a family literacy intervention program that we began 20 years ago, we posed a single overarching question: What are the effects of participation in a family literacy program on the academic experiences of children in participating families? To answer our overarching question, we asked numerous specific questions: Do children whose families participated maintain school attendance rates higher than their general education peers? Do they achieve state assessment scores that exceed those of their general education peers? Do they graduate at rates higher than their general education peers? Do they enter postsecondary program at rates higher than their general education peers? And finally, what do they say about their experiences?

The Context

The community and school system in which the ILP is implemented is a small, linguistically diverse and economically poor city just outside of Boston, Massachusetts in which 83% of the children speak a first language other than English and 87% of children reside in low-income households. Since 1989, the ILP has provided parents and caregivers of preschool or school-aged children with English literacy instruction and with strategies and materials for participating in their children's education in the public schools. The program is based on the premise that a thoughtfully designed family literacy program can serve two purposes: it can teach "the codes needed to participate fully in the mainstream of American life" (Delpit, 1995, p. 45) and, at the same time, can uncover, recognize, and build on the household funds of knowledge described by González, Moll, and Amanti (2005) as "historically accumulated and culturally developed bodies of knowledge and skills essential for household or individual functioning" (p. 72).

Since its inception, the ILP has served over 1,900 families, almost all new immigrants who journeyed to the United States from 56 different countries. The ILP's purpose is threefold: to help parents develop their own literacy, to support the practice of family literacy in the home, and, in turn, to support children's school-based success. Families learn about the project primarily through word of mouth—family members or friends who are present or former participants, their children's teachers, or acquaintances in various community groups or organizations. There is greater interest than there is space, and the ILP maintains a waiting list of about 150 families; each family is enrolled on a first-come, first-served basis.

The great majority of learners are Latino (79%) and originate from Central America (55%), but a variety of other cultures have been represented among the learner population at different times: a large number of Vietnamese families in the early years, for example, gave way to a burgeoning Afghan population in 2000, and presently, increasing numbers of families from Somalia and Burundi. There is great diversity, as well, in adult participants' levels of formal education. On average, learners have attended school for just over eight years, although individual parents' education levels vary widely: over 15% of learners have gone to school for fewer than four years and more than 14% have attended at least some college.

Nearly two thirds of adult participants are mothers, but fathers, grandparents, aunts, uncles, cousins, and siblings also take part in classes. Classes are held four mornings or three evenings per week for two hours each day. The program operates year-round, with 40 weeks of instruction broken into fall, spring, and summer instructional cycles of 12 to 15 weeks in length. Children's classes are offered in both the morning and the evening.

All of the classes, for adults and children, are heterogeneous and incorporate flexible grouping to support learners at a variety of levels. Within each class session, learners work independently, as part of a large group, and in small groups or pairs. In the children's classrooms, groupings are most often focused on children's ages. In the adult classes, however, parents are grouped in a variety of ways. Because all of the classes are multilevel and multilingual, they include parents who originate from a variety of cultures; speak several different languages as their first languages; differ in their English proficiency, level of formal schooling, and length of time in the mainland United States; and have children ranging in age from infants to adolescents. At various times, all of these criteria are used to define small groups, offering parents the opportunity to work with people with whom they share common knowledge, experiences, and goals. We accommodate the need for small-group instruction by staffing classes with teams of five teachers and tutors: two experienced teachers of literacy and three tutors who receive training in literacy tutoring. We select teachers and tutors on the basis of learners' languages and cultures, and in most cases, we are able to assemble teams on which each language represented in the class is spoken (usually fluently) by at least one staff member.

In the adults' and children's programs English is the common language of instruction, and English literacy is the parents' main goal for themselves and their children. Each week, adults read 1–2 focal texts, selected because they are of high interest to the particular group of learners. Texts are selected either because of a specific need (e.g., learning to use the newspaper to find information for daily tasks, such as weather reports or postings of community events or activities) or because a particular text provides a springboard for discussion of a topic that is likely to be of wide interest. For example, adults recently read Eleanor Estes's *The Hundred Dresses*, a story about a young girl of modest family means who is taunted by her classmates because she pretends to own the 100 dresses she has drawn; Paul Fleischman's *Seedfolks*, a story of a young girl's efforts to transform her poor, urban neighborhood by planting a garden; and Deborah Ellis's *The Breadwinner*, a story about the experiences of a young girl in Taliban-ruled Afghanistan. In addition, each week adults are introduced to a focal children's book, and they practice reading and rereading this book in preparation for sharing it with their children at home. The focal children's book relates to a theme that children are exploring in their classroom, and it is also read daily in their classroom (along with many other books), so that when children and their parents read at home, they are reading a familiar selection. Each week, parents are encouraged to select additional books from the program's lending library for sharing with their children at home, but only the focal books are introduced and rehearsed as part of weekly classroom instructional routines.

In the adult classroom, most adult texts are approached in largely the same way: before reading, the teacher prompts discussion of the topic or "big idea" in the text and elicits students' background knowledge, understandings, and points of view. The teacher might also introduce some key words or concepts that will make the text comprehensible. Then, the teacher typically reads the text aloud in part or in its entirety, depending on text length. Next, capable readers reread the text silently and jot down some notes about ideas they would like to discuss with the class; less capable readers reread the text with a partner (another student, a teacher, or a tutor), and they, too, record a few notes for discussion. Finally, the teacher reconvenes the group and adults share their ideas and pose questions for group discussion. Teachers' lessons include the use of graphic organizers, sometimes to elicit background knowledge related to a focal topic and at other times to help parents recall, organize, and discuss ideas they read about.

Routines for reading children's books typically begin with a teacher demonstrating ways to share the book with a child. These include engaging parents in a "book walk" and encouraging them to notice illustrations and respond in ways that a parent might engage a child. As the teacher reads aloud, she also calls parents' attention to interesting and important words, modeling for them ways to develop their children's vocabulary and concept knowledge and supporting the development of their children's interest in words. In addition, the teacher comments on particular actions and events, and prompts parents to make predictions and draw conclusions, again, modeling for parents the types of book-reading interactions that support children's developing text comprehension. After the read-aloud, parents practice rereading the book with a partner to develop word reading accuracy and fluency, including the types of expression that will support children's motivation and engagement.

All adult readings and children's focal books of the week are in English. During class presentations and discussions, teachers often draw upon learners' first languages to facilitate parents' and children's understanding, and learners are encouraged to write in the language of their choosing.

Each of the adult literacy classes follows the same basic guidelines—each focuses about half of class time on reading and writing around adult interests and the other half on texts of importance or of interest to child development and child learning. However, the actual content in each class may differ. While we encourage all classes to focus occasionally on specific timely issues, such as parent–teacher conferences just before they take place in the schools, most of the time teachers, tutors, and learners in any one class determine what that class will study. Specific content aside, there is a common thread underlying every lesson in every class. All teachers and tutors are focused on supporting parents' and children's understanding of strategies to improve their reading and writing and application of those strategies in their daily lives and to support children's school success.

This understanding is reinforced through several instructional routines. On a daily basis, adult learners report their previous day's literacy activities on a two-sided literacy log. On one side, parents record literacy activities of personal interest, such as reading recipes, holding conversations in English with cowork-ers, and writing letters. On the other side, learners detail literacy activities that they engaged in with their children, including storybook reading, homework monitoring, and shared television watching. A few minutes of class time each day is devoted to literacy log sharing, which allows parents to learn from the ways in which their peers use literacy at home and helps teachers and tutors build learners' understanding of what constitutes literacy. (If, for example, a parent reports having gone to the supermarket, teachers will tease out how that learner may have interacted with print while shopping.)

A second instructional routine that promotes learners' metacognitive aware-ness of their own and their children's learning is the use of graphic organizers. We make graphic organizers available for each article and book read, including several that are used in elementary classrooms, and draw learners' attention not only to how completing the organizer helps them make sense of the text and its structure but also to the fact that their children are learning the same strategies and tools in school. We are deliberate in building parents' awareness of ways in which they can apply the strategies we use in class in supporting their children at home.

Does This Model Have Sustained Effects?

Earlier studies have documented the general success of the ILP (Paratore, 1993, 1994; Paratore, Melzi, & Krol-Sinclair, 1999). Rates of attendance and reten-tion in family literacy classes have consistently exceeded those of traditional adult basic education and, in many cases, of other family literacy programs, (e.g., Bos, Scrivener, Snipes, & Hamilton, 2002; Comings, Parella, & Soricone, 1999) indicating that daily instructional practices are effective in maintaining parents' motivation to advance their own and their children's literacy knowl-edge. Parents consistently report increased use of reading and writing outside of class to achieve personal goals, thereby making print literacy a more fre-quent routine in their daily lives. As well, parents report increased time spent reading and writing with their children. In particular, by the end of program participation, parents consistently report engaging children in storybook reading at least once a week, a practice that has been found to correlate highly with early reading achievement (e.g., Bus, Van IJzendoorn, & Pellegrini, 1995; Sénéchal & LeFevre, 2002; Sénéchal, LeFevre, & Thomas, 1998; Sonnenschein & Munsterman, 2002). But all of these outcomes were measured in the short term. We wondered, then, if similarly positive outcomes would be sustained over time.

To find out, we sought data on 298 children from 163 families. All of the children were 10 years old or younger during that time period, had parents who participated in the ILP between 1996 and 1999, and resided in the community in which the program operates. We chose to study students from this period of enrollment because they had completed enough years of schooling to provide a sufficient number of data sources to examine long-term effects. All children resided in families in which parents spoke a first language other than English. Eighty-five percent of the children came from families in which Spanish was the first language; other first languages were Somali (7%); Bosnian (7%); and Armenian, Cape Verdean Creole, Haitian Creole, Khmer, Mandarin Chinese, and Vietnamese, together representing under 3% of the population. On average, the parents enrolled in the program had attended school in their countries for just under 8.8 years.

The mobility rate in the community is extremely high; in 2006–2007 alone, 29% of the students in the community transferred in or out of the school system (Bourque, 2008). As a result, only 40% ($N = 120$) of the students who were on our initial roster for the long-term effects study remained in the school system throughout their school careers, and these students served as the treatment group sample. Predictably, they were highly similar to the program population: 86% qualified for free or reduced lunch; 87% spoke Spanish as a first language; others spoke either Bosnian, Cape Verdean Creole, Haitian Creole, Khmer, Somali, or Vietnamese. The average number of years of parent education was slightly lower than the program population mean, at 7.8 years. Families had completed an average of 3.6 cycles in the ILP (above the program mean of 2 cycles). Of the 94 students still enrolled in school at the time of our study, 29% were identified for special education services (with 10% of these enrolled in substantially separate settings). At the time that data were collected (Fall 2007), grade placements ranged from grade 4 to three years postgraduation.

We used the general school population as a comparison group ($N = 5,627$). Demographically, these students were similar to those in the treatment group:

87% qualified for free or reduced lunch and 81% spoke a first language other than English (mostly Spanish). However, a far smaller percentage (13%) was identified for special education services (with 4% of these enrolled in substantially separate settings).

What Do the Numbers Tell Us?

For both treatment and comparison groups, data were drawn from existing school records and included attendance, report card grades, state assessment scores (drawn from assessments given at 4th-, 8th-, and 10th-grade years), referrals for and placement in special services, and plans to enter postsecondary education. For this chapter, we have chosen to provide only a brief summary of a more comprehensive report (Paratore, Krol-Sinclair, David, & Schick, 2009). Here is what we found: on the measure of attendance, ILP students had statistically significantly higher rates of school attendance than did their comparison group peers. Moreover, longer periods of ILP participation correlated with higher rates of attendance. We also examined grade point averages (GPA) and found that the mean GPA of ILP participants consistently exceeded that of the general school population.

Next we looked at students' achievement on the Massachusetts Comprehensive Assessment System (MCAS), the state assessment that also serves as a graduation requirement. Because of the nature of the test, we were not able to aggregate data across various years of test administration, and as a result, sample sizes in any given year were very small. However, the trends again favored ILP students. In both English language arts (ELA) and mathematics assessments at grades 4 and 8, in four of the five years for which data were available, ILP students outperformed students in the general school population. At grade 10, on both ELA and mathematics, ILP students outperformed students in the general school population in each of the five years.

Finally, we looked at data for high school graduation and postsecondary education plans (available for only 2006). Of the 10 ILP students expected to graduate, 6 completed school, 2 remained in school (both of them graduated in 2007), and 2 dropped out without having completed school, yielding an 80% completion rate, as compared with a 69% completion or "remained in school" rate for the general education population in the same year.

Of the eight ILP students who completed high school with their cohort or in the next year, all matriculated in either two- or four-year public or private colleges. This is compared with a report of the general school population, of which 73% of those who completed high school were identified as planning to enroll in two- or four-year post-secondary education.

In summary, we found positive indications of long-term effects of ILP participation on children's academic experiences. ILP students had significantly higher rates of school attendance, and a longer period of ILP participation correlated with higher rates of school attendance. ILP students consistently achieved higher scores than their general education peers in both English language arts and mathematics across years of testing and across ILP cohorts. These outcomes are especially encouraging in light of the substantially higher percentage of ILP children identified as needing special education interventions (29% as compared with 13% in the general population) and the substantially higher percentage of ILP children who are acquiring English as a second language (100% as compared with 81% in the general population). Even modest trends in the data are encouraging.

Do the Numbers "Ring True" in Family Stories?

In work of this sort, making sense of the numbers can be difficult. Although small cohort sizes in each year of high school graduation create one challenge, another lies in the diversity of the families who participate. Despite the commonalities among them (e.g., immigrants, high poverty, speakers of English as a second or even third language), they are far from a homogeneous group. They began their lives in vastly different parts of the world; they came to the United States for many different reasons, some voluntarily and some not; and they vary widely in age, in years of education, in years in the United States, in number and ages of their children, in their knowledge of the English language, in their familiarity with American schools, in their uses of literacy at home and in their communities, and in the comfort and safety of their living conditions. These differences make evaluation of this type of work both more interesting and more challenging. Although the numbers show consistent differences, these differences can be rendered relatively meaningless statistically because participants are spread across different grade levels. Yet, as we went door-to-door and listened to the stories so eagerly told, it was hard for us to accept the numbers as evidence of only small gains. In this section, we tell three of those stories.

The Peña Family. Evelin Peña came to the United States from the Dominican Republic in 1993 with two daughters, Carol, born in 1986, and Catherine, born in 1992. She arrived as a single mother with a high school diploma. Soon after her arrival, Evelin got a job in a factory that makes coats. The factory lays off employees on a seasonal basis, and Evelin first came to the ILP's morning class during one of these layoffs, enrolling in March of 1995 when Carol was 8 years old and Catherine was 2 years old. When she was called back to work, she switched to the evening class, bringing her daughters to the children's classroom, and remained enrolled for three instructional cycles. After taking one semester off, she returned for a fourth cycle. Throughout, Evelin was a dedicated learner, with an attendance rate of 87%, well above the program mean attendance of 74%. The work samples (Figures 12.1, 12.2, and 12.3) collected during Evelin's first year of study allow us to take a peek at the ways she attempted to guide her children's early literacy and language learning at home and a sense of her commitment to her children's learning.

When we revisited Evelin, we learned that she had remarried and had a third child. Her son, born in 1998, is profoundly deaf and attends a school for the deaf in Boston. Evelin now works for the Massachusetts Income Tax Center. She became a U.S. citizen in 2007. Her older daughter, Carol, graduated from high school in 2004 with a GPA of 3.27. Four years later, she graduated from

Figure 12.1. Evelin's Comment on Television Viewing

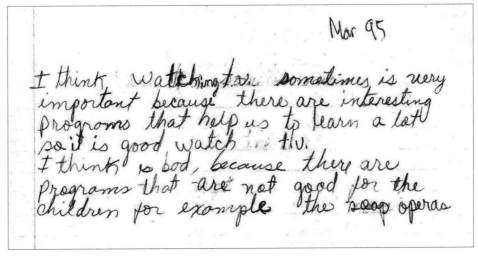

Figure 12.2. Evelin's Literacy Log

LITERACY LOG

NAME: _____
MONTH: February, 1996

DATE	Reading, Writing, Viewing and Talking Activities I Shared with My Child or Children
2-15-96	yesterday I read a book with my daughter
2-26-96	last friday I took my daughters to the park for a little while, at the park they played a lot
2-22-96	yesterday I sang with my daughters the songs. Los pollitos dicen pio pio pio "Mister sun and three little monkeys jumping on the bed.
3-11-96	this in the weekend to the to the weekend I went to the park with my daughters to play with snow and take picture.
3-12-96	yesterday I want to my daughter's school to pick her up, when we got home, I helped her with her homework
3-13-96	

Figure 12.3. Evelin's Reading Response

Reading   Response

Name: _____
Date: 1-30-96

I read the book _Happy Birthday, Moon_
(title of book)

with _Carol K._
(name of child)

This is what happened when I shared the book:

Carol enjoyed very much with this story
because. She said It's very funny
she liked a lot

Boston College. Soon after, she was hired by Chelsea Neighborhood Developers as a Program Associate for Resident Asset Development. Her sister, Catherine, is currently a high school senior with a GPA of 4.2 (because she is enrolled in more highly weighted honors courses) and is hoping to attend an Ivy League college. She has consistently scored in the Advanced category on the MCAS. For the past two years, Catherine has been employed by the ILP as a peer tutor working with elementary school–aged children during school vacations.

The Morillo Family. Fiordaliza Morillo emigrated to the United States from the Dominican Republic in 1994 to join her husband, who had come five years earlier. She brought their children: a 9-year-old girl, a 7-year-old boy, and a 6-year-old girl. Later that year, she gave birth to the couple's fourth child, a girl; in 1996, they had a fifth child, also a girl. Fiordaliza completed 10 years of schooling in the Dominican Republic, dropping out to marry before she graduated from high school. Her husband, Bartolomeo, joined the ILP first, enrolling in the evening program for one cycle, during which time he brought the three older children to the children's class. In 1995, Fiordaliza joined the morning class and dropped in and out over the years, completing a total of 8 instructional cycles (the last of which was in the spring of 2006). Her overall attendance rate was 71%, below the program average. After her children got older, Fiordaliza got a part-time job cleaning offices at night. Since 2001, she has spent at least one cycle each year working as a paid tutor in the ILP children's classroom. Fiordaliza and her three oldest children became U.S. citizens in July of 2008.

Fiordaliza's two oldest children, Luisa and Lucho, were profiled in an earlier case study (Paratore, Melzi, & Krol-Sinclair, 1999). In that study, children were judged to be academically successful, on the way to success, or unsuccessful. At that time, Luisa, then in fourth grade, and Lucho, then in second grade, were both characterized as students who were on their way to success. Data collected then indicated occasional joint parent–child reading and writing, occasional monitoring of homework, and rare attendance by parents at school meetings. Both Luisa and Lucho were achieving below grade level in English literacy, but on grade level in Spanish literacy. Luisa's teacher perceived her as a child unlikely to pursue postsecondary education, noting that she was prepared to be "a very good little mother" (Paratore, Melzi, & Krol-Sinclair, 1999, p. 53). Lucho's second-grade teacher described his academic performance as "erratic" (Paratore, Melzi, & Krol-Sinclair, 1999, p. 58).

When we looked back in on them, we found that the three oldest children, Luisa, Lucho, and Jahaira, all had graduated from high school. In a clear contradiction of her fourth-grade teacher's prediction of her academic pathway, Luisa graduated from high school with her class (in 2003) and enrolled in a two-year college. She later transferred to Suffolk University and graduated with a Bachelor of Arts degree five years after completing high school. She is presently working in a bank and hopes to attend graduate school.

Despite his earlier designation as "on his way to success," throughout his elementary and secondary school years, Lucho struggled academically. In middle school, he joined a Pop Warner football team that won a national title, and that experience seemed to focus Lucho on sports. He continued to participate in football throughout his four years of eligibility in high school. He stayed in school, graduating two years late (2007) because of insufficient credits and initially failing the MCAS. He is currently working part-time and plans to enter the local community college.

Jahaira began to experience academic difficulty in middle school, and she was retained in eighth grade. In high school she struggled to pass the MCAS, but she remained in school, eventually passed the test, and graduated one year late (2007). During her last two years in high school, she worked as an ILP children's program tutor during school vacations. She explained that her experiences as a tutor, as well as her mother's work as a tutor, prompted an interest in early childhood education. In the fall after high school graduation, she enrolled in a local community college to study early childhood education.

Karla and Sonia, the two youngest children in the Morillo family, were born in the United States and participated in the ILP from infancy. Karla is presently in 10th grade where she is enrolled in honors level classes and is already looking forward to college. Sonia is in 8th grade and she is also a good student. Both Karla and Sonia say that they "love, love, love reading."

Figure 12.4 provides a glimpse of Fiordaliza's facility with English language and literacy during her earliest days with the ILP; Figure 12.5 provides a bit of evidence of the strength of Karla's writing as she completed her eighth-grade year, and also, perhaps indirectly, some insight into the importance that Karla (and her mom, at least in the fictive story) place on the state assessment.

Figure 12.4. Fiordaliza's Literacy Log

LITERACY LOG

NAME: _____
MONTH: _10/10/95_____

DATE   Reading, Writing, Viewing and Talking Activities of **Personal Interest**

_____ I did not go any place. I stayed
_____ at home. I was with my daughter that
_____ was sick. I read books with her
_____ and she liked the books very much
_____ she likes drawings & colors
10/11/95 Yesterday I went to the School of my Son
_____ because an meeting of parents
_____ for the our child

Figure 12.5. Karla's Eighth-Grade Writing Sample

Boring Is Not So Bad!
By K_____ M., age 13
Daughter of F_____ M.

Beep! Beep! Beep! Beep! My alarm went off. I shut it off. I got up.

"Ugh, another boring day. I would give anything for something exciting to happen!" I said.

I got in the shower, but didn't wash my hair. After that, I brushed my teeth in the tub and put on my usual uniform.

"Same old, same old." I went to do my hair, I got my gel, spray, scrunchies, brush, and went to my mirror. But as I touched my head, I found out that I had no hair! "Aaah!" Now this was exciting, but I wouldn't give up my hair for something exciting.

"Oh, how horrible! What the heck am I supposed to do!" I ran frantically to my mom, who was getting ready to go to work. "Mom!"

"What?" she said, not looking up.

"I don't have hair!"

"That's what you get for using so much gel."

"No, Mom. I'm bald, as in Tony bald!" (Tony was our bald uncle.)

"What!" My mom looked up. "Oh my gosh, honey!"

I started to cry. "I'm not going to school!"

"You have to. Today's the MCAS for science, math, and history. If you don't go, you'll only have a day to finish them. Then, if you don't finish them, you won't pass eighth grade."

"Okay, okay!" I would have to lie, I though. Hmmmm, I gave my hair to cancer patients and also "the religion" I'm in makes us wear bandanas and hats. Yes, that's it.

I called my best friend and told her the story. I told her to wear a bandana on her head like I was and braced myself for the toughest days of my life to come.

The Castillo Family. Hilda Castillo and her two daughters, a 5-year-old and a newborn, came to the United States from Guatemala in 1987 to join her husband, who was already here. Two more children were born here: a daughter in 1992 and a son in 1994. Hilda completed six years of schooling in Guatemala. She confronted many challenges in her life. In Guatemala, her mother died when she was 4 years old, and she spent time in an orphanage. In the United States, her husband was abusive to her and to their daughters. He had legal residency, and, during his frequent bursts of anger, he threatened to have her and their daughters deported. On occasions when he traveled to Guatemala for visits, he had his mother stay in the house to watch Hilda. When Hilda finally filed a restraining order in 2000, her husband entered the house on a morning when she was taking the children to school and removed every stick of furniture. During the years when she lived as a single parent, she worked as a babysitter to support herself and her children.

Hilda enrolled in the ILP in its very first semester in 1989. She completed six cycles, and then left after her third child was born. She later re-enrolled, and in time completed a total of nine instructional cycles. Her attendance fluctuated over the period of her enrollment, ranging from over 90% in the earliest cycles to under 70% in cycles when she said that her husband would not let her attend class; overall, her attendance rate was 78%.

Hilda remarried in 2004, and she is often seen walking in the community holding hands with her new husband. Her oldest daughter, Lilian, struggled in middle school and was retained once during the year that her parents separated; she graduated from high school in 2001 and currently works in a retail store. Her second daughter, Yareniz, graduated on time in 2005 with a 2.2 GPA. Yareniz said that she "desperately" wanted to go to college when she graduated, but she was not immediately able to because she did not have a green card or citizenship status necessary to get financial aid. In 2008, she obtained green card status and enrolled in a community college the same week. She graduated in 2009 with a certificate in medical assisting, is working full-time, and recently married. Luz Mary, the third oldest (and first born in the United States), is presently a senior in high school, in honors courses, with a 3.3 GPA. She is involved in several school activities and is applying to universities. She wants to study in New York. Hilda's son, Francisco (known as Paquito), is in 10th grade and is enrolled in all honors classes. He, too, participates in several school-related activities and clubs and sees himself as college-bound.

Figure 12.6 provides insight into Hilda's commitment to education even as a young child and perhaps helps to explain her long-term relationship with the ILP despite the challenges in her life. Figure 12.7 provides evidence of her frequent and varied school and learning-related interactions with her children during one brief period of time.

Figure 12.6. Hilda's First Day of School Essay

My First Day of School

When I was six and a half years old I had a friend named Gloria. She invited me to go to a private school.

That day they gave me a half of a pencil and a sheet of white paper that didn't have lines. They set me to making little dots like this .... and also little lines like this ————. And this pleased me so much that I always went there everyday.

As it was a private school, one had to pay and wear a uniform. I had neither uniform nor money. I worked half the day and studied half the day. My teacher, who was very good, loved me very much.

Yes, I was feeling somewhat ashamed those first few days. But in spite of my poverty and the fact that I had never been to a school, I liked it.

And up to this very day I am grateful to my friend, Gloria, and my teacher. Thanks to them I was able to go to school. For which, today, I have my letters and I can read.

My big sister didn't like for me to study. So I would finish the chores quickly and that way she would let me go, and I would cry when she wouldn't. But if I finished quickly she would let me go, but really angrily.

The second day that I went it was raining. I covered myself, along with my friend Gloria, with a nylon. We weren't looking where we were going, as we were so small, and we passed under the legs of a burro. This was in Guatemala.

Figure 12.7. Hilda's Literacy Log Entry

Literacy Log

Name: ____________________

Month/Year: 9 - 17 - 97

Date	Reading, writing, viewing and talking activities I shared with my child or children	Child's name and age
9-16-97	Yesterday MY Son Paquito Show Me how Tu Play a Game. el Juego es que el carnisero no pued Carne:	
9-17-97	Yesturday MY Daugther and my Son We went to the library and take a BooK.	
9-23-97	Yesturday I help to My Daugter Lilian with Your home work The home work is about My country Guatemala.	
9-24-97	Yesturday I went to The Kelly School Because is openhouse.	
10-1-97	Yesturday MY Son Paquito Play with Your name:	
10-2-97	Yesturday I Reading a Book the name is Walk - Caminando Two lenguage	
10-7-97	Yesturday a I Read Never Read Your Elephant to school. MY Dauthers and my Son Likes That Book and tape.	
10-8-97	Yesturday MY Daugther Jasenie Reading For me her homework When is Finish I need to	

9/95

What We Learned

The work we describe in this chapter was designed to check back in with students whose families participated in the ILP during their early years of schooling to gain some understanding of the effects the ILP might have had on their academic progress. So, what did we learn?

The evidence indicates that, when compared with students in the general school population, the children of families who participate in the ILP have significantly higher rates of attendance and exhibit a trend toward higher grades, higher high school completion rates, higher scores on large-scale assessments of both English language arts and mathematics, and higher rates of entry into postsecondary education. Evidence also indicates that a longer period of participation in the ILP correlates with higher rate of school attendance by children. This is especially important given evidence here and elsewhere that school attendance correlates with GPA, lower school dropout rates, and overall motivation and engagement in learning (e.g., Konstantopoulos, 2006; Steward, Steward, Blair, Jo, & Hill, 2008). As such, the attendance data lend credibility to the trends observed in the other indicators (i.e., GPA, state assessment scores, graduation, and postsecondary education).

There are other reasons to be encouraged by the trends that favor ILP students. As noted previously, ILP participants start out at an academic disadvantage. In addition to substantially more children qualifying for special education services, U.S. Census Bureau data (2000) indicate that ILP parents and general education parents differ in other important ways: a substantially lower percentage of ILP parents have a high school credential (38% as compared with 60%), and a substantially higher percentage have had fewer than nine years of formal schooling (49% as compared with 22%). Moreover, whereas 58% of parents in the general education report that a language other than English is spoken at home, 100% of ILP parents report that a language other than English spoken at home. Studies have found each of these factors predicts greater risk of academic failure for children in the families.

Of course, the eventual academic success of ILP children may be accounted for in ways unrelated to their families' participation in the ILP. All of the families who participate in the ILP come voluntarily, so, at the outset, there is an apparent parental disposition toward taking actions that will support their own learning and that of their children. Some might say that, given this, the children in these families would likely have succeeded with or without the ILP. Alternatively, these children might have had the benefit of remarkable classroom teaching, and this might have made the difference in their school success. Or, for those who struggled in the face of the MCAS requirement, MCAS prep courses offered at the high school may have been the deciding factor. Moreover, many of the students were identified as having special needs—in fact, far more than the average percentage in this particular school system. Perhaps it was such identification and the special programming they received that allowed them to persist and achieve academic success. But as we talked with parents and their now adolescent children, these were not the factors they cited. Rather, they consistently linked their attitudes toward learning and achieving to their participation in the

ILP and to the literacy routines and habits of mind that participation encouraged. The words of one young woman (now attending a university on a merit scholarship) were representative of the sentiments of many:

> The ILP was a big part of my childhood. We took books from the ILP library, and my mom read with us every night, every night. She always made us do our homework; she never let us give up. I feel like the ILP is my other home.

How Might the Work of the ILP Guide Others?

As of late 2009, we are in the process of collecting additional evidence, this time using an experimental design that will allow us to more systematically examine programmatic effects. But for now, we take this first round of evidence as a very positive, if not conclusive, indicator that participation in the ILP sets students on a pathway toward eventual academic success. We believe that the ILP's success can be traced to five fundamental principles that, if adopted by others involved in work of this type, might lead to similar outcomes.

First, the ILP is grounded in the premise that the language and cultural traditions of the home setting are of fundamental importance to literacy learning. This is, of course, not a new idea. Rather, we relied on the work of many others (e.g., González, Moll, & Amanti, 2005; Heath, 1983; Taylor, 1997) to guide us as we initially planned and continue to revise and refine our routines and practices. But time and time again, our own work has affirmed the importance of discovering and building on what parents and children already know and do. We believe that several of our routines help us to learn about and from our families: the daily or weekly use of literacy logs detailing what parents do to support their own literacy and that of their children, the reading response journals that join parents and children in shared reading and response, and the writing of stories connecting the texts parents read to the texts of their own lives. Each of these literacy events provides us a window into what families know and do; even when the windows are tiny, allowing only a peek, we can often discover a tidbit of information upon which we can develop a context that is comfortable and familiar and upon which we can add new literacy practices and events.

Second, even as we strive to connect family literacy classes to events and routines that are commonly practiced at home, we also seek to connect parents and children to events and routines that are common to early childhood and elementary school classrooms. We do this in a variety of ways, among them, by deliberately adopting the language of classroom literacy instruction (e.g., *story maps*, *graphic organizers*, *reading response*); by explicitly introducing parents to ways to interact with teachers during parent–teacher conferences or other meetings; and by explaining beneficial homework routines. At times, we are able to connect to upcoming school events (e.g., preparation for state testing) and, occasionally, we can even connect to classroom curriculum (e.g., the "language" of mathematics; a social studies or science topic of study).

Third, we build on evidence that reading and writing achievement correlates with instructional intensity and focus (e.g., Allington, 2005; Torgeson, 2004). We achieve intensity by providing a significant, although still not ideal, number of hours of instruction each week (6–8), and also by requiring high levels of attendance to maintain active enrollment. Additionally, homework tasks that require extended reading and writing and require joint participation by parents and children also increase the intensity of the learning experience. Finally, as is evident in the description of classroom routines and activities, we are relentlessly focused on literacy. For the entire two-hour period, parents read, write, and respond to texts. As we learned from Worthy and Roser (2004) and Guthrie and Humenick (2004), the quality of the texts available to readers is of critical importance in reading engagement. Thus, we deliberately choose focal texts that are high interest and often consequential in their children's lives (e.g., about nutrition, crime, housing, high-stakes testing), increasing the likelihood that parents will be actively engaged in reading and responding.

Fourth, we build on evidence that some types of parent–child literacy interactions are more helpful than others (e.g., Bus, Van IJzendoorn, & Pellegrini, 1995; DeTemple & Snow, 2003; Scarborough & Dobrich, 1994; Sénéchal & Young, 2008). Although much of what we do with parents is built around storybook reading, we are deliberate about the types of books we share. That is, we intentionally choose alphabet and rhyming books for preschool children to support the development of phonological awareness and letter-name knowledge; we choose books rich in language and content to support the development of vocabulary and world knowledge; and when possible, we recommend books that will help build children's background knowledge in topics related to the classroom curriculum. Moreover, we introduce and practice strategies that are likely to help students benefit from parent–child shared reading. Parents learn strategies that encourage children to predict and respond to texts. They learn to explain and elaborate, and to engage children in talk about the text and their own experiences.

Fifth, our organization of classes into 12- to 15-week cycles builds on evidence that although family literacy interventions do not need to be large-scale, they do need to be long-lasting enough to affect sustained practices on the part of both families and schools. (e.g., Edwards, 1991; Edwards & Panofsky, 1989). Developing new strategies and establishing new routines takes time and practice; our own data tell us that there is a relationship between the number of cycles in which parents participate and children's school attendance; and attendance, by itself, has been found to correlate with academic achievement. We can predict, then, that programs that build in an extended period of participation from the start are more likely to achieve the outcomes we anticipate.

In closing, we know there is yet much to learn about ways to optimize learning opportunities afforded to parents and children who participate in family literacy intervention programs. As we await further evidence, we hope that this description of the ILP and its outcomes will provide a springboard for discussion and further development of policies and practices that will expand learning opportunities for families who, too often, are relegated to the margins.

NOTES

This work was supported by funding from the Nellie Mae Education Foundation.

REFERENCES

Allington, R. (2005). *What really matters for struggling readers: Designing research-based programs* (2nd ed). Boston: Allyn & Bacon.

Baker, L., Mackler, K., Sonnenschein, S., & Serpell, R. (2001). Parents' interactions with their first-grade children during storybook reading and relations with subsequent home reading activity and reading achievement. *Journal of School Psychology, 39*(5), 415–438. doi:10.1016/S0022-4405(01)00082-6

Bos, J.M., Scrivener, S., Snipes, J., & Hamilton, G. (with Schwartz, C., & Walter, J.). (2002). *Improving basic skills: The effects of adult education in welfare-to-work programs.* Washington, DC: U.S. Department of Education Office of Vocational and Adult Education.

Bourque, M.M. (2008). *The impact of student mobility on urban school districts.* Unpublished doctoral dissertation, Boston University.

Bus, A.G., Van IJzendoorn, M.H., & Pellegrini, A.D. (1995). Joint book reading makes for success in learning to read: A meta-analysis in intergenerational transmission of literacy. *Review of Educational Research, 65*(5), 1–21.

Clark, M. (1976). *Young fluent readers: What can they teach us?* London: Heinemann.

Comings, J.P., Parella, A., & Soricone, L. (1999). *Persistence among adult basic education students in pre-G.E.D. classes* (NCSALL Rep. No. 12). Cambridge, MA: The National Center for the Study of Adult Learning and Literacy, Harvard Graduate School of Education.

Davis-Kean, P.E. (2005). The influence of parent education and family income on child achievement: The indirect role of parental expectations and the home environment. *Journal of Family Psychology, 19*(2), 294–304. doi:10.1037/0893-3200.19.2.294

deJong, P.F., & Leseman, P.M. (2001). Lasting effects of home literacy on reading achievement in school. *Journal of School Psychology, 39*(5), 389–414. doi:10.1016/S0022-4405(01)00080-2

Delpit, L. (1995). *Other people's children: Cultural conflict in the classroom.* New York: The New Press.

Denton, K., & West, J. (2002). *Children's reading and mathematics achievement in kindergarten and first grade* (NCES 2002-125). Washington, DC: U.S. Department of Education, National Center for Education Statistics, U.S. Government Printing Office.

DeTemple, J., & Snow, C.E. (2003). Learning words from books. In A. van Kleeck, S.A. Stahl, & E.B. Bauer (Eds.), *On reading books to children: Parents and teachers* (pp. 16–36). Mahwah, NJ: Erlbaum.

Downer, J.T., & Pianta, R.C. (2006). Academic and cognitive functioning in first grade: Associations with earlier home and child care predictors and with concurrent home and classroom experiences. *School Psychology Review, 35*(1), 11–30.

Durkin, D. (1966). *Children who read early: Two longitudinal studies.* New York: Teachers College Press.

Edwards, P.A. (1991). Fostering early literacy through parent coaching. In E. Hiebert (Ed.), *Literacy for a diverse society: Perspectives, programs, and policies* (pp. 199–213). New York: Teachers College Press.

Edwards, P.C., & Panofsky, C. (1989). The effect of two training procedures on the book reading of low-SES mothers and children. In S. McCormick & J. Zutell (Eds.), *Cognitive and social perspectives for literacy research and instruction* (38th yearbook of the National Reading Conference, pp. 135–143). Chicago: National Reading Conference.

Gadsden, V.L. (2000). Intergenerational literacy within families. In M.L. Kamil, P.B. Mosenthal, P.D. Pearson, & R. Barr (Eds.), *Handbook of reading research* (Vol. 3, pp. 871–889). Mahwah, NJ: Erlbaum.

González, N., Moll, L.C., & Amanti, C. (2005). *Funds of knowledge: Theorizing practices in households, communities, and classrooms.* Mahwah, NJ: Erlbaum.

Guthrie, J.T., & Humenick, N.M. (2004). Motivating students to read: Evidence for classroom practices that increase reading motivation and achievement. In P. McCardle & V. Chhabra (Eds.), *The voice of evidence in reading research* (pp. 329–354). Baltimore: Paul H. Brookes.

Heath, S.B. (1983). *Ways with words: Language, life, and work in communities and classrooms.* Cambridge, England: Cambridge University Press.

Konstantopoulos, S. (2006). Trends in school effects on student achievement: Evidence from NLS:72, HSB:82, and NELS:92. *Teachers College Record, 108*(12), 2550–2581. doi:10.1111/j.1467-9620.2006.00796.x

Lee, J., & Bowen, N.K. (2006). Parent involvement, cultural capital, and the achievement gap among elementary school children. *American Educational Research Journal, 43*(2), 193–218. doi:10.3102/00028312043002193

Magnuson, K. (2007). Maternal education and children's academic achievement during middle childhood. *Developmental Psychology, 43*(6), 1497–1512. doi:10.1037/0012-1649.43.6.1497

Mantzicopoulos, P. (2003). Flunking kindergarten after Head Start: An inquiry into the contribution of contextual and individual variables. *Journal of Educational Psychology, 95*(2), 268–278. doi:10.1037/0022-0663.95.2.268

Mattingly, D.J., Prislan, R., McKenzie, T.L., Rodriguez, J.L., & Kayzar, B. (2002). Evaluating evaluations: The case of parent involvement programs. *Review of Educational Research, 72*(4), 549–576. doi:10.3102/00346543072004549

McCallion, G. (2006). Even Start: Funding controversy: Congressional Research Service Report for Congress, Order Code RL33071. Retrieved May 29, 2009, from www.ed.psu.edu/goodlinginstitute/pdf/crs_even_start_funding_controversy.pdf

Morrow, L.M., Paratore, J.R., Gaber, D., Harrison, D., & Tracey, D. (1993). Family literacy: Perspective and practices. *The Reading Teacher, 47*(3), 194–200.

Office of Management and Budget. (2009). Terminations, reductions, and savings. Budget of the U.S. Government, Fiscal Year

2010. Retrieved May 29, 2009, from www .whitehouse.gov/omb/budget/TRS/

Paratore, J.R. (1993). Influence of an intergenerational approach to literacy on the practice of literacy of parents and their children. In C. Kinzer & D. Leu (Eds.), *Examining central issues in literacy, research, theory, and practice* (42nd yearbook of the National Reading Conference, pp. 83–91). Chicago: National Reading Conference.

Paratore, J.R. (1994). Parents and children sharing literacy. In D.F. Lancy (Ed.), *Children's emergent literacy: From research to practice* (pp. 193–216). Westport, CT: Praegar.

Paratore, J.R., Krol-Sinclair, B., David, B., & Schick, A. (2009). *Long-term effects of a family literacy intervention: Final report prepared for the Nellie Mae Education Foundation.* Boston: Boston University.

Paratore, J.R., Melzi, G., & Krol-Sinclair, B. (1999). *What should we expect of family literacy? Experiences of Latino children whose parents participate in an intergenerational literacy program.* Newark, DE: International Reading Association.

Purcell-Gates, V. (2000). Family literacy. In M.L. Kamil, P.B. Mosenthal, P.D. Pearson, & R. Barr (Eds.), *Handbook of reading research* (Vol. 3, pp. 853–870). Mahwah, NJ: Erlbaum.

Scarborough, H.S., & Dobrich, W. (1994). On the efficacy of reading to preschoolers. *Developmental Review, 14*(3), 245–302. doi:10.1006/drev.1994.1010

Sénéchal, M., & LeFevre, J. (2002). Parental involvement in the development of children's reading skill: A five-year longitudinal study. *Child Development, 73*(2), 445–460. doi:10.1111/1467-8624.00417

Sénéchal, M., LeFevre, J., & Thomas, E.M. (1998). Differential effects of home literacy experiences on the development of oral and written language. *Reading Research Quarterly, 33*(1), 96–116. doi:10.1598/RRQ.33.1.5

Sénéchal, M., & Young, L. (2008). The effect of family literacy interventions on children's acquisition of reading from kindergarten to grade 3: A meta-analytic review. *Review of Educational Research, 78*(4), 880–907. doi:10.3102/0034654308320319

Sonnenschein, S., & Munsterman, K. (2002). The influence of home-based reading interactions on 5-year-olds' reading motivations and early literacy development. *Early Childhood Research Quarterly, 17*(3), 318–337. doi:10.1016/S0885-2006(02)00167-9

St. Pierre, R.G., Layzer, J.I., & Barnes, H.V. (1998). Regenerating two-generation programs. In W.S. Barnett & S.S. Boocock (Eds.), *Early care and education for children in poverty: Promises, programs, and long-term results* (pp. 99–122). Albany: State University of New York Press.

Steward, R.J., Steward, A.D., Blair, J., Jo, H., & Hill, M.F. (2008). School attendance revisited: A study of urban African American students' grade point averages and coping strategies. *Urban Education, 43*(5), 519–536. doi:10.1177/0042085907311807

Sticht, T.G., & McDonald, B. (1989). *Making the nation smarter: The intergenerational transfer of literacy.* San Diego, CA: Institute for Adult Literacy.

Taylor, D. (1997). *Many families, many literacies.* Portsmouth, NH: Heinemann.

Torgesen, J.K. (2004). Lessons learned from the last 20 years of research on interventions for students who experience difficulty learning to read. In P. McCardle & V. Chhabra (Eds.), *The voice of evidence in reading research* (pp. 355–387). Baltimore: Paul H. Brookes.

Worthy, J., & Roser, N.L. (2004). Flood ensurance: When children have books they can and want to read. In D. Lapp, C.C. Block, E.J. Cooper, & J. Flood, N. Roser, & Tinajero, J.V. (Eds.), *Teaching all the children: Strategies for developing literacy in an urban setting* (pp. 179–192). New York: Guilford.

Yaden, D.B., & Paratore, J.R. (2002). Family literacy at the turn of the millennium: The costly future of maintaining the status quo. In J.E. Flood, D. Lapp, J. Jensen, & J. Squire (Eds.), *Research in English and the language arts* (pp. 532–545). Mahwah, NJ: Erlbaum.

CHAPTER 13

Cultivating New Funds of Knowledge Through Research and Practice

Luis C. Moll and Julio Cammarota

For several years we have conducted work, mostly in collaboration with teachers and anthropologists, that seeks to identify and document social practices and funds of knowledge in households (González, Moll, & Amanti, 2005). We claim that such work, done as learners entering households with an ethnographic eye toward documenting knowledge, provides teachers with an important cultural framing of families and students, with implications for the teaching of literacy as meaningful practice. This framing, which in our case combines a "processual" anthropological approach (González, 2005a; 2008) with a Vygotskian cultural-historical psychology (Moll, 2000), facilitates an intellectual sensitivity to understanding thinking and learning in sociocultural context.

In relation to the teachers with whom we worked, this research offered both theory and methods to help define working-class families as possessing valuable cultural resources for instruction, challenging any perception that they would be lacking in such assets, while helping teachers establish relationships of trust with parents and students on which to base their pedagogy. From the beginning of the funds of knowledge work, we were also concerned with the social stratification of schooling, especially the rote and reductionist structures that characterize working-class schooling. Consequently, most of our work in classrooms was devoted to developing, with teachers, inquiry-based approaches to learning, inviting parents and others in the community to contribute intellectually to classroom activities, or using literature as the basis for meaning-driven literacy instruction, often in both English and Spanish (e.g., González et al.,

2005). In brief, the emphasis has been on treating diversity, as manifested in the lives of people, as a pedagogical resource.

This work has been, if we may say so, well received. The term *fund(s) of knowledge* has become part of the vocabulary of educational researchers and practitioners, often in relation to generating positive representations of students and families, enhancing social relations between families and teachers, or connecting teaching practices to student interests or family knowledge for the purpose of enhancing the academic development of students (e.g., Haneda, 2006; Moll & González, 2004). In addition, this research on funds of knowledge helped orient our observations and interviews beyond documenting just literacy events per se. Instead, it allowed us to situate such events within a richer understanding of the household ecology, including its economic base, division of labor, productive activities, relations of exchange, educational ideologies, and the production of knowledge. From the beginning, we found this concept fully compatible with the Vygotskian intent of developing a concrete psychology, one grounded in the particulars, both proximal and distal, of social life.

For present purposes, however, rather than reiterate this work, which we have presented in considerable detail elsewhere (González et al., 2005), we would like to discuss two examples of work that extend this approach by concentrating on cultivating in students new funds of knowledge and literate practices that generate additional social and intellectual resources for household or classroom life. (We use *cultivating* in the mediational sense proposed by Fuhrer and Johnson, 1998.) In both examples, the "home–school connection," as Rodríguez-Brown (2009) refers to it, remains important if not crucial, however indirect, but the emphasis is on developing expansive and varied forms of literacy with students.

In this chapter, we first reinforce the importance of the home–school connection by presenting a partial summary of Portes and Rumbaut's (2001) decade-long longitudinal research with second-generation students, the children of immigrants; this is, arguably, the most important work on the topic. We highlight the educational power of *selective acculturation*, of which fluent bilingualism and the familial relations such bilingualism facilitates is a prime indicator. We then establish the feasibility of *literate bilingualism* as an additive form of schooling for all children by borrowing from our own longitudinal work on the development of biliteracy, concentrating mostly on elementary school students. By additive schooling we mean facilitating meaningful inclusion of students' home language or cultural experiences as part of their schooling. We argue for the importance of biliteracy, which among other advantages greatly facilitates this "double move" for the students, establishing social relations with families of the sort that facilitate forms of selective acculturation while engaging them in academic activities.

We then turn to an example of participatory action research (PAR) with adolescents, work inspired in part by the funds of knowledge research (Romero et al., 2008). Using various "literacies of representation" (Paul & Wang, 2006), students conduct critical social research within their communities and schools as a central part of their schooling (Cammarota & Fine, 2008; Cammarota, Moll, Cannella, & González, in preparation; Cannella, 2009). This is research that advances an academic agenda while situating the students' work in the broader social context of household and community life.

Selective Acculturation

It is by now well established that fluent bilingualism represents both a social and intellectual asset for children. Recent evidence comes from the work of the sociologists Portes and Rumbaut (2001) with children of immigrants, referred to as second-generation students, of which Mexican Americans are the largest group in the United States. Portes and Rumbaut conceptualized and developed their decade-long survey with the goal of providing a longitudinal, multidimensional understanding of second-generation adaptation, including the interaction between immigrant parents and children. In particular, they sought to clarify the process of social incorporation, which instead of a more or less uniform process of assimilation into society, as the standard U.S. dogma has it, they found to be highly variable. They use the term *segmented assimilation* to indicate different modes of incorporation—distinct paths and consequences—depending on family resources (human and social capital), including years of schooling and income, family composition and stability, and possible barriers to incorporation, especially the sort of reception received by immigrants (the first generation) in U.S. society, whether hostile, favorable, or neutral. Needless to say, the offspring of wealthy and well-received immigrants fare better than those of impoverished and poorly received immigrants; but there is more to the story than that.

Portes and Rumbaut's (2001) sample, based mostly in Miami and San Diego—two prominent receiving communities for immigrants—consisted initially (1992) of 5,200 students who were then in ninth grade. They collected data subsequently in 1995–1996, when the students were high school seniors, and then in 2002, when they were about 24 years old, or young adults. We concentrate here on the most recent data (2006) in summarizing their argument, for which they also gathered open-ended case study interviews in both locations with a sample of respondents who overcame adverse circumstances to achieve in higher education, and with respondents' parents and (if married) spouses (see Portes, Fernandez-Kelly, & Haller, 2008).

The model proposed by Portes and colleagues (2008) captures the different "paths of adaptation" and determinants of segmented assimilation. The paths include upward assimilation, which is anchored in high parental human or social capital that is often provided by co-ethnic social networks. The paths may also include placement into working-class jobs or downward assimilation into poverty or unemployment. These researchers also identify barriers faced by second-generation children, including racism and discrimination, stratified labor markets, and recruitment into illicit activities. Portes and colleagues make the point that the advent of a knowledge-based, "hourglass" economy, with its bifurcation of top-tier jobs requiring an advanced education and technological skills, and lower-tier service occupations requiring mostly manual labor, has eliminated the previous economic structure that included an array of semi-skilled and skilled industrial occupations that facilitated options for intergenerational mobility.

A consequence, Portes and colleagues (2008) propose, is that "new entrants into the labor force, including children of immigrants...must acquire *in the course of a single generation* the advanced educational credentials that took descendants of Europeans many generations to achieve" (p. 8, emphasis in original). For those who do not achieve educationally, and with economic options limited by the bifurcation of the economy, an attractive alternative may become to engage in gang or other illicit activities with undesirable consequences, a reality these researchers label as *downward assimilation*. The interaction between family conditions, such as the level of schooling of the family, and the barriers faced by immigrants, such as those posed by racism, help mediate or determine the particular pace and modes of incorporation into society. As such, the conditions and resources of the first generation help establish the modes of incorporation of the second generation. Portes and Rumbaut (2001) explain it as follows: Children of highly educated or affluent immigrants, such as professionals, frequently undergo a process of *consonant acculturation*, where children and parents learn jointly to accommodate to the new society and, with more resources (human and social capital) and unencumbered by hostile conditions, replicate their position of privilege. In contrast, youths from working-class immigrant families, especially those who lack the social support or capital of a strong co-ethnic community (e.g., the Cuban enclave in Miami), may undergo *dissonant acculturation*, featuring adaptation to language and values of the new society while rejecting family ways and parental control and guidance. In these circumstances, children may learn English but lose or not develop fluency in the home language, often leading to a rupture of communication and alienation from family; in a sense, they must adapt on their own, bereft of much needed resources.

In sharp contrast to dissonant acculturation, especially for working-class students, stands what Portes and Rumbaut (2001) refer to as *selective acculturation*, where students learn English and U.S. ways while retaining important elements of the home culture, most notably fluency in the language. In this scenario, bilingualism is key to preserving intergenerational communications and, with it, parents' ability to provide discipline and guidance for their children, facilitate appreciation and respect for the parental culture and values, and monitor their academic progress (cf., Golash-Boza, 2005). As their data show, contrary to trenchant assimilationist and English-only ideologies, selective acculturation and fluent bilingualism are significantly associated with several positive outcomes in late adolescence, including higher school grades, self-esteem, and educational aspirations, and lesser intergenerational conflict with families (Portes et al., 2008).

In Portes et al.'s (2008) final round of data collection, they gathered interviews from respondents, few in number, who grew up in circumstances that one would expect would lead to downward assimilation but who had succeeded in school or graduated from college. They found that the most important element in common among these students, in combination with the guidance of alert parents and significant others, such as a caring teacher who would direct the student in her or his academic pursuits, was the ability to build on what we would call household funds of knowledge in overcoming barriers to advancement or mobility. In their words,

> dissonant acculturation deprives youths of this resource as they lose contact or even reject the language and culture of parents. Whatever resources are embodied in that culture effectively dissipate.... Only in the selective path of intergenerational adaptation do we find a platform to make full use of those resources brought from abroad. (p. 34)

Therefore, educational policies directed at a forced transition to English monolingualism instead of the cultivation of fluent bilingualism are seriously misguided. They deprive children of valuable resources to maintain critical intergenerational alliances—fracturing family relations as they adapt to a new society—and of their most important intellectual tool to succeed academically early in their schooling. As Portes and Hao (2002) suggest, it is the possibility of learning English

> while preserving the cultural anchor in the family's own past that lead[s] to the most desirable results. Cut the moorings and children are cast adrift in a uniform monolingual world. They, their families, and eventually the communities where they settle will pay the price. (p. 22)

Literate Bilingualism

How feasible is it to provide additive forms of schooling practices that facilitate the type of selective acculturation, including home–school connections, associated with successful social and academic outcomes? We have addressed this question through a longitudinal study of a school that produces biliteracy in all of its students, regardless of their cultural background or their home language. In this section, we summarize not the pedagogical details or particulars of how this school, located in the U.S. southwest, creates bilingual and literate persons, but the broader characteristics of this institutional setting and how practitioners, with the support of families, instantiate additive bilingual conditions for learning. This case study is even more remarkable in that the school's work is being done under hostile conditions; the state has implemented policies to ban with edicts and punitive threats precisely these forms of schooling. That the school manages to survive and thrive even in these adverse conditions is an example of what we have come to call *educational sovereignty*, the ability of a school to marshall its resources to provide an additive education for its students, even when under ideological siege by the state (Moll & Ruiz, 2002, 2005).

This story is complex and it also involves the actions of teachers and students in reaction to the impositions of the state (González, 2005b) and the full-fledged support of parents for the goals of the school. Here we summarize only some important elements of this school and its institutional arrangements. Educational sovereignty is something that is established de facto, configured in the daily practices of a school or district in response to its many challenges or constraints, but not necessarily declared by educational leaders and teachers as an explicit goal. How does the school organize itself to accomplish this goal? In our analysis we identified at least four key school practices that bolster this school's educational sovereignty (from Moll & Ruiz, 2005). They are as follows.

1. Teachers' Academic Qualifications

The school features, in contrast to most high-poverty schools, a highly qualified and diverse teaching corps. All of the instructors are certified bilingual teachers, over 70% hold a master's degree or higher, all have taken academic courses in both Spanish and English, and about 65% have taught in a dual-language program for more than seven years. We contend that this highly qualified staff helped give the school its academic emphasis and direction, especially its goal of fostering biliteracy—not simply oral bilingualism—in all students, central features of any practice of educational sovereignty.

We quote from a recent volume sponsored the National Academy of Education (NAE) that captures the point we are trying to make:

> Well prepared teachers have developed a sense of "where they are going" and how they and their students are going to get there. They are able to create a coherent curriculum that is also responsive to the needs of students and to construct a classroom community in which the "hidden curriculum" fosters respectful relations and equitable learning. They have thought about social purposes for education as well as their own visions and have integrated these so that their students can be successful in the world outside of school as well as within the supportive environment of the classroom. (Darling-Hammond et al., 2005, p. 177)

2. The Creation of Confianza

Here we are using the concept of *confianza*, or mutual trust, as borrowed from our analysis of household funds of knowledge (González et al., 2005). In the original work, we used the term to refer to the necessary trust households need in order to establish social relations of exchange; in fact we referred to *confianza* as the glue that held the households' multiple (and sometimes fragile) social networks together. Here we extend this concept to refer to the nature of the social relationships among administrators, teachers, and students that help establish the particular culture of the school, a culture of caring, if you will, to borrow from Noddings (1992), that came to define the school and that helped define who these adults are in relation to one another and the children.

The teachers in this school were entrusted to help make pedagogical and policy decisions for the school. Two examples may suffice. One is that the teachers proposed and established the proportion or distribution of use of languages for the school, where teaching in Spanish predominated; this arrangement is a deliberate attempt to protect Spanish, or to make it an *unmarked* language in the context of the school, what Luke (2009) calls establishing the school's *lingua franca*. Another example is the teachers' decision to propose an alternative language arts arrangement for Spanish—cross-age Spanish language arts sessions offered to all students, with schoolwide teacher participation, for an hour and a quarter three days a week. This innovation is widely credited within the school for privileging the development of Spanish and enhancing the biliterate capabilities of the students. The point here is that, under the conditions created by the administrators, teachers helped define themselves as a particular type of professional, and as a particular type of person, with the necessary funds of knowledge to make curricular decisions that helped define the nature of the educational relationships in the school.

3. Ideological Clarity

The school staff is well aware of the degree to which teaching is a political activity, especially after defending the children's language rights during the successful campaign by the state to establish an English-only language policy. It would be accurate to state that the school is constantly vigilant of any attempts to either alter the dual-language agenda of the school or impose an English-only curriculum. There is unanimous support among the faculty for the bilingual goals and culture of the school, and an awareness of how the school status is a political achievement and must be constantly reenacted in their practices.

An example may clarify this point. During the study a teacher approached the principal to inform her that she (the teacher) found it cumbersome to teach so much of the time in Spanish and that she planned to modify the school immersion model to teach more in English. The principal calmly replied that she (the principal) knew that the teacher was a very good teacher and that teaching in Spanish may be taxing, so she would write her an excellent letter of recommendation for her next job. The message was clear: There was broad agreement on offering students a legitimate immersion model that would result in biliteracy, and deviations would place the program at risk.

4. Extended School Ecology

The school also features an extensive after-school program loaded with cultural activities for the children and conducted in either language, with an almost 100% participation rate by the students. There is a strong emphasis on privileging Mexican cultural activities, given its location in the U.S. borderlands, including having a mariachi band, Mexican folkloric dancing, and a guitarist group. These activities are available to all students and are intended to help the children invest themselves in the school's culture regardless of their cultural background.

During the political campaign that preceded the passage into state law by popular vote of severe restrictions on bilingual education programs, which was overwhelmingly opposed by Latino and American Indian communities, we were able to document how the school became a site of resistance to the imposition of this highly constraining regulation. The campaign became a defining moment for the school, as teachers, students, and their parents became activists in defending their school from political attacks (González, 2005b). Even after the passage of the law, the school, with the support of the parents, has remained a site of defiance, so to speak, as it has continued to offer its curriculum—what they consider not only a pedagogical but also a moral choice for the students— while also adjusting its practices to the new legal conditions.

Revealingly, the father of one of the students, an attorney, offered that his firm would defend any teacher or administrator *pro bono* if the state took legal action against them, as they had threatened. Of course, not all schools can have a law firm at their disposal; this is an extraordinary example. Nevertheless, this action reflects how school leaders and teachers, as part of an extended ecology, fostered social relations with families that became resources for survival and bolstered their school as a progressive setting for learning.

Multimedia Literacy

Our final example also involves establishing a form of educational sovereignty, we could say, in this instance a social science program option for students within well-established high schools. This option is widely known as the Social Justice Education Project (SJEP; Romero et al., 2008). The SJEP began in 2003 with a classroom of 17 high school students. Currently, the program boasts more than 150 students in five courses at three different high schools. The majority of the students are from the predominantly Latino south and southwest sections of town. Most are children from poor or working-class families, and most have experienced the disadvantages of an inferior education.

The goal of the SJEP is to reverse the historical trend of failure, lowered expectations, and negligence that has plagued Latinos for generations (Cammarota, 2006; Chapa & Valencia, 1993; Sanchez, 1997; Valencia, 2002; Valenzuela, 1999). SJEP achieves this goal by, for example, allowing students to satisfy all their social science requirements for the senior year and supplementing course content with college-level material in critical race theory, critical pedagogy, and participatory action research (Cammarota, 2007). This twofold objective provides students with the opportunity to master state standards while developing the critical consciousness vital for improving their educational experiences.

The supplemental material encourages students, through a Freirean literacy perspective, to "read the world" to transform it through engaged praxis (Freire 1970, 1994, 1998). Reading the world involves the students' awareness of the sociohistorical context that fosters the circumstances of their own existence. This type of reading moves students past self-condemnation for unjust social realities to the realization that subordination or secondary status results from institutional or systematic constraints. Engaged praxis requires students to use this realization specifically for change by learning how their situation or reality is not fixed but indeed malleable with direct challenges to oppressive barriers.

Hence, the SJEP promotes critical reading and engagement, or what Freire calls "critical literacy," by teaching students how to conduct ethnographies of their schools and communities. Students observe their social realities and then document their observations in field notes, poetry, photos, and videos. They conduct observations each week for several months, etching their weekly recollections in notebooks and cameras for future analysis. The process of observing and recording eventually leads to the creation of new funds of knowledge, as students gain insight into the details of purposive injustices, insights that may not be assumed a priori. These insights further elicit change within the students by promoting stronger perceptions of efficacy to not only overcome institutional barriers but also to work toward eliminating them.

The acquisition of new funds of knowledge leads to improved academic as well as social outcomes. SJEP students outperform their peers on standardized tests while graduating at an astonishing 95% rate (Romero, 2008). Along with improving their academic performance, students have successfully lobbied the school board to update library materials, improve learning conditions for special education students, and expand SJEP course offerings throughout the district (Cammarota, 2008).

The SJEP students' first video, "Questions for Answers" is an example of how they effect change through their critical literacy and engaged praxis. The video documents how the south-end portion of Cerro High School (all names are pseudonyms) is structurally inferior to the northern, Caucasian student dominated section. Most students at Cerro are working-class Latinos and compose 63% of the student population. Caucasians are the next largest group at 19%; the Native American and African American student populations are 12% and 6% respectively. Students of color thus represent the overwhelming majority at Cerro. Although Caucasian students are the "minority," they constitute more than 50% of the students enrolled in the Advanced Placement (AP) courses. Each year students at this school receive close to one million dollars in college scholarships, but the racial distribution of this money is appalling. Eighty percent of the scholarship money is awarded to Caucasian students. It appears to many students at Cerro that there is a school within a school: a better one in the buildings located on the north side of the campus for Caucasians and the inferior south buildings for students of color.

The video shows the southern section, the space which the SJEP students and most students of color inhabit, with broken bathrooms, nonfunctioning water fountains, pipes sticking out of walls, and library shelves missing books. In contrast, the video also documents the northern section where everything works; floors and walls are immaculate, there is a fully stocked law library for the special law magnet program, and computers are everywhere. The SJEP students recorded an interview with a fellow Latino student, Juan Rodriguez, who states that the specialized Law Magnet and AP programs housed in the northern part of the school

> seem like a school within a school. And that seems wrong because most of the students from the neighborhood don't get to go to the magnet program, and most students in the magnet program are white and not from the local neighborhoods.

The video concludes with one of the many poems created from the students' ethnographic observations. The poem, entitled "Top Ten," describes the frustration of Latino students who attempt to succeed academically but encounter impediments to advancement by the system of Caucasian privilege and "greed." This prose poem by Erica Baez serves to illustrate this point:

I see the ignorant with their faces of greed and envy. They look as if they've never had any struggle. Working parents always providing the best. I watch their mouths moving cruelly and unjustly. They appear to be the ruling class. The ones with high G.P.A.s and top ten spots. I hear their greedy comments and how they eat away their tongues. They talk about a "little Mexican" that rose as young. She didn't sit in a corner wasting away. She thought well I could do it too! I could be top ten and I too could have a high G.P.A. I listen to their negativity and how they kill human beings with their words. They express with hatred "send her back let's deport her!" I think this place is ruled by the superiority. Meanwhile we are left to be the minority until some rise and take their places. They imagine we are stupid, lazy, and dumb but what they don't know is that a grade doesn't mean a thing and standardize tests don't determine your wise-ness. I believe we are capable to get good grades and that we are not stupid, lazy, or dumb. We know there's a lot of hate, and sometimes it's not the hate that numbs the pain.

Based on observations and interviews, Erica documented the experiences of her classmate, Nyeli Torres—the "little Mexican" she refers to in her poem. According to Erica, Nyeli immigrated to town from Mexico—sharing her parents' hope of high achievement in U.S. public schools. Struggling with English in middle school, Nyeli could not achieve grades higher than average. However, when she was a freshman in high school, Nyeli became a straight-A student. In her junior year in high school, Nyeli became bored with the average-level material and lobbied her counselor to enroll her in AP courses. After arguing her case several times, she received her wish and she was enrolled in AP History. Nyeli lived up to her expectations and received an A in the course. Because of Nyeli's success, her counselor had no other choice but to place her in AP Government and AP English for her senior year. The Government class was a breeze, but the true challenge for Nyeli was the English class. She entered the U.S. public school system knowing only a few words of English, but when she walked through the door of her AP English class she believed that she had mastered the language.

However, some of her classmates and the teacher for the AP English class thought differently. Nyeli learned from friends that some of her classmates spoke with the teacher and said that if Nyeli received an A in the course, she would become the valedictorian of the school. These students reportedly complained, "Nyeli wasn't born in the U.S. and only came to this country a few years back. Therefore, it wouldn't be 'right' for her to receive an A in English and become valedictorian!" Nyeli received a B in the course, which prevented her from becoming the first Mexican American valedictorian in the school's history. Many students (and some parents and teachers) interpreted Nyeli's experience as a political move by students and their teacher to limit Nyeli's success; such experiences illustrate how racist and sexist discourses encourage individuals to reinforce a hierarchical order of success. Because Nyeli was a young Mexican immigrant female, being "top ten" was simply out of the question.

The poem reminds the video's viewers that some Cerro students face direct oppression and that their lack of success is the result of injustices within the school system. After watching the video, one is supposed to sense that the problem of racial disparity is not the fault of students but of the racism that privileges Caucasians over students of color. The video also suggests that systematic transformation is necessary to engender new and better educational experiences and outcomes.

As a result of the positive outcomes, the SJEP now regularly enrolls the younger brothers and sisters of those who graduated from the program several years earlier. The enrollment of successive generations, or what we might call an enhanced generational engagement, results from bringing the students' praxis to family members. Each semester, SJEP students hold *encuentros* (public meetings) with their families to explain their research and the new knowledge that emerges from their investigations. *Encuentros* represent true forms of praxis such that transformation occurs with students as well as their families. Students, through their actualizations as public intellectuals, see themselves as knowledgeable and thus solidify academic identities. Family members, including parents and siblings, realize that SJEP students act on their behalf by producing knowledge that could potentially create better opportunities for them and their communities. Buy-in and support for the SJEP has grown considerably over the past few years because of the prevalent belief among families that the experience provided by the program (in and of itself) will improve academic and social outcomes for the schools' Latino students. Although the program receives relatively little promotion from media and school officials, younger siblings of SJEP graduates enroll each year because they have prior knowledge of its potential.

The following is an excerpt from field notes written by Cammarota (second author) after an *encuentro* held in 2006. The excerpt focuses on a conversation between an SJEP student and another student's parent and how new funds of knowledge are transmitted through engaged praxis.

The most interesting aspect of the *encuentro* was the dialogue after the presentations. Selena's mother stated that most of the time the reason students don't well in school is because they just don't care, that teachers always put their best effort into teaching and students just don't try. Validia [SJEP student] provided a contrary perspective from her own experiences. She stated to Selena's mother that there are some bad teachers out there who don't really care about the students or their job. She cited examples to support her argument much in the same way that a researcher would do, convincing me that her experiences with the SJEP provided her with the skills for effective argumentation. She said teachers had told her she should become a dishwasher, teachers had told her to drop out, teachers had told her "why bother"... she should drop out and find a job to help her family. Selena's mom didn't respond back to Validia. She seemed shocked that teachers would say such things to students. It seemed as if she assumed all teachers had good intentions and that students were the bad ones in the formula of failure. The idea that teachers could be negligent and malicious was a new revelation to her. She may have learned something new that day. Because Validia was speaking from the truthful place of her own experiences, Selena's mother could not dispute her.

It is difficult to say with any certainty whether Selena's mother had changed her perceptions about education, teachers, or students. However, the format of the *encuentro*—the honesty and reciprocity of discussions—at least put her in the position of listening to Validia as an equal and accepting her ideas as a peer. She will now likely remember what Validia had to say. Validia's knowledge may not have changed her perception, but at minimum her words were a revelation.

Certainly, Validia was transformed. When we first met Validia, her school identified her as "failing." She scored far below average on standardized tests, and although the school listed her as a junior, technically she had earned credits only equivalent to freshman status. She often contemplated dropping out. The SJEP not only motivated Validia to stay in school but instilled in her a desire to attend college. In SJEP *encuentros*, Validia publicly stated that the SJEP motivated her to work hard. She declared that she planned to study both sociology and anthropology—sociology as an undergraduate and anthropology in graduate school. She wanted to further her education because she enjoyed analyzing society and then imparting her knowledge about problems and change to other people.

The SJEP represents the opportunity to participate in critical reading and engagement. This opportunity allows students to generate new funds of knowledge that not only solidify academic identities among themselves but also influence new possibilities of change for families and communities. The students' adoption of intellectual status promotes epiphanies among those who engage and listen to them. Their knowledge reveals the sense that they are acting in the best interest of others and could potentially lead to improved conditions in schools and communities. As in the previous example on biliteracy, trust is also a key element of success for the SJEP. Families want their children to participate in the program not only for the academic benefits but also for the trust students initiate by producing new knowledge to help others read the world and transform it.

Family Participation as Process and Outcome

Within the examples provided in this chapter, then, parental participation is seen in a new light, moving away from formulaic recipes on involving parents in schools toward engaging parents and other family members as coparticipants in and contributors to the life project of educating students. Whether the home–school connection is part of a strategy for understanding families on the basis of the resources and wherewithal they possess, such as in the funds of knowledge work; or a consequence of facilitating literate bilingualism that helps retain familial relations as key resources for academic and personal advancement, as Portes and colleagues (2008) assert; or as part of the broader ecology of learning as found in the SJEP; parental participation is understood as an open ended and multifaceted activity. None of these projects provide a single structure, such as parent–teacher associations, or straightforward suggestions on how to establish favorable home–school relations. Instead, the goal is to help the students engage intellectually, where multiple forms of literacy become bona fide instruments for thinking and action, and where the participation of families becomes both process and outcome of the activities.

REFERENCES

Cammarota, J. (2006). Disappearing in the Houdini education: The experiences of race and invisibility among Latina/o students. *Multicultural Education, 14*(1), 2–10.

Cammarota, J. (2007). A map for social change: Latino students engage a praxis of ethnography. *Children, Youth and Environments, 17*(2), 341–353.

Cammarota, J. (2008). The cultural organizing of youth ethnographers: Formalizing a praxis-based pedagogy. *Anthropology & Education Quarterly, 39*(1), 45–58. doi:10.1111/j.1548-1492.2008.00004.x

Cammarota, J., & Fine, M. (Eds.). (2008). *Revolutionizing education: Youth participatory action research in motion.* New York: Routledge.

Cammarota, J., Moll, L.C., Cannella, C., & González, M. (in preparation). *Sociocultural perspectives on interpersonal relationships in school.* Manuscript submitted for publication.

Cannella, C. (2009). *Opening windows, opening doors: Marginalized students engaging in praxis to become sociohistorical analysts and actors.* Unpublished doctoral dissertation, University of Arizona, Tucson.

Chapa, J., & Valencia, R.R. (1993). Latino population growth, demographic characteristics, and educational stagnation: An examination of recent trends. *Hispanic Journal of Behavioral Sciences, 15*(2), 165–187. doi:10.1177/07399863930152002

Darling-Hammond, L., Banks, J., Zumwalt, K., Gomez, L., Sherin, M.G., Griesdorn, J., et al. (2005). Educational goals and purposes: Developing a curricular vision for teaching. In L. Darling-Hammond & J. Bransford (Eds.), *Preparing teachers for a changing world: What teachers should learn and be able to do* (pp. 169–200). San Francisco: Jossey-Bass.

Freire, P. (1970). *Education for critical consciousness* (M.B. Ramos, Trans.). New York: Continuum.

Freire, P. (1994). *Pedagogy of the oppressed.* New York: Continuum.

Freire, P. (1998). *The Paulo Freire reader* (A.M.A. Freire & D. Macedo, Eds.). New York: Continuum.

Fuhrer, U., & Joseph, I.E. (1998). The cultivated mind: From mental mediation to cultivation. *Developmental Review, 18*(3), 279–312. doi:10.1006/drev.1997.0453

Golash-Boza, T. (2005). Assessing the advantages of bilingualism for children of immigrants. *The International Migration Review, 39*(3), 721–753. doi:10.1111/j.1747-7379.2005.tb00286.x

González, N. (2005a). Beyond culture: The hybridity of funds of knowledge. In N. González, L.C. Moll, & C. Amanti (Eds.), *Funds of knowledge: Theorizing practices in households, communities, and classrooms* (pp. 29–46). Mahwah, NJ: Erlbaum.

González, N. (2005b). Children in the eye of the storm: Language socialization and language ideologies in a dual language school. In A.C. Zentella (Ed.), *Building on strength: Language and literacy in Latino families and communities* (pp. 162–174). New York: Teachers College Press.

González, N. (2008). What is culture? In A. Rosebery & B. Warren (Eds.), *Teaching science to English language learners: Building on students' strengths* (pp. 89–97). Washington, DC: National Science Foundation.

González, N., Moll, L.C., & Amanti C. (Eds.). (2005). *Funds of knowledge: Theorizing practices in households, communities, and classrooms.* Mahwah, NJ: Erlbaum.

Haneda, M. (2006). Becoming literate in a second language: Connecting home, community, and school literacy practices. *Theory Into Practice, 45*(4), 337–345. doi:10.1207/s15430421tip4504_7

Luke, A. (2009). Race and language as capital in schools: A sociological template for language education reform. In R. Kubota & A.M.Y. Lin (Eds.), *Race, culture, and identities in second language education* (pp. 286–308). London: Routledge.

Moll, L.C. (2000). Inspired by Vygotsky: Ethnographic experiments in education. In C.D. Lee & P. Smagorinsky (Eds.), *Vygotskian perspectives on literacy research: Constructing meaning through collaborative inquiry* (pp. 256–268). Cambridge, England: Cambridge University Press.

Moll, L.C., & González, N. (2004). Engaging life: A funds of knowledge approach to multicultural education. In J. Banks & C.M. Banks (Eds.), *Handbook of research on multicultural education* (2nd ed., pp. 699–715). New York: Jossey-Bass.

Moll, L.C., & Ruiz, R. (2002). The schooling of Latino students. In M. Suárez-Orozco & M. Páez (Eds.), *Latinos: Remaking America* (pp. 362–374). Berkeley: University of California Press.

Moll, L.C., & Ruiz, R. (2005). The educational sovereignty of Latino students in the US. In P. Pedraza & M. Rivera (Eds.), *Latino education: An agenda for community action research* (pp. 295–320). Mahwah, NJ: Erlbaum.

Noddings, N. (1992). *The challenge to care in schools: An alternative approach to education.* New York: Teachers College Press.

Paul, P.V., & Wang, Y. (2006). Literate thought and multiple literacies. *Theory Into Practice, 45*(4), 304–310. doi:10.1207/s15430421tip4504_3

Portes, A., Fernandez-Kelly, P., & Haller, W. (2008). *The adaptation of the immigrant second generation in America: Theoretical overview and recent evidence.* Center for Migration and Development Working Paper No. 08-02.

Retrieved from cmd.princeton.edu/papers
.shtml

Portes, A., & Hao, L. (2002). The price of uni-
formity: Language, family and personality
adjustment in the immigrant second generation. *Ethnic and Racial Studies*, 25(6), 889–
912. doi:10.1080/0141987022000009368

Portes, A., & Rumbaut, R. (2001). *Legacies:
The story of the immigrant second generation.*
Berkeley: University of California Press &
Russell Sage Foundation.

Rodríguez-Brown, F.V. (2009). *The home–school
connection: Lessons learned in a culturally and
linguistically diverse community.* New York:
Routledge.

Romero, A. (2008). *Love, hope, and tri-dimension-
alization: Toward critical compassionate intellec-
tualism.* Unpublished doctoral dissertation,
University of Arizona, Tucson.

Romero, A., Cammarota, J., Dominguez, K.,
Valdez, L., Ramirez, G., & Hernandez, L.
(2008). "The opportunity if not the right
to see": The social justice education project. In J. Cammarota & M. Fine (Eds.),
*Revolutionizing education: Youth participatory
action research in motion* (pp. 131–151). New
York: Routledge.

Sánchez, G.I. (1997). History, culture, and education. In A. Darder, R.D. Torres, & H. Gutiérrez
(Eds.), *Latinos and education: A critical reader*
(pp. 158–172). New York: Routledge.

Valencia, R.R. (2002). *Chicano school failure and
success: Past, present, and future.* New York:
Routledge/Falmer.

Valenzuela, A. (1999). *Subtractive schooling: U.S.-
Mexican youth and the politics of caring.* Albany:
State University of New York Press.

CHAPTER 14

Considering Time in the Field of Family Literacy and in the Lives of Families

Catherine Compton-Lilly

When Bradford (all names are pseudonyms) was in first grade, his mother told a story about his older brother, who was a special education high school student. Despite having perfect attendance and being on the honor role, Ms. Holt got a letter from the school indicating that her son was not going to graduate. Ms. Holt still does not understand why she received this letter. As a result, Bradford's brother dropped out of school. Ms. Holt reported,

> I'm so disgusted with my son [dropping out of school]. When something like that happens I could tell them [her other children], "Oh, you don't have to go to school 'cause this gonna happen to you when you get to twelfth [grade] and you never knew a thing." I could make them be discouraged instead of "No, you're going to work through it."

While Ms. Holt continued to encourage Bradford and his older siblings in school, her story draws our attention to time and events that occur in families over time. As she maintains, events have effects on children's lives. As family literacy researchers, I argue that we must attend to the role time plays as children construct themselves as students and readers as they move through school.

I also advocate that family literacy researchers attend to time as a contextual factor in the field of family literacy. As Adam (1990) argues, "The focus on time helps us to see the invisible" (p. 169). Time as a contextual element accompanies every moment of people's lives. Identities are constructed, development occurs, learning takes place, and life trajectories are assumed across time. Time

From *Bringing Literacy Home* edited by KaiLonnie Dunsmore and Douglas Fisher.
© 2010 by the International Reading Association.

relates to literacy practices in families—home literacy practices are adopted, adapted, and rejected; literacy identities are assumed, revised, and abandoned; and school literacy practices are embraced and devalued over time as children move through school. Considering the field of family literacy, theories are adopted and rejected; others are celebrated and critiqued. Researchers are idolized and some are dismissed; tensions are revealed.

My central question is this: How does time operate as a contextual factor in the field of family literacy and in the literacy experiences of families? To address this question, I present a general introduction to the ways time is explored in various chapters in this book and in the larger field of family literacy. I then extend these discussions by drawing on two research projects that share explicit attention to time. Specifically, I draw on an integrative critical literature review of the field of family literacy (Compton-Lilly, Rogers, & Lewis, 2009) to examine patterns across time in the field of family literacy and a 10-year longitudinal qualitative case study (Compton-Lilly, 2003, 2007, 2008). I describe each study's methodology and a sampling of findings that implicate time. Finally, I look across the two studies to consider the parallel role time plays in the field and in families.

Time Within the Field of Family Literacy and Within Families

In this section, I examine how time has been referenced in the field of family literacy. I then present the theoretical construct of timescales, which refers to the multiple dimensions of time within which people operate. I suggest that timescales have the potential to help researchers conceptualize developments in the field over time and make sense of the literacy practices and perspectives that operate, emerge, develop, and disappear within families over time.

As a relatively new field, generally traced back to Taylor's (1983) book on the subject, family literacy provides a unique opportunity to consider the emergence and construction of a field of study. Although family literacy researchers have generally not attended to time explicitly, I argue that time is implicated in family literacy studies. In the following section, I draw upon chapters in this book and the field of family literacy to identify some of the ways family literacy researchers have referenced time. Specifically, I focus on literature reviews of the field, attention to sociohistorical contexts, time as a call to action, and implications for the future of the field of family literacy.

Literature Reviews of the Field

There are several places in this book and in other texts where family literacy researchers provide their readers with reviews of the field of family literacy (i.e., Hannon & Bird, 2004; Wasik & Herrmann, 2004) that often provide a chronology of studies and findings. For example, in Chapter 5 of this volume, Roser reviews research related to the literacy experiences of children prior to formal schooling. These reviews document what has been done and what was learned. They provide an overview of the past and a reminder of questions that still need to be answered.

Time as Sociohistorical Context

In Chapter 10 of this volume, Ladson-Billings references historical time. She reminds family literacy researchers of the rich literate history of African American people in the United States by presenting the words and stories of James Albert Gronniosaw, Frederick Douglass, Septima Clark, Esau Jenkins, and others.

These histories help family literacy researchers make sense of current conditions and phenomena and remind researchers that histories are often selectively told in academia, schools, and in the larger society. As Ladson-Billings (Chapter 10, this volume) notes, some historical accounts circulate readily while others are silenced.

Time as a Call to Action

In a recent presentation, Roller (2008) directed our attention to the past to conceptualize the future. Specifically, she asked why after 40 years of research and intervention low-socioeconomic status (SES) children were "disproportionately underprepared." She revisits the Carolina Abecedarian Project (Ramey & Campbell, 1991), a longitudinal intervention that followed children from infancy through grade 5. Roller challenges family literacy researchers to conceptualize a possible future that would involve supporting policy changes and creating comprehensive intervention programs for children similar to those provided by the Carolina Abecedarian Project.

Quantitative Longitudinal Research

Quantitative researchers focusing on family literacy have used longitudinal methods to document the ways home literacy practices affect school literacy learning across time. For example, Leseman and de Jong (1998) explore various facets of home literacy experiences to examine how home literacy affects later literacy learning. Evans, Shaw, and Bell (2000) investigate both language and literacy development by following children from kindergarten through grade 2. In these three-year studies, time was treated as a methodological dimension (the length of the study) or a conditional variable (elapsed time between preschool experiences and school literacy assessments), not as a feature of participants' lived experiences.

Qualitative Longitudinal Research and Time

Some literacy researchers have conducted qualitative longitudinal studies that involve groups of participants within particular communities or families over long periods of time. For example, Heath (1983) conducted a quintessential example of long-term qualitative research. Between the years 1969 and 1978, Heath examined oral language and literacy events in two North Carolina communities. More recently, Heath (2001) returned to the research site to document the changes that had occurred in families over the past 40 years. (See Chapter 1 in this volume for Heath's description of her work.)

Also in this volume, Diane Lapp (Chapter 6) describes how a sabbatical spent in a first-grade classroom led to a 10-year relationship with Anthony and his sister, Angul. As Lapp explains, this long-term relationship with one family inspired Lapp and her colleagues (Lapp, Fisher, Flood, & Moore, 2002) to "investigate the role that these parents believed they should play in the early literacy development of their children" (Chapter 6, p. 150). Long-term relationships with families have the potential to help researchers obtain rich, nuanced, and contextualized insights into the ways parents and children make sense of school and provide educators with possibilities for intervention that reflect the challenges families face over time.

A few studies that are not longitudinal but explicitly reference the ways children and family members experience time are beginning to appear. For example, Pahl (2007) applies the construct of timescales to literacy learning within a family. She demonstrates how a Turkish child's artistic depiction of a bird operated as a semiotic artifact that crossed multiple timescales from the immediacy of his current home and school experiences to his family's history and a larger cultural history of migration, flight, and relocation. In my work, I demonstrate how one African American student draws on experiences across time at home and school, the history of African American people in the United States, and her ongoing literacy activities as she constructs herself as a reader and as a student (Compton-Lilly, 2008).

Although family literacy researchers have presented chronological reviews of the field of family literacy, referenced relevant social histories that affect families and schooling practices, and looked to the future, they have rarely focused explicitly on what it means to live temporally as researchers or as family members.

Timescales: A Theoretical Frame for Considering Time

The construct of timescales as employed by Lemke (2000, 2001, 2005) captures the various levels at which time operates in people's lives and reveals the multiple temporal worlds people inhabit and the connections they make. Lemke proposes an ecological model to explain how people function within multiple timescales that recognizes the interrelatedness of multiple dimensions of time in people's lives, understandings, and experiences. To Lemke, timescales are dimensions of an ecological system in which the lower levels are constituent of the higher levels, with the higher levels involving conceptualizations and interpretations of processes at lower levels. Human semiosis, or meaning-making experiences, involves interpretations of meanings that have been constructed and revisited over long periods of time as well as the integration of information from lower level, more quickly moving timescales.

Wortham (2006) raises the possibility of examining "cross-timescale relations" to understand long-term processes such as becoming literate; he describes sets of "linked processes across several timescales" (p. 9) that collectively explain how phenomena, such as literacy learning, draw on temporal dimensions of people's experiences. Family literacy practices can be conceptualized as simultaneously drawing upon multiple timescales. Researchers routinely draw on the day-to-day interactions with family members who participate in our research projects. At the same time, they respond to the field by recognizing historical and seminal studies as well as tensions that have been generally accepted as significant within the field. Finally, family literacy researchers are subject to the influences of larger social histories related to educational policy and practices as well as social policies connected to race, class, gender, disability, and other manifestations of difference.

For family members who participate in family literacy studies, learning is a social venture. Literacy learning involves engaging in sets of literacy practices at home and school (e.g., Cairney, 2002; Taylor, 1983), and children consciously and unconsciously draw on their experiences across time as they construct their identities as readers and writers (Ferdman, 1990; Flores-Gonzalez, 2002). However, consonant with Lemke's (2000, 2001, 2005) description of multiple interacting timescales, children draw on more than their own lived experiences. Through stories told across generations and the literacy practices enacted in their home and school, children draw on the literacy experiences of parents, grandparents, siblings, and teachers. In addition, children are also situated within larger histories related to schooling and the ways race, class, gender, disability, and other manifestations of difference have been treated in schools.

This chapter treats the construct of time as a significant contextual factor that informs literacy learning. I argue that attending to time via the theoretical construct of timescales allows family literacy researchers to recognize how time operates in the field as well as in families. In the two studies presented in the following pages, I attend explicitly to time. In the following sections, I briefly share the methodological processes used in the two studies presented in this chapter: an integrative critical literature review and a 10-year longitudinal qualitative study.

An Integrative Critical Literature Review

Methodology

Rogers, Lewis, and I (Compton-Lilly, Rogers, & Lewis, 2009) recently conducted an integrative critical review of the field of family literacy. In this section, I share data to document and analyze citation patterns over time within the field of family literacy. The complete integrative critical literature review involved five interrelated analyses. Below, I briefly describe the four analyses that will not be discussed in this chapter. This is followed by a detailed description of the fifth one, a citation coding analysis that was selected for this chapter because it explicitly addresses temporality within the field of family literacy.

1. Each of the three authors of this integrative critical literature review brought her unique history to the project. We each wrote an individual account of researchers in the field who had influenced our thinking and contributed to the sociocultural lens we brought to the project.

2. Once we had identified our shared interests and perspectives, we reviewed four databases (Academic Search, Education Full Text, ERIC, and Proquest) and the holdings of a major university library with combinations of the search terms *literacy*, *family*, *handbook*, *review*, and *home* to identify articles, books, and book chapters that contained reviews of the field of family literacy.

3. We analyzed the tables of contents, introductory materials, and editorial statements from five comprehensive handbooks of the field that focused specifically on family literacy. These materials were analyzed in terms of the topics addressed, contributors, handbook length, and terminology.

4. An analytic review template (ART) was created and used to record qualitative information from about 107 review chapters and articles. Definitions of family literacy, methodological processes, theoretical frameworks, and attention to race, class, and language were among the dimensions analyzed. Another 50 studies containing lesser reviews of family literacy were briefly summarized.

In this chapter, I focus on our fifth analysis, the citation coding scheme that we developed to identify major contributors to the field of family literacy. Early in the literature retrieval process, we used sample studies to develop and refine our citation coding (CC) scheme. The following codes were recorded beside each reference on a copy of each review's reference list.

- List References (L): The study was referenced only on a list with other references.
- Sentence References (S): The study was discussed in 1–3 sentences.
- Paragraph References (P): The study was discussed in 4 or more sentences.
- Central References (C): The study was discussed in 1 or more paragraphs and was central to the review's argument.

In this chapter, I focus on researchers whose work was coded at either the paragraph or central level in five or more of the 157 reviews; I refer to these researchers as major contributors to the field. This process provided an approximation of the centrality of researchers in the field of family literacy over time.

Findings From the Citation Coding Analysis

The citation coding procedure identified a set of 34 researchers who were major citations in at least 5 of the 157 articles. As part of the analysis process, the 34 major citations were organized chronologically (see Table 14.1).

Table 14.1. Major Citations in Reviews of Family Literacy

Rank	Number of Citations and Dates Cited	Name	Methods/Theory	Focus
1	36 1982–1995	S.B. Heath	Qualitative ethnography	Language and literacy practices
2	29 1981–1997	D. Taylor	Qualitative ethnography	Literacy practices
3	24 1988–2000	V. Purcell-Gates	Qualitative ethnography	Literacy practices
4	23 1990–2003	L.C. Moll	Qualitative ethnography	English-language learner community practices
5	18 1992–1996	T.H. Cairney	Family literacy theory	Field of family literacy
6	17 1977–2001	C.E. Snow	Quantitative causal/predictive	School literacy success
7	15 1995–2006	V.L. Gadsden	Qualitative narrative analysis Family literacy theory	Generational literacy, race, gender Field of family literacy
8	12 1996–2005	U. Bronfenbrenner	Ecological theory	Families as ecological systems
9–10	11 1987–1995	E. Auerbach	Family literacy theory	Family strengths
9–10	11 1988–2001	G.J. Whitehurst	Quantitative causal/predictive	Storybook reading
11	10 1978–1987	L. Vygotsky	Language and thought theory	Culture, thought, and language
12–16	9 1991–2000	B.D. DeBaryshe	Quantitative causal/predictive	Parent beliefs
12–16	9 1987–2006	C. Delgado-Gaitán	Qualitative	Home literacy practices
12–16	8 1960–1996	B. Berenstein	Social class theory	Class and language
12–16	8 1994–1996	S.B. Neuman	Position paper	Teacher/family collaboration
12–16	8 1996–2004	R.G. St. Pierre	Quantitative program effects	Family literacy programs
17–21	7 1994–2002	L. Baker	Quantitative causal	Home–school partnerships

(continued)

Table 14.1. Major Citations in Reviews of Family Literacy (continued)

Rank	Number of Citations and Dates Cited	Name	Methods/Theory	Focus
17–21	7 1994–2006	S. McNaughton	Family literacy theory	Home and school success
17–21	7 1994–2004	L.M. Morrow	Quantitative causal/predictive	School success
17–21	7 1991–2001	H.S. Scarborough	Quantitative causal/predictive	Storybooks and language
17–21	7 1985–1991	E. Sulzby	Qualitative observational	Emergent literacy
22–26	6 1988–2001	D. Barton	Qualitative ethnography	Local, situated literacies
22–26	6 1977–1991	P. Bourdieu	Sociological theory	Social class education, arts
22–26	6 1988–2001	M.H. van IJzendoorn	Quantitative causal/predictive	Storybook reading
22–26	6 1981–1986	S. Michaels	Qualitative narrative analysis	Children's narratives
22–26	6 1993–1999	J. Paratore	Family literacy theory	The role of family literacy in literacy learning
27–34	5 1966–1982	D. Durkin	Qualitative ethnography	Successful readers
27–34	5 1991–1996	P.A. Edwards	Implementation	Storybook reading African American community
27–34	5 1970–1988	P. Freire	Liberation theory and pedagogy	Literacy and cultural action
27–34	5 1987–1995	P. Hannon	Family literacy theory	Home–school relations Purpose of family literacy programs
27–34	5 1995–1998	M. Sénéchal	Quantitative causal/predictive	Storybook reading
27–34	5 1993–1995	T. Shanahan	Implementation	ELL program
27–34	5 1982–1984	J. Tizard	Quantitative causal/predictive	Parent/teacher collaboration
27–34	5 1985–1992	G. Wells	Qualitative language analysis	Early language learning

The most-cited researcher in the field of family literacy is Heath. *Ways With Words: Language, Life, and Work in Communities and Classrooms* (1983) appeared shortly after Taylor's (1983) introduction of the term *family literacy*, and this text alone is a major citation in 18 articles and book chapters. Although Heath's work focuses specifically on language and literacy practices in two communities and does not use the term *family literacy*, the books and articles written by Heath appear as major citations in almost one quarter of the book chapters and articles analyzed (36 out of 157 reviews).

Heath's (1983) ethnographic methods are echoed in the work of three other widely referenced family literacy scholars. In fact, the four most-cited researchers in the field are qualitative researchers whose work has documented family literacy practices in diverse families. Taylor and Dorsey-Gaines (Taylor & Dorsey-Gaines, 1988) investigate literacy practices in inner-city African American households. Purcell-Gates (1995) focuses on literacy practices within Appalachian families, and Moll and his colleagues (Moll, Amanti, Neff, & González, 1992) document the funds of knowledge possessed by Mexican American children and their families. Thus, of the 34 researchers whose work was central to the 157 chapters and articles, the top four cited researchers all conducted qualitative, ethnographic work within diverse families. In addition, Gadsden (1995, 1999, 2004), whose major citations include both qualitative analyses and position papers, is the seventh most cited researcher.

Quantitative studies of family literacy appear at about the same time as early qualitative studies, although they are rarely referenced as central resources until the late 1980s. Snow (Snow, 1987; 1993; Snow, Barnes, Chandler, Goodman, & Hemphill, 1991; Snow & Tabors, 1996) is the earliest and the most widely cited of the quantitative researchers. Although she has generally used statistical measures to examine how early literacy experiences translate into school literacy achievement, her work also incorporates qualitative methods. Other early quantitative work on parent and teacher collaboration is cited five times in the sample (Tizard & Hughes, 1984; Tizard, Schofield, & Hewison, 1982).

Between 1988 and 1996, there is a drastic increase in the number of quantitative researchers appearing as major citations (see Table 14.2). These quantitative researchers focus on causal or predictive relationships between literacy practices in families and children's school progress and included Whitehurst and Lonigan's (1998) work on storybook reading, DeBaryshe's (1995) work on parental beliefs about literacy, Scarborough and Dobrich's (1994) work on storybooks and language, and St. Pierre and colleagues' work (1995) on family literacy

Table 14.2. A Sampling of Major Citations From Quantitative Researchers

Researcher	Number of Major Citations	Dates of Cited Studies	When Studies Were Cited as Major References
C.E. Snow	17	1977–2001	1995–2007; 12 years
J. Tizard	5	1982–1984	1989–1998; 9 years
G.J. Whitehurst	11	1988–2001	1994–2004; 10 years
M.H. van IJzendoorn	6	1988–2001	1994–2004; 10 years
B.D. DeBaryshe	9	1991–2000	1994–2006; 12 years
H.S. Scarborough	7	1991–2001	1994–2004; 10 years
R.G. St. Pierre	8	1996–2004	1996–2004; 8 years

programs. Almost all of the quantitative studies first appeared as major citations in the mid-1990s. Some quantitative researchers (e.g., Bus, van IJzendoorn, & Pellegrini, 1995) have also conducted widely cited meta-analyses.

Some of the most extensively cited contributors, qualitative and quantitative researchers, offer position papers on the field of family literacy. Some of these papers critique the field by challenging researchers to address deficit assumptions about children and families from nonwhite communities (e.g., Auerbach, 1989; Cairney, 1995); others identify general patterns in the field related to the relative effects of various home literacy practices on children's school achievement (Bus et al., 1995; Paratore et al., 1995). A final group of contributors provide guidelines for the implementation of family literacy initiatives and programs (Edwards, 1995; Neuman, 1995; Shanahan, Mulhern, & Rodríguez-Brown, 1995).

Finally, it is notable that all of the most-cited contributors to the field published their first major cited articles prior to 1997. Although there are more recent contributors with three or four major citations, no researcher who entered the field in the past 12 years has five or more major citations. It took 4–12 years for the most cited researchers in the field to have at least 5 major citations.

Examining the racial and ethnic backgrounds of contributors also reveals an interesting pattern. Of the 34 major researchers identified in the current analysis, one researcher is of Puerto Rican heritage (Moll), two are African American (Gadsden and Edwards), and one is Mexican American (Delgado-Gaitán). Significantly, Moll, Gadsden, and Delgado-Gaitán work in communities of color. The other 30 major researchers are Caucasian. Various nationalities are represented in the sample, including British, New Zealander, Dutch, Australian, and Welsh; the researchers representing all of these nationalities are of European heritage.

Analysis of Findings Based on Citation Coding

Findings from the citation coding process reveal insights about how time operates as a contextual factor in the field of family literacy. It is possible to conceptualize the development of the field of family literacy as occurring at multiple timescales. While Lemke (2000, 2001) argues for the existence of countless timescales that people draw upon, in the following analysis, I examine how researchers draw upon three timescales: historical timescales, community timescales, and ongoing timescales.

Historical Timescales. Researchers in the field of family literacy reference theories and ideas that predate the field of family literacy (e.g., those of Berenstein, Bourdieu, Freire, Vygotsky). These theoretical frames that extend far beyond the field of family literacy are grounded in psychology, sociology, and liberation pedagogy. These historical formal theories build upon preexisting academic and naïve theories that extend across much larger periods of time, referencing theorists including Dewey, Froebel, and Marx as well as naïve beliefs about race, gender, and social class. Historical timescales operate both consciously and unconsciously and incorporate ways of thinking that rely on preexisting social theories and ideologies.

For example, it has been a historically accepted and generally unquestioned belief that schools exist to teach children and that teachers are considered experts who share knowledge. Therefore it was logical for family literacy educators to assume that teaching parents school-valued literacy practices would address the needs of families whose children struggled in schools. Existing biases related to race and social class have been documented in some family literacy programs and methodological practices (i.e., Auerbach, 1989; Cairney, 1995). Academic fields are susceptible to historical discourses that operate within societies; one of the challenges of a field is to be consciously aware of the power of these discourses and constantly vigilant in monitoring the field.

Community Timescales. In addition to the theories promoted by the formal theorists I have mentioned, family literacy researchers also draw upon theories emerging from closely related fields, including literacy (Sulzby, 1985) and language studies (Michaels, 1981; Wells, 1986). In contrast to the theories discussed here, these theories emerged alongside family literacy and presumably were reciprocally informed by work in family literacy; these theorists (Sulzby, Michaels, and Wells) do not appear as major citations until the mid-1990s.

Community timescales are particularly evident when considering researchers whose work has been referenced in numerous review papers. The fact that the work of some family literacy researchers consistently appears as major citations provides information about how the field has constructed itself over time. In particular, the finding that all four of the most commonly cited major researchers are qualitative researchers who focus on families in diverse communities is revealing. The work of these four qualitative, ethnographic researchers first appeared between the years 1982 and 1990 and has informed the field of family literacy in terms of both the questions asked and the types of research projects designed. Questions about existing literacy practices in diverse homes not only documented the range of literacy practices but also may have contributed to the privileging of particular practices that were associated with successful groups of children. Overall, 12 of the 34 major contributors produced qualitative research studies.

Ten quantitative researchers are also represented among contributors with major citations. Most of these quantitative researchers entered the field beginning in the late 1980's, 5 to 14 years after the earliest qualitative researchers. Their work built on the findings of early qualitative scholars by asking how the early literacy practices documented via qualitative methods affect, predict, or cause later school literacy achievement. These causal and predictive studies highlighted literacy practices that correlated with later school success and privileged particular literacy practices and types of family literacy programs.

Tensions within the family literacy field related to ideology, methodology, causation, pure description, generalizability, and the collection and analysis of data from diverse communities have contributed to alliances and divisions. These divisions are particularly apparent when examining intervention programs and the ways families are positioned within these programs. While many family literacy researchers tend to reference the seminal qualitative studies discussed above, there are clear alliances in citation patterns, with quantitative and causal studies tending to reference similar studies and qualitative researchers tending to reference other qualitative studies. Alliances are also apparent when we consider coauthorships and contributions to particular journals.

Finally, analyses of community timescales reveal a relative lack of family literacy researchers from diverse cultural backgrounds. With the exception of four major researchers, prominent family literacy researchers have tended to be Caucasian researchers who examine the literacy practices of people of color. Because the voices of people of color are not widely heard within the research community, the field is left open to the danger that historical assumptions and attitudes about diverse families may be operating through our analyses, conclusions, and recommendations.

Ongoing Timescales. Ongoing timescales reference the everyday interactions through which family literacy researchers and educators come to define themselves. The perspectives that researchers critique and adopt, the language they use and reject, and the anecdotes they tell and dismiss are informed by the identities that researchers continually construct and reconstruct. Although the field presents certain possibilities, researchers choose among those possibilities by not only drawing selectively upon the past and existing studies but also by envisioning possible futures for the field.

A Longitudinal Qualitative Study

Although the integrative literature I have described highlights the role of time in the field of family literacy, the following section focuses on time in the life of one student. Timescale analysis will be used to explore Bradford's school and literacy experiences.

Methodology

Most ethnographic accounts of literacy in families extend over a few months or perhaps a few years. Neale and Flowerdale (2003) argue that longitudinal qualitative research captures increasingly comprehensive accounts of people's lives— in their words, producing "a movie rather than a snapshot" (p. 191). Similar to Lapp in her account of Anthony and Angul (Chapter 6 in this volume), I follow one African American boy over a 10-year period. Here I present the methodology for that study and a sampling of findings related to time.

The Research Process. The qualitative longitudinal study described in the following sections draws upon all four phases of a 10-year research project, each occurring three or four years apart. In these sections, I follow Bradford from first grade through high school. In 1995, I randomly chose 10 students in my first-grade class and their parents to participate in the study. In this chapter, I present only an overview of the study; more detailed accounts are available elsewhere (Compton-Lilly, 2003, 2007, 2008).

The families participated in the study during the children's first-grade (phase 1), fourth-/fifth-grade (phase 2), seventh-/eighth-grade (phase 3), and tenth-/eleventh-grade (phase 4) years. In first grade, the students attended what I will refer to as Rosa Parks Elementary School, a large urban school where 97% of the students qualified for free or reduced-price lunch. The school served children from the lowest socioeconomic population of a mid-sized northeastern city that had the 11th highest child poverty rate in the nation. Rosa Parks Elementary School was on the state's list of schools in need of improvement. Consistent with the district's high mobility rate, four years later, many of the students in my study had left Rosa Parks Elementary School to attend other schools in the same district. By high school, 7 of the 10 students remained in the study and attended schools across the district. Only 1 of my former students was in grade 11 at age 17. Four children left school without graduating; 2 of these students, including Bradford, left school when they were assigned to the eighth grade at age 17.

The initial study was planned as a one-year study. Because I was the students' first-grade teacher, it involved a rich range of data, including four interviews with children and parents, field notes containing classroom observations and reflections, student portfolios and classroom assessments, and audiotaped class discussions. Phases 2 and 3 involved two interviews with students and parents, analyses of reading assessments (see Clay, 2002; Ekwall & Shanker, 1993; Leslie & Caldwell, 2006), and analyses of writing samples completed during the interviews. Phase 4 of the research project involved interviews with parents and students, classroom observations, and analyses of student-created reflective texts, including reflective writing, photographs, drawings, and audio journals. Reading assessments in phase 1 involved running records of leveled texts and story retellings. Reading assessments in phases 2, 3, and 4 involved informal reading inventories that included word lists, reading passages, and comprehension questions.

Analysis of Longitudinal Data. Audiotapes were transcribed and coded during each phase of the study to identify salient categories of information. During the first and third phases, data was coded into categories and contrastive analysis methods were used to organize these categories across cases to identify themes and patterns. During the second and fourth phases, data was coded separately for each case, and case summaries were constructed for each family. I then looked across the cases to identify intercase patterns and larger categories of data.

Findings: Bradford and His Family Over Time

I tell Bradford's story to examine how time operates in the life of one student and in his family. I argue that school success entails a strict set of temporal expectations and that reading and schooling success are contingent on meeting these temporal expectations. Specifically, school and literacy success is not about what students know or can do; it is about when they know and can do it. As a special education student, Bradford encountered disjunctures between the temporal expectations enacted in his self-contained classroom and the general education program, as well as tensions related to report card grades, standardized testing, the pace of instruction, and grade-level retention. In what follows, I introduce Bradford and his family. I then look across time to present his educational trajectory and issues related to the pace of instruction.

An Introduction to Bradford and His Family. Bradford entered my first-grade class after spending a year in pre-first. He was acutely aware of being a year older than the other children. Due to his previous year of schooling, he entered the class with reading abilities that the other children did not possess. However, the other children soon surpassed him. He was reluctant to engage in reading and described it as difficult.

Bradford was the youngest of seven children. When I first met Ms. Holt, Bradford's mother, she described herself as a "sports person rather than a reader." She remembers being "made to read" books when she was in school and recalls writing book reports on *Shane* (Schaefer, 1949/1983) and *Old Yeller* (Gipson, 1956/1995). Although she read the newspaper every day and recipes in her job as a dining room manager, she reported, "I'm not a reader." Ms. Holt grew up in a suburban community and described the emphasis her mother placed on reading and school success. On several occasions, Ms. Holt reminded me that she and all of her siblings had graduated from high school; she attributed this to her mother.

Although Ms. Holt maintained that she could read everything that she needed to read, her sister had recently reminded her of the difficulties she faced when learning to read.

She said "Treeka, you know when you were coming up, your reading never was that good." You know, I said, "Really?" She said "Remember?" This was locked up inside there [pointing to her heart]. I said, "OK, I remember those days."

Revisiting these memories caused Ms. Holt think about Bradford: "It never even ever dawned on me that this might be what his problem is. [It's] hereditary."

In fifth grade, Bradford was acutely aware of his reading difficulties. He got nervous when he read and was "scared when I don't know how to pronounce every word." He said he preferred to read by himself because other people "distract" him. By grade 8, Bradford's mother reported that Bradford "won't pick up a book to save his life. Cause he can't read." Ms. Holt argued that the teachers should not be "more lenient, but more understanding and be more helpful than they would be with a normal child." Instead of just handing him a book and saying, "you read this," she suggested that they have Bradford read about his favorite sports. She explained that his teacher had recently sent a book about Martin Luther King Jr. home with Bradford. Ms. Holt suspected that Bradford "destroyed that book." As she explained,

> He said, "I'm not trying to read it. I already been through that damn book." I figure if you give him a soccer book or a baseball book you might have him. Couldn't you do the same thing reading-wise with a soccer book as you do with a Martin Luther King book?

It was during the final interview, when Bradford was 18 years old, had dropped out of school, and had just been released from a incarceration facility for drug charges, that he first identified texts that he enjoyed reading. Bradford mentioned *King*, a gentleman's magazine, as his favorite. He had also enjoyed books by Donald Goines while he was incarcerated. Donald Goines was his mother's favorite author; he wrote books featuring African American characters that Ms. Holt described as "street stories."

Bradford's six older siblings experienced various degrees of success in school. Eventually all of the children, except Bradford and an older brother who was also a special education student, graduated from high school. A second brother, who had also been a special education student, graduated from a four-year college. Bradford was the first member of the family to have run-ins with the law.

Bradford's Educational Trajectory Over Time. After her son had been in a self-contained special education classroom for grades 3 and 4, Ms. Holt was excited because his fourth-grade special education teacher reported that Bradford would be mainstreamed into general education classes. However, when I went back to visit the family the following spring, Bradford remained in the special education classroom. Ms. Holt was very disappointed and reported that his current teachers were not even considering the possibility of mainstreaming Bradford.

Report card grades and policies related to standardized testing were particularly confusing. Although Bradford was bringing home good grades on assignments from his special education classes, he was "getting all D's on his report cards." Ms. Holt worried about the effects of these low grades, but she was particularly concerned about standardized testing. She explained, "I see [why you] test all those kids and see where they belong. That's good, that's right there. I don't have any problem with that. But in the meantime don't discourage him." Ms. Holt worried that Bradford's test scores failed to reflect his progress in school.

> They should have two tests. You [are] in a special class...then when you're in a regular class, they're not in the same class so why give them the same test? You know what I'm saying? If you're going to give him a fifth-grade test, put him in fifth grade.

By the end of eighth grade, Bradford had been arrested and spent over two years in a juvenile detention center. While Ms. Holt was extremely upset, she was hoping that "they scared him straight." She was relieved that he would be placed on probation for three or four years and that the judge would make it mandatory for Bradford to attend school.

Both Bradford and Ms. Holt spoke extensively about the juvenile detention center. At the facility, Bradford eventually took high school classes and was doing well. Ms. Holt was excited about Bradford's grades; "I never seen Bradford with A's and B's before. When I saw that report card, oh my God!" Bradford reported that when he was released he was prepared to take college-level math courses.

> I was taking mad math and they gave you a test right before you leave [the facility]— reading, math.... And they said my math was a 12th grade level [going] into college and my reading was like 9th.

However, when Bradford was released from this facility, the public school district refused to recognize the gains he had made while incarcerated and placed him in seventh- and eighth-grade classes. As Ms. Holt reported, "You know Bradford, he won't go to middle school when he's like 17 years old....

When they told him seventh and eighth grade he hit the ceiling and he ain't been back that way since." Bradford described the public school district as trying to "play" him.

In the final interview, Ms. Holt reported, "Bradford's not doing anything but being Bradford." She suspected that if Bradford had stayed at the juvenile facility he would have graduated from high school. One of Bradford's brothers graduated from a tutoring center that served students with behavioral problems. However, as Ms. Holt explained, he could not be admitted into that program without first getting into trouble at school. Bradford wanted to pursue his GED, but the local school district would not allow him to enroll in the GED program until after he was scheduled to graduate. As Bradford explained, "I'm just chillin."

Pace of Instruction. In addition to an educational trajectory that did not fit the temporal expectations of schooling, the pace of the instruction Bradford received in the special education program was problematic. Specifically, Bradford and Ms. Holt contended that teachers lacked patience, failed to provide students with the time and help they needed, and exhibited low expectations.

Ms. Holt spoke about meeting Bradford's fifth-grade special education teacher. She described this teacher as having a "military style" and explained that Bradford needed someone who was "patient." She noted, "You know with kids, I call then special kids, you have to have patience. Because they're, I know it's [their] brainwaves [that] don't move as fast as normal." She emphasized the need to take time and work with Bradford:

> When he gets it he's got it. But if you throw it to him and say like, "Do you got it?" [He'll say] "Yeah, I got it" and he don't really have it. You lost him. But if he's interested, if the teacher takes time and just explains it to him, I don't see them wait sometimes. It's just like [he's thinking], "What's that?" "What's she saying to me?"

In the spring of eighth grade, Bradford was finally mainstreamed into a regular math class. Although he had a B+ average in his special education math class, his grades dropped to F's and D's in the general education class. Ms. Holt described Bradford as complaining that the teacher was "making me go too fast." Ms. Holt and Bradford were both very disappointed. In contrast, Bradford described the teachers in the juvenile facility as "nice" and "willing to teach you so that you could get out of that program." He complained that the teachers in the public high school would just "slap the work on [while] they [were sitting] at they desk."

In addition to not getting the help he needed, Bradford described his experiences in special education classes as redundant and insulting:

> [In] self-contained [classes] you don't do nothing there. They just give you the same work...stuff that I could already do they will just keep on giving it to me because I could do it and I could zip right through it...they ain't never try to challenge you or [extend] what your skills is basically.

Bradford believed that the teachers were underestimating him the whole time he was in school, saying, "They just wanted me to stay in the same class."

Ms. Holt connected Bradford's experiences to the rhetoric that surrounded schooling at the time of the study. "He's been in that program, no kids left behind. [But] they keep leaving him behind.... I can't understand, I never did understand that. I still don't." She noted the irony of her son's situation: "Every year he was in the same class" and the district's decision to place him in seventh and eighth grade was the last straw. She describes the school as

> putting him somewhere and holding him down so they won't succeed. And that's what they do too. Just keeping him in that same class every year. They [the students] get disgusted. Because I'd be disgusted seeing the same teacher every year.

Throughout Bradford's school career there was a mismatch between the pace of instruction and Bradford's abilities. While a quick-paced military style was not the answer, failing to challenge Bradford did not work either. As Bradford's case illustrates, with help and support he could be successful, but until he was incarcerated, he did not get that assistance.

Discussion of Findings From the Longitudinal Case Study

This chapter opened with Ms. Holt wondering whether the experiences of Bradford's older brother would affect Bradford when he was in high school. While it is not clear that his brother's experiences had a direct impact, Bradford's literacy experiences have cumulated over time, contributing to his situation. I maintain that Bradford and Ms Holt draw upon a multiple timescales as they make sense of Bradford's school and literacy experiences. Specifically, I focus on ongoing, familial, and historical timescales.

Ongoing Timescales. Throughout the longitudinal study there are numerous references to events that are happening at the time of the interviews. Bradford's ongoing struggles with schooling, placement in special education and Ms. Holt's efforts to have him mainstreamed, low report card grades, run-ins with the law, and experiences in the juvenile detention center were all ongoing events at the time of the interviews. Both Ms. Holt and Bradford struggled to make sense of these events.

Familial Timescales. Familial timescales include Ms. Holt's childhood experiences, the experiences of Bradford's brothers, and Bradford's own past experiences. Familial timescales draw upon the sense that families make of their collective experiences. Thus the stories that are told and retold in families become salient. Specifically, Ms. Holt connects the stories of her own difficulties with learning to read to Bradford's struggles. She notes agency when she emphasizes the role her mother played in ensuring that she and her siblings graduated from high school. She tells the story of Bradford's brother dropping out of school and worries that this experience might negatively affect Bradford's school success. The stories of Bradford's other brother's success in college, despite his special education status, are told to suggest possibilities for Bradford.

Temporal expectations relative to schooling and literacy learning are integral to how Bradford conceptualizes his success as a student. Being a successful student involves being promoted to the next grade level, meeting learning standards at particular points in time, passing grade level reading tests, passing standardized tests, and achieving the learning expectations of teachers. Success means being able to learn material and move through curricular materials at appropriate rates. However, Bradford's ability to meet the temporal expectations of schooling were complicated by the time he spent in pre-first grade, his placement in special education, his ability to keep pace with academic expectations, and ultimately his placement in seventh and eighth grade at age 17. These temporal ruptures impacted Bradford's identity as a learner and as a reader. They also impacted Bradford's visions of the future. Despite these challenges and his ultimate failure in public school, Bradford found texts that he enjoyed reading (i.e., *King* magazine and books written by Donald Goines) and took pride in his success with math. Unfortunately, institutional temporal expectations provided no option that allowed Bradford to build upon these successes and he was left "chillin" with few options.

Historical Timescales. Bradford's experiences are grounded in larger social histories related to special education, the treatment of juvenile offenders, testing policies, and the rhetoric around educational standards, as well as historical positionings related to race, class, and gender. Special education has historically played a problematic role in relation to the general education program. Most children placed in special education remain there until they leave school, and many do not graduate. Although recent initiatives involving standardized testing are designed to ensure that "no kids are left behind," as Ms. Holt explained, this was not a reality for Bradford.

Urban schooling brings another history. Large urban schools appeared at the turn of the 19th century to efficiently assimilate immigrant children and their families to American society (Cremin, 1990). These schools required children to adapt to the official expectations of schooling rather than providing opportunities for students from diverse backgrounds to develop their cultural and linguistic strengths. In addition, contemporary urban schools, including the schools attended by Bradford, have suffered from long histories of underfunding (Kozol, 1992). Specifically, the school district Bradford attended struggled to hire certified teachers, provide current educational materials, and offer experiences, including sports, that might engage disenfranchised students.

Finally, issues related to race, class, and gender were also relevant. When Bradford eventually found texts that he enjoyed reading, they were not schoolbooks but texts that recognized his identity as a young African American male. Like the traditional texts Ms. Holt complained about in school, school texts left Bradford unengaged and uninterested. Traditional school curricula are part of a long history of schooling and literacy instruction that relate little to Bradford, his emerging identity, and his experiences.

Family Literacy Over Time

Whether discussing academic fields or families, attention to time references how people make sense of their worlds. Not only do ongoing events inform people's understandings, but the ways communities and families collectively make sense of their worlds affects the trajectories and meanings constructed by researchers and family members. Furthermore, ongoing events and familial/community experiences are contextualized within larger social histories that bring ways of thinking and knowing that frame people's understandings of themselves and their social worlds. Recognizing academic communities and families as evolving communities complicated by tensions, acts of agency, inconsistencies, and challenges prevents us from essentializing groups of researchers or diverse families. Instead, we view researchers and families as operating within larger social histories that involve experiences, ideologies, histories, policies, goals, and relationships.

Poor and diverse families bring resilience and agency to literacy learning classrooms, yet they often live in difficult communities, endure challenging work schedules, suffer economic setbacks, reside in substandard housing, attend underfunded schools, and experience challenges with health care. These difficulties accumulate over time and contribute to the difficulties children face in school and with literacy learning. Likewise, members of research communities bring particular educational histories, professional affiliations, institutional challenges, theoretical frameworks, ideological beliefs, and professional interests to their work that often divide research communities (i.e., qualitative versus quantitative; preschool versus school-age; skills-based versus experiential).

Recognizing families and academic fields as systems that extend over time allows us to recognize how families and research communities are constructed within constantly evolving educational and social histories. Ultimately, attention to time presents possibilities. For example, academic fields can come together around the shared goal of helping children to succeed in school and to envision possibilities for the future that draw on past multiple perspectives while challenging negative assumptions that researchers and educators often bring to the families they serve. By focusing on families and their interests and actions over time, researchers can conceptualize families as agents for progress and growth who have access to resources that enable them to act on behalf of their children.

Most importantly, by viewing both fields and families as temporally bound systems we begin to envision what is really needed to help children. I suggest that the solution is not only about teaching Bradford's mother how to parent or support his literacy development. Helping Bradford and millions of other children involves larger issues related to healthy communities, employment opportunities, educational opportunities for children who do not thrive in schools, channels for parental advocacy, accessible resources, changes in staffing policies that allow teachers to truly help students, individualized and focused reading instruction for students beyond the primary grades, and supporting and extending library services so that all children have easy access to books that are not traditionally available in schools. This is more than an educational issue. Social policies that allow some families to live in untenable situations and face impossible challenges are relevant. Family literacy research cannot only focus on literacy for young children. Family literacy educators need to advocate for a comprehensive and longitudinal investment in families and communities over long periods of time and at an enormous scale. Although this might appear impossible, until we can muster the determination to recognize family literacy as extending beyond young children and assumedly deficient parents, the educational system will fail to support children like Bradford.

REFERENCES

Adam, B. (1990). *Time and social theory*. Oxford, England: Polity Press.

Auerbach, E.R. (1989). Toward a socio-contextual approach to family literacy. *Harvard Educational Review, 59*(3), 165–181.

Bus, A.G., van IJzendoorn, M.H., & Pellegrini, A.D. (1995). Joint book reading makes for success in learning to read: A meta-analysis on intergenerational transmission of literacy. *Review of Educational Research, 65*(1), 1–21.

Cairney, T.H. (1995). *Beyond tokenism: Parents as partners in literacy*. Portsmouth, NH: Heinemann.

Cairney, T.H. (2002). Bridging home and school literacy. *Early Child Development and Care, 172*(2), 153–172. doi:10.1080/03004430210883

Clay, M.M. (2002). *An observation survey of early literacy achievement*. Portsmouth, NH: Heinemann.

Compton-Lilly, C. (2003). *Reading families: The literate lives of urban children*. New York: Teachers College Press.

Compton-Lilly, C. (2007). *Re-reading families: The literate lives of urban children, four years later*. New York: Teachers College Press.

Compton-Lilly, C. (2008). *Learning to read across time: Negotiations and affiliations of a reader, grades 1–8*. WCER working paper No. 2008-9. Retrieved November 27, 2009, from www.wcer.wisc.edu/publications/workingPapers/Working_Paper_No_2008_09.php

Compton-Lilly, C., Rogers, R. & Lewis, T. (2009). *An integrative critical literature review of family literacy*. Manuscript submitted for publication.

Cremin, L.A. (1990). *American education: The metropolitan experience, 1876–1980*. New York: HarperCollins.

DeBaryshe, B.D. (1995). Maternal belief systems: Linchpin in the home reading process. *Journal of Applied Developmental Psychology, 16*(1), 1–20. doi:10.1016/0193-3973(95)90013-6

Edwards, P.A. (1995). Empowering low-income mothers and fathers to share books with young children. *The Reading Teacher, 48*(7), 558–564.

Ekwall, E.E., & Shanker, J.L. (1993). *Ekwall/Shanker reading inventory* (3rd ed.). Boston: Allyn & Bacon.

Evans, M.A., Shaw, D., & Bell, M. (2000). Home literacy activities and their influence on early literacy skills. *Canadian Journal of Experimental Psychology, 54*(2), 65–75. doi:10.1037/h0087330

Ferdman, B.M. (1990). Literacy and cultural identity. *Harvard Educational Review, 60*(2), 181–204.

Flores-Gonzalez, N. (2002). *School kids/street kids: Identity and development in Latino students*. New York: Teachers College Press.

Gadsden, V.L. (1995). Representations of literacy: Parents' images in two cultural communities. In L.M. Morrow (Ed.), *Family literacy: Connections in schools and communities* (pp. 287–303). Newark, DE: International Reading Association.

Gadsden, V.L. (1999). Family literacy practice and programs. In D.A. Wagner, R.L. Venezky, & B. Street (Eds.), *Literacy: An international handbook* (pp. 258–264). Boulder, CO: Westview Press.

Gadsden, V.L. (2004). Family literacy and culture. In B.H. Wasik, (Ed.), *Handbook of family literacy* (pp. 401–426). Mahwah, NJ: Erlbaum.

Hannon, P., & Bird, V. (2004). Family literacy in England: Theory, practice, research and policy. In B.H. Wasik (Ed.), *Handbook of family literacy* (pp. 23–39). Mahwah, NJ: Erlbaum.

Heath, S.B. (1983). *Ways with words: Language, life, and work in communities and classrooms.* Cambridge, England: Cambridge University Press.

Heath, S.B. (2001). The children of Trackton's children: Spoken and written language in social change. In E. Cushman, E.R. Kintgen, B.M. Kroll, & M. Rose (Eds.), *Literacy: A critical sourcebook* (pp. 156–172). New York: St. Martin's.

Kozol, J. (1992). *Savage inequalities: Children in America's schools.* New York: Harper Perennial.

Lapp, D., Fisher, D., Flood, J., & Moore, K. (2002). "I don't want to teach it wrong": An investigation of the role families believe they should play in the early literacy development of their children. In D. Shallert, C. Fairbanks, J. Worthy, B. Maloch, & J. Hoffman (Eds.), *The 51st yearbook of the National Reading Conference* (pp. 275–286). Oak Creek, WI: National Reading Conference.

Lemke, J.L. (2000). Across the scales of time: Artifacts, activities, and meanings in ecosocial systems. *Mind, Culture, and Activity, 7*(4), 273–290. doi:10.1207/S15327884MCA0704_03

Lemke, J.L. (2001). The long and short of it: Comments on multiple timescale studies of human activity. *Journal of the Learning Sciences, 10*(1&2), 17–26. doi:10.1207/S15327809JLS10-1-2_3

Lemke, J.L. (2005). Place, pace and meaning: Multimedia chronotopes. In S. Norris & R. Jones (Eds.), *Discourse in action: Introducing mediated discourse analysis* (pp. 110–122). New York: Routledge.

Leseman, P.P.M., & de Jong, P.F. (1998). Home literacy: Opportunity. *Reading Research Quarterly, 33*(3), 294–318. doi:10.1598/RRQ.33.3.3

Leslie, L., & Caldwell, J.S. (2006). *Qualitative reading inventory-4.* Boston: Pearson.

Michaels, S. (1981). "Sharing time" Children's narrative styles and differential access to literacy. *Literacy in Society, 10*(3), 423–442.

Moll, L.C., Amanti, C., Neff, D., & González, N. (1992). Funds of knowledge for teaching:

Using a qualitative approach to connect homes and classrooms. *Theory Into Practice, 31*(2), 132–141.

Neale, B., & Flowerdale, J. (2003). Time texture and childhood: The contours of longitudinal qualitative research. *International Journal of Social Methodology Research Methodology, 6*(3), 189–199. doi:10.1080/1364557032000091798

Neuman, S.B. (1995). Reading together. *The Reading Teacher, 49*(2), 120–129.

Pahl, K. (2007). Timescales and ethnography: Understanding a child's meaning-making across three sites, a home, a classroom and a family literacy class. *Ethnography and Education, 2*(2), 175–190. doi:10.1080/17457820701350558

Paratore, J.R., Krol-Sinclair, B., Homza, A., Lewis-Barrows, T., Melzi, G., Sturgis, R., et al. (1995). Shifting boundaries in home and school responsibilities: The construction of home-based literacy portfolios by immigrant parents and their children. *Research in the Teaching of English, 29*(4), 367–389.

Purcell-Gates, V. (1995). *Other people's words: The cycle of low literacy.* Cambridge, MA: Harvard University Press.

Ramey, C.T., & Campbell, F.A. (1991). Poverty, early childhood education, and academic competence: The Abecedarian experiment. In A. Huston (Ed.), *Children reared in poverty* (pp. 190–221). New York: Cambridge University Press.

Roller, C.M. (2008, October). *Building the political will to reduce the achievement gap.* Presentation for the Ball Foundation Family Literacy Symposium, Chicago, Illinois.

Scarborough, H.S., & Dobrich, W. (1994). On the efficacy of reading to preschoolers. *Developmental Review, 14*(3), 245–302. doi:10.1006/drev.1994.1010

Shanahan, T., Mulhern, M., & Rodríguez-Brown, F. (1995). Project FLAME: Lessons learned from a family literacy program for linguistic minority families. *The Reading Teacher, 48*(7), 586–593.

Snow, C.E. (1987). Factors influencing vocabulary and reading achievement in low-income children. In R. Appel (Ed.), *Toegepaste Taalwetenschap in Artikelen Speciaal*

(Feestbundel voor B. Th. Tervoort, pp. 124–128). Amsterdam: ANELA.

Snow, C.E. (1993). Families as social contexts for literacy development. In C. Daiute (Ed.) *The development of literacy through interaction* (pp. 11–24). San Francisco: Jossey-Bass.

Snow, C.E., Barnes, W.S., Chandler. J., Goodman, I.F., & Hemphill, L. (1991). *Unfulfilled expectations: Home and school influences on literacy.* New York: Cambridge University Press.

Snow, C.E., & Tabors, P. (1996). Intergenerational transfer of literacy. In L.A. Benjamin & J. Lord (Eds.) *Family literacy: Directions in research and implications for practice* (pp. 73–80). Washington, DC: Pelavin Research Institute.

St. Pierre, R.G., Swartz, J.P., Gamse, B., Murray, S., Deck, D., & Nickel, P. (1995). *National evaluation of the Even Start Family Literacy Program: Final report.* Washington, DC: U.S. Department of Education, Office of the Under Secretary.

Sulzby, E. (1985). Children's emergent reading of favorite storybooks: A developmental study. *Reading Research Quarterly, 20*(4), 458–481. doi:10.1598/RRQ.20.4.4

Taylor, D. (1983). *Family literacy: Young children learning to read and write.* Portsmouth, NH: Heinemann.

Taylor, D., & Dorsey-Gaines, C. (1988). *Growing up literate: Learning from inner-city families.* Portsmouth, NH: Heinemann.

Tizard, B., & Hughes, M. (1984). *Young children learning.* London: Fontana.

Tizard, J., Schofield, W.N., & Hewison, J. (1982). Collaboration between teachers and parents in assisting children's reading. *British Journal of Educational Psychology, 52*(1), 1–15.

Wasik, B.H., & Herrmann, S. (2004). Family literacy: History, concepts, services. In B. Wasik (Ed.), *Handbook of family literacy* (pp. 3–22). Mahwah, NJ: Erlbaum.

Wells, G. (1986). *The meaning makers: Children learning language and using language to learn.* Portsmouth, NH: Heinemann.

Whitehurst, G.J., & Lonigan, C.J. (1998). Child development and emergent literacy. *Child Development, 69*(3), 848–872.

Wortham, S. (2006). *Learning identity: The joint emergence of social identification and academic learning.* Cambridge, England: Cambridge University Press.

CHAPTER 15

Rethinking Family Literacy Through a Critical Lens: A Focus on Culturally and Linguistically Diverse Families

Rosario Ordoñez-Jasis

Reflecting upon the literacy programs he developed with marginalized groups in São Paulo, Brazil, Freire (1973, 1994) envisioned a literacy pedagogy that focused on reading and writing activities—together with reflection and dialogue—that were based on themes situated in participants' real-life experiences. He argued against the notion of "banking education," where the educator's discourse and agenda is privileged and knowledge is viewed as an entity to be deposited into "patient recipients." Over 30 years ago Freire (1973) wrote,

> From the beginning, we rejected...a purely mechanistic literacy program and considered the problem of teaching adults how to read in relation to the awakening of their consciousness.... We wanted a literacy program which would be an introduction to the democratization of culture, a program with human beings as its subjects rather than as patient recipients, a program which itself would be an act of creation, capable of releasing other creative acts, one in which [families] would develop the impatience and vivacity which characterize search and invention. (p. 43)

Freire's (1973) work reveals a more democratic framework for literacy and learning, one that views participants as active creators of their own knowledge and in which literacy skills emerge as consciousness is raised. Approached from this perspective, literacy programs would consider the linguistic milieus and emphasize the social worlds where learning and literacy emerge, embracing a dynamic view of how culture, language, and social interaction mediate literacy and learning (Vygotsky, 1978). Describing this as a critical stance toward literacy (Gee, 2005; Giroux, 1983, 1988; Gutiérrez & Rogoff, 2003), Freire believed that literacy skills are not only functional in society but also are the essential tools to critically analyze the dialogical relationship among words and worlds, knowledge and power, and between ideology and practice. His transformative *theory of education* centralizes opportunities for the literacy learner to consider his or her own attitudes, beliefs, and values and thus highlights the advancement of human potential and social empowerment.

Grounding my analysis in the theoretical discussions put forth by Auerbach (2001) and Lareau (1994), who, among others, have attempted to reconceptualize family literacy to necessarily include issues of power, voice, and ideology, this chapter responds to the need to embrace a more critical stance toward literacy and families to help reimagine the possibilities for family literacy programs, research, agendas, and practice. Defined by Giroux (1988), critical literacy "functions as a theoretical tool to help students develop a critical relationship to their own knowledge," to "learn how to read the world and their lives critically and relatedly...and, most importantly, it points to forms of social action and collective struggle" (p. 49). Applying this critical approach to family literacy, then, begins with an in-depth understanding of sociocultural theory; that is, it acknowledges that the discourse patterns, linguistic practices, and cultural ways of knowing and experiencing are essential aspects of literacy learning (see Chapter 13). Within oppressed communities in the United States, and among culturally and linguistically diverse communities in particular, the need to meaningfully incorporate a profound respect for their culture, linguistic codes, and worldviews into the learning environments of family literacy programs has been clearly delineated in the literature (Ada & Zubizarreta, 2001; Delgado-Gaitán, 1994; Ortiz & Ordoñez-Jasis, 2005; Valdés, 1996). However, family literacy redefined from a sociocritical pedagogy views these inclusionary practices as only a necessary first step—as an infrastructure for a true nurturance of social critical thought and a participatory exchange of knowledge. Concerned with educational justice and human agency, a critical approach to family literacy goes beyond what Freire (1973, 1994) refers to as mechanistic programs and engages parents and other caregivers as active learners who have the potential to question dominant institutional and ideological structures within schools and society with the goal of achieving a more active voice in the education of their children.

Ample research on Latino families' experiences in U.S. public schools suggests feelings of isolation and marginalization (Darder, 1991; Delgado-Gaitán,

1994; Jasis, in press; Ordoñez-Jasis & Jasis, 2004; Valdés, 1996). Through the lens of a more critical orientation to family literacy, Latino families have the opportunity to remake themselves within sociocultural-historical-political patterns of meaning as they embark on both new and familiar literacy practices. Critical family literacy programs, in this sense, have the potential to help families—via reading, writing, listening, speaking, viewing, and sharing activities—to reflect on the current realities shaping their capacity to analyze, critique, and transform their access to literacy and their relationships to schools and, quite possibly, to help change the conditions under which they live.

Moving Beyond Remediation

In her analysis of successful practices in working with Spanish-speaking Latino families in Chicago, Rodríguez-Brown (Chapter 9 in this volume) discusses the need to move beyond what she refers to as functional approaches to family literacy. She describes functional programs as those developed without the input from the communities for which the programs were designed. Similar to Freire's (1973, 1994) description of mechanistic programs, functional perspective programs do not consider the needs, concerns, or interests of participants nor are they concerned with the internal dynamics of the home (Valdés, 1996). Rodríguez-Brown further explains that the content, focus, and goals of these types of programs do not address the daily realities or future aspirations of families and, as a result, the programs are short lived. Program such as these—particularly those targeted toward low-income and culturally and linguistically diverse families—have been shown to adopt materials, curricular models, pedagogical approaches, and participant structures that serve to marginalize the voices, concerns, expectations, and overall needs of their participants (Auerbach, 2001).

I would further argue that a disproportionate number of functional perspective programs tend to target poor and nondominant communities where, despite evidence to the contrary (Ada & Zubizarreta, 2001; Delgado-Gaitán, 1994; Garcia, Jensen, & Cuellar, 2006), parents are assessed as nonsupportive of their children's literacy attainment, and their home literacy practices are viewed as inadequate or counterproductive. As a result, family literacy programs are designed and implemented as "intervention" programs where both the child and the family are perceived as requiring "remediation" (Ordoñez-Jasis & Jasis, 2004). Unfortunately, these family literacy programs follow a history of educational initiatives targeted toward Latino students and their families that have been synonymous with programs for poor, lower class, immigrant, at-risk, or dropout students (Garcia, Jensen, & Cuellar, 2006). As a result, the majority of work in schools has taken the form of specific compensatory-like programs aimed at remediating the Latino family with basic skills that would allow them to only get by in school and in society (Ordoñez-Jasis, 2002).

These remediation-focused programs also tend to adopt a language-as-a-deficit discourse whereby English-language learner (ELL) families and speakers of nonstandard varieties of English are viewed as lacking cognitively, academically, linguistically, or culturally, and the use of the primary or home language is discouraged (Cain, 2005; Gutiérrez & Rogoff, 2003). Moreover, a skills-based, standard-English-only prescriptive curriculum is rationalized in a way that privileges schooled literacy over out-of-school home literacy practices (Taylor, 1997). This approach works to change parents' abilities and beliefs about the role literacy plays in their lives, proposing only school-like literacy interactions with their children (Auerbach, 2001). In addition to promoting language correctness over cognitive complexity, remedial family literacy programs underestimate the cultural literacies within the home (e.g., oral traditions, faith-based practices) that may serve to enhance a strong cultural identity or competency while building strong academic literacy skills as well (see Chapters 7 and 10 in this volume). According to Paratore's (2003) research synthesis of past and present practices in family literacy, these programs do not produce long-term sustainable gains because the

> burden of change rests, primarily, often even exclusively, on the shoulders of parents. They are expected to incorporate school-like literacy and learning routines within the fabric of their everyday lives.... [However] increased efforts by [schools] to learn about and build on the multiple ways in which parents and children use literacy outside school may help children maintain, even increase, the gains they make during initial family literacy interventions. (p. 23)

Interestingly, these deficit-based programs and ideologies are rarely encountered in programs designed for upper middle class and mainstream families (Lareau, 1994). Instead, family literacy programs aimed toward dominant social groups closely mirror the more "advanced" school curriculum that students of these families generally receive (Cain, 2005; Moreno, 1999). That is, mainstream families in these programs are more likely to engage in sociocultural literacy practices that promote critical thought in natural, meaningful, and authentic settings. In developing literacy programs for culturally and linguistically diverse families, it is imperative to reexamine unexpressed assumptions about and approaches toward nondominant families. It is within this space that new learning environments could be imagined, where culturally and linguistically diverse families receive meaningful opportunities to engage in critical inquiry rather than rote learning, where their language and literacy practices are meaningfully incorporated into program design, and where the relationships between homes and schools are strengthened and reconstructed on a more equal basis.

Sociocultural Approaches to Family Literacy

As an alternative to deficit-based ideologies found in many functional or remedial family literacy programs, a sociocultural framework would allow program developers to design family literacy initiatives based on the strengths and needs of a particular community. Sociocultural theory is the proposal that individual learning and social interaction are interconnected. According to Vygotsky's (1978) theory of social constructivism, learning is shaped by an individual's process of constructing his or her thoughts, ideas, and beliefs through social activity with others. Within this sociocultural framework, literacy learning is best understood not only as the acquisition of a set of certain technical skills and subskills (e.g., letter recognition, decoding, fluency) but also as an exchange of worldviews and experiences with others. Reading, writing, speaking, listening, and viewing, then, are not isolated and decontextualized activities; instead, they are a medium of participation and are embedded in social practice (Gee, 2005).

Sociocultural theory offers a lens to understand "literacy as the relationship between learners to the world, mediated by the transforming practice of this world taking place in the very general milieu in which learners travel" (Freire, 1996, p. 106). A sociocultural framework for understanding this dialectical process of literacy development via family interaction necessarily considers the dynamics of the community where families live, their linguistic realities, and the goals that parents or caregivers wish to achieve in sharing literacy activities with their children (e.g., educational, recreational, political, or economic). Taylor (1997), in acknowledging the role of the community and culture on family literacy use, writes,

> It is essential that literacy programs recognize and honor not only the diversity of literacies that exist within families, but also the communities and cultures of which

they are a part. The culture of the community and the experiences of the families who live in the community are an essential part of all literacy programs. (p. 4)

The emphasis placed on "diversity of literacies" is an important one. Gutiérrez and Rogoff (2003) remind us that Latinos in the United States are not a homogeneous community; rather, variations exist and are situated within each family's history of engagement with specific culturally mediated linguistic activities. Within sociocultural theory, the specific literacy-related activity, the value a family places on it, its setting, and its purpose must all be taken into account. And, although there are regularities in the ways that cultural groups participate in the everyday practices in their respective communities, the "characteristics of those environments are in constant tension with the emergent goals and practices participants construct, which stretch and change over time...[and] contribute to the variation and on-going change within an individual's and a community's practices" (Gutiérrez & Rogoff, 2003, p. 21). It is this formal and informal participation within these diverse linguistic practices (e.g., Spanish, Spanglish, English, dialects such as Calo) that further mediates literacy learning within and among Latino families (Gutiérrez, Baquedano-Lopez, & Tejeda, 1999). Sociocultural theory views families as powerful socializing agents as they introduce their children to the words and worlds (Freire, 1994) of the complex and varied linguistic communities to which they belong. Crossing cultural, linguistic, and social boundaries, families and children transverse multiple worlds, develop multiple identities, and forge new literacies along the way.

Project FLAME and Sociocultural Theory

Highlighting her work with Project FLAME (the acronym stands for Family Literacy: *Aprendiendo, Mejorando, Educando* [Learning, Improving, Educating]), Rodríguez-Brown (Chapter 9 in this volume) reveals the possibilities of drawing upon sociocultural theory to establish a comprehensive model for the long-term engagement of an entire family unit in literacy-related activities. Rodríguez-Brown and her colleagues' work exemplifies how a program can be designed to be linguistically and culturally relevant for Latino families when the culture of the community is at the forefront of program design. She draws heavily upon the work of Moll (see Chapter 13 in this volume), who highlights the positive impact of culturally relevant literacy programs that incorporate students' funds of knowledge and intentionally include the social/intellectual resources and other dimensions of social life that enter into a family's meaning-making processes as they engage in literacy-related activities. Project FLAME is also grounded in Gay's (Chapter 7 in this volume) theoretical perspectives on cultural responsivity, that is, teaching and learning that is situated within multiethnic cultural frames of reference. To enhance program effectiveness and sustainability, Project FLAME draws upon the Latino families' funds of knowledge and cultural ways of knowing and doing that already exist in the community, including their linguistic background, personal knowledge, cultural preferences, and views of literacy. Rodriguez-Brown notes that rather than attempting to change existing language and literacy practices, family literacy programs that draw upon sociocultural theories and insights demonstrate a renewed understanding and appreciation for the depth and diversity of home-based knowledge as they attempt to add new practices to the ones that parents bring to the program.

Project FLAME also attempts to establish strong personal relationships with families with the goal of building continuity between homes and the schools. Indeed, the research conducted by Hoover-Dempsey and Whitaker (Chapter 3 in this volume) on the processes of parental involvement reveals that the development of trust, ongoing positive and mutually supportive interactions, and a school or program's responsiveness to families' "life context variables" (e.g., time, energy, language, cultural modes) have a strong positive influence over the degree to which parents become involved in their children's education. Likewise, in her work with the Latino immigrant families who participated in Project FLAME, Rodríguez-Brown identifies the interactional patterns, or cultural modes, of sharing that are key to program success and parent participation. They include *confianza* (mutual trust) and *respeto* (respect). Similarly, research (Ordóñez-Jasis, Flores, & Jasis, in press), reveals that the working class Latino families who participated in a family literacy program in Los Angeles also benefited from the personal advice, or *consejos*, they received from other Latino parents and teachers via their participation in a literacy-based, culturally responsive learning community. Taken together, these interactional patterns appear to be critical elements that help to nurture and sustain a sense of community among many Latino parents and schools while enhancing program effectiveness and sustainability via a family's active engagement with the program.

In sum, family literacy from a sociocultural perspective is a means of recognizing, validating, and meaningfully integrating a community's multiple perspectives, diverse realities, varying discourse patterns, and "diversity of literacies" into the heart of its program's curricular design. Programs within this paradigm reject deficit-based practices and approaches aimed at remediating families; rather, informed by a deeper reading of a community, they embrace a strength-based perspective that meaningfully and authentically incorporates the ideas, needs, concerns, worldviews, and aspirations of its families as they discover new ways to support their children's literacy learning.

Reframing Family Literacy for Diverse Families: A Sociocritical View

Critical theory, as put forth by Gee (2005), Giroux (1983, 1988), Freire (1973, 1994), and, more relatedly, in the field of family literacy by Auerbach (2001), highlights some fundamental components that can be integrated into family literacy initiatives. For these theorists and others, a critical perspective necessitates a closer consideration of knowledge, power, social action, language, voice, and ideology within family literacy programs and openly "takes sides in the interest of struggling for a better world" (Gee, 2005, p. 19).

For example, Giroux (1988) argues that schools and school-sponsored programs are often characterized by a plurality of conflicting languages, struggles, hopes, and expectations. Giroux further explains that, potentially, our interactions with families from underrepresented communities can become sites where dominant and subordinate cultures collide. As a result, family literacy program planners and families may differ as to how school and home literacy practices are to be defined and understood. Rodríguez-Brown (Chapter 9 in this volume) and others have proposed culturally and linguistically responsive instruction to address this site of contestation by attempting to fully incorporate the knowledge, aspirations, dreams, concerns, and expectations of students and their families, creating a form of cultural congruency that holds the potential to develop cohesive learning communities. Sociocritical theorists such as Darder (1991) argue for the transformation of traditional pedagogical structures where asymmetrical power relations are questioned and power is shared among all program participants. In addition to cultural responsivity and the development of mutually respectful relationships, critical theory pushes for a serious rethinking of the relationship between and among social groups and social institutions, including the inequities that exist in schools and school-sponsored programs.

Critical theory also attempts to politicize knowledge, interrogating its non-neutrality, the legitimacy of certain types of knowledge over others (Bourdieu, 1991), and the ability or inability of certain groups to "produce, distribute, and legitimize their shared principles and lived experiences" (Giroux, 1983, p. 74). A critical approach toward family literacy takes the point of view that the knowledge that families hold is, itself, an object of analysis and not just a means to analyze other phenomena (Giroux, 1988). As important as it is to acknowledge, respect, and integrate knowledge from diverse families into family literacy agendas, equally important is the ability to gain insights into family and community knowledge as possibilities for new forms of understanding. To put it another way, in the words of Giroux (1983), critical approaches to literacy argue for "looking at knowledge critically, within constellations of suppressed insights that point to the ways in which historically repressed cultures and struggles could be used to illuminate radical potentialities in the present" (p. 36). As such, family literacy in this regard may have a transformative impact on diverse families' ability to construct and reconstruct themselves historically as social, political, and literate beings.

Likewise, reframing family literacy from a sociocritical perspective clearly differentiates between language inclusion and the development of voice, where *voice* is defined as the "capacity to enter into a dialogue and make oneself heard" (Darder, 1991, p. 44). More recent research conducted within linguistically diverse communities by sociocultural and sociolinguistic researchers and educators have embraced linguistic responsivity (Ada & Zubizarreta; 2001; Delgado-Gaitán, 1994; Valdés, 1996). Rather than viewing ELLs and speakers of nonstandard varieties as a problem, a more strength-based approach to primary or heritage languages is one where educational programs view language diversity as a resource for all (Hornberger, 2005). In the field of family literacy, such inclusive practices are not only necessary to build important bridges to linguistically marginalized and oppressed communities (Darder, 1991), but from a sociocultural theory of learning, they become an essential element of literacy development.

Indeed, language expresses the culture from which we emerge. It is a powerful means of transmitting our personal and collective histories and our current realities (Bourdieu, 1991). However, Ramirez (as cited in Hornberger, 2005) warns that a mere inclusion of language might coincide with the exclusion of a particular group's voice. Similarly, Darder (1991), who speaks from the point of view of a critical educational theorist, writes, "It is simplistic and to our detriment to...believe that simply utilizing a student's primary language guarantees that a student's emancipatory interests are being addressed" (p. 102). She explains how our primary language is a significant human resource, for it contains "the codification of our lived experiences" (p. 101) and therefore functions as a critical starting point for families to dialogue about and engage in literacy-related activities that "affirm, contradict, negotiate, challenge, transform, and empower particular cultural and ideological beliefs and practices" (p. 101). In the context of family literacy, reflection and dialogue in the participant's primary language can serve as a powerful tool to engage parents in a critical investigation of the role literacy plays in their lives and the lives of their children. The transformative potential of family literacy then, lies not only in the mere inclusion of language and culture with text-related activities, but also in the use of language, literacy, and culture to dialogue, understand, and reflect upon how families shape and are shaped by their worlds (Freire, 1994).

A critical perspective, as proposed here, approaches family literacy pedagogy as an active, challenging approach to literacy (Gutiérrez & Rogoff, 2003). Additionally, it aims to broaden our understanding of literacy and literacy instruction so we may approach reading, writing, speaking, listening, and viewing as permeated by social and political issues. Exploring Freire's ideas of the power of literacy, Giroux (1983) writes,

> Literacy in this sense in not merely linked to the notion of relevance; instead it is grounded in a view of human knowledge and social practice that recognizes the importance of using the cultural capital of the oppressed to authenticate the voices and modes of knowing they use to negotiate with the dominant society. What is at stake here is the goal of giving working class [families] the tools they need to reclaim their lives, histories, and voices. (p. 226)

A critical perspective approach to family literacy, then, critiques a skills-only based pedagogy as stripping the possibilities of engaging families in critical and active thought and inquiry (Darder, 1991). As Freire delineates, a serious consequence of predefined authoritarian curriculum is a failure to examine how literacy could be embraced as a tool to allow families to fully participate in society. In this framework, family literacy pedagogy should not go unquestioned and "effective practices" must move beyond Eurocentric literacy practices (e.g., reading 20 minutes with your child each day) to include a deeper understanding of literacy as a cultural tool to awaken and liberate (Freire, 1994) with the possibility of reclaiming the voice of families. Although few would dispute the need to learn grammatical skills to function in society, what is questioned here are family literacy pedagogy and practices that omit critical thought and reason. The concern expressed is that instead of benefiting from reflective dialogue and instruction that can promote higher levels of comprehension or political insight, too many families who participate in literacy programs targeting culturally and linguistically diverse communities, in particular, are subjected to a reductionist pedagogy that pushes for the mastery of specific decontextualized skills (Ordoñez-Jasis & Ortiz, 2006).

A Pedagogy of Transformation and Social Action

What is needed in family literacy, as Paratore (2003) so aptly explains, is a movement from a pedagogy of transmission to a pedagogy of transformation. Similarly, Auerbach (2001) describes a model of family literacy where social change replaces skills training, or the "transfer of information from experts to learners," and "stresses an exchange among peers [where] participants share their experiences in order to give a critical understanding of their social nature" (p. 105). As such, a serious rethinking of family literacy would attempt to explore the discursive construction of reality given the variety of interpretations that exist within the individual literacy learner (Gee, 2005) while promoting a collective analysis of power, language, voice, and access within schools and society, without which issues of racism, classism, language dominance, sexism, and xenophobia persist (Lareau, 1994; Macedo, Dendrinos, & Gounari, 2003).

As such, an essential aspect of critical theory as it applies to family literacy agendas is the allowance for social action, which may include creative expressions of opposition or even some forms of resistance (Giroux, 1983). Much can be gained from Giroux's discussion of resistance and critical pedagogy. Specifically, it points to the need to "understand more thoroughly the complex ways in which to mediate and respond to the interface between their own lived experiences and structures of domination and constraint" (p. 108). Applied toward a critical reframing of family literacy, participants, particularly those from underrepresented and oppressed groups, are viewed as communities continually in flux, constantly influenced by a number of economic, social, political, historic, linguistic, and personal factors that are woven into the fabric of their everyday lives. Given the opportunity to develop analytic and practical skills in a problem-posing literacy curriculum, Latino families could reflect, dialogue, and become critically conscious (Freire, 1994) of why hierarchical structures exist, whose purpose they serve, and how these structures could be penetrated to allow for greater access.

Within the literature, some more recent examples of Latino parent organizing exist that challenge stereotypes of Latino parents as passive and inactive.

A powerful element of Rodríguez-Brown's (Chapter 9 in this volume) Project FLAME is its focus on parents as leaders via a beyond literacy module that focuses on parent-selected topics, such as parents' rights, immigration issues, and community activism. Similarly, Delgado-Gaitán's (1994) ethnographic work with *Comite de Padres Latino* (COPLA, Latino Parents Committee) documented how a family literacy program could also serve as a vehicle for Spanish-speaking immigrant families, many of whom felt socially isolated from school participant structures, to organize themselves to collectively learn about the school system and to advocate on behalf of their children. Further, Jasis and Ordoñez-Jasis (2004) examine the process of change among Latino parents at three public schools in California who engaged in community organizing to improve their children's education. Their research explored the multilevel interactions and the process of consciousness raising taking place as these parents engaged in a process of organizing independently with the goal of achieving a more active voice in the education of their children, and thus in the school community. The study chronicled how

> Latino families who have been traditionally under-served by the educational system participate effectively in the education of their children when the conditions for their involvement are facilitated and how, through the development of a collective voice, minority parent organizing can serve as a platform to establish meaningful school-community partnerships and educational leadership via supportive school programs. (p. 9)

These projects reveal how historically marginalized communities, through their organizing, can gain awareness, question, challenge, or even resist hierarchical structures and open symbolic spaces of participation in schools and in society. Likewise, family literacy programs can potentially have the same transformative effect on parents, particularly on how they view the role of literacy in their lives and the lives of their children.

The Impact of Ideology on Family Literacy Programs

A sociocritical framing of family literacy in the ways outlined above calls for the Freirean (Freire, 1994) notion of "ideological clarity." It requires program developers to have an ideological orientation to take on the political work necessary for a transformative pedagogy. This necessarily leads to a discussion of the importance of ideology in family literacy programs, for ideology shapes the manner and extent to which family literacy programs incorporate and can critically deconstruct within their pedagogy families' knowledge, their voice, and issues of power. Ideology is, generally, a view that subscribes to a common-sense idea of how our social, cultural, and political world is and ought to be (Flores, 2003). For Trujillo (1996), ideology in education is a "connected set of systemically related beliefs and ideas about what are felt to be the essential features of teaching...[it] involves the task of educating and a set of prescriptions for performing it" (p. 127). Moreover, the practical ideologies arise from the dialectic between an educator's beliefs and his or her praxis. "Practical ideologies are made as people live out their lives in the real world. In this framework, ideology is the practice through which individuals are produced, and in turn, produce their orientation to the social structure they inhabit" (Trujillo, 1996, p. 137). Examination of ideologies is critical to interrogating assumptions about our roles as family literacy researchers, practitioners, and educators as well as program goals, agendas, and objectives.

Auerbach (2001) points out that if consideration of access and power is omitted, family literacy programs developed from an inclusionary, strength-based perspective will unintentionally take the shape of functional or deficit-based programs that place the burden of change on parents. For example, many well-intentioned programs that claim to be responsive to cultural and linguistic diversity implement a pedagogy that includes as its end goal the teaching of European American middle class ways of reading with their children, talking with their children, and interacting as a family unit. Programs that aim to capitalize on "cultural ways of knowing" as a bridge to the attainment of new information but do not simultaneously address issues of access, marginalization, and voice within nondominant groups can be a pretext for the practice of "remediating" families. Rather than respecting and valuing families' funds of knowledge, the delicate internal dynamics may become disrupted (Valdés, 1996). Arguing that family literacy programs are becoming a "single-solution approach" to complex and multifaceted social concerns (e.g., illiteracy, poverty, crime, drop-out rates), Auerbach explains,

> The goal in a social change view focuses more on changing the institution and adding the conditions which give rise to poverty (and other social issues) than changing families. This view posits that children's literacy acquisition is shaped by many forces, only one of which is parental input. (p. 105)

Auerbach further warns that unless the ideological positioning of the program or approach is made evident, culturally and linguistically inclusive programs may inadvertently reproduce the status quo rather than produce an informed and democratic citizenry. Although many family literacy practices have been shown to have a strong positive impact, particularly in the area of early childhood education (see Chapter 5 in this volume), inclusive practices should be viewed as only a foundation for the creation of democratic participatory spaces for the families. The idea put forward is that unless the pedagogy for family literacy includes a serious consideration of issues related to power, ideology, and voice, it may not fully realize its considerable transformational potential.

Opening a Democratic Space for the Voices of Families

Family literacy framed within a sociocritical framework calls into serious question the ideologies and pedagogical structures which shape both the program design and resulting experiences of program participants. It critically examines curricular approaches to literacy to determine the inclusion of not only the language, culture, and knowledge of the participants, but also their voices. The issue here then is to not to create a false dichotomy between culturally and linguistically responsive pedagogy and a more critical one; instead, the goal is to embrace an inclusive curriculum that also creates pedagogical spaces for parents to question key issues that impact their families on a daily basis. Recognizing families' multiple identities, multiple literacies, varying discourses, and their complex ways of "reading" their worlds is an integral aspect of our political work with culturally and linguistically diverse families. Indeed, a transformative view of family literacy, at its core, views the potential of families to remake themselves within sociocultural patterns of meaning. For this to occur, programs must accept and actively incorporate what families bring with them to the learning situation.

Unveiling the political possibilities for culturally and linguistically diverse communities also includes a pedagogy of empowerment that allows families to use literacy in ways that are meaningful to them as they journey toward self-defined destinations. Family literacy viewed through a critical lens nurtures a true democratic framework for literacy and learning, an "act of creation" in which families speak with their own voices and draw upon their own sociohistorically situated knowledge and experiences to become, more fully, a part of a democratic and literate society.

REFERENCES

Ada, A.F., & Zubizarreta, R. (2001). Parent narratives: The cultural bridge between Latino parents and their children. In M.D. Reyes & J.J. Halcón (Eds.), *The best for our children: Critical perspectives on literacy for Latino students* (pp. 229–244). New York: Teachers College Press.

Auerbach, E. (2001). Considering the multiliteracies pedagogy: Looking through the lens of family literacy. In M. Kalantzis & B. Cope (Eds.), *Transformation in language and literacy: Perspectives on multiliteracies* (pp. 99–111). Canberra, VIC, Australia: Common Ground.

Bourdieu, P. (1991). *Language and symbolic power* (J. Thompson, Ed., G. Raymond & M. Adamson, Trans.). Cambridge, MA: Harvard University Press.

Cain, C.J. (2005). (Re)writing inequality: Language of crisis implications in California education reform. In T.L. McCarty (Ed.), *Language, literacy, and power in schooling* (pp. 263–282). Mahwah, NJ: Erlbaum.

Darder, A. (1991). *Culture and power in the classroom: A critical foundation for bicultural education*. Westport, CT: Bergin & Garvey.

Delgado-Gaitán, C. (1993). Parenting in two generations of Mexican American families. *International Journal of Behavioral Development*, 16(3), 409–427.

Flores, S. (2003). *Connecting the life experiences of Latino educators with their praxis: Five narratives*. Unpublished Dissertation, University of North Carolina at Chapel Hill.

Freire, P. (1973). *Education for critical consciousness* (M.B. Ramos, Trans.). New York: Continuum.

Freire, P. (1994). *Pedagogy of hope: Reliving Pedagogy of the Oppressed* (R.R. Barr, Trans.). New York: Continuum.

Freire, P. (1996). *Letters to Cristina: Reflections on my life and work* (D. Macedo with Q. Macedo & A. Oliveira, Trans.). New York: Routledge.

Garcia, E.E., Jensen, B., & Cuellar, D. (2006). Early academic achievement of Hispanics in the United States: Implications for teacher preparation. *New Educator*, 2(2), 123–147. doi:10.1080/15476880600657215

Gee, J.P. (2005). Literacies, schools, and kinds of people in the new capitalism. In T.L. McCarty (Ed.), *Language, literacy, and power in schooling* (pp. 223–240). Mahwah, NJ: Erlbaum.

Giroux, H.A. (1983). *Theory and resistance in education: A pedagogy for the opposition*. New York: Bergin & Garvey.

Giroux, H. (1988). *Schooling and the struggle for public life*. Minneapolis: University of Minnesota Press.

Gutiérrez, K.D., Baquedano-López, P., & Tejeda, C. (1999). Rethinking diversity: Hybridity and hybrid language practices in the third space. *Mind, Culture, & Activity*, 6(4), 286–303.

Gutiérrez, K.D., & Rogoff, B. (2003). Cultural ways of learning: Individual traits or repertoires of practice. *Educational Researcher*, 32(5), 19–25. doi:10.3102/0013189X032005019

Hornberger, N.H. (2005). Student voice and the media of biliteracy in bi(multi)lingual/multicultural classrooms. In T.L. McCarty (Ed.), *Language, literacy, and power in schooling* (pp. 151–168). Mahwah, NJ: Erlbaum.

Jasis, P. (in press). *Todo por nuestros hijos*/All for our children: Migrant families and parent participation at an alternative education program. *Journal of Latinos and Education*.

Jasis, P., & Ordoñez-Jasis, R. (2004). Convivencia to empowerment: Latino parent organizing at La Familia. *High School Journal*, 88(2), 32–42. doi:10.1353/hsj.2004.0023

Lareau, A. (1994). Parent involvement in schooling: A dissenting view. In C.L. Fagnano & B.Z. Werber (Eds.), *School, family and community interaction* (pp. 61–73). San Francisco: Westview.

Macedo, D., Dendrinos, B., & Gounari, P. (2003). *The hegemony of English*. Boulder, CO: Paradigm.

Moreno, J.F. (Ed.). (1999). *The elusive quest for equality: 150 years of Chicano/Chicana education*. Cambridge, MA: Harvard Education Publishing.

Ordoñez-Jasis, R. (2002). *Chicano families and schools: Tensions, transitions and transformations*. Unpublished doctoral dissertation,

Graduate School of Education, University of California at Berkeley.

Ordoñez-Jasis, R., Flores, S., & Jasis, P. (in press). *En confianza*: Co-constructing professional strength and voice with Latina early childhood educators. *Journal of Early Childhood Teacher Education.*

Ordoñez-Jasis, R., & Jasis, P. (2004). Rising with De Colores: Tapping into the resources of la comunidad to assist under-performing Chicano/Latino students. *Journal of Latinos and Education, 3*(1), 53–64.

Ordoñez-Jasis, R., & Ortiz, R.W. (2006). Reading their worlds: Working with diverse families to enhance children's early literacy development. *Young Children, 61*(1), 42–48.

Ortiz, R.W., & Ordoñez-Jasis, R. (2005). *Leyendo juntos* (reading together): New directions for Latino parents' early literacy involvement. *The Reading Teacher, 59*(2), 110–121. doi:10.1598/RT.59.2.1

Paratore, J. (2003). Building on family literacies: Examining the past and planning the future. In A. DeBruin-Parecki & B. Krol-Sinclair (Eds.), *Family literacy: From theory to practice* (pp. 8–27). Newark, DE: International Reading Association.

Taylor, D. (1997). *Many families, many literacies: An international declaration of principles.* Portsmouth, NH: Heinemann.

Trujillo, A.L. (1996). In search of Aztlán: Movimiento ideology and the creation of the Chicano worldview through schooling. In B.A. Levinson (Ed.), *The cultural production of the educated person: Critical ethnographies of schooling and local practice* (pp. 119–148). Albany: SUNY Press.

Valdés, G. (1996). *Con respeto: Bridging the distances between culturally diverse families and schools: An ethnographic portrait.* New York: Teachers College Press.

Vygotsky, L.S. (1978). *Mind in society: The development of higher psychological processes* (M. Cole, V. John-Steiner, S. Scribner, & E. Souberman, Eds. & Trans.). Cambridge, MA: Harvard University Press.

CHAPTER 16

"I Don't Want You to Die in Your Entire Life. If You Do I'll Bring You Flowers": Words in Families and Word Families at School

Denny Taylor

Words. "Words are the most subtle symbols which we possess and our human fabric depends upon them.... The living and radical nature of language is something which we forget at our peril," as Murdoch (1971, p. 33) reminds us. At one of the most intense moments of language learning, when children are deeply engaged in the exploration of their sensory and nonsensory understandings of the world, they go to school. At a time when they are creating their own appreciations and interpretations of language and metaphors, these activities, which are central to human existence, are interrupted. Words that have no connection are connected, and little attention is given to the importance of the language and thinking of children in their making and remaking of the world.

In *The Life of the Mind,* Arendt (1978) writes, "The work we do around language is central to the human experience" (p. 110). She focuses our attention on the role of sensory and nonsensory experience. She writes of the experience of being here, seeing, feeling, touching, tasting, and smelling, the things we do every day, the kinds of things children focus on in their early development. She contrasts these sensory experiences with nonsensory experiences—how we think and understand, how life is experienced through metaphor. "Analogies, metaphors, and emblems are the threads by which the mind holds on to the world," Arendt writes, "even when, absentmindedly, it has lost direct contact with it, and they guarantee the unity of human experience" (p. 109).

So, it is Murdoch and Arendt, together with Simone Weil, Elaine Scarry, Veena Das, and Toni Morrison, who have held my hand as I have contemplated and meditated on the ideas in this chapter. I focus on the relationship between sensory experience, what we touch, taste, smell, hear, and see, and nonsensory experience, thinking and knowing, what makes us human *and inhumane*. And in this meditation on life and language, I reflect on the experiences that children have as they connect their sensory world with the nonsensory world through reading and writing at home and in school.

This chapter is grounded in my ethnographic research in family, community, and school settings in multiple contexts, including studies of children living in areas of urban and rural poverty, and research in areas of armed conflict and natural disasters. It also reflects my focus in the past 10 years on medical and psychiatric research on adverse childhood experiences in which language and complex trauma are regarded as organizing principals. More recently, these efforts have taken a philosophical turn. Living and working in environments in which human suffering is so extreme has shaped who I am and who I have become. For me this is an intense time, driven by a desire to see and to know. What follows originates in this struggle. Except for the last conversation between a grandmother and her grandchild, every utterance is verbatim.

Everybody's Child

This is a story about a little girl, her mother, and her grandmother. The little girl could live next door to you. You might have seen her with her mother at the supermarket. Her grandmother could be your friend. Her family might come from Cambodia. Her great, great grandmother might have been transported before abolition and sold as a slave. Her family might live a subway ride from New York City in Queens or in Jefferson Parish, across the Huey P. Long Bridge from New Orleans.

I choose not to name this little girl. Instead, I will call her Everybody's Child. I imagine that she is Haitian, Cuban, Peruvian, Sudanese, Nepalese. Her family is Muslim, Jewish, Christian, orthodox, secular, white, black, and every color in between. She is Irish, Italian, Greek. She is Palestinian, Israeli, Indian, Pakistani. Her father is a doctor, a lawyer. He is a farm worker, a dish washer. He is in prison. He has recently been deported. Everybody's Child is a U.S. citizen. She has a green card. She is undocumented. Her family can trace their ancestry to the *Mayflower*. Uprooted, she is an émigré, a refugee, an evacuee, displaced, replaced, dislocated, relocated, but *she is here* in America, like everybody else's child.

Calling her Everybody's Child speaks to our humanity. She is one of us. She is our child. But being Everybody's Child also gives us some indication of the ways in which we position her. She has made her appearance on a stage that we have set before her (see the interview with Stephen Toulmin in Kayzer, 1999, for more information about the stage we have set). This year, she is in first grade. We can imagine her classroom. It does not matter if she is in Queens or Jefferson Parish. It does not matter if she speaks Hindu or Saek. The reading programs will be similar or the same. Today is Monday and in her classroom all the children are practicing their spelling words. After the workbook activities, they write each word in their spelling books. Tonight all the children, *every child*, will take the words home to practice, and on Friday they will have a spelling test to make sure they have learned to spell them.

The mother of Everybody's Child takes a train, catches a bus. She drives her car to work. She has an MBA. She is a physicist, an epidemiologist. She works for the municipality. She wears a hard hat, a neon vest, holds the flags and directs the traffic when the crew paints yellow lines or fills in potholes in the roads. She cleans houses. She has no papers. She rents two rooms above a dry cleaning store. On Mondays, she works late.

Gate and *Fate*

At the end of the school day, Everybody's Child climbs on a school bus, which transports her to an after-school program, and she plays with her friends until her grandmother picks her up at 5 o'clock. She goes to her grandmother's house and plays with her grandmother's dogs while her grandmother cooks dinner. When they have eaten, she helps her grandmother clear the dishes off the kitchen table, and she gets out her homework. Her grandmother knows the routine. Monday night is spelling night. Everybody's Child writes each word three times and then closes her eyes and she spells the words as her grandmother says them. This Monday, on the list are *gate* and *fate*.

"Gate," her grandmother says.

"G-a-t-e," Everybody's Child says with her eyes closed.

"Fate," her grandmother says.

"F-a-t-e," Everybody's Child says.

Now Everybody's Child has to write each word in a sentence. Gate? She knows the meaning of the word *gate*. She has opened and closed the gate to her grandmother's backyard more times than she can count. She has swung on it and climbed over it. She can see it in her mind. She can almost feel the roughness of the wood and feel the coolness of the metal latch that she lifts when she opens the gate. If the dogs are in the back yard, she opens the gate just enough to squeeze through. She can hear the dogs barking, pushing against the gate as they jump up. She thinks about making sure the gate is closed. And then she writes, *The gate is open*. She looks at what she has written. She knows that handwriting counts and so checks that all the letters are sitting on the line. She wants to write a more complicated sentence about the dogs getting out, but it would be more risky. Her handwriting might be crooked, or she might misspell some of the words.

She looks at the next word. Fate? No images come to mind. She has no way to think about the word, no sensory experience for nonsensory thought. She cannot see it, feel it, touch it. She cannot taste it. It has no smell. She cannot hear it. She has lost contact with the world. She focuses on the sounds, the graphophonics, elongating the *a* and not making any sound for the *e*. She inspects the way she has written the word. She erases the *e* at the end of her third *fate* and rewrites it carefully so that the curve at the bottom sits neatly on the line. "Fate," her teacher will say on Friday when the test is given, and she will have no problem spelling the word.

Everybody's Child erases the *e* at the end of her second attempt to write *fate*. She thinks about silent *e* and moves her pencil carefully to make sure the *e* sits on the line. In silence, she looks back to her first attempt to write *fate* and once again she erases the *e*. Her grandmother watches her as she sips her cup of tea.

"I don't know what to write," Everybody's Child says. "What's fate? What does it mean?"

Her grandmother smiles. She is not sure what to say. After a few moments she says, "It's a very big word."

Her granddaughter looks puzzled. "It only has four letters," she says. "It's not a big word."

"Fate is a word we use to talk about what happens to us in our lives," her grandmother says. "It has a big meaning. It is a huge word."

In this story about Everybody's Child, we can imagine her grandmother's life history. She grew up in a small town. Her family lived in the same community for generations. Her mother and father had high expectations for her and they were very strict. It was the sixties. She wore flowers in her hair and took part in antiwar demonstrations. She remembers the shouting, doors slamming. She argued with her parents about free will. Freedom. She wanted to be free. She was torn between loyalty and liberation, loving them and leaving them, which she did.

We can imagine that the grandmother of Everybody's Child is from the Dominican Republic. When she was growing up, her father was involved in the underground against the Trujillo dictatorship. Many of her uncles and cousins disappeared. It is not easy for her to put into words what had happened to her family. "Fate?" she asks herself. "What does it mean? What does it mean to be free?"

We can imagine her coming from South Korea and settling in Southern California, learning English, finding work, making sure the mother of Everybody's Child worked hard in school. She remembers sitting with her daughter as she practiced her spelling words. Back then she could not read the words her daughter had to spell. All she could do was make sure she remembered the letters that made up each word. Now, when her granddaughter asks, "What is the meaning of *fate*?" she wonders what she should say. When she came to America, she wanted to understand Western ways of thinking, but as she gets older she thinks more and more about her childhood in Korea and she is not so sure.

We can imagine that the grandmother of Everybody's Child's comes from Tunisia and grew up speaking Arabic and French. She is Jewish, Arab, African, and American. She reads Sartre and Camus. She embraces her multiple identities and celebrates them with her daughter and granddaughter, but she does not to tell her granddaughter that she doesn't believe in fate. It might irritate her daughter, who rejected her mother's existential eccentricities.

"It is fate," Everybody's Child writes, and her grandmother smiles and nods her head.

We might ask why she wrote "It is fate." Syntax? Perhaps. "It is hot." "It is cold." It's a pattern she knows that tells us very little about her understanding of the word.

Everybody's Child puts her spelling words away and eats a cookie while her grandmother finishes her tea. They talk about the dogs and laugh, but suddenly Everybody's Child looks sad.

"I don't want anyone in my family to die," Everybody's Child tells her grandmother while they are still sitting at the kitchen table.

'I know," her grandmother says, not surprised by this unexpected turn in the conversation. Everybody's Child often makes these shifts in thinking. Her grandmother remembers that her daughter had done the same. When she listens to her granddaughter, it's as if a window opens revealing what Everybody's Child is really thinking, what is puzzling or worrying her, and what her ideas are about the world.

"I don't want you to die in your entire life," Everybody's Child continues.

"I will die one day," her Grandmother says, "but not for a long time," she adds reassuringly.

"If you do I'll bring you flowers," says Everybody's Child.

"I will like that," her grandmother says. Her eyes connect with her granddaughter's and, in a tender moment, she says, "We'll all die one day, that's our fate."

Gate and *Fate* Are in the Same Word Family at School

On Wednesday, Everybody's Child's teacher talks with the children in her class about word families, and she uses *gate* and *fate* as an example. On Friday, they take the test. "Gate," her teacher says, "gate." For a brief moment, Everybody's Child thinks about her grandmother's dogs before she focuses on the sounds. The graphophonics. She tries to sit the *e* on the line as she writes the word. "Fate" her teacher says, and Everybody's Child remembers talking with her grandmother about dying and her grandmother saying something about fate, but it is a new idea and the connection is easily broken. In less than a moment, she is back to the test. She remembers what her teacher said on Wednesday about word families. All she has to do is write *f* instead of *g* and she will have spelled the word. She writes the letter *f* and makes the sound. At a critical moment in the development of her understandings of life and death, her thoughts are diverted. Just as she is beginning to get an idea about the meaning of the word *fate*, the connection is broken. For Everybody's Child, the link between sensory and nonsensory experience is lost. Linking the words *gate* and *fate* becomes a source of confusion, creating an unrealistic reconception of fate and establishing a spurious and deceptive relationship between *gate* and *fate*.

Given the potential for confusion, it is important that we ask, What happens when we turn *fate* into a spelling word and link it to another word with which it has no connection?

Fate. Gate. If children are encouraged to focus on superficial connections between sounds and graphic marks on paper at a critical moment in human development, how does that affect their relationships with the world? Before we respond to these questions, it is important that we consider the meaning of the word *fate*.

Fate Is a Philosophical Word Embedded in Ideologies and Mythologies

Fate is a philosophical term and, as such, is metaphoric. It is a poetically frozen analogy in the sense that it, as Arendt writes, "has as much to do with human thinking as it does to our sensory world" (see Arendt, 1978, p. 106). Deeply embedded in ideologies and mythologies, it is an abstraction filled with ambiguity, connected to life and death, an abstraction rooted in religion and contested in science. If we are fatalistic, or realistic, or both, fate is contingent and conditional on our multiple identities, our positionalities—cultural, ethnic, racial, religious, geographic, political. Depending upon our life histories, we might ask if our fate is predetermined or if we have free will. For some, it is not even a question.

"Human life has no external point," Murdoch writes (1971, p. 77). This idea, she explains, "has already in fact occasioned a whole era in the history of philosophy, beginning with Kant and leading on to the existentialism and the analytic philosophy of the present day" (pp. 77–78).

So she is not misunderstood, Murdoch (1971) is critical of Kant. She does not position herself with existentialists or analytic philosophers. Instead, she acknowledges her "debt" to Weil (2002), who writes in *Gravity and Grace*, "The mind, is not forced to believe in the existence of anything" (p. 64). But Murdoch and Weil are not always on the same page, for Weil also pens the following:

> Man's greatness is always to recreate his life, to recreate what is given to him, to fashion that very thing which he undergoes. Through work he produces his own natural existence. Through science he recreates the universe by means of symbols. Through art he recreates the alliance between his body and his soul. (p. 178)

It is unlikely that Murdoch (1971) believed in the idea that man has a soul. Perhaps that is her fate. No matter. The point is made. Language is not incidental. It is central to the human condition, to who we are and our ways of being in the world. Some of the little words we reduce to word families to test first-grade children's ability to read and write *are huge*.

"Metaphors are not merely peripheral decorations or even useful models, they are fundamental forms of our awareness of our condition," as Murdoch (1971) writes.

"The sheer naming of things, the creation of words, is the human way of *appropriating* and, as it were, disalienating the world into which, after all, each of us is born as a newcomer and a stranger," Arendt writes, as if in response (1978, p. 100, emphasis in original).

"Metaphors can be a mode of understanding, and so of acting upon, our condition," Murdoch (1971, p. 91) continues, in this imaginary conversation.

Metaphors bridge "the minor truth of the seen to the major truth of the unseen," Arendt writes (1978, p. 106, citing Ernest Fenellosa, 1918), including Fenellosa in the conversation.

When children go to school, these activities, which are central to human existence, are interrupted. The bridge is blocked and their learning is diverted, subverted, and their thinking changed. Words that have no connection are connected. *Gate* and *fate*. For many children, learning to read becomes a meaningless activity. This is not to say that the mechanics of reading and writing are not important, they are, but at *no time* should learning to decode or recode supercede the focus on the importance of children's language and thinking.

Rain and *Pain* Are in the Same Word Family at School, but *Pain* Is a Very Complicated Word

Let's return to Everybody's Child and sit with her at her grandmother's kitchen table. It's Monday night, and they have just finished dinner. Everybody's Child is now in second grade and the spelling patterns of the words she has to learn are a little more complicated.

"Rain," the grandmother says after Everybody's Child has written each word three times.

Everybody's Child closes her eyes. "R-a-i-n," she says, spelling the word.

"Pain," her grandmother says.

"P-a-i-n," Everybody's Child says.

In her workbook she writes, "It is raining." Then without hesitation she writes, "I have a pain."

Her grandmother reads the sentences that Everybody's Child has written. She understands why they are so short, but she wishes they were longer, that there were more to them, that they meant something, that she felt the words in her heart, that she lived them.

"What sort of pain?" she asks.

"Just a pain," Everybody's Child says, looking puzzled.

"Pain is a very complicated word," her grandmother says.

You can imagine the rest of the conversation. Let's consider *rain*. It's a sensory word. It's raining as I write. We can stand in the rain together, tip our heads back and feel the raindrops on our faces, splash in the puddles, maybe put up our umbrellas. We can share our experiences of rain but not pain, *even though* they belong to the same word family.

For Everybody's Child, pain is nothing more than a tiny toothache or a sore throat that is an irritating tickle. But for the child sitting next to her, pain is being hit, punched, kicked. It is a violent, bone-breaking word.

In the United States, more than 3 million children are reported abused or neglected every year. That's the population of Chicago. More than 13 million U.S. children live in poverty and their families do not have the financial resources to take care of their basic needs. In 2005 more than 1,460 children died as a result of abuse or neglect, but the actual number is thought to be much higher. Seventy-seven percent of these fatalities were children under 4 years of age. Don't hide. Think of three schools filled with dead children.

There is no way to sugarcoat it. Pain separates us. We cannot feel one another's pain. It is the most complicated of words, presented to children alongside *rain* as if it is nothing more than a tear drop falling on a wet page in their spelling book.

Pain. Emotional? Physical? How do we tell one another about the pain we are experiencing if we cannot share the experience? Even though there have been many research studies, assessing pain is still an enormous problem for the medical profession. There are questionnaires translated into many languages that focus on the location, quality, and duration of pain. The level of pain is requested in numbers on a scale of 0–10. Patients are shown faces (see Figure 16.1). We divide pain into thermal and temporal. We describe pain as burning, throbbing, pinching, cramping, crushing. Scarry (1985) in *The Body in Pain* writes,

> Though the total number of words may be meager, though they may be hurled into the air unattached to any framing sentence, something can be learned from these verbal

Figure 16.1. Pain Assessment Scale

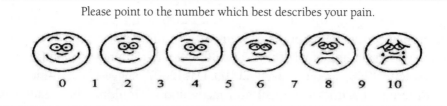

fragments not only about pain but about the human capacity for word-making. To witness the moment when pain causes a reversion to the pre-language of cries and groans is to witness the destruction of language; but conversely, to be present when a person moves up out of that pre-language and projects the facts of sentience into speech is almost to have been permitted to be present at the birth of language itself. (p. 6)

In England, I spend time in a hospital with my mother. In the room next to hers a man is moaning and making guttural sounds. When he wakes, he cries out. His pain is so extreme that we cannot even begin to imagine how he feels. The noises he makes start low and end in high-pitched screams. Sometimes when it is too soon for his next intravenous injection of pain medication, the nurses encourage the man to sing old songs with them from the 1940s and 1950s and in this way he gives language to his pain. Perhaps singing gives the man a few moments of relief. For others, nurses and patients, the songs that he grunts and groans are easier to hear than his screams.

In his Foreword to *Life and Words*, the breathtaking book by Das (2007), Cavell reminds us that Wittgenstein (1948, cited in Cavell) wrote in *Culture and Value*, "The whole planet can suffer no greater torment than a single soul" (p. xiv). Cavell focuses on the ways in which Das helps us appreciate that there are no standing words for pain and that language is inherently unreliable in the expression of pain. Das herself writes of the language of pain "having all the phonetic excess of hysteria that destroys apparent meanings" (p. 55). She writes,

> Pain in this rendering is not that inexpressible something that destroys communication or marks an exit from one's existence in language. Instead, it makes a claim on the other—asking for acknowledgment that may be given or denied. In either case, it is not a referential statement that is pointing to an inner object. (p. 40)

When Everybody's Child writes "I have a pain," pain becomes referential, a noun, an object. It's the way we teach children to read in school. When we reduce words to graphophonic patterns and match them with other words with similar patterns, no claims are made on the other. Words become discrete, autonomous. We change the *r* at the beginning of *rain* to the *p* at the beginning of *pain* without consideration of the consequences. Children write the word without any understanding of what it means. It's not a trivial problem. Building on Wittgenstein (1948, cited in Cavell, 2007), Das (2007) suggests we think about pain in terms of acknowledgment and recognition. Thinking about language in this way raises questions about teaching and learning. Das writes, "In the register of the imaginary, the pain of the other not only asks for a home in language, but also seeks a home in the body" (p. 57). The rejection of the Cartesian mind–body separation (Modell, 2003) allows us to consider again the relationships between the ways in which children "language" life in their families and the ways in which they are taught to language life in schools.

In the Hospital, *Fate* and *Pain* Belong to the Same Word Family

To take these ideas about life and words a little further, we need to leave the kitchen table where Everybody's Child is studying her spelling words with her grandmother. Studying them in school won't help us. It has to be in another place, where everything that is familiar to us is made strange. In the summer of 2008, I spent every day in a critical care unit of a hospital, and for just a few paragraphs I am going to take you there. In the quiet moments, and there were a few, I spent my time reading the chapter "Language and Metaphor" in Arendt's (1978) *The Life of the Mind* and pondering the spelling words of Everybody's Child. In the hospital, *fate* and *pain* create a different "word family." In life and death words are more than referential, they live. After several days of reading, I started writing ethnographic notes with no intention of using them except for contemplation and meditation, but there are insights to be gained about the ways in which we language life when the unseen of living and dying is seen.

My friend, J, is paralyzed and he has lived the last 22 years in excruciating pain. On June 16th, he became seriously ill, and he has been in the hospital ever since. In the beginning, his aide, Otto, and I provided round-the-clock support. Otto was with him at night, and I was with him during the day. We are still at the hospital every day, but we now have more help. What follows are from the early days of his hospitalization. I have read my notes to J, and he will read the chapter before I present or publish it. As you read, keep in mind Wittgenstein's

(1948, cited in Das, 2007) idea of "the bodying forth of words," and of the ways "language makes claims on the other" (Das, 2007, p. 40). Consider the bodying forth of words like *fate* and *pain* and the ways in which both words make claims on the other. In this instance, "the other" is you.

J has tubes draining both lungs, oxygen tubes in his nose, another tube in his nose that goes down into his stomach to feed him, a catheter to urinate, three IVs—two in his right arm and one in his left arm—a heart monitor with all the leads, a finger monitor for oxygen, and special leg massagers to make sure his blood is circulating.

"I don't think we'll go to Central Park this year," J says. "Next year."

J is gasping for every breath. His lungs are filled with fluid. He has a tube draining his right lung and tomorrow they will insert a tube and drain his left lung. Liters of fluid will fill both bags, and the doctors will have no explanation.

"I'm drowning inside," J rasps. Each word is labored whisper. "What am I supposed to do?"

"Ice! Get the ice!" he whispers. I know this means he is going to cough and he needs to sit up. The pain will be intense. I make sure the wires and tubes are not tangled. He grabs the side rails, and I work my hand under his back and get ready. "Push!" he says, gasping for breath. I push. He's up. Coughing. His spine is crushed so when he sits up his head falls forward. I hold him up, keeping my hands still. I do not rub or pat. His pain is too intense for that. "Back!" he rasps, "Back!" and I try to hold him steady as he uses the rails to lower himself onto the pillows piled on the bed. "Ice! Ice! I can't breathe!"

"Oxygen saturation 96," I tell him. "Breaths 33, 34." I breathe out slowly, blowing loudly so he can hear and perhaps feel, "29, 30."

"I can't breathe!" I blow and his breathing slows. 20, 19, 18, 20.

Exhausted, J closes his eyes and focuses on his breathing. "I'm here in the moment," he whispers. "I'm just trying to breathe. I'm struggling for every breath. One gasp. One breath. It's so painful. I don't want to die. I want to live."

The nurse is talking to Henry, who lies behind the curtain in the next bed. He is moaning. It is a deep sound. Not harsh. "Can you stop moving your arm please? You're going to pull these needles right out of our arm. We're going to have a bloody mess here. We can't take the needles out."

"Take, take, take," Henry says, appropriating the word and giving it a familiar meaning. "Never give. Take, take, take, never give, take, take, take."

"Come assist this gentleman," Henry says, living past experiences in an imaginary telephone call. He pauses between utterances for the other to speak. "I want to go to the Fifth Precinct."..."They'll charge him."..."Give me a hand man."..."It'll take five minutes to get here."

Henry cries out. "Can someone help me out here?" he shouts, needing help in bed. "Can I have a hand please? I can't get down from the building."

Henry speaks in metaphors and analogies, bringing sensory and nonsensory experience together. The complexity of his utterances goes unnoticed. No one listens or tries to understand. I speak with his son and his sister, try to explain. They smile at me and thank me for the lemonade I gave to Henry when he asked for some.

"Hey, what you do?" Henry shouts. "Did you rob this place?"..."Okay"..."Yeh, I heard you"..."Hey man"..."I heard you"..."I need back up! Police!"

"Can I interrupt your procedure?" he says to a nurse. "Oh, I don't know what's going on here. I don't understand this. Who's looking after me?"

Henry is quiet on the day he is told he's going to be sent to a nursing home. The following day his sister Rita says, "He's had a set back." Doctors come and go. Later when his sister has gone, Henry cries out.

"All right! All right! Open the door!" he shouts. "Open the door! Open the door! Rita! Rita! Please open the door!" And then in a broken voice that sounds like a sob, Henry cries, "Oh, I'm going to be lost forever." Henry is crying. "I'm going to be lost forever!"

In the Step Down room it is quiet. J stretches out his arm and pulls the curtain back to look for Henry. His bed is empty. J closes his eyes as he lets go of the curtain. That day J is diagnosed with Wegener's, a rare vascular disease. After eight days of intensive nursing in Step Down, he is "moved up" to a critical care unit where he spends the next six weeks in a glass room.

J talks on the telephone with a young psychiatrist who was his intern. "I'm doing well," he says, "I just have to remember that I am not giving up."

Later, I ask J how he feels. "Right now," he says, "I am spaced out, but I am not spaced out anywhere. It is not even three dimensional. I am trying to make it real, reality, there's no foundation. It's hard to imagine being here."

The nurse comes in and tells J he will start dialysis today or tomorrow. She talks with me about the level of toxins in his body and about making sure he is conscious. J's eyes close. "I'm watching him," she says. "Get me if you have any concerns."

J is sleeping more. He is less alert. In a lucid moment he says, "I'm an island. It only exists when you are here." He traces the island in the air, the bed, the chair. He points at my eyes and then his own and says "eye-land." He is fading. "When I am alone I'm not here."

Later, J talks about pain, being in pain, having pain in his back, his chest, his stomach. "I'm frightened," he says.

An alarm goes off. The woman is dying in the room next to J's. A square appears on the heart monitor screen in her room. A flat line runs across it. "999." A team of nurses comes running. There is shouting. Commands. Action. The woman's husband and daughter are crying. The curtain gets caught and is pulled back. We can see the lifeless woman, the nurses with pain and grief on their faces are moving quickly, and grim-faced doctors are frantically trying to revive her and bring her back. Two people die in the glass room next to J's, one after another, a man dies the following week, just 15 feet away from where J lies.

In his glass room the lights are always on; there are constant beeps that are punctuated by the loud speakers broadcasting "999." The days and nights lose definition. Weeks go by and J asks one of the doctors if he is going to live. She says there is a slim chance he might recover. She talks at length about Wegener's Disease and in the stream of talk she uses the word "miracle."

"Is it going to take a miracle?" J asks.

She nods her head.

In August, J leaves critical care for a room in the new wing of the hospital. The nurses smile and wish him luck. "It's a miracle," one of them says, and we talk about what the doctor said. At the beginning of October, J is still there. The pain is almost constant now. He says it's a seven or an eight; he never says nine. He hopes to go home next week. He will have home dialysis and round-the-clock nurses and a lifetime of moments to live. But November comes and J is still in the hospital. His suffering is so extreme that one of the nurses says he can not take care of him, and a doctor says it is difficult for several of her colleagues to come and see him. Still, others embrace him, tell him they love him, that he is "family," and they sometimes cry when they leave his room.

The Fate of Children Who Live in Pain

Fate. We do not know what will happen to J or to Henry but their stories have become a part of our lives. We cannot hide from them or hide them. In many countries the frailness of those who are sick and the fragility of those who are injured is more visible. When I am working in regions where there is armed conflict or in which a catastrophic event, such as Katrina, has taken place, there are moments when the closeness to death connects the living.

"I feel sad," a third-grade child writes one month after Hurricane Katrina. "I saw people dead in the water." Figure 16.2 shows a drawing by this third-grade child made at that time.

More than three years later, children are still suffering. In May of 2009, I returned to Louisiana to spend time with the teachers and children in St. Bernard Parish (Elliot & Taylor, 2006; Taylor & Yamasaki, 2006) and Jefferson Parish (Taylor & Yamasaki, 2005). In Chalmette in St. Bernard Parish, teachers talk about children needing time to discuss what's happening and share feelings.

"Some children stayed and some saw death right in front of them," a teacher says.

"We came back on a Tuesday night," one of the teachers says, telling her own story. "We moved into our trailer. That night, my sister came banging on

Figure 16.2. I Feel Sad. I Saw Dead People in the Water

the door crying 'Daddy is dead.' He wasn't sick. I think he just couldn't rebuild again."

"One catastrophe can lead to another," a teacher says. She recounts, "A child holding on to a tree with his mother and father was coping okay, and then his mother tried to commit suicide."

More than three years after Hurricane Katrina, tragedies are still occurring.

"Catastrophes happen and children might cope," another teacher says, "but a year later, two years later, problems surface."

A psychiatrist (Pandya, 2006) provides verification of the experiences of the Louisiana teachers when he speaks of the expectation of symptoms during the acute phase of an emergency that become transient and fluid, often recurring weeks, months, or years after the disaster happened. Pandya (2006) speaks of the let down, and so did the Louisiana teachers, who talk at length about the changes they were observing in their students' behaviors as they began to understand that their families, schools, and communities would never be the same.

The teachers talk of Katrina becoming part of children's identity.

"Hi. I'm John and I was in Katrina," a teacher says, as an example.

"They live the storm," another says.

In a trailer, Everybody's Child is sitting at the table with her grandmother. It is Monday night, and they have just had dinner. Everybody's Child has written her spelling words three times.

"Rain," her grandmother says.

Everybody's Child closes her eyes.

"R-a-i-n," she says.

"Pain," her grandmother says. Everybody's Child opens her eyes. She looks at her grandmother, who puts her arms around her granddaughter. They are both crying. Pain is a family word that is connected to rain by chance, only because of a hurricane, which is a word that does not fit into the word family Everybody's Child is learning in school.

When we connect the surface features of words like *pain* and *rain* or *gate* and *fate*, we divert children away from their sensory and nonsensory experience. We shift meaning from the bodying forth of words. Instead, we refocus children's attention on the surface features of words.

And So, Questioning the Question

If children are forced to focus on superficial connections between sounds and graphic marks on paper, how does this affect their relationships with the world?

Essentially, I am asking you to explore the proposition that the ways in which reading and writing are taught in school have the potential to interfere with the human drive for meaning. I am encouraging you to consider the consequences of the shift that takes place in school away from the deep connections that exist between language and life, to the surface structures, the visual features and auditory patterns of words, like *gate* and *fate*, *rain* and *pain*.

It is important that we ask, What happens when we turn *fate* and *pain* into spelling words? What happens to language? What happens to Everybody's Child?

And now the questions behind the question: Could it be that it is not only children who are diverted? What about us? Have the ways in which we have been taught to read and write in school affected our thinking? Can we body forth words? Feel when we think? Do the threads that hold our minds together bind us? Can we connect the sensory and the nonsensory? Do we feel empathy? Are we aware of the pain of others?

Toni Morrison, in her 1993 acceptance speech for the Nobel Prize in literature, tells the story of a woman who is old and wise. She is the daughter of slaves, black and American, and she is blind:

> She is worried about how the language she dreams in, given to her at birth, is handled, put into service, even withheld from her for certain nefarious purposes. [This woman] thinks of language partly as a system, partly as a living thing over which one has control, but mostly as agency—as an act with consequences. (n.p.)

Morrison's (1993) Nobel acceptance speech brings me back to the beginning of this chapter and the quote from Murdoch (1971). "Words are the most subtle symbols which we possess and our human fabric depends upon them," she writes. "The living and radical nature of language is something which we forget at our peril" (p. 33).

Morrison (1993) leaves us in no doubt what the consequences are of such forgetfulness. She writes of the death of language, of dead language that is "content to admire its own paralysis."

> However moribund, it is not without effect for it actively thwarts the intellect, stalls conscience, suppresses human potential. Unreceptive to interrogation, it cannot form

or tolerate new ideas, shape other thoughts, tell another story, fill baffling silences. Official language smitheryed to sanction ignorance and preserve privilege is a suit of armor polished to shocking glitter, a husk from which the knight departed long ago. Yet there it is: dumb, predatory, sentimental. Exciting reverence in schoolchildren, providing shelter for despots, summoning false memories of stability, harmony among the public. (n.p.)

It is painful, but this is our fate and the fate of everybody's child unless we take up the challenge and rethink the ways in which language, given to us at birth, is handled and put into service in schools without consideration of the consequences for grandmothers and granddaughters, and grandsons, *all our children*, suppressing their potential by the ways in which they are taught to read and write, and thus, changing their relationships to and with the world.

REFERENCES

Arendt, H. (1978). *The life of the mind* (M. McCarthy, Ed.). San Diego, CA: Harcourt.

Cavell, S. (2007). Foreword. In V. Das, *Life and words: Violence and the descent into the ordinary* (pp. ix–xiv). Berkeley: University of California Press.

Das, V. (2007). *Life and words: Violence and the descent into the ordinary*. Berkeley: University of California Press.

Elliot, C., & Taylor, D. (2006). Leading in the worst times. *Educational Leadership, 64*(1), 82–86.

Kayzer, W. (1999). *A glorious accident: Understanding our place in the cosmic puzzle*. New York: W.H. Freeman.

Modell, A.H. (2003). *Imagination and the meaningful brain*. Cambridge, MA: MIT Press.

Morrison, T. (1993, December 7). *The Nobel lecture in literature*. Retrieved November 9, 2009, from nobelprize.org/nobel_prizes/literature/laureats/1993/morrison-lecture.html

Murdoch, I. (1971). *The sovereignty of good*. New York: Routledge.

Pandya, A. (2006, April 19). *The psychological impact of disaster and terrorism: Tending to the hidden wounds*. Presentation to the American Medical Association convention, New York, NY.

Scarry, E. (1985). *The body in pain: The making and unmaking of the world*. Oxford, England: Oxford University Press.

Taylor, D., & Yamasaki, T. (2005). *The Kate Middleton elementary school: Portraits of hope and courage after Katrina*. New York: Scholastic.

Taylor, D., & Yamasaki, T. (2006). Children, literacy and mass trauma: Teaching in times of catastrophic events and on going emergency situations. *Penn GSE Perspectives on Urban Education, 4*(2). Retrieved October 20, 2009, from www.urbanedjournal.org/archive/Unsorted%20Archives/articles/article0029.pdf

Weil, S. (2002). *Gravity and grace* (A. Wills, Trans.). New York: Putnam. (Original work published 1947)

AUTHOR INDEX

Note. Page numbers followed by *f* or *t* indicate figures or tables, respectively.

Hemphill, L., 315
Henderson, A.T., 154
Henderson, R., 31
Herman, P.A., 250
Heron, E., 188
Herrmann, S., 308
Heubach, K., 255
Hewison, J., 315
Hicks, D., 28
Hicks, L., 67
Hiebert, E., 188
Hilferty, A., 188
Hill, M.F., 283
Hirsch, E.D., Jr., 139
Hobbs, R., 37
Hoffman, J., 33
Hoffman, J.V., 85, 109,112, 126
Holland, D., 138
Holliday, L., 166
Hollingsworth, J.R., 139
Hoover-Dempsey, K.V., 54, 55f, 56, 58, 59, 60, 61, 67, 80
Hornberger, N.H., 340
Horton, M., 228
Huang, C.W., 249
Huerta-Macías, A., 214
Huey, E.B., 191
Hughes, M., 315
Humenick, N.M., 285

I

Ice, C.L., 56
International Reading Association, 142
Irby, M.A., 22
Irvine, J.J., 184
Ivey, G., 72, 246, 248, 249, 252, 254, 255, 256, 257

J

Jacob, E., 248, 251
Jacobs, J.A., 50
Jacobs, L., 210
Jasis, P., 334, 338, 343
Jensen, B., 334, 335
Jeynes, W.H., 68
Jiménez, R.T., 195
Jo, H., 283
Johnson, V.R., 62
Johnston, P.H., 257
Jones, L.T., 190
Jordan, C., 209, 210
Joseph, I.E., 290

K

Kaiser Family Foundation, 204
Kastler, L., 109
Kastler, L.A., 112
Katz, L.F., 137
Kaufman, S.Z., 191
Kayzar, B., 266
Kee, C., 138
Kemple, J.J., 248
Kennedy, A.M., 246
Kessler, D., 34
Kingsolver, B., 37
Kirby, D.L., 257
Kirkland, K., 168
Kirsch, I., 249
Kirton, E., 210
Klass, P., 99
Klindienst, P., 37
Klingner, J., 236
Knapp, C.E., 173
Knoblauch, C.H., 139
Kohl, H., 228
Kohl, H.R., 19
Kohl, J., 228
Konstantopoulos, S., 283
Kozol, J., 19, 327
Krashen, S., 250
Kreider, H., 45, 62
Krol-Sinclair, B., 83, 271, 277
Kubicek, L.F., 99
Kuhn, M.R., 85, 86, 92
Kunjufu, J., 145, 236

L

Labbo, L., 190
Lachicotte, W., Jr., 138
Ladson-Billings, G., 139, 150, 229, 231, 236, 239
Lake, C., 247
Lake, R., 163–164
Landry, S.H., 63
Langman, J., 22
Lansberg, M., 140–141
Lapp, D., 43, 57, 138, 144, 153, 309, 319
Lareau, A., 24, 48, 50, 140, 333, 335, 342
Larner, M.B., 24
Lasch, C., 16, 17, 22, 29, 30
Laureau, A., 203
Lave, J., 139
Lawrence-Lightfoot, S., 184
Layzer, J.I., 266
Lazar, A.M., 190

Scherff, L., 246
Schmidt, P.R., 190
Schneider B., 42
Schofield, W.N., 315
Schreiber, P.A., 85
Schwannenflugel, P.J., 85, 92
Schweinhart, L.J., 68
Scoblionko, J., 84
Scott, J.A., 188
Scrivener, S., 271
Seale, D., 163, 164
Sénéchal, M., 64, 266, 272, 285, 314t
Serpell, R., 266
Severino, C., 154
Shafer, D., 84
Shanahan, T., 213, 220, 314t, 316
Shanker, J.L., 320
Shannon, S.M., 207, 208
Shaw, D., 309
Shockley, B., 192
Simon, J., 99
Simpkins, S., 62
Sipe, L.R., 122, 124–125, 126, 127
Skinner, D., 138
Slater, W., 246
Slavin, R.E., 247
Smith, D., 110
Smith, E.W., 105
Smith, K., 116
Smith, K.E., 63, 115
Smith, M.W., 122, 125, 127
Smyth, L., 22, 24
Snipes, J., 271
Snow, C., 192, 210, 315
Snow, C.E., 34, 192, 247, 285, 313t, 315, 316t
Sonnenschein, S., 64, 65, 138, 191, 266, 272
Soricone, L., 271
Spindler, G.D., 17
St. Pierre, R.G., 266, 313t, 315–316, 316t
Stahl, S.A., 85, 86
Stapin, B., 163, 164
Stauffer, R.G., 255
Steward, A.D., 283
Steward, R.J., 283
Stewart, R., 256
Sticht, T.G., 265–266
Stinnett, N., 46
Stokes, S.J., 190, 192
Street, B.V., 192
Strickland, C.S., 62
Strickland, D.S., 194
Suárez-Orozco, C., 45, 48

Suárez-Orozco, M.M., 45, 48
Sulzby, E., 138, 314t, 318
Super, C.M., 191
Sutton-Smith, B., 33
Swanson, M.C., 142
Sweet, L., 153
Swords, R., 149
Swygert, H.P., 178–179

T

Tabors, P., 315
Tamarkin, C., 233
Tamis-LeMonda, C.S., 99
Tan, A., 85
Taylor, B.M., 186
Taylor, C., 31, 32, 141
Taylor, D., 138, 141, 143, 152, 190, 192, 194, 284, 307, 311, 313t, 315, 335, 336–337, 362
Taylor, H.B., 63, 65, 71
"Teacher Demographics," 44
Teale, W.H., 138, 190, 191, 212
Tejeda, C., 337
Tembo, M.S., 141
The New London Group, 221
The Pew Hispanic Center, 204, 205
Thomas, C., 192
Thomas, E.M., 266, 272
Thomas, W.P., 140
Thomas-El, S., 27
Thompson, D.F., 37
Tilly, C., 31
Tizard, B., 315
Tizard, J., 314t, 315, 316t
Todorova, I., 45, 48
Toker, K.H., 99
Tomasello, M., 36
Torgesen, J.K., 85, 285
Tough, P., 49
Tracey, D., 266
Tracey, D.H., 83
Trevino, R.E., 61
Trueba, H., 206, 208, 209, 210
Trujillo, A.L., 344
Turner, J.D., 138, 184
Turner, M., 249
Tutwiler, S.W., 143
Tyack, D., 151

U

U.S. Census Bureau, 148
U.S. Department of Education, 204, 213

V

Valdés, G., 203, 205, 206, 207, 210, 333, 334, 340, 344
Valencia, R.R., 298
Valencia, S.W., 251
Valenzuela, A., 298
van IJzendoorn, M.H., 65, 71, 272, 285, 314t, 316, 316t
Van Voorhis, F.L., 59
Vásquez, O.A., 208
Venkatesh, S.A., 24, 28
Vukelich, C., 194
Vygotsky, L.S., 84, 313t, 317, 332–333, 336

W

Wagner, R.K., 85
Walker, J.M.T., 54
Walpole, S., 186
Wang, Y., 291
Wasik, B.H., 84, 308
Weil, S., 354
Weisberg, R., 190
Weisner, T.S., 191, 210
Weiss, H.B., 45, 62
Wells, D., 117, 119, 122, 124
Wells, G., 124, 314t, 318
Wenger, E., 139
Wertsch, J.V., 139
West, J., 266
Westberg, L., 84
Wheeler, R.S., 149
Whitaker, M.C., 56
Whitehurst, G.J., 313t, 315, 316t
Whitmore, K.F., 154
Wigfield, A., 66, 72, 249

Wigginton, E., 173, 174
Wilcox, L., 188
Wiley, T.G., 189, 190, 191
Wilkins, A.S., 54
Wilkinson, I.A.G., 188
Willis, A.I., 230
Wilson, P.T., 250
Winter, M., 191
Winters, W.G., 196
Wolf, S.A., 257
Wolos, C., 136
Wortham, S., 311
Worthy, J., 249, 256, 285

X

Xu, J., 67

Y

Yaden, D.B., 143, 267
Yagelski, R.P., 246
Yamasaki, T., 362
Yang, Y., 141
Yeakey, C., 31
Young, J., 57, 59, 64, 70, 71, 84, 94
Young, L., 266, 285
Young, S., 37
Young, V.H., 17

Z

Zeichner, K.M., 234
Zentella, A.C., 31, 205, 207
Zimmerman, B.J., 67
Zipporoli, L., 24
Zubizarreta, R., 333, 334, 340

SUBJECT INDEX

Note. Page numbers followed by *f* or *t* indicate figures or tables, respectively.

A

AAVE. *See* African American Vernacular English
ABC books, 108
academic learning: cultural competence as conduit for, 164–167; Foxfire approach to, 175–176
academic literacy, 180–181
academic qualifications, 295
Academic Search, 312
academic self-efficacy, 66
access to meaningful reading and writing, 241–242
access to texts, 104–106
accommodation, 188
acculturation: dissonant, 293; selective, 290, 291–294
achievement gap, 27–28
Achievement Via Individual Determination (AVID), 142
acquisition literacy, 167
activities: with books children bring home from school, 88*f*, 88–89; family literacy activities, 83; *Highlights for Children* magazine, 95–96; home activities, 61, 76, 88*f*, 88–89; literacy-supportive home activities, 76; Project FLAME, 219–220; school involvement activities, 77; teacher-directed reading/writing activities, 254–255
adaptation, 188, 190, 191–192, 194–195; intergenerational, 293; paths of, 292
adolescent literacy: additional interventions for, 258–259; books for, 258; connecting inexperienced teenage readers with books, 245–261; creating literacy-rich contexts for, 249–250; engagement-focused interventions for, 252–257; formative experiments, 250–252; inexperienced adolescent learners, 255–257; inexperienced adolescent readers, 259; inexperienced teenage readers, 245–261; status of, 245–248
Advanced Placement programs, 299, 300
affection, 46–47
African American Vernacular English (AAVE), 142, 144, 163
African Americans, 17, 20, 24, 108–109, 140, 141, 151, 161–162, 165, 173, 181–182, 226–227, 242–243; adolescents, 163; demand for success in, 236; early readers, 107; enslavement of, 227–229; ethnically specific institutions for, 176, 178–180; family literacy, 227; family literacy programs, 184–202; high-achieving, 166; literate slaves, 227–229; mothers, 113–115, 114*f*, 118, 120, 121; multidimensional needs of students, 178; poor parents, 185–187, 196–197; in urban classrooms, 237
Afrocentric Educational Academy (Minneapolis), 176
Afrocentric programs, 176
after-school programs, 297
Aid to Families with Dependent Children (AFDC), 105
Alliance for Excellence in Education, 246–247
American Medical Association, 46
American Psychiatric Association, 46
analogies, 360
analytic review template (ART), 312
Angul (student), 144–149
Anthony (student), 143–144, 144–149

anthropology, linguistic, 15
Appalachia, 172–173
application literacy, 167
appreciation, 46–47
Arizona, 204
art, 171–172
artists, 27
Ashley (student), 147, 148
Asian Americans, 107, 161–162, 165, 173, 181–182
Asian-Pacific Islanders, 151
Asians, 140
assessment: Family *Highlights* Program, 96–98; of fluency, 89–90, 90f; StimQ assessment, 100
assimilation: consonant, 292–293; downward, 292; segmented, 291
authentic literacy, 229
"Authors Spot," 95
autobiographies, 190
AVID. *See* Achievement Via Individual Determination

B

Baez, Erica: "Top Ten," 299–300
"banking education," 332
Beacon Centers, 50
behavior: central to learning success, 63–64; learning-related, 63; parents' modeling of, 63; parents' reinforcement of, 63–64
BELLE Project, 44, 98–100, 100–101; program, 99–100; results, 100
Bellevue Hospital Center Clinic, 99
Bellevue Project for Early Language, Literacy, and Education Success (BELLE Project), 98–100
Bible, 107, 108, 228, 231
biculturalism, 165
Big Books, 125, 126
bilingual classes, 125
bilingualism: fluent, 294; literate, 290, 294–297
block schools, 19
book conversations, 124–125
book floods, 105
book talks, 127–129
book walks, 270
books: ABC books, 108; access to, 104–106, 241–242; Big Books, 125, 126; that children talk about, 119–121; connecting inexperienced teenage readers with, 245–261; home storybook talk, 118–119; importance for adolescents, 258; meaningful reading and writing, 241–242; parent-child book reading, 187–195; picture books, 109, 116–121; reading activities to do with books children bring home from school, 88f, 88–89; for self-selected reading, 253–254; social and cultural purposes served by, 111–112; in support of children's language and literacy, 110–121; as talking, 226–227; talking over, 104–135; texts in support of children's language and literacy, 110–121; types in homes, 106–110; types of texts in homes, 106–110
Bossman, Anthony (student), 143–144, 144–149
Boston University: Intergenerational Literacy Project, 117
Boy Scouts, 27
Boys and Girls Clubs, 22, 23, 27
Bradford (student), 321–325
Bravo, 23
Breadwinner (Ellis), 269

C

California, 204, 205
California Test of Basic Skills, 96
Canada, Geoffrey: Harlem Children's Zone (HCZ), 49–50
caring pedagogy, 173
Carolina Abecedarian Project, 308
Castillo, Hilda, 280–282; first day of school essay, 281, 281*f*; literacy log, 281, 282*f*
Castillo family, 280–282
Caucasians, 151
causal/predictive research: quantitative, 312–317, 313*t*, 314*t*
CDS. *See* Child development specialist
Cerro High School, 299
child care, 220; after-school programs, 297
child development specialist (CDS), 99
children, 350–351; books they talk about, 119–121; early readers, 107; getting to know, 149–154; of immigrants, 291, 292; interviews with, 92–94, 96–97; invitations from, 74–75; parent-child relationship, 70–71; parents' communications with, 61; reading with, 116–121; responses to Family Fluency Program, 92; school-aged, 44; who live in pain, 361–363, 362*f*. *See also* Students
children's magazines, 109
choral reading, 88*f*
citation coding: analysis of findings based on, 317–319; findings, 312–317, 313*t*–314*t*
Citizenship Schools, 228, 229
civic agents, 27
Civil Rights movement, 228
Clark, Septima, 228, 229, 308
classroom literacy, 186
classroom literacy instruction, 285
classrooms, 240–241
collaborative relationships, 69–70
Colorado, 204
Comité de Padres Latinos (Latino Parents' Committee) (COPLA), 209, 343
commitment, 47
communication: book talk, 127–129; books children talk about, 119–121; culturally bound styles, 48–49; family-school communications, 61, 76; home storybook talk, 118–119; interactive and mutually respectful, 69–70; parents with children, 61; positive, 48–40; preschoolers' book conversations, 124–125; talking over books, 104–135
community: in action, 22–28; culturally and linguistically different, 203–225; urban, 226–244
community learning, 15–41
community literacy, 37
Community Literacy Journal, 37
community timescales, 317–319
Concept-Oriented Reading Instruction (CORI), 250
confianza (mutual trust), 206, 208, 212, 295–296, 338
consejos (personal advice), 338
consonant assimilation, 292–293
contextual motivators, 57–59, 74–75
conversations: book talk, 127–129; preschoolers' book conversations, 124–125; talking over books, 104–135
coping with crises, 49–50
COPLA. *See* Comité de Padres Latinos (Latino Parents' Committee)
CORI. *See* Concept-Oriented Reading Instruction

Cosby, Bill, 153
crises: abilities for coping with, 49–50
critical literacy, 298, 333; Project FLAME program, 220–221
critical literature review, 311–319
critical theory, 339–340
cultural capital, 197–198
cultural competence, 161–162; as conduit for academic learning, 164–167; development of, 182; as foundation for teaching literacy, 163–164; as literacy, 164–167
cultural consciousness: critical, 167–172; developing, 167–172; exercises for developing, 168–170, 170–171
cultural differences, 197; family literacy with, 203–225; and parental involvement, 205–209
cultural diversity, 332–347
cultural diversity talking quilts, 171–172
cultural ethnography, 172–173
cultural hybridity, 165
cultural identity, 169–170
cultural journalism, 173–174
cultural literacy: essential, 177–178; students', 179; teaching to ethnically diverse students of color, 180–181
cultural misunderstandings, 208
cultural models, 210–211, 230
cultural pride, 172–173
cultural reciprocity, 185, 196–197
cultural responsivity, 338
cultural self-analysis, 190
cultural ways of knowing, 344
culturally responsive literacy: Foxfire approach, 172–176; in higher education, 176–177; professional literacy, 167; teaching, 167; through ethnically specific institutions, 176–180
culture: communication styles, 48–49; ethnically diverse, 162–163; family culture, 60; home culture, 159–261; Latino, 203–225; multicultural education, 170; of power, 192–193; of school, 123–124
curriculum: advanced, 335–336; hidden, 295

D
data analysis, 320–321
Davidsonville Elementary School (Louisiana), 187, 195
demand for success, 236, 239
democratic values, 345
demographics, 272–273; national, 44
Devereaux, Julia, 232–233, 233–234, 241, 242
Dewey, John, 20
differences, 140
digital images, 257
Dine College (Navajo Reservation), 177–178
discourse: Discourse, 137, 138, 211; discourse, 137–138, 211–212; primary discourse, 211; secondary discourse, 211
discussion: book conversations, 124; book talk, 127–129; talking over books, 104–135
display, 124
dissonant acculturation, 293
diversity: cultural, 332–347; ethnic, 161–162, 162–163, 180–181; family literacy for diverse families, 339–345; family literacy programs in diverse communities, 221–223; linguistic, 332–347; of literacies, 337, 338–339; Teach for Diversity (TFD), 234–235

double consciousness, 194–195
Douglass, Frederick, 184, 308
downward assimilation, 292
Dr. Seuss, 109
Dreamkeepers, 231
dreams, 197–198
dropouts, 140, 141

E
early readers, 107
Ebonics, 163
echo reading, 88*f*
ecological theory: major citations in reviews, 312–317, 313*t*
ecology: school ecology, 297
economic differences, 28–31, 140
education, 205–206; "banking education," 332; block schools, 19; higher, 176–177; importance of, 266; Latino schooling, 203–225; multicultural, 170; parental, 266, 272; postsecondary plans, 273; special education, 324, 325; transformative theory of, 333. *See also* Literacy programs
Education Full Test, 312
educational sovereignty, 294; key school practices that bolster, 295–297
educational toys, 33
edutainment, 33
effective practices, 341
efficacy, 56–57
Ellis, Deborah, 269
empowerment, 345
encouragement, 63
encuentros (public meetings), 301–302
engaged reading, 249, 258–259
engagement: in creating literacy-rich contexts for adolescents, 249–250; time and space requirements for, 258–259
engagement-focused interventions, 252–257; for inexperienced adolescent learners, 255–257; for middle school English-language learners, 252–255
English as a Second Language (ESL) classes, 215, 218
English language: definition of, 175; importance of, 204; literacy instruction, 267–268
English-language learners, 140, 335, 340; engagement-focused interventions for, 252–255; middle school, 252–255
English monolingualism, 294
entertainment orientation, 113
environmental stewards, 27
equality: believing in, 19–21; partnerships of, 154–155
ERIC, 312
essential questions, 256
Estes, Eleanor, 269
ethnic diversity, 161–162; literacy practices with, 162–163; teaching literacy with, 180–181
ethnic heritage programs, 176
ethnically specific institutions, 176–180
ethnicity, 116, 140, 151
ethnography, qualitative, 312–317, 313*t,* 314*t*
European Americans, 24, 107, 141, 161, 165–166, 173, 181–182
Even Start, 266–267

F

facilitative roles, 113

familia, 205, 214

familial timescales, 326

families, 29; activity domains mediated by literacy, 111; capacities for effective parental involvement, 72–80; characteristics of, 45–50; components of, 28; concept of, 205; diverse, 340–346; ethnically diverse, 162–163; as extended groups of individuals, 229; getting to know by joining, 142–149; importance of, 137; Latino, 209–212; linking literacy to students' family lives, 242–243; literacy practices in, 162–163; participation of, 303; research findings, 321–325; resilient, 46; respecting and working with, 69; responsiveness to life context of, 59–61, 75; in school-based literacy practices, 13–158; school communications, 61, 76; school partnerships, 143; self-understanding of, 175; strategies for accommodating, 190; support for values and goals of literacy learning from, 76; supporting, 13–158; time issues, 306–331; in 21st-century economy, 28–31; voices of, 345; ways to offer encouragement and effective support to, 77–78; word families, 353–354, 358–361; words in, 348–365; working-class, 28. *See also* Parents

family culture, 60

family dinner, 35

Family Fluency Program. *See* Family Literacy Fluency Program

Family *Highlights* Program, 94–98, 100–101; assessments, 96–98; family program, 95–96; feedback from children, 96–97; feedback from parents, 98; feedback from teachers, 97; results of, 96–98; school program, 94–95; value of, 98

family literacy, 1–3, 15–41, 188–189; activities, 83; in African American culture, 227; concept of, 16; with culturally and linguistically different community, 203–225; description of, 83–84; for diverse families, 339–345; functional approaches to, 334; in future, 31–35; history of, 16–28; integrative critical literature review, 311–319; literature reviews, 308; long-term effects of, 265–288; major citations in reviews, 312–317, 313t–314t; over time, 327–329; practice of, 16; quantitative longitudinal research, 309–309, 309–310; research and practice, 263–365; rethinking, 332–347; sociocultural approaches to, 336–337; term introduction, 315; time issues, 306–331

Family Literacy: *Aprendiendo, Mejorando, Educando* (Learning, Improving, Educating) (FLAME), 212–221, 337–339, 343

Family Literacy Fluency Program, 85–94, 100–101; emergence of, 86–90; feedback from parents, children, and teachers, 92–94; goal of, 85; parent workshops, 87–90; results of, 90–94

family literacy programs, 193, 266; African American, 184–202; challenges for, 100–101; characteristics of, 83–103; in diverse communities, 221–223; ideology and, 343–345; as intervention programs, 334–335; parents on, 195–196; possibilities for, 100–101; remediation-focused, 335; school-initiated, 84; as single-solution approach, 344; sociocultural framework for, 221–223. *See also specific programs by name*

family literacy theory: major citations in reviews, 312–317, 313t, 314t

family stories, 275–282

family systems theory, 46

fate, 350–353, 353–354, 354–355, 361–363

field experiences, early, 190

financial differences, 140

FLAME (Family Literacy: *Aprendiendo, Mejorando, Educando* [Learning, Improving, Educating]), 212–221, 337–339, 343

Fleischman, Paul, 269

Florida, 204

fluency: assessing, 89–90, 90f; how parents help their children develop reading fluency, 92, 93t

Fluency Oriented Reading Instruction (FORI), 85; Family Fluency Program from, 86–90; school study, 86

fluent bilingualism, 294

Horton, Myles, 228
The Hundred Dresses (Estes), 269
Hurricane Katrina, 30, 362

I

J

K

L

language and thought theory: major citations in reviews, 312–317, 313t

language arts, 296

Language Experience Approach, 255, 257

Latino Parents' Committee (Comité de Padres Latinos, COPLA), 209, 343

Latinos, 140, 141, 151, 161–162, 165, 173, 181–182, 334–335; culture and schooling, 203–225; ethnically specific institutions for, 176; families, 209–212; population, 204, 338; second-generation, 204; in United States, 203–205

Law Magnet program, 299

leadership: Parents as Leaders (Project FLAME module), 219

learning: academic, 164–167, 175–176; community learning, 15–41; cultural competence as conduit for, 164–167; distal outcomes, 67–69; Foxfire approach to, 175–176; intrinsic motivation for, 66; literacy learning, 72–80, 112–116; mechanisms of, 54, 77–78; model-based suggestions for enhancing, 72–80; outcomes supported by parental involvement, 64–69; parent-child relationship and, 70–71; parental involvement and, 62–64, 64–69; parents as learners, 218–219; parents' beliefs about, 112–116; parents' modeling of, 63; proximal outcomes, 65–67, 78–79, 79–80; social constructivist theory of, 336

Learning at Home, 208

learning literacy, 234–237

learning words, 364–365

legal parents, 28

Lewis, Ann, 231–232, 232–233, 241, 242

liberation theory and pedagogy: major citations in reviews, 312–317, 314t

lingua franca, 296

linguistic anthropology, 15

linguistic diversity, 203–225, 332–347

literacy: academic, 180–181; adolescent, 245–248; in African American culture, 227; authentic, 229; beliefs about, 210–211; children's, 110–121; classroom, 186, 285; community, 37; critical, 220–221, 298, 332; cultural, 177–178, 179, 180–181; cultural competence as, 164–167; culturally responsive, 167, 176–180; for diverse families, 339–345; diversity of, 337, 338–339; in ethnically diverse families and cultural contexts, 162–163; in ethnically specific institutions, 176–180; family, 1–3, 15–41, 188–189, 227, 265–288, 306–331, 332–347; family activities, 83, 111; functional, 220–221; guiding principles for support, 69; importance of, 184; as key, 227–229, 231–234; learning, 234–237; linking to students' family lives, 242–243; meaning of, 229; modeling, 215; multimedia, 297–303; opportunity for, 215; professional, 167; Project FLAME program, 220–221; real, 229–240; of representation, 291; sociocultural theory of, 336; supportive activities at home, 76; teaching, 161–183; in urban classrooms and communities, 226–244

literacy development: culturally responsive, 176–177; foundation for, 73; in higher education, 176–177; motivations and skills essential for, 71–72; parental involvement and, 69–72; student, 79–80

literacy instruction: classroom, 285; English literacy instruction, 267–268; language of, 285

literacy interactions, 215

literacy learning: guiding beliefs, 213–214; model-based suggestions for enhancing, 72–80; parents' beliefs about, 112–116; ways to offer encouragement for family involvement and effective support for, 77–78

literacy log: samples, 278f, 279, 281, 282f

literacy programs: characteristics of, 83–103; family literacy programs, 83–103, 266, 343–345; family-school communications, 76; functional, 334; general invitations from, 58, 74–75; ideology and, 343–345; intergenerational, 266; mechanistic, 333; reading programs for middle and high schools, 247; remediation-focused, 335; responsiveness to family life context, 59–61, 75; school-initiated family literacy programs, 84; support for parents' active role construction and positive sense of efficacy, 73–74; support for parents' choice of involvement forms, 76–77;

support for parents' understanding of links between proximal learning outcomes and students' literacy development, 79–80; support for parents' understanding of students' perceptions of involvement, 78; support for parents' understanding of students' proximal outcomes, 78–79; support for parents' use of learning mechanisms, 77–78; two-generation programs, 266. *See also specific programs by name*

literacy-rich contexts for adolescents, 249–250

literacy teaching: in cultural context, 161–183; culturally responsive, 167; to ethnically diverse students of color, 180–181

literary heritage, 120

literate bilingualism, 290, 294–297

literate slaves, 227–229

literature reviews, 308; analytic review template (ART) for, 312; integrative critical, 311–319; major citations in reviews, 312–317, 313t–314t

Little Golden books, 109

lived partnerships, 143

longitudinal research: case study findings, 325–327; data analysis, 320–321; findings, 321–325; qualitative, 319–327; quantitative, 308–309, 309–310

Louisiana, 362

M

mainstream homes, 137

Malcolm X Academy (Detroit), 176

Massachusetts Comprehensive Assessment System (MCAS), 273

MCAS. *See* Massachusetts Comprehensive Assessment System

Meadows-Livingston School (San Francisco), 176

meaningful reading and writing, 241–242

metaphors, 355, 360

Mexican Americans, 210–211, 291, 300–301

Mexicans, 210–211

middle school English-language learners, 252–255

Midtown Family Place, 49–50

minorities, 27–28

modeling literacy, 63, 215

Moore, Kelly, 143

Morehouse College, 179–180

Morillo, Fiordaliza, 277-279; literacy log, 279f

Morillo, Karla, 278, 280; eighth-grade writing sample, 279, 279f

Morillo family, 277–280

mothers, 113–115, 114f

motivation for learning, 66

motivation for literacy development, 71–72

motivation for parental involvement, 54, 56–61; contextual, 57–59, 73–75; personal, 56–57, 73–75; from responsiveness to life context, 59–61, 75; supporting, 73–75

multicultural education, 170

multimedia literacy, 297–303

mutual respect (*respeto*), 206

mutual trust (*confianza*), 206, 208, 212, 295–296, 338

mythology, 354–355

N

NAE. *See* National Academy of Education

NAEP. *See* National Association of Educational Progress

narrative analysis: qualitative, 312–317, 313*t*, 314*t*

National Academy of Education (NAE), 295

National Association of Educational Progress (NAEP), 226, 246, 266

National Council of Teachers of English, 246

National Family Literacy Center, 19–20

National Reading Panel, 248

Native Alaskans, 177

Native Americans, 17, 161–162, 163, 164, 165, 173, 181–182; ethnically specific institutions for, 176; heritage colleges, 176–177

Native Hawaiians, 176

native language effects, 120–121

Navajo Nation: Dine College, 177–178; Rock Point and Rough Rock Community demonstration schools, 176

Nevada, 204

New Jersey, 204

New Mexico, 204

New York, 204

New York University School of Medicine, 99; BELLE Project, 98

newspapers, 115

No Child Left Behind Act, 27

nonmainstream students, 136–158

O

Obama, Barack, 37, 153

observational research: qualitative, 312–317, 314*t*

Open Court series, 233

opportunity for literacy, 215

organizations, 22

P

pain, 355–358, 358–363; children who live in, 361–363, 362*f*; faces assessment scale, 356–357, 357*f*

PAR. *See* Participatory action research

parent-child book reading, 187–195

parent-child relationship, 70–71, 113–115

parent handouts: assessing fluency, 89–90, 90*f*; reading activities to do with books children bring home from school, 88*f*, 88–89

parent workshops, 87–90

parental involvement, 198; activities at home, 61; activities at school, 77; choice of forms, 76–77; contextual motivators of, 57–59; cultural differences and, 205–209; distal learning outcomes, 67–69; family capacities for, 72–80; forms of, 61–62, 76–77; foundation for, 73; invitations from school or program for, 58, 74–75; invitations from students or children for, 58–59, 74–75; invitations from teachers for, 58, 74–75; learning outcomes supported by, 64–69; and literacy development, 69–72; model of, 54, 55*f*; motivation for, 54, 56–61, 73–75; parents' use of learning mechanisms during, 77–78; personal psychological motivators of, 56–57; process of, 53, 54–69, 69–72; proximal learning outcomes, 65–67, 78–79, 79–80; rationale for, 265–267; role construction for, 56–57; at school, 61–62; and student learning, 62–64; student perceptions of, 54, 78; teachers' reports of, 91; ways to offer encouragement and effective support, 77–78

parents: beliefs about literacy learning, 112–116; communication with children, 61; education, 266, 272; getting to know, 149–154; "good" and "supportive," 45; handouts for, 88*f*, 88–89; how they help their children develop reading fluency, 92, 93*t*; importance, 188; instruction by,

64; interviews with, 92–94, 98; as learners, 218–219; legal, 28; modeling of learning-related
values and behaviors by, 63; on Parents as Partners in Reading program, 195–196; reading
with children, 116–121; reinforcement of student behaviors, 63–64; responses to Family
Fluency Program, 92–94; roles, 73–74, 126, 188; skills and knowledge, 60; surveys, 91–92;
as teachers, 216–218; time and energy, 60; understanding of links between proximal learning
outcomes and students' literacy development, 79–80; understanding of students' perceptions
of involvement, 78; understanding of students' proximal outcomes, 78–79; use of learning
mechanisms by, 77–78
Parents as Leaders (Project FLAME module), 219
Parents as Learners (Project FLAME module), 218–219
Parents as Partners in Reading: A Family Literacy Training Program, 193, 195–196, 198
Parents as Teachers (Project FLAME module), 216–218, 219
Parents as Volunteers (Project FLAME module), 220
participatory action research (PAR), 291
partner reading, 88f
partnerships: of equality, 154–155; lived, 143; true, 154–155
pedagogy, 234, 341; caring, 173; of cultural reciprocity, 185, 196–197; of empowerment, 345;
    major citations in reviews, 312–317, 314t; of transformation and social action, 342–343
Peña, Evelin, 275–277; comments on television viewing, 275, 275f; literacy log, 275, 276f; reading
    response, 275, 276f
Peña family, 275–277
permission to fail, 239
personal advice (consejos), 338
personal life stories, 190
personal motivations, 73–74; psychological motivators, 56–57; role construction and efficacy, 73–74
personal psychological motivators, 56–57
personality traits, 48–49
phonemic awareness, 237
photographs, 190
picture books, 109, 116–121
PISA. See Programme for International Student Assessment
poetry: for developing cultural consciousness, 167–172; teacher education, 170–171; "Top Ten"
    (Baez), 299–300
political possibilities, 345
position papers: major citations in reviews, 312–317, 313t
postsecondary education plans, 273
poverty, 115; African American parents in, 185–187, 196–197; welfare population, 115; working
    poor, 28
power: culture of, 192–193
preschoolers, 124–125
professional literacy, 167
Programme for International Student Assessment (PISA), 249
Project FLAME (Family Literacy: Aprendiendo, Mejorando, Educando [Learning, Improving,
    Educating]), 212–221, 337–339, 343; activities, 219–220; assumptions, 214; child care, 220;
    functional or critical literacy program, 220–221; guiding beliefs, 213–214; instructional
    program, 216–219; literacy interaction, 215; literacy modeling, 215; literacy opportunity, 215;
    objectives, 214; Parents as Leaders module, 219; Parents as Learners module, 218–219; Parents
    as Teachers module, 216–218, 219; Parents as Volunteers module, 220; theoretical design,
    214–216; Training of Trainers module, 219–220
Proquest, 312
public meetings (encuentros), 301–302
Puente Academy for Peace and Justice, 176

Q

qualitative research, 318; major citations in reviews, 312–317, 313t, 314t
quality time, 50
quantitative research, 308–309, 318; major citations, 312–317, 313t, 314t, 316t; and time, 309–310
Question Answer Relationships (QAR) strategy, 196
"Questions for Answers" video (SJEP), 299

R

race, 237
Reach Out and Read (ROR) program, 49, 98–99, 100
read-aloud styles, 127
readers: inexperienced adolescent readers, 259; inexperienced teenage readers, 245–261
Readers Theatre, 22–23
reading: activities to do with books children bring home from school, 88f, 88–89; assessing fluency, 89–90, 90f; with children, 116–121; engaged, 249, 258–259; essential questions that lead to, 256; home storybook talk, 118–119; how parents help their children develop reading fluency, 92, 93t; meaningful, 241–242; purposes of, 111; self-selected, 253–254; shared reading, 125; story reading, 116–117; teacher-directed activities, 254–255
reading programs: for middle and high schools, 247. See also Literacy programs; specific programs by name
Reading Recovery, 144
reading response, 285; sample, 275, 276f
reading the world, 298
reciprocal enculturation, 196
reinforcement, 63–64
remediation, 334–336, 344
remediation-focused programs, 335
repeated reading, 88f
representation, 291
requests for display, 124
research, 289–305; adolescent literacy, 250–252; benefits of, 289–291; family literacy, 263–365; formative experiments, 250–252; integrative critical literature review, 311–319; literature reviews, 308; participatory action research (PAR), 291; in practice, 212–221; qualitative, 312–317, 313t, 314t, 318; quantitative, 300–309, 309–310, 312–317, 313t, 314t, 316t, 318; on schooling and Latino families, 209–212; studies of real literacy, 229–240
researchers, 316–317
resilient families, 46
respect (respeto), 206, 338; for families, 69; mutual, 206; for teachers and school, 206
Riley, Richard W., 193
Rock Point and Rough Rock Community demonstration schools, 176
Rodriguez, Juan (student), 299
role construction, 56–57
role playing, 216–217
ROR program. See Reach Out and Read program
Rosa Parks Elementary School, 320

S

scaffolding, 165, 192
school(s): advanced curriculum at, 335–336; Afrocentric schools, 176; block schools, 19; culture of, 123–124; ethnic heritage schools, 176; extended ecology of, 297; family literacy programs initiated by, 84; family-school communications, 61, 76; family-school partnerships, 143; home-school connection, 215–216, 290; home-school relationship, 136–158; institutions

for particular ethnic groups, 176; invitations from, 58, 74–75; involvement activities, 77; key practices that bolster educational sovereignty, 295–297; *lingua franca,* 296; as more like home, 43–45; parental involvement at, 61–62; research on, 209–212; respect for, 206; responsiveness to family life context, 59–61, 75; Sunday School, 107; support for parents' understanding of students' perceptions of involvement, 78; support for parents' use of learning mechanisms, 77–78; talking over books at, 121–127

school-aged children: national demographics, 44. *See also* Children

school-based literacy practices, 13–158

school survival skills, 185–186, 196

second-generation students, 291

Seedfolks (Fleischman), 269

segmented assimilation, 291

selective acculturation, 290, 291–294

self-analysis, 190

self-efficacy: academic, 66; social, 66, 67

self-regulation, 66, 67

self-selected reading, 253–254

shared reading, 125

sharing, 257

SJEP. *See* Social Justice Education Program

skill development, 54; school survival skills, 185–186, 196; self-regulatory skills, 67

skills orientation, 113

slaves, 227–229

social action, 343–344

social class theory: major citations in reviews, 312–317, 313*t*

social competency, 163–164

social constructivism, 336

Social Justice Education Program (SJEP), 297–298, 299, 300, 301, 302–303; *encuentros* (public meetings), 301–302; "Questions for Answers" video, 299

social self-efficacy, 66, 67

sociocritical view, 339–345

sociocultural theory, 336; approaches to family literacy, 336–337; framework for family literacy programs in diverse communities, 221–223; Project FLAME and, 337–339

sociological theory: major citations in reviews, 312–317, 314*t*

space requirements, 258–259

Spanish language: cross-age language arts sessions, 296; linguistic diversity in, 337

special education, 324, 325

Spelman College, 178, 179

StimQ assessment, 100

story maps, 285

story reading, 116–117

storybook reading: home storybook talk, 118–119; roles teachers and parents take in, 126–127

Striving Readers Program, 245

students: attendance rates, 273; dropouts, 140, 141; early readers, 107; engagement of, 54; ethnically diverse students of color, 180–181; high school graduation rates, 273; interviews with, 92–94; intrinsic motivation for learning, 66; invitations from, 58–59, 74–75; linking literacy to family lives of, 242–243; literacy development, 79–80; middle school English-language learners, 252–255; multidimensional needs of, 178; nonmainstream, 136–158; parental involvement and, 62–64, 78; perceptions of, 65, 78; preschoolers, 124–125; proximal learning outcomes, 65–67, 78–79, 79–80; second-generation, 291

success: demand for, 236, 239

Sunday School, 107

urban classrooms and communities, 226–244; lessons learned, 240–243
U.S. Department of Education, 213

V

VEEP. *See* Voluntary Enrollment Exchange Program
Video Interaction Project (VIP), 99–100
visual art, 171–172
vocabulary, 355; learning, 364–365; word families, 353–355, 358–361
voice(s), 340, 345
Voluntary Enrollment Exchange Program (VEEP), 146, 147
volunteers, 220

W

Washington, Booker T., 184
welfare population, 115
Whites, 140
whole language (WL) movement, 231
Wigginton, Eliot, 172–173
wilderness, 33
WL movement. *See* Whole language movement
word families, 353–355, 358–361
words, 364–365; in families, 348–365; learning, 363; surface features of, 363
working-class families, 28
working poor, 28
workshops, 216–217; parent workshops, 87–90
writing: eighth-grade sample, 279, 279*f*; functions of, 218; meaningful, 241–242; sample first day of school essay, 281, 281*f*; teacher-directed activities, 254–255

Y

YMCAs, 22
youth organizations, 22–23